CRESCENDO!

---

75 Years of the
City of Birmingham
Symphony Orchestra

CBSO
75 YEARS

Beresford King-Smith

CRESCENDO!

75 Years of the
City of Birmingham Symphony Orchestra

Best wishes!

Methuen

1 Nov 2006

The publication of this history was made possible by generous donations from the S & D Lloyd Charitable Trust and from the City of Birmingham Orchestra Endowment Fund. The Directors of the CBSO Society Ltd are most grateful for this support.

First published in Great Britain 1995
by Methuen London
an imprint of Reed Books Ltd
Michelin House, 81 Fulham Road, London SW3 6RB
and Auckland, Melbourne, Singapore and Toronto

A CIP catalogue record for this book
is available at the British Library
ISBN 0 413 69740 1

Phototypeset by Intype, London
Printed and bound in Great Britain
by Clays Ltd, St Ives plc

This book is dedicated to the memory of

Stephen and Dorothy Lloyd.

Their love of music and of things made
in Birmingham was joined to their support
for the CBSO, whose concerts they attended
with great regularity for more than fifty
of the seventy-five years covered by this history,
and in whose affairs they both played an active part.

Contents

Foreword by Sir Simon Rattle, CBE ix
Preface and Acknowledgements xi
1 Elgar's button-up boots 1
2 William Stockley – George Halford 4
3 Granville Bantock – Thomas Beecham 13
4 Genesis 21
5 Appleby Matthews – Innovator 27
6 Adrian Boult – Orchestra builder 36
7 Consolidation 43
8 Leslie Heward – 'A very gifted musician' 52
9 The BBC link 60
10 The wartime years 67
11 George Weldon – Going for broke 78
12 Peace and productivity 86
13 Unlucky for some 95
14 Rudolf Schwarz – Creativity and crisis 103
15 'Ideas and ideals' 112
16 Andrzej Panufnik – New thinking 121
17 Hugo Rignold – Complete professional 131
18 Discord and Harmony 142
19 Louis Frémaux – 'A wrist second to none' 154
20 'The best French orchestra in the world' 166
21 All change 176
22 Simon Rattle – Making music an adventure 190
23 The Development Plan 204
24 Symphony Hall 217
25 Towards the Millennium 227
Tables 242
Notes 245
Index 278

Foreword
by Sir Simon Rattle, CBE

So, the story of the CBSO is finally told, and what a heroic task Beresford King-Smith has completed. He has been a one-man respository of this information for so many years that he must feel a little wistful to have it all in one permanent form at last. And what a compulsively readable story it is, even if some of the tales of musicians struggling against impossible financial odds have a strangely familiar and repetitive ring about them. How many more generations of British musicians will spend their lifetimes miraculously managing to fly, despite being seemingly shackled to the runway?

Oh, to have been a fly on the wall, or maybe one of Julian Barnes' all-seeing, all-hearing woodworm! How I would love to have heard, for instance, Sir Adrian Boult's CBO Mahler performances, despite a characteristically wry conversation I had with him some 20 years ago:

AB: You know, people came from miles around to hear our Mahler and Bruckner performances.
SR: I didn't know they were favourite composers of yours.
AB: No, not at all, I thought they were terrible rubbish!

How sad not to have experienced the consummate musicianship of Leslie Heward, who seems to have commanded such unanimous love and respect. For many musicians, and myself in particular, the chapter on Rudolf Schwarz will be a touching reminder of one of the most compassionate and thoughtful musicians of our time. I would also like particularly to pay tribute to the work of my distinguished predecessor, Louis Frémaux, who did so much for the CBSO in every way, and bequeathed to me an instrument of such flexibility and finesse.

At the end of it all, of course, it is Beresford's triumph to have woven all this tapestry together, and reminded us all of the integrity and adventurousness which have been the hallmark of the orchestra throughout, even against the odds. It is now, more than ever, a story of teamwork – musicians, management, audience, all bound together by the unusually enlightened support of the city.

The very best crescendos are the slowest burns of all – there is already so much to be proud of, but I know we have so much more to look forward to, and that we should adapt the old saying 'it is better to journey than to arrive' to a phrase both defiant and optimistic – 'Let us never consent to arrive!'

To all involved in this story, this whole inspiring community, my profoundest admiration and gratitude.

Simon Rattle

Birmingham, 1995

Preface and Acknowledgements

'How quickly the years slip by, and how little of history rests with us if it is not written down.'[1] Records of the Birmingham orchestra's early years are, indeed, far from complete and for that reason no one can be certain how many concerts it has given over the past 75 years, though a tally of 10,000 cannot be far off the mark.[2]

Viewed in that light, it is perhaps not surprising that the first draft of this history was almost twice the length of the finished book; that longer and more detailed version has now been placed in the CBSO Archives, where it may be consulted by appointment.[3] Inevitably, this process of abbreviation has meant that some anecdotal material and a lot of programme detail have been set aside along the way; hopefully, the baby has been retained and only the bathwater discarded.

Similarly, limitations of space have prevented the inclusion of a bibliography, but principal sources are credited in notes at the end of the book. Where passages have been quoted or photographs reproduced, every effort has been made to contact the copyright holder; where this has not proved possible, apologies are extended. The inclusion of an exhaustive CBSO discography, too, would have had the effect of shortening the main text still further; it is to be hoped, however, that one will be forthcoming at a later date.

The fact that the CBSO has experienced only one day of industrial action in its 75 years to date speaks for itself, but inevitably there have been times when the *crescendo* has been interrupted by a *fermata*. In some cases – notably the events of 1978, when both the general manager and principal conductor left within hours – many of those who were involved in the drama are still alive. I have interviewed them where possible and have done my best to present the facts fairly and squarely. I would sincerely hope that nothing I have written could cause any offence; if it should, however, I offer my apologies.

Sadly, I cannot acknowledge here the names of all who have contributed to this history in one way or another; they have been credited where possible but, even where they are not, I am greatly indebted to each and every one.

To mention any by name might seem invidious, but I list here some who have provided me with access to important documentary material:

Sir Adrian Boult, CH, and Harold Gray, OBE, both donated their press-cuttings books to the CBSO during their lifetime; Mrs Anne Griffith-Jones kindly gave me access to the scrapbooks and programmes of her father Appleby Matthews; Miss Fiona Bantock allowed me to browse through the Granville Bantock diaries; Miss Helen Berry kindly copied out for me copious extracts from the diaries (1927–60) of her aunt, cellist Gwen Berry; Frank Young kindly shared with me the fruits of his detailed researches into Leslie Heward's career; Miss Karen Heward loaned me her father's pocket-diaries (1938–43) and her mother's diaries (1942–3).

During her lifetime, Miss Ethel Hatton donated some of her George Weldon concert diaries to the CBSO and, since her death, her sister Miss G. M. Hatton and Miss W. Burdett-Coutts have kindly presented to the orchestra the remaining relevant items from Miss Hatton's collection; Mrs Barbara Hatheson (*née* Jones) allowed me to borrow and copy her articles and reviews for the *Birmingham Despatch*; Mrs Sheila Campbell kindly presented to the CBSO two scrapbooks containing newspaper articles and reviews for the *News* and the *Birmingham Weekly Post* by her father, the late W. S. A. Taylor; John Waterhouse generously allowed me to borrow eleven columns of press cuttings containing his father's *Birmingham Post* reviews and articles (1946–64); the collection includes a number of interesting letters written to Waterhouse in response to his notices; Kenneth Dommett was also kind enough to lend me a collection of his *Birmingham Post* press cuttings (1965–72).

James Lloyd kindly allowed me to study correspondence dating from 1950 onwards between his father, the late Stephen Lloyd, and a number of distinguished conductors and composers; Kenneth Matchett let me borrow and copy a file of documents referring to his General Managership, 1952–3; Patrick Baird and his staff in the Local History Department of Birmingham Central Library have shown me unfailing courtesy in my researches; as a former Financial Controller of the CBSO for many years, Graham Escott put his specialised knowledge at my disposal by analysing published accounts and preparing a financial table; his successor Cheryl Gentry kindly produced an Income and Expenditure graph from Graham's figures; I must also acknowledge the special help of my friend Lyndon Jenkins, who read much of this book in draft and made countless suggestions to improve it – I still hope that one day he will find the time to put on paper the in-depth biography of Leslie Heward that only he could write.

I am also deeply indebted to the CBSO's Chief Executive Edward Smith, and to his Deputy, Richard York, who made it all possible, and to many members of the CBSO and its staff, past and present, for their helpful contributions and unfailing support. I must also express my thanks to Penny Hoare, Kate Goodhart, Alex Lankester and Ilsa Yardley of Methuen, who have helped so much to bring this project to fruition. Finally, a word of special thanks to my wife Kate for all her loving help, patience and encouragement over the long period during which this book has taken shape.

Beresford King-Smith
Sutton Coldfield, March 1995

I

Elgar's button-up boots

On Wednesday, 10 November 1920, England's senior and most respected musician, Sir Edward Elgar, OM, mounted the rostrum in Birmingham's historic Town Hall to conduct the inaugural symphony concert of the City of Birmingham Orchestra, which comprised three of his finest and most complex late works: the Symphonic Study *Falstaff* (into which he had poured so much of himself); the Cello Concerto, with soloist Felix Salmond (who had given its first performance a year before)[1] and the Second Symphony, in which Salmond joined the orchestral cellos as a tribute to the great man. It was a long programme, and one which would have challenged any orchestra, let alone one which had only been working together for a few weeks; but, as John Denison (who played the horn in performances conducted by the composer during his later years) recalls, 'Elgar developed great expertise in not wasting time by just playing through a programme. Every minute was used to maximum advantage in explanation; setting and testing the right effect at key passages, tricky moments or pitfalls; and adjusting the impact of a climax to his satisfaction.'[2] The *Birmingham Mail* reported that 'the work of the orchestra bore witness to the careful preparation and frequent rehearsal on which its performance was based. Its playing was a credit to the city.'[3]

Before the concert, in the course of a Civic Reception held in his honour in Birmingham's splendid Victorian Council House, Elgar reminisced about those happy, busy days back in the early 1880s when he would commute by rail from Worcester to Birmingham to play as a back-desk first violinist in William Stockley's orchestra – known locally as 'Mr Stockley's Band'. He was conscious how much he had benefited from the experience, familiarising himself with the symphonic repertoire and acquiring lessons about orchestration 'from the inside' which would remain with him for the rest of his creative life. Referring to his rehearsal earlier in the day, he remarked to the Lord Mayor, 'I almost expected to see myself come on with the fiddle!'[4]

Impressed by the young man's enthusiasm and undoubted gifts, Stockley had provided him with his earliest opportunity to hear one of his works performed by a professional orchestra – the *Intermezzo: Sérénade Mauresque*, premièred in Birmingham Town Hall on 13 December 1883. As Stockley later recalled, 'I am very proud of having had the honour and pleasure of initiating a musician of such great merit into a larger sphere of action. Mr Elgar's modesty, on the occasion referred to, was of the kind that so often accompanies great talent, for I could not persuade him to conduct his *Intermezzo*, or even to listen to its performance from the auditorium, but he insisted on playing in his place in the orchestra, from whence he came to the front in response to a most cordial demand from the audience.'[5]

Elgar maintained close links with Birmingham, whose triennial Musical Festival commissioned and staged the first performances of four of his most important choral-orchestral works, between 1900 and 1912. For a variety of reasons, the première of *The Dream of Gerontius* was not an unqualified success, but the fact that the composer felt able to accept subsequent commissions for *The Kingdom, The Apostles* and *The Music Makers* is eloquent testimony in itself that he held neither the city nor the Festival responsible for that.

It goes without saying that the appearance in Birmingham of England's most distinguished musician (not seen there as a conductor since the early days of the Great War)[6] created a great deal of local interest. As the musical journalist and composer Havergal Brian wrote, Elgar's prestige in the city was unrivalled: 'Of course, he was everything in our eyes, of greater stature than the most notable foreigners, and at least the equal of Richard Strauss. There was a lot of civic pride about: and had not Elgar disclosed his vision of Birmingham as an art centre for music, rivalling Leipzig both in its Conservatorium and its Gewandhaus concerts? A permanent orchestra of a hundred and a resident conductor whose name would be known throughout the land.'[7]

When Elgar conducted that first CBO symphony concert, his 'vision of Birmingham as an art centre for music, rivalling Leipzig . . . in its Gewandhaus concerts' still seemed a mere pipe-dream. Seventy-five years on, however, as Sir Simon Rattle commences his sixteenth season in charge of the City of Birmingham Symphony Orchestra, it begins to look uncommonly like prescience. *Crescendo* is a story of continual growth, in the face of many difficulties, from the part-time band of the Twenties to the major international orchestra of the Nineties.

There is a curious footnote to the Elgar concert. Clutching a friend's autograph book, Mr. J. S. Swann of Stourport remembers finding his way to the principal artists' room in Birmingham Town Hall after the concert. He knocked, received no reply, waited a while and entered, only to find the CBO's Principal Conductor, Appleby Matthews, apparently kneeling in homage at the elderly composer's feet. 'Feeling that, if Mr Matthews knelt in the great man's presence, then this was certainly no place for him to be, he beat a hasty retreat and thereby missed the opportunity of getting Elgar's autograph. Only later did he realise that Matthews had been helping him to undo his button-up boots!'[8]

2

William Stockley – George Halford

1897 was the year of Queen Victoria's Diamond Jubilee. All over Britain, kitchen dressers were being adorned with commemorative cups and saucers, whilst small but inexpert fingers were embroidering 'Sixty Glorious Years' samplers for brightly coloured cushion covers. Thousands of troops from every country in the Empire paraded before the old Queen, and through the new-fangled miracle of electricity she was able, by pressing a single button, to telegraph a message of thanks over distances previously unthinkable. Marconi had just arrived in England, and wireless communication, too, would soon become a reality. The Jubilee also provided Edward Elgar with his first London success: the *Imperial March*, whose blend of pomp, dignity and self-confidence seems perfectly to encapsulate the Victorian era that was drawing gradually to its close.

In Birmingham it was a Musical Festival Year. Well-heeled patrons from the city and from its surrounding shire counties were looking forward to their triennial celebration, with all its well-tried formulæ. Sir Arthur Sullivan, in a Presidential Address to Birmingham's Clef Club, remarked that the town reminded him of 'a huge boa constrictor that took an enormous gorge every three years, and fasted in the interim'.

Orchestrally, the 1897 Festival certainly broke new ground: the Birmingham Town Hall organ had been tuned down to the standard European low pitch of the day, and the instruments followed suit. Repertoire was less adventurous, though Fuller-Maitland's version of Purcell's *King Arthur* attracted a certain amount of interest (with Arnold Dolmetsch and his wife playing his recently constructed harpsichords, then regarded as very quaint).

Nevertheless, the Jubilee Year was to prove a milestone for orchestral music in the city. The 40-year-old Elgar, for example, premières of whose oratorios would dominate succeeding Festivals, knew Birmingham well from his days as a freelance violinist; but for some of the others, the name probably conjured up nothing much beyond a smoky view of New Street station, *en route* for somewhere more enticing, farther down the line.

While Thomas Beecham Senior was vigorously promoting his Pills ('Worth a Guinea a Box') in the *Birmingham Daily Post* as a sovereign remedy for every known complaint from 'Blotches on the Skin' or 'Fulness and Swelling after Meals' to 'Disturbed Sleep and Frightful Dreams', his 18-year-old son was being launched on an undergraduate career at Wadham College, Oxford, where he used his time profitably, slipping surreptitiously over to Dresden to attend the occasional opera performance and during the vacations forming his own orchestra in St Helens, a sound preparation for his unconventional Hallé debut in 1899.[1] Thomas Beecham Junior was to play a significant rôle in the establishment of a professional orchestra for Birmingham.

Leslie Heward, who would pilot the City of Birmingham Orchestra with consummate musicianship through the difficult days of the 1930s, was actually born in 1897. Adrian Boult (his mentor and distinguished forerunner at the CBO) was only seven. Appleby Matthews, the CBO's very first conductor, was Boult's senior by some three years, though he too would be glad to take a few conducting lessons from him later on. Landon Ronald – one of a succession of musical knights who made regular appearances in the city – was 24 and (with Nellie Melba's influential support) just launching out on twin careers as accompanist and conductor.

At 29, Henry Wood (a regular Birmingham visitor both before and after World War One) was starting his third season of Proms at Queen's Hall, but for Granville Bantock (a year older than Wood, and still three years away from his appointment as Birmingham School of Music's first stipendiary Principal), 1897 was a crucial year. It marked his first orchestral post, at the Tower, New Brighton, where he rapidly upgraded what was then 'a wretched musical establishment',[2] 'little more than a light music group',[3] into a capable little orchestra. With this ensemble 'Mr Bantock's enthusiasm led him to give whole programmes to individual British composers',[4] who were often invited to conduct their own music.

It is easy to imagine that a century ago Birmingham's cultural life was a pretty low-key affair, but the facts really do not bear that out. For a start, Joseph Hansom's splendid Town Hall of 1834, now surrounded by an impressive cluster of buildings – the Council House, Christ Church, the Post Office, Queen's College, the Midland Institute, the Public Library, Mason College – provided a prestigious venue for concerts of every sort.

In 1871, Percy Harrison and his uncle Thomas had started a successful series of Subscription Concerts, 'the only other series then existing being that of the Festival Choral Society . . . They were prepared to educate the musical tastes of the people, and to do this they, among other things, engaged the celebrated Hallé's band.'[5] Harrison's opening events of the 1897–8 season featured recitals by Melba and Paderewski, with Clara Butt and a host of famous artists to follow. Grieg took part in a recital of his own chamber music, promoted by Priestley's.[6] At the Prince of Wales Theatre (on the site where Symphony Hall now stands) Sir Henry Irving was playing in *The Bells*, whilst Hans Richter, Europe's leading conductor, friend of the great and the good, had charge of his fifth Birmingham Festival.

William Stockley's Orchestral Concerts

The Festival apart, Birmingham's major musical talking-point in 1897 was the retirement of William Stockley, who had worked closely with Richter since 1885. He had dominated most aspects of the city's musical life since the middle of the 19th century: as conductor of the Birmingham Festival Choral Society from 1855 to 1895; chorus master to the Birmingham Triennial Musical Festivals since 1858; conductor from 1873 to 1897 of his own series of Orchestral Subscription Concerts featuring 'Mr Stockley's Band', in which Elgar had been a violinist for seven years; organist of Carrs Lane Church, *inter alia*, and, from 1886, honorary principal of Birmingham School of Music.

There is ample evidence to show that he was an inspirational choir trainer. In his book, Stockley makes a great deal of his orchestral concerts, but we should remember that he only promoted three or four each year, which would hardly have set the town on fire; a glance at the Munns portrait in the Foyer of Birmingham's Adrian Boult Hall reveals a real Victorian gentleman, and his recall (following his successor's untimely death) to train the Festival Chorus for the unhappy 1900 *Gerontius* première suggests that he was out of touch with new developments in music. Even so, his withdrawal left a sizeable vacuum in Birmingham's musical life, with several contenders vying to fill it. He makes it abundantly clear[7] that he would have continued his orchestral concerts beyond 1897 had it not been for 'the formation of a syndicate to give concerts similar to mine', and something akin to moral (and financial) blackmail on the part of the Festival Committee for him to pull out.

Thus it was that, within a few days in late 1897, it was possible to attend concerts in Birmingham Town Hall presented by three different orchestras.

On Thursday, 2 December, Dr Charles Swinnerton Heap ('a splendid musician', according to Richter),[8] who had replaced Stockley as Festival Chorus

Master, launched a new venture by the Birmingham Festival Choral Society: not a choral programme but its 'First Orchestral Concert' – a substantial programme with Schubert's *Great C Major* Symphony as its main work, but also including the *Tragic* Overture and a short choral item by Brahms, who had died earlier in the year; this was the *Song of Destiny* (which Richter had conducted at the recent Festival), and it was clearly intended to attract the Society's traditional oratorio-loving audience. During the season the Society promoted three choral and three orchestral concerts, much as Stockley had done whilst wearing two of his three principal 'hats'. Sadly, Heap's orchestral series did not survive a sudden onslaught of pneumonia in December 1898, and his subsequent death.

A week later, 'Dr Rowland M. Winn's Second Orchestral Concert' was advertised – 'Admission One Shilling'. This was the direct successor to 'Mr Stockley's Band', featuring rather shorter, more popular repertoire, with two soloists: a violinist and the well-known baritone Ffrangcon-Davies. Rowland Winn, a pupil of the Birmingham-born composer A. R. Gaul, had been Stockley's pianist and amanuensis for many years, but he lacked his rôle-model's charisma. Despite some eminent soloists (Vladimir de Pachmann in the Chopin F minor Concerto) attendances were disappointing and the experiment lasted only two seasons.

Finally, on Tuesday, 14 December, the 'syndicate' of which Stockley had written (carefully avoiding naming names) was promoting 'Mr Halford's Fourth Orchestral Concert', including Schubert's *Unfinished* Symphony and Beethoven's *Emperor* Concerto played by Alexander Siloti, paying 'his first visit to the City'. George Halford (1858–1933) had been a pupil of Swinnerton Heap, and conducted the Birmingham Choral and Orchestral Association's concerts for many years until 1889. His important annual series of ten orchestral concerts will receive more detailed attention in due course.

These three new orchestras, competing for the same audience, promoted between them during the 1897–8 season seventeen mid-week concerts in the Town Hall.

Birmingham's 19th-century musical history lies well beyond the scope of this book, but we do perhaps need a few pointers to the state of orchestral playing in this country at that time, to set the scene for the story to come.

> 38 Bull St, Birmingham, September 17th 1832 – My dear Grimshaw – I must now give you instructions how to conduct your 'progressing' expedition to Kidderminster. In the first place you must send off your Dble Basso, well packed, by Canal, addressed to 'Mr Harvey, Secretary to the Musical Festival, Kidderminster' – You must leave Manchester with Mr Cudmore on Saturday

so as to be in Wolverhampton on Saturday night or Sunday morning. Go on in one of the coaches from Wolverhampton to Kidderminster. We shall be in Kidderminster on Sunday morning to meet you. I hope we shall all meet in good health & spend a pleasant week. Till then adieu – God bless you. Very faithfully, Joseph Lyon.'[9]

The author of this letter (written two years before Birmingham Town Hall was opened) was a part-time violinist who kept a shop in Digbeth, on the old London Road out of the city. His friend Sam Grimshaw was a Preston solicitor who played cello and bass in many of the leading Festivals of the day; at York he received a fee, but in Birmingham, where a charity stood to profit, he played gratis. Just a few years later he would have been able to bring his 'Dble Basso' quite safely by train, but with the state of the turnpikes in 1832, a horse-drawn narrow boat offered the only safe option.

What were performing standards like at these early Festivals? Local newspaper reviews of the day tend to be self-congratulatory, but where the witness is acknowledged to be a great musician, his opinion will carry extra weight. A composer, for example, may be glad to accept a commission, or flattered to receive an invitation to conduct one of his own established works, but he will hardly accept a second or third invitation unless his first experience proved satisfying. Mendelssohn visited Birmingham four times, and after the third visit (the 1846 *Elijah* première) he wrote that 'No work of mine ever went so admirably at the first performance or was received with such enthusiasm both by musicians and the public as this.'[10] Greig and Gounod came twice each to the Birmingham Festival, Dvořák three times, and Saint-Saëns was another who sent back glowing reports of performance standards. Later, Sibelius was a fairly frequent visitor, always staying with the Bantocks.

Apart from a few back-desk semi-professionals like Lyon and Grimshaw, most of the orchestral players at the Festivals came either from the 'Hallé Band' or from one of the London orchestras, so a glance at London standards would not be out of place. Here is Bernard Shaw: 'The German orchestra [an *ad hoc* group of continental musicians presenting Wagner's *Siegfried* under Gustav Mahler at Covent Garden and Drury Lane] is rough; but the men know the work, and are under perfect and willing discipline. In readiness and certainty of execution they are fully equal, if not superior, to the ordinary Covent Garden orchestra. But I cannot say as much for them in the matter of purity and individuality of tone. I still cannot accept this imported orchestra as being up to the standard of tone quality we have become accustomed to expect in London.'[11]

For a view of orchestral standards at the Birmingham Festivals at the turn of the century, we can turn to Beecham's hugely entertaining autobiography *A Mingled Chime*. After taking a swipe at Hans Richter, 'for whom the world of creative effort had stopped about 1895', Beecham took the opportunity to lambaste the Birmingham Festivals, at which 'the level of performance was rarely higher than adequate, as the time and facilities for rehearsal were never anything like sufficient. Over everything hung what Berlioz once described as the fatal disability of all English musical institutions, the curse of the *à-peu-près*, and often the proceedings resembled a race meeting more than an artistic celebration.'[12]

But Beecham – master, as ever, of the sweeping generalisation – was writing with 40 years' hindsight. Indeed, one wonders whether he had actually attended those Festivals so long ago. The *Post*'s immensely detailed reviews, not only of the performances but of all the pre-rehearsals, challenge his assertions. Things had come a long way since the days of Lyon and Grimshaw. Richter was about to take over the Hallé, from which many members of the Festival Orchestra were drawn; for the 1897 Festival he had three and a half days of 'London Band Rehearsals' (leaving them in the hands of the guest composer-conductors while he came briefly to Birmingham, by rail, for a choral rehearsal) and then two seven-hour days of *tutti* rehearsals in Birmingham. This compares favourably with the rehearsal allocation for the Three Choirs' Festivals during the 1970s, when the CBSO was their regular 'house orchestra'.

Whilst the Festival Orchestra was undeniably *ad hoc*, and only a comparatively small number of the players were local, there is no doubt that Richter worked meticulously with them and that he seemed very happy with the results, describing them as 'splendid, a real joy for me to work with these sensitive people.'[13] Rehearsing Tchaikovsky's *Pathétique* Symphony (new to most of the players) he put down his baton after the first movement and 'expressed his satisfaction with a hearty "Bravo", and by hand-clapping',[14] and then, having started the 5/4 movement, proceeded to let the orchestra play it unconducted. A little showmanship for the benefit of the Press, maybe, but such confidence in his players, on the part of the leading European conductor of the day, hardly suggests the scratch band that Beecham's comments evoke.

It is possible to identify twenty or more separate Birmingham orchestras which existed, in one form or another, prior to the establishment of the City of Birmingham Orchestra in 1919–20. Some were professional, some amateur, some a mixture of the two. Some were adjuncts to the many choral societies, while others existed in their own right. Ten of them, in particular, demand our attention:

William Stockley's Orchestral Concerts	1873–1897
Festival Choral Society Orchestral Concerts	1897–1898
Dr Rowland M. Winn's Orchestral Concerts	1897–1899
Mr Halford's Orchestral Concerts[15]	1897–1907
Birmingham Promenade Orchestral Concerts	1905–1920
Birmingham Symphony Orchestra	1906–1919
Birmingham Orchestral Concerts	1907–1908
Birmingham Concerts Society	1907–1909
Birmingham Philharmonic Society	1910–1913
Sir Thomas Beecham's New Birmingham Orchestra	1917–1918

Of the first three something has already been said, but we need now to look more closely at Halford, whose orchestra alone bridged the gap from the 19th into the 20th century.

George Halford's Orchestral Concerts

Looking back over thirty years, Sir Henry Wood wrote, 'Birmingham has always taken pride in its music, and when the full history of its activities comes to be written the name of George Halford should not be overlooked. Birmingham owes him a great deal.'[16] Halford's obituary in the *Birmingham Post* added, 'But for him the Birmingham of his day would have had no high-class music except that to be found at the annual Sir Charles Hallé concert and the Triennial Festival.'[17]

Halford was an idealist, prepared to challenge his audience. At a time when encores were the norm, he would never allow one – not even on an occasion when Arthur de Greef was recalled some twenty times after the Grieg Concerto. Havergal Brian described him as 'A man of wide sympathies, knowledge, and experience . . . Rarely does he conduct without the score, but it is patent to the veriest onlooker that the score is in his head, and not his head in the score.'[18]

As a composer whose music Halford programmed from time to time, Brian may not have been a totally disinterested party, but he was nobody's fool, and in any case Halford's record speaks for itself. In two seasons (1898–9 and 1904–5) he conducted all nine Beethoven Symphonies; in another, all Brahms's orchestral works. He often invited composers to conduct their own music: on 21 January 1902, Elgar conducted *Cockaigne* and a couple of *Pomp and Circumstance* marches. The Birmingham musical journalist Sydney Grew recalled many years later that 'Mr Halford played cymbals in the latter, and he looked very uncomfortable'.[19] 'The composer, who had a great reception, secured a magnificent performance.'[20] At the same concert Bantock conducted his *Songs of the East*.

Halford also engaged many eminent soloists: Busoni, Ysaÿe, Percy Grainger, Egon Petri, Kreisler, Dohnányi, Godowski, Lamond, Joachim, Brodsky – an international line-up that speaks for itself. Even Richard Strauss conducted an entire programme of his own music.

In the end, Halford's brave venture failed, for financial rather than artistic reasons. In a retrospective of Halford's orchestra in the *Gazette*, Robert Buckley wrote, 'The programmes were too good . . . [but] Siloti, the friend of Tchaikovsky, after playing with the Halford Orchestra, and Fritz Kreisler on many occasions privately expressed to the writer a high opinion of the Birmingham instrumentalists.'[21]

Landon Ronald's Promenade Orchestral Concerts

Halford's season finished each year around Easter. The Dutch-born violinist Max Mossel,[22] a former Leader of the Amsterdam Concertgebouw Orchestra who taught at Birmingham School of Music from 1895 to 1920 and ran the city's leading string quartet (in which Johan Hock, another ex-Concertgebouw player, was the cellist), presented from 1905 onwards a popular series of 'Promenade Orchestral Concerts' each spring, conducted by Landon Ronald, who soon built up a considerable following locally. Eighteen orchestral concerts were presented in the space of three weeks at the newly rebuilt Theatre Royal in New Street, which accommodated 2200 (the capacity of latter-day Symphony Hall). Ronald, dapper and shrewd, was a first-rate musician, and with Hamilton Harty as his associate conductor, this series was in safe hands. Archie Camden (principal bassoon in Ronald's orchestra at the age of 21) recalled that 'in Birmingham I was once again playing under two conductors for whom I had immense admiration and respect'.[23]

In her biography of Ronald,[24] Bridget Duckenfield includes a detailed description of these Proms by Grew, who was impressed by programmes 'of architectural firmness'. Standard 19th-century classics were leavened with Richard Strauss, Rachmaninov, Delius and Elgar. Nevertheless, public support remained patchy and, after the 1909 series, Brian was reporting that 'support has been so meagre that they have already come to be looked upon as the last season of promenade concerts'.[25] But continue they did, until 1914, when a combination of financial problems and the Great War supervened. Subsequently, Mossel and Ronald did resuscitate these Promenade Concerts, though they were given earlier in the year.

The Birmingham Symphony Orchestra

In 1909, Brian noted that the members of Halford's orchestra 'have formed themselves into the Birmingham Symphony Orchestra, which, we believe, is being run on co-operative lines'. This ensemble had made its appearance just a year before the Halford Concerts Society gave its final orchestral concert, which was also Halford's hundredth.[26]

On 4 April 1906, Wood conducted the new orchestra's inaugural concert, in the Town Hall, 'Under the patronage of the Lord Mayor of Birmingham', with a fairly safe programme, Tchaikovsky No. 5 being the main work. The listed players include about fifty of Halford's regulars, who had given a Beethoven–Wagner programme with him only a week before, but an explanatory leaflet stated that 'with the exception of one or two Saturday Night Popular Concerts, they only intend to give an Annual Concert in Birmingham, and this with the object of becoming known as an Orchestra, to enable them to undertake concerts and accept engagements outside Birmingham'. In November 1907 we find the BSO playing for many different choral societies, under Elgar, Sinclair[27] and Henry Coward, who brought his famous Sheffield Choir to the Town Hall for a one-off concert. Inevitably, this Birmingham Symphony Orchestra, from the early part of the century, has occasionally been confused with the principal subject of this book – the much later City of Birmingham Symphony Orchestra – but any connection between them was only one of title.

In 1909, the BSO gave concerts under Richter and Vassily Ilyich Safonoff ('the baton-less conductor', whose readings of Beethoven and Tchaikovsky had greatly impressed the 18-year-old Adrian Boult in London, two years earlier),[28] and it continued to give occasional Saturday night Popular Concerts under Wood, Ronald, Halford, Wymark Stratton and Julian Clifford.

3

Granville Bantock – Thomas Beecham

George Halford's declared intention to pull out of orchestral concert-giving gave rise to a situation not dissimilar to that of a decade earlier, in 1897, when William Stockley had retired. In 1907, Birmingham City Choral Society, which had been giving its major concerts[1] under Wood, invited Beecham to become its conductor; under its gifted Chorus Master Fred Beard (whose violinist nephew Paul was to lead the City of Birmingham Orchestra in Boult's day) it was proving a lively rival to the Festival Choral Society. But things were still developing on the orchestral front: in addition to the Birmingham Symphony Orchestra, founded a year earlier, two other new organisations materialised that summer.

Birmingham Orchestral Concerts

The first, a series of Birmingham Orchestral Concerts, launched in June 1907, had powerful backing: Richard Peyton and George Hope Johnstone were pillars of the Musical Festivals; Elgar and Bantock were amongst the sponsors of the scheme, as was Max Mossel, the moving spirit behind this new venture. The idea was to import a series of high-class concerts, using the Hallé and Queen's Hall orchestras, augmented with local players. An eight-concert season was announced, Richter and Henry Wood conducting their respective orchestras, with Max Fiedler (another signatory) and Landon Ronald conducting the remaining programmes.

Ernest Newman, the recently appointed music critic of the *Birmingham Post* (a 'new man' indeed, for the *nom-de-plume* disguised William Roberts, a former Liverpool bank clerk) gave a glowing review to the first of these concerts (an all-Wagner programme), but the series did not survive into a second season.

Birmingham Concerts Society

This series of 'imported' symphony concerts really put the cat amongst the pigeons where Birmingham's professional musicians were concerned, and doubtless a good deal of pressure was put upon Halford to resume his orchestral series. As a result, a Birmingham Concerts Society was launched in 1907, advertising itself as a merger of the Halford Concerts Society and the Birmingham Symphony Orchestra, and announcing a series of eight concerts, given variously under Halford, Stanford, Beecham and Henri Verbrugghen.

The *Post*'s review[2] of the first concert was far from enthusiastic, but Halford did announce a further series of eight concerts for 1908–9, using the Birmingham Symphony Orchestra and some eminent soloists: Elman, Zimbalist, De Greef, Siloti, Godowsky, Santley. Big names were what sold recitals, too – in November 1908, Mossel was promoting Ysaÿe and Irene Scharrer in the Grosvenor Room, whilst Priestley's staged a Town Hall recital with a star-studded cast: Nellie Melba, John McCormack, Wilhelm Backhaus and Joseph Szigeti.

Eventually Halford decided that enough was enough, but not before leaving an indelible mark on Birmingham's orchestral history, for which, as Sir Henry Wood remarked, we should feel eternally indebted to him.

From this point onwards, until the establishment of the City of Birmingham Orchestra in 1920, a name that keeps cropping up is that of Granville Bantock. Up to now he had been too busily engaged in putting the Birmingham School of Music on to a proper footing to give much time to other matters, but once involved in the short-lived Birmingham Orchestral Concerts scheme, he became increasingly drawn into the orchestral debate. Bantock was a man with a mission. He yearned to see a top-class locally based band, and less conservative programme planning; but he was also the ideal entrepreneur. Havergal Brian described him as good-humoured and friendly, without prejudice.

In 1908 Elgar resigned his University Professorship; Newman was a candidate, but Bantock was appointed to replace him. Brian described him as an outstanding Professor, who 'framed a complete system of musical education at the university, on modern lines'.[3]

Birmingham Philharmonic Society

Bantock retained his position at the School of Music, the two organisations working in close liaison. Now in an unassailable position in the city's musical life, he soon conceived the idea of a Birmingham Philharmonic Society. With a little gentle persuasion on his part, a meeting was convened in November

1909 which agreed to enrol guarantors (at one guinea [£1.05] a year, for five years) to provide a financial reserve. Even for that period, the level of guarantee seems extremely modest, but references to opera and to the Festival show that Bantock's plans were ambitious indeed. Margaret Handford notes that 'The Birmingham Philharmonic Society was formed in 1910 with seventy players, mainly derived from the Birmingham Symphony Orchestra, which was still playing the popular Saturday evening series.'[4]

Its inaugural season of eight concerts in 1910–11 was successfully completed under Wood, Safonoff and Beecham (a typically adventurous programme including *Ein Heldenleben*, the Finale from *Elektra, L'après-midi d'un faune* and Delius's *Paris*). By the end of the initial 1910–11 season Beecham's involvement had, in fact, become crucial to the project.

From mid-1911, Bantock started to keep a diary, in which we find him attending Philharmonic concerts, expressing concern about a scathing Newman review of Beecham's Elgar concert ('What was the cause of the thorough badness of the performance we can only conjecture'), pouring oil on troubled waters, involving Neville Chamberlain in a series of meetings and finally persuading Beecham to put up a guarantee of £6000 (a prodigious sum in 1912) to fund the BPS.

Whether this offer was ever taken up is not clear, but if it was, it failed to secure the orchestra's future beyond one further season. The *Post*'s account of the winding-up meeting makes dismal reading, but it is worth quoting, since it touches on matters which will crop up again and again in this book: 'A decision to wind up the Birmingham Philharmonic Society yesterday was come to at a meeting held at Queen's College. Last season's report, already published, disclosed a serious deficiency, and the committee stated they did not feel able to ask for a continuation of large payments on guarantees or for subscriptions to raise a permanent fund from a comparatively small number of liberal donors when there was no indication of public interest to justify the hope that the concerts would eventually become self-supporting.' A thinly-veiled reference was made to Newman's less-than-enthusiastic notices ('the criticism that dwelt in the ethereal atmosphere somewhere up above, where there was no box office') and a vote of thanks was expressed to the organising committee; but nobody seems to have thanked either Beecham or Bantock, despite all the hard work and commitment they had put into the BPS.

The New Philharmonic Society

The outbreak of hostilities in 1914 had a predictably disruptive effect on the city's music. Plans for the 1915 Festival were dropped, and this essentially 19th-century institution did not survive the War. However, 1915 did see the advent of yet one more local orchestra: a 'New Philharmonic Society', directed by Mathew Stevenson, jun., son of the founder of the Midland Musical Society. Ernest Newman considered that 'the name seems a little ambitious for an orchestra that is largely amateur', but Neville Chamberlain was sufficiently impressed to accept its Presidency, and its programmes displayed considerable originality; but by 1917, the New Philharmonic Orchestra's players were entirely supplied by Sir Thomas Beecham's entrepreneurial New Birmingham Orchestra, and it is to that short-lived but influential body that we must now turn our attention.

1917 was the year of the Russian Revolution. The Great War dragged on remorselessly, bogged down in the awfulness of the Flanders mud. Since 1914, Birmingham University campus had been commandeered as a military hospital, and local musicians (together with visitors such as principals of the Beecham Opera Company) rallied round to provide free entertainment for the troops.

Meanwhile, three major planets moved into conjunction in Birmingham: Ernest Newman, Granville Bantock and Neville Chamberlain, the city's musical and political big guns. Although the initial venture that brought them together was to survive only one season, it bore within it the seed of another to follow, which was to fulfil – and eventually to exceed – their wildest dreams. Today we know it as the CBSO.

Newman, Bantock and Chamberlain did not always see eye to eye about methods. Newman may still have harboured some resentment stemming from Bantock's preferment for the University professorship in 1908; Chamberlain and Bantock (a friend of Keir Hardie and a pillar of the Independent Labour Party) were at opposite ends of the political spectrum. But on some things they could all agree: Birmingham needed a first-rate professional orchestra; to achieve it, substantial funding would be required; and the best person to direct it would be Sir Thomas Beecham.

Chamberlain invited Beecham to address a meeting, 'at which all the trite sentiments ever uttered upon such a subject anywhere since life began were rolled out by one speaker after another . . . But of any idea how to put it into practical operation there was little evidence; certainly no one seemed ready to spend any of his own money on it, and the Lord Mayor, Mr Neville Chamberlain, was very clear that the present was not the time to add one farthing to the rates in the interests of the fine arts.'[5]

Beecham goes on to describe how he invited the leading lights of every choral society within a thirty-mile radius to a meeting and struck a deal with them whereby he would engage an orchestra for six or seven months a year, if they in their turn would agree to engage it to play for their concerts, at a cost no greater than they had been paying for freelance players in the past. He also approached the guarantors of the now defunct Birmingham Philharmonic Society to support the new venture.

Writing nearly 30 years on, Beecham cast himself as 'onlie begetter' of the orchestra that emerged in 1917 from these preliminary meetings. He certainly played a crucial rôle as 'front man', but all the evidence points to Bantock and Chamberlain having been the prime movers. Chamberlain (a genuine, if somewhat blinkered, music-lover, who admired Beethoven above all others, and 'knew every note of the quartets'),[6] put his weight behind the formation of a Midland Concert Promoters' Association.

Meanwhile, Bantock was at work behind the scenes, as his meticulous diaries show: '4 October 1916: Handed to Lord Mayor a Memorandum on Orchestral Music for the Midlands.'

A working party was set up, consisting of Bantock, W. Ellary Warden and Gerald C. Forty, to sort out the details of the scheme; Chamberlain approached Beecham to become Musical Adviser and Bantock's Memorandum was issued to the Press.

'18 December: In evening Mr Forty came in for an hour & we discussed Newman's article in today's "Post", attacking my Memorandum.' The article was in response to an anonymous piece in *Musical Opinion* which had hinted that Bantock's Memorandum had given rise to discord in the city's musical world. Newman pointed out that, as long ago as August 1913, he had suggested in the *Post* that the old 'guarantee' system was discredited, and that a combination of a subvention from the rates plus an endowment fund 'of at least £2000' (the annual interest from which would be used to fund the orchestra) would be a better solution. He referred to two Hallé concerts which he had supported 'with a view to keeping the feeling for orchestral music "warm" until the time came for appealing to the endowment fund'. At the second of these concerts, on 22 March 1916, Chamberlain had made a speech during the interval, endorsing Newman's idea and suggesting a contribution from the rates. 'This last was an old idea of mine and though it can't be done now I thought I might as well start the ball rolling . . . I should very much like to see a really good local orchestra formed in Birmingham.'[7]

In his article of 18 December, Newman also pointed out that more than a year before he had mooted a scheme for a new complex, to include a large and a small concert hall, and had received a promise of support for this from Beecham. He now suggested that when the proposed orchestra was established, local musical bodies should be encouraged to engage it; that Beecham be engaged as Musical Director, having charge of the major concerts jointly with other internationally known conductors; and that 'the most promising of the younger English conductors' should be engaged for the Saturday Popular concerts.

Seeing that Forty, Warden and Chamberlain were precisely those with whom Bantock had himself been consulting, it seems odd that he had not gleaned all this already, but perhaps he was better at dreaming up his own schemes than at listening to others' ideas. In effect, Newman was saying that Bantock was a Johnny-come-lately – that in his Memorandum, which had mooted an endowment fund of £10,000 and annual expenditure of £5000, he had done neither his homework nor his sums properly, and that 'The whole scheme suffers from elephantiasis'. It must have taken all Gerald Forty's tact to persuade Bantock that there was a lot of sense in what Newman was saying, but eventually, on 20 February 1917, he wrote to Newman, 'offering to bury the hatchet'.

Shortly before this, plans for the new orchestra had been approved, the most significant proviso being 'that it should be partly or entirely supported from the rates . . . The anticipated cost might work out at £190 per week.'[8] What followed was the logical outcome of all this groundwork: '2 March: Present at conference in Queen's Hotel at 4.00pm in Beecham's room, when he made his generous offer to the Midland Concert Promoters' Association to provide a permanent local orchestra for 3 years.'

With this exciting new development, Bantock's object appeared to have been achieved, and after noting that he received a visit on 10 March from Sir George Kenrick, when they 'talked over Beecham Orchestra scheme', he seems to have bowed out for a while, leaving Priestley and Forty (listed in the programmes as 'Sir Thomas Beecham's Representatives') to get on with making the practical arrangements.

The New Birmingham Orchestra[9]

For its initial season, 1917–18, the Midland Concert Promoters' Association announced a series of nine Wednesday Symphony Concerts, using an orchestra of up to 77 players. Beecham had evidently struck a deal with the Hallé Orchestra, who supplied a dozen or so strings for each of the Wednesday Symphony Concerts.

Wood, Ronald and he were to conduct three Wednesday Symphony Concerts each, with Sammons, Moiseiwitsch and de Greef amongst a strong line-up of soloists. Many vocal items were still given with piano, Appleby Matthews being the regular accompanist. Beecham's own programmes were the most adventurous, with *Brigg Fair, Petrushka*, Rimsky-Korsakov's *Antar* and Lalo's *Symphonie Espagnole*. The ten Sunday Concerts were more run-of-the-mill, using an orchestra of around 60 musicians playing under a mixture of visitors and local conductors. Remarkably, the CBSO's far-from-comprehensive Archives do contain the Account Book for Beecham's orchestra, meticulously handwritten by A. H. Shephard, its 'Librarian and Orchestral Secretary'. Shephard was one of the great survivors, the City of Birmingham Orchestra's ever-resourceful 'fixer' and secretary. A few key musicians were paid on a weekly basis, the remainder *ad hoc*. 'Rank and file' string players received one guinea for a rehearsal and a concert. The Leader, T. H. Smith, received two guineas. On the same fee (sometimes more, up to three guineas a concert) was the principal cellist Johan C. Hock, a brilliant but temperamental Dutchman who dominated the orchestral scene in Birmingham for some thirty years.

Between September 1917 and June 1918, the New Birmingham Orchestra was involved in nearly 60 concerts, of which only 19 were self-promoted, the remainder involving the supply of musicians to various promoters around the Midlands. On Monday, 24 September 1917, the front page of the *Birmingham Post* was dominated by impressive double-column advertisements for the New Birmingham Orchestra's own Wednesday and Sunday concerts; for the New Philharmonic Society's series; and for an enterprising Appleby Matthews concert in which Elgar's *The Fourth of August* received its first complete performance. All of these concerts used the NBO. The Birmingham Symphony Orchestra's little advertisement for its own series of four Saturday concerts looks rather apologetic by comparison. Chamberlain was also working hard to get the NBO off the ground; 'I shall be really pleased', he had written, 'if I can get something done for music, because it is the one thing I always had in mind to attempt if I ever did become Lord Mayor.'[10] On 5 November he addressed a meeting of all Birmingham's leading music-traders – eleven in all – and secured their co-operation in a non-competitive ticket-selling scheme for the NBO.

Newman gave favourable reviews both to the new orchestra's very first appearance on 29 September (under the ægis of the NPS, with Stevenson and Eugene Goossens sharing the conducting) and to Beecham's first concert on 10 October. But he also had to report 'a regrettably large number of empty seats at the Town Hall'. Bantock's diaries show that Beecham was grooming his patroness, Lady Cunard, to underwrite the project, but at this juncture, 'My representative in the town [Forty] notified me that the Government had taken possession of every building where music could be given and asked what was to be done about it. I replied that the proposition was transparently clear: no hall, no music; no music, no orchestra; and that it was for Birmingham to decide if this was what it wanted.' The Town Hall was used (for a few months only, up to the end of the War) by the Food Control Department for the issue of ration books. Chamberlain decided not to intervene, and the New Birmingham Orchestra was precipitately wound up.

With a quarter-century's hindsight, Beecham wrote that he had not incurred 'more than a reasonable loss', but from the fact that he made no attempt to resuscitate the scheme when the Town Hall was made available again in November 1918, it seems very likely that the orchestra was already in financial difficulty. From 1920, his personal financial problems absorbed all his energies for a year or two, though he later made occasional guest appearances for the City of Birmingham Orchestra and for its successor the CBSO, in addition to frequent visits to the Town Hall with his own orchestras. Sir Thomas never really forgave Birmingham for its failure to support his various orchestral enterprises in the city, into which he poured a considerable amount of money and effort, and in his customary end-of-concert speeches he would often pull the legs of the local politicians. But he was also able to claim that 'the effort was not entirely in vain. I had demonstrated that the thing could be done in a practical and fairly economical way, and a few years later the city council came forward with a grant which brought about the establishment of an actual municipal orchestra.'[11]

So there it is. We have examined ten precursors of the City of Birmingham Orchestra, and we could have glanced at ten more. The New Birmingham Orchestra came nearest to succeeding, and most of its 'back-room boys' – Bantock, Chamberlain, Forty, Warden, Shephard, Matthews, Wassell – went on to found the City of Birmingham Orchestra. Imported and locally-based orchestras had been tried in the city, with varying degrees of success. Amongst the latter, there was considerable continuity between each ensemble and its successor, in terms of playing personnel and of management. But even with guarantors, and a substantial number of engagements from other promoters, none was able to subsist for more than a few seasons on Box Office takings alone. It had become increasingly evident to Bantock – and by now to Chamberlain too – that public funding alone held the key to long-term success. The stage was set at last for that bridge to be crossed.

4

Genesis

'At the end of the First World War, Birmingham was the second city of the British Empire. It was three times the size of Glasgow, and twice the size of Manchester and Belfast.'[1] The huge corporate sigh of relief resulting from the Armistice in 1918 gave rise to a spate of plans for a spanking new, up-to-date Birmingham. One of these involved a Civic Centre, designed to include Municipal Offices, a Public Library and a 5000-seat multi-purpose hall. Baskerville House, a much-modified version consisting entirely of City Council offices, was eventually embarked upon in 1938. Chamberlain and his associates repeatedly promoted the idea that if Birmingham only had a big enough concert hall, its orchestra could eventually make ends meet without any public subvention, ignoring the uncomfortable fact that, despite very modest seat prices, none of Birmingham's previous professional orchestras had even been able to fill the 1750–seat Town Hall on a regular basis.

Granville Bantock's 1918–19 diaries give a distinct impression of *déjà vu*, as we find him chairing a series of unofficial meetings, very similar to those he had held in 1911–12 and 1916–17. But this time the stakes were higher, and those invited consequently more high-powered. On 17 December 1918, a few weeks after the Armistice, they included Warden; Newman; G. W. Hubbard (editor of the *Birmingham Post*, 1906–33) and the City Treasurer, Arthur Collins. January 1919 saw a further series of meetings, now with Forty present, discussing financial estimates and ultimately producing the final draft of a scheme to be submitted to the City Council.

Sensing that the support of the *Post* would be crucial, Bantock cultivated Hubbard and Newman especially. He and Alfred Hayes, long-serving Principal of the Midland Institute, visited the widow of John Feeney (philanthropic son of the founder of the *Post* and its Proprietor for many years) at her home in Berkswell, near Coventry, to seek her support. He drew in Clayton Cooper[2] and the piano-store proprietor Joseph Riley; he also visited Neville Chamberlain at the House of Commons, and would doubtless have taken the chance to lobby Henry Wood when he found himself sitting next to him at a Festival Choral Society concert.

On Monday, 17 March, Bantock, Warden and Forty submitted the draft Orchestral Scheme to the Lord Mayor, Sir David Brooks, at the Council House. On 23 May, Brooks provided Bantock with a list of guarantors; effectively, the new orchestra was in business, and on 27 May 1919 the *Gazette* reported 'that the committee which had been considering the question of establishing a permanent orchestra for the city had now received the necessary financial guarantees, and that therefore the Corporation was in a position to proceed with the scheme'.

This is first time we hear of the City Council becoming involved, but already the Old Boy Network that operated amongst the old Birmingham families which exercised such a powerful influence over the city's commercial, cultural and political life had clearly been at work, discreetly signing up guarantors, who were invited to underwrite the scheme up to a stated limit, for the first season at least. This may sound like good news, but it is worth remembering that Bantock's stated aim for Beecham's 1917 orchestra was 'that it should be partly or entirely supported from the rates'. Nothing about guarantees, or private patronage, or a 'municipal orchestra' (with staff and musicians as local government employees) – just an independent body receiving a limited amount of public funding in order to bridge the gap between income from the Box Office and solvency. There is no doubt that Chamberlain and his associates had extremely high ideals, envisioning a post-war Birmingham worthy of a brave new world. Bantock would have gone along with that, too, but not with its hidden agenda: nowadays we would call it Private Sector Funding.

Private patronage had operated in well-to-do Birmingham through the Musical Festivals. Now the long-discredited guarantee system was being dragged inexorably into the funding scheme for the city's new orchestra. Even Bantock found himself drawn into the process: there are several references in his 1919 diary to guarantors whom he had successfully lobbied, including the Lloyd family, which has staunchly supported the City Orchestra to the present day.

Needless to say, orchestras are grateful to receive funding from any source, but it is crucial to their artistic and financial health that any sponsorship should be without strings attached; patronage can so easily become either patronising or paternalistic.

The scheme was an exciting one, but it fell far short of the 'permanent orchestra' of which everyone had been talking for so long. It provided for 'an orchestra of 70 instrumentalists, composed as far as possible of local players, who will be employed under conditions approved by the Musicians' trade union. The season will be from October to May, a period of 30 weeks.' The players could readily find summer employment in the little orchestras maintained by the spa and seaside towns. In addition to a series of twelve Wednesday Symphony Concerts in the Town Hall, regular 'Popular Saturday and Sunday Concerts' were proposed, but the orchestra was also 'to devote other performances to light music for dancing', besides 'free concerts for Council School children' and concerts in the city's parks.

The annual estimated cost of running the orchestra was put at £8500 and the revenue at £6000, leaving a deficit of £2500 to be met half by guarantees and half by an annual grant from the rates, initially for a five-year period. This was the first time that a fully independent symphony orchestra had been in receipt of public subsidy in this way, anywhere in Britain.

A leading article in the *Birmingham Post* on 28 May added a footnote to the effect that, after those five years, 'it might be expected that the undertaking would be self-supporting'. But everything pointed to the fact that if it were to be both worthwhile and fully professional, it could *not* be totally self-supporting. Not in five years. Not in seventy-five years.

An interview with Bantock concentrated on the urgent need to catch recently demobbed young servicemen who were musically qualified, before they took jobs elsewhere. He claimed that, in 'Beecham's orchestra',[3] 70% of the players had been former students of his at Birmingham School of Music. As to a permanent orchestra for the city, Bantock went on to say, 'There was pretty general agreement as to the most suitable appointment for the permanent conductorship, but it would be premature to make any statement on that point.' If he had Beecham in mind yet again, he was going to be disappointed.

The City of Birmingham Orchestra

In the summer of 1919, Ernest Newman left Birmingham, to be replaced at the *Post* by A. J. Sheldon. On 19 June, the guarantors met at the Council House under the chairmanship of Sir David Brooks. Neville Chamberlain and Sir George Kenrick were elected Vice-Presidents and a small Sub-Committee was set up, whose brief was to appoint a manager, a paid secretary and a worthy conductor for the new organisation, which was to be known as the City of Birmingham Orchestra. Probably the name stemmed from a wish on the council's part to stamp the name of the 'City of Birmingham' indelibly into the new body's persona. At all events, they succeeded in giving it a title which was already uncomfortably clumsy in 1920 and was to become almost unmanageable when the 'Symphony' was added, at George Weldon's behest, after World War Two. To most concert-goers it soon became 'The City Orchestra' or 'the CBO', and (after 1947) 'the CBSO'.

By a happy chance, the CBO's first Minute Book, long assumed lost, came to light in the early 1980s – an unpretentious affair, the first entry (reproduced in Note 4) handwritten by Warden, the Honorary Secretary. The committee formed an experienced group, but it made terribly heavy weather of the task of setting up the CBO. The brief Minutes of the second meeting reveal a number of tensions and misunderstandings; Forty and Mossel, for example, were understandably put out to discover that Bantock had been sounding out some of the local conductors off his own bat. Councillor George Johnson was elected Chairman, but as meetings proceeded and Bantock gradually eased back, it is Gerald Forty's beneficial influence that one begins to sense above all. Nevertheless, as the Committee tried to pursue the City Council's brief, its suggested budget began to look increasingly unattainable and any thoughts either of engaging a major international figure as the CBO's first conductor or of taking on an experienced orchestral manager soon faded.

Beecham's term 'Municipal Orchestra' is used in the Minutes from time to time, but the CBO was never that. It took a long time for the Council's preferred title of 'City of Birmingham Orchestra' to gain general acceptance, and when in mid-November advertisements were placed for a conductor,[5] it was under the headline 'Birmingham City Orchestra'. The position was offered in the first place for one season only; applicants were invited to apply by 1 January 1920, stating the salary required and their experience.

Numerous applications were received, but the Minute Book lists only the four who were shortlisted by the Sub-Committee on 5 January: Edgar Bainton, Julius Harrison, Appleby Matthews and Richard Wassell. Bantock knew all the candidates well, so he declared an interest and withdrew from the selection panel. The two leading local music critics – A. J. Sheldon and Robert Buckley – were brought in to replace him at the interviews on 12 January. At these, it emerged that neither Bainton nor Harrison 'would feel justified to leave their present work[6] and remove to Birmingham for one season's engagement only', but the Sub-Committee did not feel that they could extend the tenure 'as the Grant from the Rates is dependent upon the generosity of a number of Guarantors whose enthusiasm for the movement may possibly dwindle'. So the two local men were left to fight it out.

Sheldon, who had succeeded Newman at the *Post* only in 1919, was far more familiar with Matthews's work than with Wassell's, and both he and Buckley spoke up forcibly in favour of Matthews. Indeed, 'Mr Sheldon expressed the view that Mr Appleby Matthews was likely to become one of the leading conductors of the day.' A week later, Matthews and Wassell were interviewed again, this time in the absence of the music critics, and it was unanimously agreed that a recommendation should go forward to the Executive Committee to appoint Matthews 'at a salary of £450 for the thirty weeks' season, or £600 for the year'.[7] Wassell was to be offered eight concerts during the season (making him, in effect, the CBO's Assistant Conductor) and 'well-known visiting conductors' were to be invited 'to conduct all or part of the Symphony Concerts'. On the same day, Monday, 19 January 1920, these proposals were accepted.

Thomas Appleby Matthews, the first conductor of the City of Birmingham Orchestra, was quite a character. 'He was rather like a little peacock,' said Leon Goossens, who played principal oboe for him at several CBO concerts in the Town Hall in 1920–1. 'He was a very short man, and he always tried to walk a little bit taller than he really was.'[8] Edna Iles, who studied with Matthews and played her first Concerto with the CBO under his direction in 1921, at the age of 15, feels that Goossens overstated this aspect, but the extant photos seem to lend some support to his assertion. A 13-year-old when Stockley retired, Matthews had witnessed virtually all the changes in Birmingham's musical scene described in the foregoing chapters. A first-class keyboard player, he played viola in Halford's orchestra and could also turn his hand to the violin. His wartime 'Appleby Matthews Concerts' were characterised by some imaginative programme building – a series including all Debussy's latest chamber works, for example – which had attracted favourable notices from Ernest Newman.

He was an experienced choir trainer (with his own 'Appleby Matthews Chorus', also acting as local chorus master for the Beecham Opera Company) and had conducted the Hallé Orchestra in Manchester in 1916. In the same year he won Elgar's confidence by his performances of *The Spirit of England*, conducting the second and third movements in Birmingham Town Hall a month after Elgar had conducted their first performances in Leeds and London. Newman gave him a pretty good review, observing that 'all he needs is technical experience'. Then, on 4 October 1917, Matthews secured a notable *coup* by conducting the première of the recently completed first movement, *The Fourth of August*, in Birmingham, with Rosina Buckman, the Appleby Matthews Chorus and the New Birmingham Orchestra. Newman wrote that 'Elgar's confidence in Mr Matthews was not misplaced. Those of us with a knowledge of all the musical centres can say that nowhere in England could last night's performance have been bettered.' Praise indeed, from one of the leading music critics of the day.

Matthews was well aware, though, that his technique needed refinement, and shortly after his appointment was announced, he contacted Adrian Boult, seemingly about the possibility of having a few private lessons, and received a friendly and positive reply. Boult attended Matthews's rehearsal and concert in the Futurist Cinema on Sunday, 25 April, and, according to John Crowder, some lessons ensued.

Appleby Matthews also conducted the City of Birmingham Police Band. In a personal letter dated 18 June 1920, Lady Brooks, the Lady Mayoress (who was to prove a loyal supporter of the CBO), congratulated him 'most heartily on the metamorphosis that has taken place since you took the Band in hand . . . You have made of it a thing that is capable of giving a live interpretation of whatever it is called upon to handle.' Harold Burnett, another good friend of the orchestra over half a century, had 'many happy memories . . . of the band concerts in Cannon Hill Park . . . our very fine police band was the pride and joy of the Chief Constable, Sir Charles Rafter, himself a competent flute player.'[9]

Matthews was a workaholic with quick fingers, a quick brain and (sometimes to his cost) a quick tongue. Accustomed to the nitty-gritty of the freelance world, wheeling and dealing came as second nature to him, but you really have to admire the cheek of anyone who could undertake 'to place his services entirely at the disposal of the City Orchestra', on the basis of a fee of £450 for 30 concerts, and then turn up at his first Committee Meeting, only three months later, with a completely new and far more ambitious scheme, involving the guarantors in a potentially far higher level of commitment and a fee for Matthews himself of £1000 for the season, inclusive of 'the cost of necessary Secretarial and Management expenses'. He even succeeded in persuading the Committee to backdate his salary to the beginning of the year.[10] Matthews had rolled two jobs into one for himself, as a sort of 'actor-manager', and the Committee must have felt that they were getting excellent value for money. With hindsight, we can see that the decision to appoint as both conductor and manager a man who had only limited experience in either field was dictated by financial and practical considerations rather than by artistic ones; but now it was up to Matthews to deliver the goods, if he could.

5

Appleby Matthews – Innovator

Genesis came within an ace of becoming *Exodus.* Matthews was well aware that there was only a limited pool of competent local professionals, most of whom were earning their living playing in the hotels, restaurants, theatres and cinemas.[1] A key element in his scheme was that whenever more than two wind players were required in a section, he would be able to call upon his Police Band players[2] to fill the vacant seats, thus economising both on fees and on the additional cost of importing 'extras' from out of town. Not surprisingly, when the Amalgamated Musicians' Union got wind of this, all hell broke loose, and during the summer of 1920 it began to look as if the CBO might achieve the unhappy distinction of becoming the only orchestra to have a strike on its hands before it had played a note of music! However, Matthews succeeded in holding them at bay long enough to plan and launch his 1920–1 season, for which he planned eight Saturday Popular and six Wednesday Symphony Concerts in the Town Hall, plus 38 Sunday Popular Concerts in a less expensive venue. To keep costs down even further, some of the Popular programmes were to be chamber concerts.

Time was short, but on 18 June Matthews was able to report that he had succeeded in negotiating a deal with Philip Rodway, Manager of the Theatre Royal, New Street, for Sunday evenings throughout the season. This was a shrewd move, not only because the theatre was capacious, centrally located and well suited to orchestral concerts but also because it was already associated in the minds of Birmingham's older concert-goers with Landon Ronald's popular and long-running Promenade Concerts.

Matthews's estimates implied the use of a modest-sized orchestra of local players for the Sunday series, augmented with players from London and elsewhere for the Wednesday Symphony Concerts.[3] Obviously they would need to work together as much as possible before meeting either the Town Hall audience or the distinguished guest conductors engaged for the Symphony

Concerts; but, keen to make as favourable an initial impression as possible (and doubtless relishing the prospect of conducting a large orchestra), he actually engaged 75 performers for the first few Sunday Concerts, taking him way over budget. Finally, at 9.30 a.m. on Saturday, 4 September, in the Police Band Room at Steelhouse Lane, Appleby Matthews rehearsed the City of Birmingham Orchestra for the very first time, and after another rehearsal in the theatre on the following morning, the 'Grand Opening Night' took place at 7 p.m. on Sunday, 5 September 1920, in Birmingham's Theatre Royal.

1920–1

Appropriately, the very first music to be played by the CBO, with Matthews's regular leader Alex Cohen, was Bantock's Symphonic Overture, *Saul.* Tchaikovsky's Fourth Symphony was the main work, with Wagner's *Tannhäuser* Overture to finish the concert on a triumphant note. In the *Post*, Sheldon praised both the quality of the new orchestra and Matthews's handling of it, views echoed by the *Gazette*, the *Dispatch, Musical Opinion* and the *Daily Post.*

Smoking was allowed at Sunday concerts, but Matthews was determined to get away from those old 'Smoking Concerts', in which few items exceeded five minutes in duration, so he routinely included a symphony, even in his Sunday Popular Concerts. Bantock and Holst conducted major scores of their own, the orchestra augmented by players from the Beecham Opera Company, then playing at the Prince of Wales Theatre.

A soloist was a *sine qua non* on Sundays, but the public preferred vocalists, who generally sang an item with orchestra in the first half, and a group of songs with piano in the second. Many were local artists, but their choice of songs was a law unto itself, so even if Matthews programmed an all-Tchaikovsky or all-Beethoven night, listeners might well find themselves treated to 'A Brown Bird Singing' between the items.

Having launched his Sunday concerts (some of which were conducted by Wassell), Matthews announced in October a monthly series of Symphony Concerts, 'musically the finest which has ever been offered to Birmingham'. He put together as strong a team as his resources would allow, buying in, for his first series of Symphony Concerts, most of Henry Wood's Queen's Hall Orchestra wind principals. Leon Goossens (oboe), Haydn Draper (clarinet), Wilfred James (bassoon) and Alfred Brain (horn) were representatives of the four most famous families of English instrumentalists at that time, all members of the London Wind Quintet, which made acoustic recordings for the Edison Bell label at this time.[4]

Birmingham's own musical families were also well represented: Paul Beard, who led the violas, with his father Albert alongside him, replaced Alex Cohen as Leader a year later, still aged only 19. There were three Cockerills (double bass and harp), three Yorkes (all horns)[5] and, in time, three generations of Heards (a violinist and three flautists).

The Elgar concert was followed by Hamilton Harty conducting one of his 'party pieces' – Berlioz's *Symphonie Fantastique* – and Vaughan Williams, who directed his own *London Symphony.* Boult (who would play a major rôle in the CBO's later history) and Ronald conducted the Second Symphonies of Rachmaninov and Brahms respectively, while Matthews took on a Beethoven concert in which his choir joined the orchestra in the *Choral* Symphony. On Sunday, 20 February 1921, Jean Sibelius conducted a programme of his own music in the Theatre Royal, including the Third Symphony, which was dedicated to Bantock.[6]

Matthews had gambled on taking Birmingham's concert-goers by storm, and he was able to claim that 'The amount subscribed for Symphony Concerts constituted a record for any similar series of concerts in this city'; but attendances at all the series stubbornly refused to fulfil his estimates, and by the end of the year, with the deficit already standing at £1432, we find a note of inevitability creeping into Finance Committee Minutes: 'Mr Matthews asked if he might alter the form of his programmes in future, and make them as popular as possible.' The Feeney Trust (which would later play a major rôle in commissioning new works for the orchestra) came in with a gift of £250, but a month later the shortfall was over £2000; the Sunday Series was foreshortened and a bank overdraft negotiated, to tide the orchestra over until a call could be made on the guarantors. Sunday attendance had averaged between 1500 and 1600 – roughly a two-thirds house, but the expensive seats were not selling; indeed, Matthews's patience with Birmingham's 'top people', with whom he had to deal, was wearing extremely thin.

In December, the vexed question of Police Bandsmen playing with the CBO was raised in the House of Commons, and in January 1921 the matter came up again in a question to the Home Secretary. Matthews must have felt embattled indeed, but he soldiered on, although Sheldon (in the *Post*) and William Beeson (in the *Musical Standard*) were critical both of his conducting and of his managership. The last straw came when Buckley (in the *Gazette*) hailed Ronald's concert in April as 'the brightest and best of the five symphony evenings. Everyone knows which was the dullest and worst.'

Poor old Matthews! It had been Sheldon and Buckley whose recommendations had carried the day in his favour at the original interviews, and now they seemed to be spearheading the local campaign against him. But from the London critics he fared better: the *Telegraph* was generally complimentary about the first season's work, and several praised him warmly for his direction of the initial run of Rutland Boughton's extraordinarily successful *Immortal Hour* at the Rep, for which he assembled an excellent orchestra which included many of his London players, including Leon Goossens and Alfred Brain.

Matthews also introduced a successful series of Saturday afternoon Children's Concerts in the Town Hall, and Clayton Cooper brought forward proposals for the foundation of a City of Birmingham Choir, which was duly formed, with Bantock as President, Matthews as Director of Music and Joseph Lewis as Conductor. At its first performance (Rutland Boughton's *Bethlehem*) Matthews, who conducted, was moved to tears by the performance of Gwen Ffrangcon-Davies as Mary.

1921–2

During the summer of 1921, Matthews evidently regained the confidence of the Committee (now chaired by Councillor R. R. Gelling, who had had dealings with him and his Police Band when Chairman of the Parks Committee) and his plans for the 1921–2 Season attracted a rave review from an unlikely source – the *Manchester Guardian*: 'The striking thing about [the programmes] is that they are all concerts of serious ambition, and are wholly free from the taint of hackneyed popularity which tells of too purely commercial considerations . . . in face of this amazing prospectus, even Manchester may well envy Birmingham its municipal music.'[7]

The Town Hall Symphony Concerts included visits from Albert Coates (who sent Matthews a nice letter congratulating him on the orchestra's rapid progress), Eugene Goossens and Hamilton Harty. The Sunday series moved from the Theatre Royal to the Grand Theatre and included Glazunov's Sixth Symphony and the provincial première of Butterworth's fine orchestral song cycle *Love blows as the wind blows*. Arthur Bliss directed three of his most experimental works: *Rout, Two Studies for Orchestra* and the Storm Music from his incidental music for *The Tempest*. Matthews priced the house as high as he dared, leading one CBO patron to complain to the *Evening Despatch* of 'the excessive charges . . . For 1s. 3d. one has to endure the discomforts of the gallery.'[8]

The playing of the City Police Band had greatly improved since Matthews had taken it over, and on 28 September 1921 he conducted the first commercial gramophone recordings to be made in the city. He did not confine his activities to this country; with his choir he took first prize at the Paris International Musical Festival, where he was awarded a special prize for conducting. In April 1922 he conducted the Berlin Philharmonic, no less, in two adventurous and well-received programmes in the Beethoven-Halle, including what the *Birmingham Mail* described as 'Strauss's "Till Eulens Piegel" '. Six months later, he was back in Paris, in the Salle Gaveau, conducting the Lamoureux Orchestra in an all-British programme; again the notices were excellent, and Matthews saw to it that they were reproduced by the Birmingham papers.

However, the CBO's finances continued to exist on a knife-edge. Paul Beard[9] recalled that since (as Leader) he received the largest pittance, Matthews would pay him first and would then borrow something back from him to pay the next chap, and so on, down the line! By December 1921, a series of small-ads in the *Mail* emphasised that 'The financial anxieties of the City Orchestra would be dispelled if audiences were increased by only 20 per cent. That is all that is asked to preserve an institution which has called forth the approval and envy of the whole country.' Nobody could accuse Matthews of not trying, but it was bad psychology: people buy tickets because they want to attend concerts, not 'to preserve an institution', however worthy.

The remaining Sunday concerts at the Grand were abandoned in favour of a series of twelve 'Suburban Concerts', in cinemas around the region. Matthews, no stranger to such venues, targeted his advertisements at 'My Police Band Audiences' and drew some good houses, at very low prices (1/3d and 1/10d). More out-of-town venues (Cheltenham, Tamworth, Wolverhampton) were also introduced, and the Children's Concerts continued to thrive (at 9d a seat).

1922–3

In 1922 the City of Birmingham Orchestra was constituted as a Specially Authorised Society under the Friendly Societies Act. Councillor G. F. Macdonald became its third Chairman in as many seasons, but he had staying power, and would remain in the post until 1931. Joseph Lewis was appointed Deputy Conductor and allotted a few concerts, but crisis was in the air. In December 1921, the appointment of the new General Secretary, H. S. Goodwin, had finally been confirmed at a salary of £350, deducted from Matthews's £1000. At the same time Matthews had been relieved of all financial responsibilities. Increasingly he was being marginalised by the Committee, which issued, in April 1922, a printed 'Appeal to all those who are interested in music', outlining the CBO's achievements in its first two seasons and setting out the dates for the next. Matthews was instructed to get this printed and distributed, but he must have found it a galling experience, for it mentioned him not once!

To reinforce the Appeal, a Propaganda Committee was set up under the energetic leadership of Lady Brooks; this divided the area into 21 districts, each with a representative responsible for drumming up local support. Gerald

Forty was closely involved in a development which would have far-reaching consequences for the CBO: the establishment of a Birmingham studio for the newly founded British Broadcasting Corporation, at Witton.

By now the basic permanent orchestra for Sunday concerts had shrunk to 35 players – half the planned size – and although Matthews included, as usual, a few novelties, prospects looked bleak. Early in 1923 the Committee received a strongly worded message from Sir David Brooks (now a Trustee), warning them that unless they put their financial house in order they were in danger of losing the City Council grant. They resolved to scrap the loss-making Sunday series, but the players, for whom these weekly programmes were a lifeline in those hard times, offered to undertake them on a co-operative basis. A series of 24 concerts was therefore reinstated, though at a different venue: the Futurist Cinema; John Crowder recalls that its acoustics were 'very good'.

The number of out-of-town promotions was still increasing, too,[10] and local authorities, choral societies and other promoters in the region were circularised about engaging the CBO for their concerts. Summer dates were particularly suggested, in an attempt to move towards the 'permanent orchestra' that Matthews knew could provide the only long-term solution to improved standards and to solvency. The BBC was approached for possible broadcasts, and another positive and far-sighted move was to establish a CBO Library, rather than spend money on hiring orchestral material; some orchestral sets bought from Matthews at that time are still there to this day. But by May 1923, with the deficit standing around £3000, desperate measures were called for and the Secretary, Goodwin, was given notice.

1923–4

On 5 December 1923, the CBO and City Choir gave the first-ever BBC broadcast from the Town Hall, including the première of a work by Christopher Edmunds. Beethoven's *Choral* Symphony had by now become an annual event, but in this season it climaxed performances of all the symphonies, in order, in the Sunday series (excepting only, for some unexplained reason, the First). Otherwise, the programmes stuck to well-trodden paths, though Matthews slipped in a few novelties such as Debussy's *Danse sacrée et danse profane*.

By now, Matthews and the Committee were increasingly at loggerheads. In July 1923 the Committee received a letter from his solicitors, and promptly appointed an honorary legal adviser of their own. On 27 October notice was sent to Matthews 'to terminate the present Agreement between us'. To replace him, they had two names in mind: Eugene Goossens and Adrian Boult. Each had conducted CBO concerts and had proved popular both with the public and the players, but Goossens had recently taken up a well-paid conducting position in the USA, with the Rochester Philharmonic. The Birmingham Committee still had hopes that he might accept an offer from them, and for the 1923–4 season put up an interim package deal – four of the six Symphony concerts, at 100 guineas, his name appearing in equal billing with Matthews in the advertisements for the series. Goossens could only accept three of these dates.

The plot thickened in the autumn of 1923, when 'Sir Henry Wood resigned . . . as conductor of the Birmingham Festival Choral Society and nominated Boult as his successor'.[11] Wood had become increasingly frustrated with the inadequate conditions of the Festival Choral's concert giving but, in his autobiography, *My Own Trumpet*, Sir Adrian remarks that he 'was in no mood to pick or choose and cheerfully accepted the difficulties'. John Crowder joined the Festival Choral Society for a short time when he came down from Cambridge (where he had been a Choral Scholar at King's under A. H. Mann) because Boult was in charge and he had met him there. Michael Kennedy suggests that in accepting the Festival Choral position, Boult was already aware 'that the orchestral scene in Birmingham might soon alter dramatically'. Certainly the fact that the City Orchestra played for BFCS concerts will have influenced his decision to accept. He had made his first appearance with the CBO as long ago as 9 February 1921, getting a warm reception from public and press alike, especially from A. J. Sheldon of the *Post*; he considered Boult's handling of Brahms's Second Symphony at that first Town Hall concert 'a triumph of flexibility, suggestion and control'. Boult appeared again in the Town Hall on 14 November 1923 as a late substitute for Matthews, released 'in compliance with a special request from Birmingham Repertory Theatre . . . to enable him to conduct the opening performance of the *Immortal Hour* in London'.

There is nothing in CBO Minute Books to suggest that Goossens was ever formally offered the conductorship when Matthews resigned, but he was certainly on friendly terms with Gerald Forty and there seems little doubt that the job was his for the taking. However, 'Because of his commitments in Rochester he declined the solo post as well as a suggestion that he should share it with Boult.'[12]

Appleby Matthews conducted his last CBO concert on Sunday, 30 March 1924, in the Futurist Cinema. The main work was Mozart's G minor Symphony, but his choice of three works by Wagner can scarcely have been accidental: '*Träume*' (for the unfulfilled dreams of what might have been); *Wotans Abschied* (for the painful parting of the ways); and, to go out on a note of triumphant defiance, the *Meistersinger* Prelude. Bearing in mind that Matthews and his Committee were by now involved in litigation, the final irony was contained in the Futurist's own advertisement, on the facing page: they were currently showing a film called *Let-not-man-put-asunder*.

Matthews's case against his erstwhile employers was based on the premise that the orchestra's legal advisers had been careless in drafting the letter giving him notice. His solicitors saw a possible action for damages, arising from wrongful dismissal, and in the summer of 1924 this went to Birmingham County Court, where Judge Ruegg found in favour of Matthews and awarded him one month's salary: just over £54. The CBO Committee would have been well advised to have left the matter there, but they decided to take it first to the Divisional Court and then to the Court of Appeal, where it came up in November. However, even the famously persuasive advocacy of Norman Birkett, KC, who appeared for the orchestra, was unable to convince the Judge that their dismissal of Matthews had been within the terms of his contract. The three Lord Justices upheld the original decision, and on 8 December 1924 the CBO Committee, egg all over their faces, authorised the payment into Court of £600.[13]

On this acrimonious note, the City of Birmingham Orchestra and its first Conductor parted company, permanently and irrevocably, though Matthews continued to play an active rôle in the city's musical life for many years to come. The more one looks at his achievements up to 1924 and studies his programmes, the more impressive they seem, and he well deserved the signal honour of becoming, in 1921, the first recipient of Birmingham Civic Society's prestigious Gold Medal. He may not have been the easiest of characters, but he was a man of immense energy and undoubted gifts, who has never really had his due. He was presented with a sticky wicket on which to play, regularly strapped for cash at a time when the Depression was already beginning to bite. Always happier running his own show than working with others, he undoubtedly found the politicians and top businessmen who made up the CBO Committee uncongenial and inflexible, and they in their turn tended to find him unbiddable and uncooperative. There is evidence that 'he had a terrible temper and often lost it with the orchestra'.[14] But undoubtedly he was an expert and versatile musician, and 'a very sincere person, and kind', but no great administrator, generally fonder of bookmakers than of bookkeeping.

From the standpoint of Matthews's lasting reputation, it was to be his misfortune not only that his successor in Birmingham would be of a rather different temperament, able to work with the CBO Committee without strain on either side, but that he was to become, even during his time at the CBO, a major figure in the orchestral life of this country. For its part, the Committee heaved a sigh of relief, and invoked the city's motto: 'Forward!' With hindsight, we can afford to be more generous in our assessment of a remarkable little man, who set high standards and established the CBO's pattern of concert giving for many years to come.

6

Adrian Boult – Orchestra builder

By February 1924 the ground was shifting in Adrian Boult's favour. Two of his friends – Gustav Holst and Sir Hugh Allen – had put in a good word for him with Forty, and whilst in Birmingham for Festival Choral Society rehearsals of Ethel Smyth's *Mass in D* he was able to arrange a short but crucial meeting with him. By the middle of March, an announcement was made in the local press, and on 8 September the Committee confirmed his appointment as the CBO's next Director and Conductor, at an annual salary of £800.

The Annual Meeting was postponed to 29 September, as a result of the Matthews lawsuit; it revealed a financial situation which still gave cause for concern, although the long-term deficit had been reduced by nearly £1000. After the meeting, Chamberlain spoke of music as 'the Cinderella of the Arts' – one which 'would have to remain in the kitchen until some kind fairy godmother would take her to the ball'. He talked, too, of the need for a new concert hall for the city, but a leading article in the *Birmingham Mail* made the point that the City Orchestra could not support itself, though 'wireless' might yet come to its rescue. The *Post* was more positive in its tone, remarking that the orchestra deserved a larger grant to help it over 'the rather long awkward period which must be passed through' before an adequate new concert hall would be forthcoming. Had any of those involved realised that it would be another 67 years before that would occur, they might well have abandoned the struggle.[1]

Bantock sent Boult a letter of congratulation ('one of the kindest I ever received') which spoke of his long-term dream 'to make our city an English Weimar . . . Your advent will bring new life and culture into the place.'[2] Despite his larger-than-life manner, Bantock could always spot real musicianship, and his faith in the CBO's new conductor was not misplaced.

*

Adrian Cedric Boult was born in Chester on 8 April 1889 into a well-off Unitarian family. Two characteristics became apparent from an exceptionally early age: precocious musical awareness, and a sometimes wicked temper. Just thirteen years later, still a Westminster School day-boy, he saw Artur Nikisch conduct a Wagner–Tchaikovsky programme, and knew that he must become a conductor.

The 18-year-old's diary affords an insight not only into his astonishing musicality, but also a glimpse of the rich musical world of London in which he then found himself:

> 23 November 1907: Tetrazzini in *Rigoletto*. She is far finer than Melba, but still I think rather overrated. Her voice is worn, but her runs are beautifully clear still and she acts well. John McCormack and Sammarco both splendid.
> 1 February 1908: Debussy's first appearance in London. He conducted an exquisite performance of *L'Après-midi* and a new thing *La Mer* which seemed too long.

Then came Oxford (lots of rowing and choral singing) and a formative period at the Conservatory in Leipzig, also attending Nikisch's Gewandhaus rehearsals. Then more and more conducting, including the famous private première of *The Planets* in 1914 and work with the British Symphony Orchestra, combined with teaching conducting at the Royal College of Music (Constant Lambert and Leslie Heward amongst his students) and his first venture into print: the admirable *Handbook on Conducting*. By 1924, Boult was ready and eager to take over the musical direction of a symphony orchestra, and to be in a position to plan his own programmes.

He wasted no time in moving to Birmingham, as required by his new contract; he retained his London home, but was hardly ever there. He paid for an office (on the corner of Bennett's Hill and Colmore Row) out of his own pocket, as he did for the services of a secretary and musical amanuensis. The post was filled by an enthusiastic young local pianist and organist, fresh from the Royal College of Music, a tour of the leading German opera houses and an extended visit to Bayreuth, paid for by kind friends; thus began the 55-year-long association with the City Orchestra of Harold Charles Gray (born 1 December 1903).

1924–5

Though Chamberlain and Bantock could now only keep a benevolent eye on proceedings, due to their other commitments, Boult still found himself at the head of a very strong team. Albert H. Shephard had been promoted from the position of Librarian and general dogsbody to become the CBO's devoted and hard-working General Secretary (filling in as 'extra' trumpet from time to time). The Chairman, G. F. Macdonald ('Mr Mac' to the players), also served the orchestra loyally for many years, lobbying his fellow City Councillors and cajoling influential and public-spirited citizens[3] on to the CBO Committee. The link between the administrator and the politician – indeed, the real force behind the orchestra's policy-making – was Gerald Forty, whose innate musical and business sense kept the ship on a straight course even when seas were rough.

Before the season got under way, Forty had good news for the Committee: the Lord Mayor had given permission for the Town Hall to be used for eight Tuesday Symphony Concerts and six Saturday Popular Concerts, free of charge. The Symphony Concerts had necessarily been partly planned before Boult took up his position; he was allocated four, the remaining four being divided between Ronald (now Sir Landon), Goossens (two) and an exciting guest: Bruno Walter. But Boult's influence on the programmes is clear above all, and it was certainly his idea that two of the concerts should be given 'twice-nightly', at 6 p.m. and 8.30 p.m., and at a lower price. But A. J. Sheldon of the *Birmingham Post* haughtily dismissed the idea as 'absurd'.

Adrian Boult chose to open his first Town Hall season, on 7 October 1924, with an orchestra of sixty players[4] and a characteristic mixed bag: Wagner, Armstrong Gibbs,[5] Strauss and Brahms's First Symphony. For the first time, the concert was broadcast by the BBC (an historic occasion, indeed, for it seems to have been the very first 'Outside Broadcast' orchestral concert to have taken place anywhere).[6] Sheldon gave notice straight away that he was not going to prove easy to please, finding 'Mr Boult's *Don Juan* too sober a rake to be a likeable fellow', and the *Mail* was only marginally more enthusiastic. Robert Buckley of the *Gazette*, however, made considerably more encouraging noises about the Saturday and Sunday concerts at the end of the same week, though Boult's spoken introductions on the Saturday did not go down too well with some of the audience.

Boult was very conscious that, as the Depression started to take its toll, his players would need more than just a Sunday concert each week in order to make ends meet. As he told Barrie Grayson in 1980, 'I bought an old "banger" and went around the area, to public schools like Rugby, Oundle, Shrewsbury, Repton and Cheltenham, cadging work for the orchestra. We had to get money and that meant more and more dates.' He was perfectly prepared to share the conducting if that would secure an engagement.[7]

Matthews and Boult were both hard-working and resourceful in promoting the CBO, but they came from rather different social backgrounds (more significant in the 1920s than nowadays). Matthews had skilfully exploited the musical world that he knew, and fought his Committee tooth and nail to achieve his ends; Boult could talk their language and was able to take them along with him as he tried to expand the CBO's horizons. But he was also more at his ease dealing with public schools or the big festivals. Boult built on Matthews's foundations, but he expanded them too.

Ever eager to experiment, he introduced a series of four lunch-time concerts in the Town Hall, at sixpence a time. Musical education was of paramount importance to him and he soon established close links with the local branch of the British Music Society, giving lectures under its auspices on the Thursday before each Symphony Concert, at which he and Michael Mullinar would play excerpts from the music to be heard on the following Tuesday. He also persuaded Sir Hugh Allen to let him conduct one of the Royal College of Music's annual 'Patron's Fund Rehearsals', which had never been held outside London, at the Midland Institute – a considerable feather in the CBO's cap.

The weekly Sunday Concerts showed evidence of Boult's careful planning, too. 'Every evening when he wasn't conducting he would go and listen to recitals by local singers, and the best of them he would invite to sing in this series.'[8] Whilst the programmes remained fairly popular in character, the first half of each programme featured music by a single composer, and he was even able to persuade solo singers to toe the line in this regard.

Myrrha Bantock recalled that it became a custom for the family 'to troop down to the Futurist Cinema to attend his rehearsals. We were often accompanied by some of my father's music students from the University. We sat with our feet on the seats in front, bent over miniature scores . . . Boult was a very polite and pleasant man, and conducted in an easy, natural manner. He never objected to this invasion of his rehearsals by young musical enthusiasts.'[9]

Boult looked back on these 'cinema concerts' with great affection, although he admitted that the Futurist had 'the extra disadvantage of allowing us no platform for a pianoforte, thus depriving us of one of the most popular forms of music'.[10] 'There was no artists' room at all and I used to walk in through the main door, take off my coat in the front row and climb onto the platform. I remember, one foul day, when I had just finished the overture, Paul Beard leaned over and said "Do you realise you're still wearing your rubber wellingtons?" '[11]

Eugene Goossens's first Symphony Concert on 27 January 1925 (in which Fanny Davies played a Mozart Concerto) included Bantock's *Hebridean* Symphony. On the following day, the CBO players trooped into Riley Hall on Constitution Hill to record the work for Columbia, not with Goossens but with Boult on the rostrum. Sadly, these acoustic recordings became the victim of modern technology, for electrical recording came into general use later that year. The master discs were evidently destroyed, and all that survives of the historic occasion is a hazy newspaper photograph in the *Birmingham Weekly Post*.

In his book about the great horn player Dennis Brain,[12] Stephen Pettitt mentions that in the winter of 1924–5 the BBC 'formed a permanent Wireless Symphony Orchestra of thirty-seven players, which could be augmented to between sixty and seventy. With the Birmingham Symphony Orchestra, four concerts were given at Covent Garden.' The first three of these were billed in *Radio Times* as 'International Symphony Concerts', for which the CBO seems to have supplied around 30 players.

The first programme, in December 1924, was conducted by Pierre Monteux; the second, in January 1925, by Ernest Ansermet; and the third, in February, by Bruno Walter (who had conducted what Boult described in his autobiography as 'a thrilling concert' with the CBO in Birmingham on the day before the BBC series had opened: 9 December 1924). These must have seemed heady days for the Birmingham players – busy ones, too, for the Ansermet concert was slotted in between a series of Boult's Children's Concerts in Birmingham Town Hall, on the Monday, Wednesday and Friday mornings.

Boult's first CBO season ended with an orchestra dinner, of which a faded photo survives. He was able to give the Committee a reasonably buoyant report, despite a deficit of £2068 on the year's work. Sheldon had proved right about the 'twice-nightly' concerts, which had only drawn two half-houses on each occasion; a few of his other criticisms will have given cause for concern, but in two detailed *World of Music* articles at the end of April he summed up Boult's contribution, not unfairly, as 'a conductor to whose future with us we can look forward with high hopes, provided we accord to him the support his abilities deserve'. Indeed, the Press in general were becoming more upbeat in their tone, both locally and nationally. In a letter to Mrs Coats, CBO Committee member and enthusiast, Ernest Newman wrote, 'I am glad to hear that the orchestra is looking up in Birmingham. Music seems to be in a pretty bad way everywhere, so you need not despair.'

In the *Gazette*, Robert Buckley wrote of 'a wonderful season' and favourable leading articles appeared in the *Birmingham Post*, the *Yorkshire Post*, *The Times* and the *Observer*, all of them urging Birmingham City Council to renew and increase its five-year grant to the CBO. On 7 April 1925 it doubled it, to £2500 annually.

*

1925–6

Boult's second season of Symphony Concerts was dogged by ill-luck. Bantock invited Sibelius to Birmingham in October 1925, to conduct 'his New Symphony' (No. 7). But in a letter to 'My dear old friend', Sibelius politely declined, on the grounds that he was seeing the Sixth Symphony through the press.[13] Instead, Boult asked Holst to share the concert with him, but it was undeniably a disappointment. Then the illness of the soloist (Lidus van Giltay) caused the cancellation of the first performance of Cyril Scott's Violin Concerto. Next, Bantock himself failed to come up with another heralded première, his 'New Symphony' having to be replaced by a performance of the *Four Pagan Chants*, featuring Frank Mullings. A further blow fell when a great Czech conductor also had to pull out of his CBO concert. With disarming candour, the announcement read, 'M. Váčlav Talich has an engagement to conduct in Stockholm on February 28th. Under the impression that there were thirty-one days in February he accepted the Birmingham engagement, which he now finds it impossible to fulfil.' And finally, in October 1925, the ceiling of the Town Hall fell in and while urgent repairs were carried out, the Symphony Concerts were transferred to the rather smaller Central Hall in Corporation Street.

This unfortunate combination of events left Boult's 1925–6 Tuesday Series looking slightly tattered and a touch bland, despite a fine line-up of soloists: Arthur Catterall, Leff Pouishnoff, the Harrison sisters and an impressive performance of the Beethoven concerto by the CBO's own Leader, Paul Beard. But the real novelty of the season came when Priestley's engaged Sir Landon Ronald and the CBO to play for a concert in which Harold Bauer played the Saint-Saëns Second Piano Concerto – except that Bauer was not there at all; he had pre-recorded the work on a Duo-Art piano-roll, 'and in the very difficult task of accompanying the recorded interpretation, the players were often like fairies on the end of Sir Landon's baton'.[14] Ronald 'expressed himself as highly impressed with the improvement since he conducted the orchestra twelve months before.'[15]

The financial situation continued to give rise to concern, but generous offers of £1000 from Sir George Kenrick and £500 from Adrian Boult's father[16] were encouraging to the Committee. Boult went on building up the CBO's out-of-town diary, with some twenty engagements during the season. Occasionally a concert would even take place between seasons: in April 1926, for example, they appeared at the Westmorland Festival in Kendal, and a month later Sir Hugh Allen booked Boult and the CBO for the opening concert of a week-long festival celebrating the 300th anniversary of the Heather Chair of Music at Oxford University.

In West Bromwich, the CBO's Leader, Paul Beard, found himself faced with an inept local conductor whose *tempi* in Dvořák's *New World* Symphony were so laboured that it seemed likely that the players would miss the last train back to Birmingham. His whispered 'Follow me, boys!' spread like wildfire through the orchestra, as he led off the *finale* at a cracking pace, leaving the unfortunate conductor waving his arms in rotary backward circles and protesting loudly, in a broad Black Country accent, '*Yow'm* going too fast! *Yow'm* going too fast!'

In a typical month in 1926, the CBO's Birmingham programme included two Symphony Concerts, one Saturday Concert, two Midday Concerts and one for the Festival Choral Society,[17] plus weekly Sunday Concerts at the Futurist and two Children's Concerts. The BBC was still relaying some of these. Only a month after the ceiling had collapsed, the Town Hall was reopened for concert giving, but repairs were only temporary, and it was apparent that a far longer closure could be expected. In March 1926, the City Council approved an outlay of £37,000 for repairs and alterations. Sir David Brooks used the opportunity to raise again the question of a new Civic Hall. Sir Adrian told Lyndon Jenkins that Chamberlain had assured him, 'Don't worry, Dr Boult, you'll have your new concert-hall before you leave Birmingham.' Inevitably, the considerable cost of remodelling the Town Hall pushed plans for a new hall into the background once again but, bearing in mind what it would have been like,[18] we can probably be grateful that it was not built at that time.

One of Boult's experiments was to play the same work at consecutive Symphony Concerts. On 23 March, the programme stated that 'in response to many requests', Bartók's *Dance Suite* would be repeated at the end of the advertised programme, though, in reality, it had received quite a mixed reception a fortnight before. He rounded off his Sunday programmes with a different kind of repetition, including in consecutive concerts Handel arias from *Israel in Egypt* and *Orlando*, in which different words were set to the same music. His report on his second season noted that 'hardly a rehearsal takes place without a request coming from the orchestra for a repetition of some passage in a work'. Some of the players had even asked if they might have their instrumental parts in advance, so that they could put in some individual practice. This was outside his experience at that time, at least in England.

7

Consolidation

1926–7

The centenary of Beethoven's death loomed large over the season; between the various series of concerts, Boult managed to programme all nine symphonies[1] and a number of shorter works. The Sunday concerts were transferred from the Futurist to the somewhat larger West End Cinema, whose platform allowed the inclusion of works for piano and orchestra – including a few rarities such as the Strauss *Burleske*. Whilst the fee for a local soloist at these concerts was set at two guineas, a big-name artist at a Symphony Concert would routinely receive fifty guineas. This kind of ludicrous imbalance still plagues concert promotion.

Restoration work continued at the Town Hall. Unfortunately, the architect, Sir Charles Allom, had not felt it necessary to consult any of the city's leading musicians about the proposed alterations. To Boult's horror, the balustrades of the lower gallery continued right across the platform so that it effectively cut the playing area in half. Bantock wrote a letter of protest to the Lord Mayor, saying that unless he had a reply within three hours he would send his letter to the *Birmingham Post*.[2] He got his reply, but news of the problems had already reached the *Post*, and for once Sheldon made himself useful, contributing a leading article,[3] demanding that the scheme be rethought, which it duly was; the offending balustrades were modified so that they could be removed for concerts and put back afterwards. Meanwhile, the early Symphony Concerts of the season took place once again in the Central Hall. Bruno Walter agreed to return (a testimony in itself) with a programme whose main work was the Schubert *Great C major* Symphony.[4] The *Mail* observed, 'Everybody was impressed by the way Mr Paul Beard and the others worked to give expression to Mr Walter's thought, and the conductor himself showed clearly how pleased he was with them.'

Boult conducted all the other concerts in the series. For once, Sheldon was driven to superlatives by his reading of *Don Quixote*, with Johan Hock, still the city's leading cello teacher,[5] as soloist. But the real, and highly original, climax of the season had taken place a few days before. Hard on the heels of the Scherzo from the Bruckner Sixth, Boult introduced the music of Gustav Mahler to Birmingham: the Fourth Symphony, with the bright, clear voice of Dorothy Silk in the solo rôle. It was only the work's second performance in this country, and it attracted several London critics, who were complimentary. Even Sheldon conceded that 'after hearing it one could think of little else'.

The season was marked by two important out-of-town excursions. The first, in October 1926, was to accompany a three-week season of opera in Bristol's historic Theatre Royal, underwritten by Philip Napier Miles.[6] This included the première of Ethel Smyth's *Entente Cordiale*, conducted by its redoubtable composer, who afterwards 'stated that . . . the orchestra had fulfilled their task with notable skill'.[7]

Other operas in the season included Purcell's *Dido and Æneas.* Napier Miles's own *Markheim* and *Fire Flies* (the chorus wearing battery-operated blue lights in their head-dresses) and the two major successes of the season, *Così fan tutte* (in which Boult had Bernhard Ord accompanying the recitatives on a two-manual harpsichord dated 1777) and *The Travelling Companion* by Stanford, who had died two years before.

Boult and his forty players[8] had an excellent reception from the local press and public for what must have been an exceptionally intense period of work for them. They had six pre-rehearsals in Bristol, then six evening performances and two matinées each week (24 sessions in all), for which principals were paid twelve guineas a week, others ten guineas, with everyone receiving five guineas to cover the three days of pre-rehearsals. These rates were slightly subsidised by the CBO in order to secure this prestigious job in a highly competitive market, but Shephard reserved the right to demand some reciprocal unpaid rehearsals during the following season.

The second major outing of the season took place on 22 March 1927 and was to Cheltenham, for a pair of concerts in honour of Gustav Holst, the town's best-known musical son. These were organised by Lewis Hann, who taught violin at the Ladies' College; some £400 was raised to pay for an orchestra of 75 players, which had three three-hour rehearsals in Birmingham for an enterprising programme (the same, afternoon and evening) in which Boult conducted the ballet music from *The Perfect Fool* and the *Two songs without words.* Holst (who later described the occasion as 'the most overwhelming event of my life') conducted *A Somerset Rhapsody*, the *Fugal Concerto* and a complete performance of *The Planets.* Correspondence between Hann and

Shephard reveals that there were many problems in setting up this day – Boult had to make a special journey to Worcester in an attempt to persuade the autocratic Sir Ivor Atkins to release some CBO players from a choral concert, and arrangements had to be made for a train to stop specially in Cheltenham to pick up the players and enable them to get back by midnight, thus avoiding heavy overtime payments.[9]

The following Sunday, 27 March 1927, saw a special concert to mark the centenary of Beethoven's death, at which the singer (in '*Ah! Perfido*' and a group of songs) was Dorothy D'Orsay, an old friend of Boult and one of the stars of the Bristol Opera Season. Boult still ran a successful series of Children's Concerts, on Saturday afternoons throughout the season, with repertoire ranging from Haydn to Robin Milford.

The Town Hall was finally reopened after its refit on 12 April 1927. The City Council had accepted Allom's proposals to increase the seating capacity by ripping out the original Great Gallery and replacing it with two new ones. As a result, Hansom's impressively tall windows at the rear of the hall were unforgivably cut in two, creating acoustic dead-spots at the back of the Lower Gallery and the Ground Floor. Sheldon was dubious about the alterations: 'Everything sounded strange, and the effect . . . differed considerably according to the position in which one happened to be.'[10] At a concert marking the reopening, the prodigious total of £26,000 was raised in aid of local hospitals – that would have been more than enough to have cleared the CBO's accumulated debt and established a substantial endowment fund for the future.

But, all in all, it had been an exciting and promising season. Despite the continuing nation-wide recession, members of the Committee were achieving some success in attracting gifts to reduce the accumulated deficit, with firms such as Mitchells & Butlers and Lewis's making helpful donations. Another good friend of the CBO, Harry Keep, underwrote a Saturday Concert at the Digbeth Institute, with tickets priced at only 3d and 5d; the weather was bad and he had to meet a considerable loss. Through the good offices of Sir Charles Rafter, Richard Wassell's Police Band raised £925 towards the City Orchestra – a remarkable effort, which enabled the Committee to take up Sir George Kenrick's offer at last, and thereby see off the debt. But on the downside, to Boult's considerable dismay, the Committee did 'not yet feel confident to engage a permanent orchestra'.

1927–8

Every time things seemed to be looking up, they started to go wrong. The BBC had already stopped broadcasting CBO promotions, as the result of a national dispute with the Musicians' Union, whose members had up to now earned nothing from these relays. Having recently taken over the London Promenade Concerts, it was looking to put regional music on to an organised basis, especially as in 1928 its Birmingham station (5IT) was upgraded to become 5GB, serving the entire Midland area. Sixteen of the CBO's best players were now offered full-time BBC contracts, which, understandably, most accepted.

Secondly, when the great Al Jolson could at last be both seen and heard on the screen, there was a double knock-on effect for the orchestral players: those who still earned a regular living in the cinema ensembles were soon out of work; and the novelty of the 'Talkies' provided even more competition from the cinemas in respect of orchestral concert attendance.

Finally, Adrian Boult was taken ill at a concert in the West End Cinema on 9 October. His deputy Joseph Lewis was sent for, and meanwhile Paul Beard conducted ('with more than credit') Dvořák's *New World* Symphony. When Lewis arrived, he had the even tougher assignment of conducting (sight unseen) the accompaniment to Birmingham's first hearing of Falla's *Nights in the Gardens of Spain*; but he 'rose to the occasion magnificently'. Boult tried to shrug off his illness, and gave his usual report to the Annual Meeting three days later, but despite a holiday in the USA earlier in the year, he had been seriously overdoing things,[11] and was forced to take three weeks off. He returned for a few more concerts but was soon taken ill again, and packed off to Egypt by his doctor, for a much needed rest. In his absence, Joseph Lewis kept things ticking over, and in January 1928 Boult returned, much refreshed, and on Sunday the 22nd had a terrific reception from the audience: 'the row at the concert was really surprising', he wrote.

The season came to an end on a fairly positive note, with a further £739 contributed from Police Band concerts, and a salary increase for the CBO's General Secretary and Librarian A. H. Shephard, to £500.[12] But attendances were down again,[13] and, reading between the lines, it is clear that the unsettling influence of a number of different problems had also had some effect on overall standards of playing, and had led to some heart searching on Boult's part.

1928–9

Times were still hard. A document called *Birmingham and its Civic Managers, 1928* lists matters of concern to the City Council, presumably in order of importance. It ends: 'Cemeteries; Sewage disposal; Mental defectives; City of Birmingham Orchestra.' As the combined effects of the Depression and the 'Talkies' bit ever deeper into the players' scope for employment, Boult tried harder than ever to increase the number of CBO out-of-town dates, still hoping for that elusive full-time contract. The musicians continued to disappear from Birmingham entirely during the summer, and he 'always dreaded the first few weeks of the season, when root principles had to be restated and seaside habits unlearned'.[14]

It was doubtless for this reason that he called two extra rehearsals for the first Symphony Concert of the 1928–9 season.[15] He was frustrated, too, by a shortage of quality local talent; some 23 engagements were fulfilled, but often with many players from London or elsewhere. This aggravated a long-term problem: CBO contract players had always thrown in pre-rehearsals for Symphony Concerts free of charge, but now might find themselves sitting next to an extra player being paid the proper going rate. The Musicians' Union announced that this practice must cease, but a Players' Committee (which continues to this day) was formed and, complaining that the Union had not consulted its own members, agreed to continue the practice for the time being.

Boult rounded off the season with Beethoven No. 9, and two performances of what was at that time a far rarer choral masterpiece, Bach's *St Matthew Passion*, with a team of top-class soloists: Dorothy Silk, Margaret Balfour, Steuart Wilson and Arthur Cranmer. The critic of *The Times* wrote, 'The great merit of this performance was its consistency, a quality obtainable only where orchestra and choir are permanently under the same conductor, so that players and singers are equally alive to his methods.'[16]

1929–30

By the spring of 1929, rumour was rife about who might succeed Percy Pitt,[17] who had announced his imminent retirement after many years in charge of music at the BBC; the job was to be upgraded to Director of Music, part of whose responsibility would be to conduct the new BBC Symphony Orchestra of over a hundred players. Gordon Beckles wrote, 'All eyes are on Mr Adrian Boult – and no wonder! Though he looks younger than his forty years, he is a man of great experience. He has conducted every orchestra in the country. He lacks platform presence and his personality is not a vivid one. But English composers have no better friend.'[18]

On 10 June the CBO Committee was given news both good and bad. The financial position (boosted by a further £534 from Police Band concerts) showed a surplus, permitting the Lunch-hour and Sunday series to be extended and a continuation of the free Children's Concerts. Furthermore, the well-known local pâtisserie, Pattison's, was to supply refreshments at the Symphony Concerts – a great innovation. But they were also told that Boult had tendered his resignation, with effect from Easter 1930, in order to take up the BBC post. Sir John Reith put pressure on him to take up his position immediately, but that would have involved a breach of faith with the CBO of a kind which Boult could never countenance.

In the July issue of the *British Musician*, Sydney Grew (a close confidant of Boult) observed that 'Three young British conductors come to mind as suitable successors to him. Of these, one is easily prime favourite in the minds of the local musical public.' He added that there were at least 150 others who would like the job, 'for while it is no "plum", it is a situation of vast possibilities'.

By September 1929, Macdonald and Forty had begun interviewing possible replacements; we only know that Stanley Chapple and Leslie Heward had been shortlisted by then, and that they had yet to talk to four more, from whom they shortlisted Julius Harrison, who was well known locally and had indeed been a candidate for the original conductorship in 1920.[19] At some point Basil Cameron's name was added to the list, and during November and December these four candidates were offered trial concerts in the Sunday Series. Boult said, on a later occasion, that 'Heward very easily won the palm'. The February 1930 issue of the *British Musician* included a verse of doggerel about each competitor:

> The second, alert Leslie Heward,
> Of music was proved a just steward;
> For he'd found out the way
> To make his folk play
> As if most things were easy, and few hard.

Gwen Berry was a cellist in the CBO, and later the CBSO, from 1929 until the 1960s; she died in 1974. Her diaries, though incomplete, make fascinating reading. She had already been earning a modest living as a jobbing musician when, in October 1927, she attended a Sunday night concert at the West End Cinema, at which Johan Hock had played Dohnányi's *Konzertstück* for cello and orchestra. She noted in her diary, 'Should rather like to be in the City Orchestra, but still have really enough to do with Trios and Quartets and Picture House.' Two years later Gwen decided to audition for the CBO, 'swotted up' the Dohnányi and on the morning of Monday, 10 September 1929 took it along to play for Adrian Boult: 'He was so jolly you simply couldn't feel nervous. I only played bits of the Dohnányi and then he gave me some reading. My hat! The *Don Juan* thing of Strauss. But I managed to keep in and evidently haven't done so very badly as I have received a notice to play in the eight Symphony Concerts! Isn't it glorious – I could fairly sing for joy.'

The diary really helps to bring these CBO concerts to life for us. On 12 December 1929 she was clearly over the moon about Boult's Wagner concert on the previous evening – especially the Funeral March from *Götterdämmerung*: 'I shall have it played full orchestra over me when I've pegged out, if I can afford it. For one thing it will be a parting engagement gift to a lot of pals and also I ought to be able to hear the racket in that middle section wherever I've got to. The Tubas sounded fine, the tone glorious – just like sitting down on about 20 eiderdowns. Came home in George's car, bellowing bits of Valkyrie.' The soloists at the concert were two great Wagnerians, both trained at Bantock's Birmingham School of Music, whose voices and frames were of truly Wagnerian proportions. 'But Gosh! You ought to see Frank Mullings and Rosina Buckman close up! They insisted on bringing Mr Boult on between them hand in hand, true operatic style, and they made him look like a skinned rabbit.'

The Symphony Concerts looked 'safer' than usual, with few excursions into the unfamiliar, but some well-known names helped to draw the customers. Dr Malcolm Sargent[20] conducted Elgar's First Symphony and Boult included Vaughan Williams's *Pastoral*, but the musical highlight of the season was unquestionably his performance of Mahler's *Song of the Earth*, with Astra Desmond and Steuart Wilson as soloists.[21] This was only the second British performance, the work not having been heard since Henry Wood had given it in London in 1914, so when Sheldon, from his Olympian heights, averred in the *Birmingham Post* that 'the tempi were frequently too slow', Boult finally decided to take him on through the columns of his own paper: 'How does he know? Has he formed a standard by comparing the renderings of various conductors? If so, his experience cannot include Mengelberg's,[22] whose association with Mahler over his own works was probably as close as Bruno Walter's. His performance has on two occasions, to my certain knowledge, taken several minutes longer than we did on Thursday.'[23] The letter must have provided Boult's many admirers with a great deal of amusement, and it would certainly have given him considerable satisfaction to write.

In January 1930 Gwen Berry reported that 'the BBC orchestra will probably be drafted into the CBO and the places will have to be played for by audition! I s'pose I shall have to swot up a concerto again, to be prepared. Oh dear, what an effort!'

Another development with long-term consequences was the first flowering of Harold Gray as a conductor. Up to this time, his association with the CBO had been as Boult's amanuensis, secretary and jobbing pianist, but for some time he had been commuting to London for Sargent's conducting classes at the RCM, gaining local experience meanwhile with various choral societies. In December 1929 he called a meeting in Sutton Coldfield (where he was organist and choir-master of the Parish Church) at which Boult spoke enthusiastically, as a result of which a 'Sutton Coldfield Musical Committee' was formed, and a series of concerts initiated.[24] On 30 January 1930 Gray conducted the CBO in the first of these, with the great Australian baritone Peter Dawson as soloist. Gray's mentor Malcolm Sargent sent him a congratulatory note and Boult was in the audience, as was Sheldon, who noted a trifle condescendingly that 'Mr Gray provided evidence sufficient to suggest that there should be a conductor in him'.[25]

Adrian Boult's official Farewell Concert took place in the Town Hall on Thursday, 27 March 1930. It was a Beethoven programme, and Gwen Berry noted in her diary: 'The last of the Symphony Concerts and the farewell dinner to Mr Boult at which our new conductor was present, Mr Leslie Heward . . . We got through the concert all right and there was much speechifying afterwards by Councillor Macdonald as Chairman of the Committee and the Lord Mayor and Mr Boult who was given a desk and a chair. He said he felt sure he ought to feel business-like sitting at it. The Lord Mayor "'oped our noo conductor Mr Yeward . . ." – how Father[26] would have writhed!' Gwen's sense of humour punctures the formality of the occasion at every turn:

> We then toddled round to The White House, where all the men clung together in a terrified herd and the ladies were left to do likewise . . . Further speeches. Mr Forty's very amusing. He was going to prolong the time as far over hours as he could as he was hoping the place would be raided and he would be found with a glass of alcoholic liquor in his hand, in the company of the Chief Constable. They presented Mr Boult with a score of Mahler's *Song of the Earth*, from the Orchestra, and Mr Heward, who looks awfully nice, was dying to have a look at it . . . At the end Mr Macdonald boomed 'How are you getting home, Miss Berry?' and, as I didn't like to confess that I intended to roll home along the tram lines with the boys, he said 'Oh well, you come along with me, I'll see you home.' Went to break the news to Harry[27] and found that he'd just been roped in too, so we both sat very refined and proper in the taxi, and as I sat beside Mr Mac's boiled shirt, I longed to ask him if his dull top hat was the kind that conked in.

Boult's last Sunday concert, on 30 March, included Bach, Beethoven, Mozart, Brahms's Fourth Symphony and, to end with, one of his favourite scores: Parry's *Symphonic Variations*. They characterise perfectly both the man and

Birmingham Council House and Victoria Square:
the fashionable audience leaves the Town Hall (out of picture, left)
after a Triennial Musical Festival concert during the 1890s.
Photo: John Whybrow Collection.

The Halford Orchestra (Leader: Ernst Schiever), with soloist Fritz Kreisler in the Town Hall, 1903. George Halford is on the rostrum and Appleby Matthews (bespectacled) amongst the violas.
Photo: CBSO Archives.

Sir Edward Elgar, with Sir Granville Bantock, c. 1910.
Photo: CBSO Archives.

The New Birmingham Orchestra
in the Town Hall, 1917. On the rostrum
(left to right): Sir David Brooks (Lord Mayor);
Sir Thomas Beecham; and Neville Chamberlain.
Photo: CBSO Archives.

Gerald C. Forty, founder member
of the CBO Committee and Chairman, 1931–1950.
Painting by Bernard Munns, 1918.

Birmingham Town Hall,
from Paradise Street, c. 1920.
Photo: L. W. Lewis, Walsall.

Appleby Matthews,
c. 1920.
Photo: Birmingham Post & Mail.

Appleby Matthews (hand on drum) and the City of Birmingham Police Band, c. 1920. During the 1920s the Band raised huge sums to support the City Orchestra, and bandsmen often played as 'extras' with the Orchestra.
Photo: CBSO Archives.

Adrian C. Boult, c. 1920.
Photo: CBSO Archives.

Adrian Boult and the CBO (Leader: Paul Beard), Birmingham Town Hall, c. 1925. *Photo: CBSO Archives.*

Gustav Holst – a copy of the Herbert Lambert photograph, inscribed by the composer to commemorate the Festival of his music in Cheltenham, 1927. *Photo: CBSO Archives.*

Leslie Heward and the CBO
(Leader: Paul Beard),
Birmingham Town Hall, c. 1931.
Note the suspended microphone.
Photo: CBSO Archives.

Leslie Heward.
Photo: CBSO Archives.

Leslie Heward and Harold Gray – a picnic *en route* for a CBO concert.
Photo: CBSO Archives.

Victor Hely-Hutchinson, who conducted most of the CBO's concerts during Leslie Heward's illness, 1939–40.
Photo: BBC.

The Theatre Royal, New Street
(where the CBO's very first concert had taken place, September 1920)
photographed from Bennett's Hill, following an air-raid in April 1941.
Photo: Birmingham Post & Mail.

the uncompromising artistic integrity which he brought to his six seasons in Birmingham (the only time in his long career, as he often remarked, that he could plan his own programmes without someone else looking over his shoulder).

Although Sir Adrian's treatment of his time with the CBO in his autobiography *My Own Trumpet* is rather laconic (occupying a mere three pages out of 200), he always looked back on those years with great nostalgia and affection, and Birmingham took him to its heart, both during his residency in the Twenties and on his frequent return visits over the following 40 years and more. He worked tirelessly to promote orchestral and choral music in Birmingham, often providing discreet financial help to engage extra players or enable additional rehearsals. He brought many fine soloists to the city, and his musicianship was never in doubt. He would doubtless have given a wry smile as he pasted into the last page of his Birmingham scrapbook A. J. Sheldon's valedictory article, in the April issue of the *Monthly Musical Record*, considerably more upbeat than anything he had written in the *Post*: 'He leaves [the CBO] in a stronger position than when he came to it . . . and takes his leave of us in the happiest possible manner. He was won respect on all sides.'

Sheldon was probably right, however, when he pointed out that Boult had never entirely taken hold of the public's imagination – Birmingham would have to wait until the Forties for a charismatic figure of that kind – but he gave a fair assessment of six years of continuous growth. None the less, Boult will have thought it ironic that, shortly after this, Sheldon retired from the *Post* and was replaced by the balanced and more supportive Eric Blom.

The Public Orator, at the Congregation a few months later at which Adrian Boult received his Honorary Mus.D. from the University of Birmingham got it right when he remarked that in 1925 Birmingham had 'looked for much more than a skilled and inspiring conductor of an orchestra in its cradle. We needed a humanist technician to teach us that music of the right kind is an essential element in a true and progressive citizenship . . . We found that teacher in Mr Boult.' He would have liked that.[28]

8

Leslie Heward – 'A very gifted musician'

In her engaging memoir *As I Remember*,[1] Mildred Boulton recalls that 'One of the clearest memories of the CBO I have is of the night Sir Adrian Boult left us in 1930, having been principal conductor since 1924 . . . I can remember him saying that he was leaving us "in good hands". How right he was. Our next conductor was Leslie Heward.' And in his contribution to the memorial volume[2] published after Heward's death in 1943, Boult wrote of his favourite pupil: 'There are few musicians who cannot treasure in their minds a piece of perfect re-creation from him. I think I would choose an exquisite reading of Wagner's "*Träume*", when he brought the Cape Town Orchestra to Birmingham in 1925. It was one of the loveliest things in my experience.'

In the late 19th century it was left to a trio of German-born conductors – Charles Hallé (b. 1819), August Manns (b. 1825) and Hans Richter (b. 1843) – to set the standard of high-class orchestral music in Britain. They were followed by the first generation of great British conductors: Henry Wood (b. 1869), Landon Ronald (b. 1873) and Thomas Beecham (b. 1879), all of whom were (like Richter) closely involved in Birmingham's musical life at some point in their careers. Of the outstandingly gifted generation born between 1889 and 1899 – Boult, Goossens, Sargent,[3] Heward, Barbirolli – two had charge of the CBO, in a golden period that lasted nearly two decades, from 1924 to 1943.

Leslie Hays Heward was born on 8 December 1897 in Littletown, Liversedge, Yorkshire and showed remarkable early promise. On his eighth birthday he played the organ for Handel's *Messiah*, conducted by his father Herbert, in the Moravian Church, Lower Wyke, Bradford.[4] Sydney Nicholson spotted him playing at a competitive festival in Morecambe in 1910 and arranged a scholarship for him to join Manchester Cathedral Choir School. Nicholson took him to hear his first orchestral concert: Richter and the Hallé. Afterwards, he said, 'Shouldn't I like to conduct that band some day, sir!' He became an avid concert-goer (score in hand) and later attended many of Beecham's British National Opera performances.

Even as a boy, Leslie Heward had poor health: eczema led to asthma and, in time, to the tuberculosis that would bring about his tragically early death. At least his asthma prevented him becoming trench-fodder in the horrors of World War One. Stanford heard him play and recommended him to Parry, whose comment was that 'This is the kind of phenomenon that appears once in a generation'. In 1917 he became an assistant music master at Eton College (where he started a lifelong friendship with Victor Hely-Hutchinson), and for a short while in 1920–1 took charge of the music at Westminster School.[5]

For some time he had been making weekly trips to London to study composition at the Royal College of Music, with Stanford and Herbert Howells,[6] and in due course he became a founder member of Adrian Boult's conducting class, accompanying him on an expedition to watch Artur Nikisch rehearse and conduct the Concertgebouw Orchestra in Amsterdam.

Following a promising conducting début at the Gaiety Theatre in January 1921, Percy Pitt provided him with valuable experience as an assistant conductor with the British National Opera Company.[7] Then, in 1924, Heward took over the orchestra in Cape Town, on the recommendation of Basil Cameron, following the retirement of Theo Wendt. Here he renewed his acquaintance with Hely-Hutchinson (then 23, and born in Cape Town, where his father was Governor of Cape Colony; a fine all-round musician who had been composing since the age of ten, he was to play a major rôle in the CBO's wartime history). Heward, who was also Musical Director of the South African Broadcasting Corporation, did excellent work with the Cape Town Orchestra for two or three years, including a tour of England, at the end of which he married his wife Lenore (whom he had met whilst working for the BNOC) in Westminster Abbey. Sadly, it was also in South Africa that he contracted the TB that was to dog his health for the remainder of his life. In 1927 he returned to London, where he made a meagre living as a freelance pianist[8] and occasional BNOC conductor, until Boult, absolutely convinced of his potential, encouraged him to apply for the Birmingham vacancy.

The CBO players, who had much enjoyed Heward's trial concert, had a further taste of his outstanding gifts (and his innate generosity) in April 1930, when he offered to conduct their annual Pension Fund concert. Gwen Berry remembered that 'It was really very exhilarating playing *1812* with our orchestra of 100[9] plus the Police Band and Mr Cunningham on the organ, and three sets of bells. It's a wonder we didn't crack the nice clean roof of the Town Hall . . . Mr Heward conducted, and by Jove he is fine. I shall howl if I'm not in next year.' And if Heward had a generous nature, he had a great sense of humour too: 'Mr Gerald Forty sent a Questionnaire to South Africa, asking Mr Heward to fill it in as the basis of a Biographical Note for the Press and the printed programmes. In reply to the question, "What is your favourite flower?" he wrote, 'Cauli"! Mr Forty was . . . a bit formal in the Office, but when I showed him Mr Heward's replies to his questions, he couldn't help roaring with laughter.'[10]

1930–1

On 1 September 1930, when he took up his position as Conductor and Musical Director of the City of Birmingham Orchestra, Leslie Heward was only 32, and the Committee was taking a gamble, for at the time of his trial concert, his name could have been known only to a tiny minority of the orchestra's regular concert-goers. His annual salary was fixed at £1000, plus 'reasonable travelling expenses' for out-of-town dates, half of any conducting fees paid to the CBO 'when conducting the orchestra at the Birmingham Station of the British Broadcasting Corporation', and separate fees if commercial gramophone recordings should be made. The contract was terminable at six months' notice on either side.

Heward's gifts were different from those of Matthews or Boult, both of whom enjoyed talking to audiences, experimenting with new series of concerts and going out to look for business for the CBO. 'I never, under any circumstances whatever, get up on my hind legs and talk, to however small a crowd.'[11] By the same token, he had little interest in conducting for schoolchildren, which involved talking to them about the music, but he soon found someone else to look after that aspect of the CBO's work. However, even if administration was not really Leslie Heward's 'scene', he was never short of ideas, and it was he who invited Peter Warlock to write programme notes for the CBO.[12] Whatever he was *not*, he was unquestionably a prodigious musician, a wonderful conductor and a man of great charm.

The rumour that Gwen Berry had heard in January 1930 proved well founded. Gerald Forty had spent months brokering a mutually beneficial agreement with the BBC's Percy Edgar, who had been in charge of the Corporation's Birmingham operation since 1922. In a talk broadcast in 1947, Forty recalled that eventually 'A deputation, of which I was one of three members, went to the headquarters at Savoy Hill. We were received by that awe-inspiring person Sir John Reith . . . and a formidable array of musical and financial experts. Speaking for myself, I confess that I felt rather as I imagine David did, when he first caught sight of Goliath; but our anxieties were soon allayed – indeed, we found that we were pushing at an open door.'

The BBC agreed to increase the fee paid to the CBO for broadcasts, with the right to broadcast all CBO promotions. In return, the CBO undertook to provide an orchestra of 40, at cost, to undertake 13 studio concerts during each winter season. It was a real step towards the long-awaited permanent contract for all the musicians. The Corporation agreed to reduce its own Birmingham orchestra (which had absorbed several good CBO players in 1927) to an octet, and the redundant players (along with existing CBO players) were auditioned by Heward and Boult, who represented the BBC. At Sir John Reith's suggestion, Percy Edgar subsequently joined the CBO Committee.

Heward elected to conduct seven of the eight Symphony Concerts (advertised with '75 Performers') in his first season, the remaining date being allocated to Albert Coates, with a predictably all-Russian programme. Unfortunately Coates had to pull out, marooned in Moscow with acute bronchitis; Heward simply took over Coates's advertised programme *ad notam*, and had a considerable success with it. Distinguished visitors in this series included the pianists Arthur de Greef and Nikolai Orloff, cellist May Mukle and violinist Arthur Catterall, who played the Sibelius Concerto. Lenore Heward recalled 'an awful moment', Catterall 'dramatically whipping his bow right off the fiddle, and returning it *under* the strings!' Of the 41 pieces advertised, no fewer than 28 carried an asterisk denoting 'First performance at these concerts' – a bold move indeed. Sunday programmes were solidly based in mainstream repertoire – nothing that could be termed 'light orchestral music', though some novelties crept in: Dohnányi, Ethel Smyth, Sinigaglia, Moeran, William Wallace – even Hermann Goetz's Symphony in F.[13]

No sooner had Boult moved to the BBC in London than his deputy Joseph Lewis (the BBC's senior conductor and an experienced administrator) followed him, leaving a significant gap in the CBO's armoury. Heward would have heard from Boult about his young assistant Harold Gray, and he lost no time in turning up incognito at one of Gray's Sutton Coldfield concerts with the CBO. He evidently liked what he saw, and from that time forward gave him as much encouragement as possible.[14] In November 1930, Gray conducted a complete performance of Gounod's *Faust* for a BBC broadcast, with the Birmingham Grand Opera Society and the CBO.

Leslie Heward's first season proved more successful musically than financially. Sir Charles Rafter was still able to provide a remarkable annual boost from Police Band concerts (over £750 in 1930) and this was now earmarked as the basis of an Endowment Fund, but things still looked ominous. Councillor Macdonald's deteriorating health had forced him to retire as CBO Chairman, after nine seasons of dedicated work, and the opportunity was now taken to appoint separate Chairmen for the orchestra's two Committees, the vastly experienced Gerald Forty leading the Executive Sub-Committee and Alderman

W. Byng Kenrick taking over the Chair of the Management Committee; these two were to provide stability and maturity over the next twenty years.

At the Annual Meeting, Heward remarked that some people who had previously supported the orchestra were now staying at home, listening to concerts on the BBC and imagining that, when the Depression had passed, they would be able to come back to hear the CBO again; but there might not be a CBO to hear.

1931–2

From the beginning of the season, the name of Harold Gray appears with increasing frequency in the Minute Book. First, he took over the CBO's Children's Concerts, for a fee of £30,[15] drawing on his experience of Boult's sterling work in this area; he took to his new responsibilities like a duck to water, delighting the City's Education Department with his work. The BBC also invited him to give a number of broadcast talks, illustrated at the piano. Whilst Heward never entirely overcome his distaste for speaking in public, Percy Edgar was able to persuade him, too, to give a series of short talks, a day or two before each of the Symphony Concerts, all of which were broadcast, along with many other CBO concerts. Heward proved an able broadcaster. In June 1932, on Heward's recommendation, Gray was appointed Deputy Conductor, fulfilling the rôle that Joseph Lewis had in Boult's time, but without any remuneration (save that for concerts actually undertaken on the CBO's behalf). His title changed later to Associate Conductor and there was to be a hiccup in the Forties, but, to all intents and purposes, Harold (as he was universally known) would remain the orchestra's No. 2 conductor, with great distinction, for almost the next fifty years.

The personality cult operated just as effectively as a crowd-puller in those pre-war days as it does today, and the best-attended of the 1931–2 Symphony Concerts was Sir Henry Wood's disappointingly lightweight programme, in which Beethoven's First Symphony was the only item of substance.

Leslie Heward was an able (if self-critical) composer. In a 1979 interview with the author, Gray remembered joining the pianist William Murdoch for lunch at the Hewards' home on a day when Murdoch was due to play the Mozart D minor Concerto at a BBC Studio concert. The choice of cadenzas came up, and Murdoch suggested some of his own. 'Leslie rummaged around in a drawer and emerged with a scruffy old manuscript copy of some cadenzas he had written years before; Billy was a wonderful sight-reader and he played them straight off. At the concert, Leslie turned to the audience and said, "So far as we know, there are three sets of cadenzas for this work: one by Beethoven

– very good; one by Murdoch – even better; and one by Heward – better still, and that's the one that Mr Murdoch will play!" '

Studying scores with Heward must have been a revelation. As Harold Gray recalled, 'He could easily have made a career as a concert pianist, but the remarkable thing was his insight into complex scores; he could sit at the piano and give an extraordinarily realistic performance – an amazing person!'[16] The final Symphony Concert of the season affords a fine example of Heward's daring programme building: three unfamiliar works by Haydn, then Delius's *North Country Sketches* and finally Elgar's *Falstaff.* In April 1932, soon after playing under Elgar in *King Olaf*, the CBO gave the opening concert at the new Shakespeare Theatre in Stratford-on-Avon, under Heward, who reported that he had received 'wide-spread congratulatory reports of the concert' and considered it to have been 'a feather in our cap'.

1932–3

In the summer of 1932, Sir Thomas Beecham invited the CBO's Leader, Paul Beard, to fill a similar rôle in the London Philharmonic Orchestra, which he was then forming; Beard accepted. It could, perhaps, be seen as another 'feather in the CBO's cap', if an unwelcome one. Beard, who had made an invaluable contribution to Birmingham's musical life, was replaced by Alfred Cave. The singer Maggie Teyte described him rather unkindly as looking 'just like an orang-utan',[17] but nobody doubted that Cave was a first-class violinist. Reviewing the first Symphony Concert of the season, the critic of the *Birmingham Weekly Post* noted that he 'had an opportunity to display his quality, for in the *Job* masque of Vaughan Williams he had a solo passage which enabled us to hear a beautiful tone and some sensitive phrasing well out of the ordinary. He should easily justify Mr Leslie Heward's choice.'

Times were hard for musicians in the early Thirties. Those out of work banded themselves into bodies such as the 'Birmingham Citizens' Orchestra'. A visit to Lewis's cafeteria might be accompanied by piano solos played by the CBO's first conductor, Appleby Matthews.[18]

The Annual Meeting in October 1932 learned of a worrying shortfall of some £600 on the previous season's work. Under its agreement with the CBO, the BBC made up £500 of this, but average attendance at the 24 Sunday Concerts had dropped 15% – from 956 to 816 – and Heward found himself having to resist the pressure to move further 'down-market' in his programming.

In an article entitled 'Fifty Years of Progress?', the composer-journalist Havergal Brian observed that 'One thing that hasn't happened successfully during the past fifty years is the Municipal Orchestra. Leeds determined to try one, and the writing-men of the time beatified the effort, prophesying greater births. Another was born in Birmingham, but both have had to struggle for material existence: evidently municipal milk is not sufficiently rich in vitamins LSD.'[19]

Heward also put forward the idea that 'the orchestra should be recognised as the body for the whole of the Midland area'; he hoped to 'persuade them to regard us as a family affair worthy of cultivation'. He was on absolutely the right lines, and the idea has been repeated at regular intervals, but the message still goes largely unheeded. He also suggested the appointment of an advertising agent. This does not seem to have been implemented, but more strenuous efforts were made in that direction, and the new Ladies' Council was able to report that through its efforts some 40 extra serial tickets had been sold for the Symphony Concerts; appeals for more subscribers were made at concerts, by Byng Kenrick and Mrs George Cadbury.

Guest conductor in the Symphony series was Adrian Boult, with the best-attended (but perhaps the least interesting) concert of the eight, Holst's *Perfect Fool* ballet music sitting somewhat uncomfortably between Weber, Schumann and a group of Wagnerian 'pops'. Weber was also what the Programme Committee thought that Heward was suggesting for the concert on 16 February 1933; what they actually heard was Anton Webern's Symphony!

In April, G. D. Cunningham and the City Choir gave the first performance in the Midlands of Walton's *Belshazzar's Feast*, with Roy Henderson as soloist. Harold Gray gained valuable experience as assistant conductor for Albert Coates's London Wagner Season, but Leslie Heward was not well; the TB he had contracted in South Africa, aggravated by heavy smoking, was beginning to take its toll; at this stage it only laid him low for a few days, but it was a development that was to have ominous echoes in the following seasons.

1933–4

Heward worked hard to improve standards. Some attempt was made to stifle 'Big Brum' (which always seemed to chime the hour during *pianissimo* passages) and the dismal platform lighting in the Town Hall was improved.[20] An extra cello and bass (overall cost: about £50) were engaged for the Sunday Concerts, which featured May Blyth, Trefor Jones, Frank Mullings and Robert Maitland in the ever-popular Wagner Night and the splendid Robert Easton in Mozart (Osmin and Sarastro, of course). Heward appeared as composer (Evelyn Stevenson singing a group of his songs) and as pianist in the Beethoven Triple Concerto, with Alfred Cave and Harry Stanier. Cave also played the Sibelius Concerto – a measure of the confidence Heward placed in his technique. There was great interest in the visit of Artur Schnabel to play Beethoven's G major Piano Concerto, his 80-guinea fee partly underwritten by an anonymous donation.

Sir Granville Bantock retired from his Professorship and left Birmingham; since 1900 nobody had worked harder to establish orchestral music in the city, and he must have taken some quiet satisfaction in seeing the CBO still there, after fourteen years.

1934 was a seminal year for British music; the deaths of Elgar, Holst and Delius had left Vaughan Williams and his contemporaries feeling isolated, surrounded by younger men of a very different mould (William Walton, Constant Lambert) who were just starting to make their mark. But 1934 was to prove a crucially important year for the CBO, too. At its May meeting, the Committee found itself faced with worrying news. The Sunday Series, 'the first one in which we have had the cinema in direct opposition to us', had made a substantial deficit and further economies were called for, notably in the size of the orchestra. It was crisis time again, and this time the prognosis looked grim. A knight errant was required and, as in all the best stories, one duly appeared, though only in the nick of time.

9

The BBC link

The knight errant, improbable as it might sound, was the BBC. In the summer of 1934, Edgar and Forty, with the full co-operation of Reith and Boult, were finally able to agree on the establishment of a BBC Midland Orchestra of 35 players, with Heward as its conductor in addition to his CBO position. Heward himself played an important rôle in the negotiations,[1] which would have been further eased by the BBC's local Director of Music Victor Hely-Hutchinson, who was soon to take Bantock's place as Professor of Music at the University, and would remain close to Heward and to the CBO for the next decade.

The new arrangement meant that the CBO would now have to book many of its former players through the BBC, which in turn invoiced them to the orchestra. The bill for 35 players for a typical Sunday Concert amounted to around £60 and for a Lunch-hour Concert around £23, but that presupposed that the BBC was not already needing those players for its own broadcasts, and Shephard's job in fixing out-of-town engagements was undoubtedly made far more complicated; but it was a small price to pay for relative financial stability.

1934–5

From 1 October 1934, Heward was engaged by the BBC to conduct its Midland Orchestra for an average of two concerts a week from October to March each year, and three concerts a week from April to September, at an annual salary of £750, and on that day the new orchestra, which provided many of the CBO's best players with a 12–month contract, at last broadcast its first concert. This was also the day of the CBO's Annual Meeting, and it provided a welcome note of optimism to offset the customary gloomy financial results – a deficit for the fourth season in a row. But as so often, more encouraging news was followed by renewed anxieties: on 18 November 1934,

Heward was taken ill after completing the morning rehearsal for a Sunday Concert. Gray could not be traced until an hour before it was due to begin, but he stepped into the breach and acquitted himself creditably.

Choral societies in this country were going through a rough patch in the mid-1930s.[2] Nevertheless, the 1934–5 season included some major choral concerts, including a Civic Concert marking the centenary of Birmingham Town Hall, which involved the City Choir and Festival Choral Society. In February 1935, Gray conducted the Festival Choral and the CBO in an exacting all-Delius programme, including the first Midland performance of the *Songs of Farewell*, and in May the orchestra was also involved in the extensive local celebrations of the Silver Jubilee of King George V and Queen Mary.

Rossini's *Cambiale di Matrimonio* Overture; Mozart's *Prague* Symphony; Delius's *Paris*; Sibelius's Second Symphony – such a programme could only mean Beecham, and he drew the expected full house, justifying his 100–guinea fee. Ernst Wolff, Arthur Catterall, Egon Petri, Frederic Lamond[3] and Henry Holst,[4] with Paul Beard and Anthony Pini in the Delius 'Double', added lustre to an extremely distinguished Symphony season.[5] Heward also included an all-Sibelius programme of unusual interest: the *Karelia* Overture; the Fourth Symphony;[6] the Violin Concerto and the two *Lemminkäinen Legends* then published.

After a succession of gloomy results, the Annual Meeting at the end of the season at last had some more encouraging news. The Chairman, Alderman Byng Kenrick, reported that, as the result of the new links with the BBC, 'Financial anxiety was almost entirely relieved', but attendance at the 22 Sunday evening concerts (now given in the Town Hall) was still disappointing (averaging 624), though that for the Saturday Popular Concerts was appreciably better (1164). The customary eight Symphony Concerts were now drawing excellent houses, with an average attendance of 1403 (boosted, admittedly, by a 2000 house for Beecham's concert), and although the cost per concert (with well-known guest artists) was slightly higher, it is very hard to see why the CBO Committee obstinately stuck with the familiar pattern instead of increasing the number of week-night Symphony Concerts and reducing the number of week-end events.

Lunch-hour Concerts were still felt to be worthwhile, but attendance at the Saturday afternoon Children's Concerts had declined steadily over the previous ten years, and they were now dropped. In their place there was a series of eight free weekday afternoon concerts in the Town Hall, introduced and conducted by Gray, to which schools would send children by coach. Thus were the seeds sown of post-war CBSO Education Concerts.

1935–6

The great advantage of working with his musicians, week in, week out, summer as well as winter, was that Heward could really start to build on the groundwork of the CBO's previous 15 years. He reported to the Committee that 'we seem to be making a name for ourselves in performing the music of Sibelius, as the Hallé Orchestra did with Berlioz'.

One of the major events of Heward's tenure (comparable in importance to Boult's Mahler performances) took place in the Town Hall on 22 November 1935, when he conducted the CBO in what was only the second complete performance of Walton's B♭ minor Symphony, less than three weeks after Sir Hamilton Harty had given its first performance. After it, the composer's publisher, the shrewd and influential Hubert Foss of OUP, wrote to his wife, 'It really was a magnificent performance – the band is not really full of good players, but they went all out for this and pulled it off. The tears were rolling down my cheeks during the Epilogue, so they were down many others! In some ways it was better than Hay's,[7] but not in breadth of experience. The thing that pleased me was the way it gripped the public: Willie had an ovation.'[8]

Sibelius's Sixth Symphony, which Heward had dropped from the previous season, now had its first Birmingham hearing, in a Symphony Concert. Long-serving CBO violinist Muriel Tookey recalled the rehearsal: 'Leslie asked our indulgence if he made mistakes, as he had not had time to look at the score and had not done the work before. There were no mistakes, and he was able to call out corrections to the parts as he went along.'[9]

Heward's phenomenal score-reading ability is well documented, as is his professionalism in rehearsal. Diagnosis was instant and absolutely practical: 'Wrong clef!' 'Trumpets in F, there!' Albert Sammons recalled, 'One of his time-saving devices at rehearsal was to transfer his baton to the left hand and continue to beat time while he wrote down marks and notes in his score with the right.'[10] Flautist Gordon Heard, whose father and grandfather also played flute in the CBO, remarks that 'I have never known a conductor who was so much respected by the players as he was'.[11]

A distinguished guest conductor (paying his second visit to the CBO) was Ernest Ansermet, with whom Heward had worked several times as a keyboard player. Adolph Busch drew the largest audience of the season with the Beethoven Violin Concerto. At the penultimate Sunday Concert of the season, Arthur Bliss conducted his *Music for Strings*, and at the last, the City Police Band, which had been supporting the CBO financially over so many years, joined the orchestra in a roof-raising *1812* Overture.[12]

*

1936–7

After the more upbeat tone of the 1935 Annual Meeting, the figures in the 1936 Report revealed a working deficit in excess of £500, typical of the first four years of the decade. It had been an exceptionally cold, hard winter, and attendance had suffered. Heward must have been depressed by talk of the need to avoid the unfamiliar – the best-attended Saturday Concert (1400) had been one called 'Popular Symphonies' (the *Unfinished*, Beethoven's Fifth and the *New World*) and a questionnaire to Sunday audiences had produced similar requests for 'safe' repertoire – but he was encouraged to see more young people at the Sunday Concerts, for which prices had been reduced. But slightly increased sales had not compensated for this, and takings were down. Furthermore, the players (who had voluntarily accepted a 10% cut in their wages for three seasons, due to the Depression) had been restored to their rightful remuneration, so costs had risen steeply.

Victor Hely-Hutchinson, Musical Director of the BBC's Midland Region, was invited to join the Committee. A thriving City Orchestra Club now met fortnightly, and 'VH-H' repeated his existing series of Birmingham University lectures for its members, introducing the following Thursday's Symphony programme. Hely-Hutchinson and Heward also gave BBC talks. Hely-Hutchinson introduced one of the season's highlights – Egon Petri playing the Busoni Piano Concerto. When Nicolai Malko conducted Shostakovich's First and Tchaikovsky's Fourth Symphonies, Heward gave the talk. In the *Post*, Eric Blom noted that the CBO played 'admirably' for Malko, though he was distinctly sniffy about Shostakovich's music: 'Having no impress of personality, it will merely typify a branch of a Russian school from which no creative individualities stand out.'[13]

Solomon, Jean Pougnet, William Primrose and Isolde Menges also appeared during the season, which saw the completion of Heward's Sibelius Symphony cycle, with No. 7.

The Swiss composer Ernest Bloch had agreed to conduct the première of a new orchestral work in Birmingham in March 1937. Whilst working on it at his home in France, he chanced to pick up on his radio a broadcast concert from Birmingham, in which Heward conducted his *Winter–Spring* tone poems, and promptly wrote to Heward: 'My wife and I were extremely moved by the very beautiful performance. It is very rare for me to hear one of my works interpreted as I intended it to be, not only the music itself but what lies *behind* the notes. We felt that you loved it and that you could impart your love and understanding to your musicians.' In the upshot, Bloch was ill and failed to complete his new work in time for his promised appearance. The new work – a three-movement suite entitled *Evocations* – was eventually completed, but

Heward must have been disappointed that it was Pierre Monteux and the San Francisco Symphony Orchestra who gave its first performances, on 11 and 12 February 1938. Heward and the CBO gave its European première[14] in the Town Hall on 10 March, and two weeks later Dr G. D. Cunningham, the City Choir and the CBO gave the first British performance of Bloch's *Sacred Service*, coupling it with *Belshazzar's Feast*, Roy Henderson the soloist in both works.[15]

In May 1937, the Coronation of King George VI and Queen Elizabeth was marked by great celebrations across the city, and later that week the CBO, City Choir and Festival Choral Society combined to give two special Civic Concerts in the Town Hall. Heward and Gray conducted music by Purcell, Handel and Elgar, while Victor Hely-Hutchinson directed the first performance of his setting of 'I vow to thee, my country', composed for the occasion.

1937–8

By the late 1930s, the Sunday Series had been progressively reduced from 24 to either 19 or 20 concerts, for which a neat little 16–page booklet was produced at the beginning of each season. Saturday afternoon Children's Concerts had been reinstated, but still averaged less than 1000 young people; four free concerts were still given on weekday afternoons also. But as the Third Reich dominated Central Europe more and more, CBO concerts were increasingly seen as a welcome escape from the worrying news that filled the papers. The Town Hall sported a massive poster, the full height of its columns, appealing for volunteer air-raid wardens, and the News Theatre, High Street, was showing *Chamberlain the Peacemaker*, billed as 'The screen story of Birmingham's greatest living citizen, who by his courage and steadfastness averted a world catastrophe'![16]

The independent activities of the BBC Midland Orchestra lie beyond the scope of this book, but since Heward was its conductor and its players were also members of the CBO, it as well to remember that remarkable work was taking place in the Broad Street studio. Violinist Muriel Tookey remembered especially 'the night when Béla Bartók came to the Birmingham studio of the BBC to play his latest Piano Concerto with us. Leslie was marvellous and followed that most complicated score and fiendishly difficult piano part as though it were easy. Bartók was greatly excited and made a charming little speech afterwards.'[17]

Philip Henderson recalls that 'The Town Hall was far from ideal as a concert hall, by modern standards. The starlings were a great pest. One minute there would be peace (except for the 1930s traffic) and two minutes later all hell would be let loose as the starlings all arrived together!'[18]

The septuagenarian Felix Weingartner (commanding the first 100-guinea fee since Beecham) was the guest conductor in the 1937–8 Symphony Series. Harold Gray recalled that 'Leslie Heward being away at the time, he asked me to "do the honours". I remember during the first awkward moments managing to convey to him that the first-ever performance of Mendelssohn's *Elijah* was given in the Town Hall. There were no awkward moments after that. "This, then, is Holy Ground," said Weingartner, as he literally stroked the walls of the Town Hall.'[19] There was a record attendance of 2050 for what Heward described as 'authoritative and inspiring' performances of Haydn and Beethoven. Another distinguished visitor was Edwin Fischer.

In the summer of 1938, Heward's health was giving cause for some anxiety – he suggested that Gray and Walter Stanton should conduct some out-of-town programmes, to ease the pressure on him. The 20 hours a week that he and the players were putting in at the BBC Studios in addition to their CBO work were beginning to take their toll.

Relations between the Society and the City Council were somewhat ambivalent at this time. No Lord Mayor had attended a CBO promotion for many years, but the Council was still happy enough to use the orchestra for its own purposes. In 1938 the city celebrated the centenary of its incorporation as a borough and in January the City Orchestra, City Choir and Festival Choral Society combined to give a Civic Concert to mark the occasion. The highlight of the celebrations came in July with a massive pageant, staged in Aston Park. Over 6000 people were involved in this theatrical re-enactment of Birmingham's history. The CBO was approached to take part, but its BBC commitments made this impossible. However, Heward, Gray, the two choirs and the CBO gave yet another celebratory concert (the fourth such joint affair in five years) on 16 July 1938 – all music first performed in the Town Hall: Part 1 of *Elijah* plus works by Sullivan, Dvořák, Parry and Elgar.

1938–9

To glance through successive *Birmingham Post* reports of the CBO's Annual Meetings in Heward's day is to have a distinct sense of *déjà vu*. The headlines have a monotonous ring about them, and October 1938 was no exception: 'Future of the City Orchestra – Bigger attendances at concerts essential.' Heward told the meeting that 'he would like, under better conditions, to give a lot more concerts free. He realised that if art was to do any good in the world today it must be for the masses.' He also urged the priority of putting the musicians' contracts on to a 12-month basis: 'I am of the opinion . . . that Birmingham could just manage to do with some music in the summer, and probably will some day.' It would be another seven years, though, before his successor would introduce the CBSO Proms.

Heward, always aiming at the highest possible standards, was none too happy with some of the orchestral playing. Good players were hard to find. When the CBO's long-serving harpist retired, he reported to his Committee that 'the girl in her place will never be first-class'. W. S. Yorke, principal horn, had been away ill for three months, and the playing of his deputy had proved so inadequate that one particularly unfavourable press review had resulted in the player bringing a libel action; he lost, but it reflected poorly on the CBO. The shortcomings of the same deputy led to Heward having on one occasion to stop the orchestra, during a live broadcast, apologise to the audience ('I'm sorry – we can do better than that') and restart the piece. This incident illustrates not only the drawbacks of the old 'deputy' system but also how the BBC link could itself have unfortunate repercussions on recruitment. When it became apparent that Yorke might not play again, Heward engaged John Denison as Acting Principal, but the BBC would not offer him a permanent contract, so the appointment fell through.[20]

In his January 1939 Symphony Concert, Heward invited Albert Sammons to perform a work which he had by then made virtually his own – the Elgar Violin Concerto – and Brailowsky, Moiseiwitsch,[21] Leon Goossens, Orrea Pernel and Suggia (she of the famous Augustus John portrait) were the other soloists in the series, which also included what was only the second performance of E. J. Moeran's Symphony, Heward having conducted its première in Queen's Hall, with the LPO, shortly before.

Serious musician though he was, Heward's sense of fun was never far beneath the surface. When the cellist May Mukle asked him to accompany her in an encore, he agreed only on condition that 'you give me something I've not heard or seen before and that we play it without a rehearsal'.[22] And E. F. Vale remembers Harold Gray 'conducting Haydn's *Military* Symphony, with Leslie playing the cymbals! On another occasion, Hely-Hutchinson was booked to play Falla's *Nights in the Gardens of Spain*. He failed to turn up, and Heward told the audience that "VH-H" had got lost in the Gardens, so Heward would play some piano music, to fill the time in!'[23]

By the summer of 1939, the CBO's financial position looked comparatively sound again, and a freelance Publicity Officer was appointed, in an attempt to build up the number of subscribers. The future for the CBO looked as bright as it had ever done, but, as Noël Coward sang, 'Bad times are just around the corner'. These would involve not only Leslie Heward's precarious state of health but negotiations between two international leaders: one – Neville Chamberlain – had been a founding father of the CBO; the name of the other was Adolf Hitler.

10

The wartime years

During the orchestral holiday, Leslie Heward took up an invitation to visit Canada and the USA, embarking from Liverpool on 26 August and arriving in Montreal on Sunday, 3 September, the day that Chamberlain was telling the people of Britain that they were at war with Germany. Diary entries imply that he conducted there and in Toronto, visited Niagara Falls and in New York met John Barbirolli, the viola-player William Primrose and the conductor Eugene Goossens, who had just returned from England for his next season in Cincinnati. Heward's return sailing was delayed four times, doubtless due more to wartime rescheduling than to his deteriorating health; nevertheless, by the time he reached Southampton on 30 September his diary records that he was 'v. ill', and the next day: 'Went home to Brum. Bed.' Heward was suffering from a serious attack of TB, aggravated by a great deal of hard work, coupled with chain-smoking and fairly heavy drinking. There follow a series of deleted engagements and blank pages until 25 October, when he went into Romsley sanatorium, where he remained for more than six months until 18 May 1940. By July he was taking some active part in planning concerts, but apart from a recording session with the LPO in July, it would be October before he could conduct an orchestra again.

Meanwhile, Heward's illness was only one amongst many problems facing Shephard, Forty and the CBO Committee as they strove to keep orchestral music ticking over throughout those unreal days of the 'Phoney War' during the autumn of 1939.

The BBC's knee-jerk reaction to the outbreak of hostilities had been to lay off nearly all its musicians and disband most of its regional groupings, including the Midland Orchestra.[1] By the time the CBO's Executive Committee could meet, on 11 September 1939, the Town Hall (in front of which there were already sandbags and auxiliary water-tanks) had been commandeered for the war effort. Shephard was instructed to cancel all engagements and commitments entered into; the young Denis Matthews was especially disappointed that these included what was to have been his début performance with the CBO – a Brahms D minor, with Heward, in January 1940. The Committee decided to keep Shephard on, 'in order that we might be in a position to resume activities at the earliest moment', but felt that it must give the ailing Heward six months' notice, under the terms of his contract. The 1938–9 Annual Report closed with the hope that, despite everything, 'the need for that refreshment of mind and spirit which these arts supply remains. It is hoped that at an early date a way may be found by which some modified service may be organised by your Committee for the benefit of the General Public and the relief of those Artists whose loss of occupation and livelihood is one of the many sad happenings in this disordered world.'

1939–40

The Committee was as good as its word. From 28 October, concerts were resumed, under the title 'City of Birmingham (Emergency) Orchestra'. A series of weekly Saturday afternoon concerts (four at first, then extended to six) was announced, to take place in the Large Theatre of the Midland Institute in Paradise Street, adjoining the Town Hall; Heward's name still appeared as Musical Director, but the concerts were conducted by Victor Hely-Hutchinson,[2] with local soloists and some ambitious programming which included Vaughan Williams's *London Symphony* and Strauss's Suite *Le Bourgeois Gentilhomme*. The single-sheet printed programmes cost one penny, and contained information about the location of air raid shelters; the orchestra, however, intended to play on regardless.

'VH-H' was full of praise for guest conductor Basil Cameron, 'sensitive and dynamic in the highest degree', but rather less so for Julius Harrison. Despite a slight falling-off in attendance, 'due to the gradually advancing hour of black-out', the public's warm response to these concerts encouraged the Committee to look for a larger venue, and by moving them from Saturday to Sunday afternoons, Shephard was able to negotiate, from the beginning of 1940, the use of the West End Cinema. Heavy snow in January 1940 notwithstanding, Boult, who knew the cinema so well from his CBO days in the 1920s, conducted the first concert.

W. K. Stanton, Harold Gray, Julius Harrison, Basil Cameron and Clarence Raybould all made appearances, but Victor Hely-Hutchinson was the preeminent conductor. The series also featured a tremendous array of top-line soloists, including Eileen Joyce, Arthur Catterall, Thelma Reiss, Louis Kentner, Kathleen Long, Leon Goossens, Adila Fachiri, Kendall Taylor, Irene

Scharrer and Benno Moiseiwitsch. To mark the completion of Heward's first decade (and conscious that he had been unable to earn his living or support his family for almost a year), Boult returned to conduct a Benefit Concert for him on Sunday, 14 April 1940, with Myra Hess as soloist; artists and orchestra gave their services. The *Post* carried a jolly photo of Heward sitting up in bed, now sporting a bushy moustache and beard; but 'he doubts if he will have the courage to appear next season plus the beard'. He was looking forward to listening to the BBC's relay of the first part of the concert.

The final concert, given on 26 May 1940,[3] as the German army advanced remorselessly through the Low Countries *en route* for Dunkirk and the anticipated invasion of Britain, was the twenty-fifth to be presented in the seven months since the series had begun – no small achievement, in the circumstances. The CBO had made a quick recovery following the anxieties of September 1939, and for that Hely-Hutchinson, with his great musical and administrative abilities, must take much of the credit.[4] A cultured and generous-minded man, he would accept no payment, either for his work as a conductor and pianist or for some hundreds of excellent (and anonymous) programme notes which he gave to the orchestra, as he did the proceeds of his series of lunch-time piano recitals at the Midland Institute, in which he performed all the Beethoven Piano Sonatas.[5]

Confidence returned quickly. Since the end of January, the word 'Emergency' had been dropped from the title, and in March 1940 the Committee felt able to retain Heward's services on a temporary contract, and to apply to the City Council for a further grant of £2500 a year for the next five years. It was duly agreed, despite the complaint of one councillor that 'This highbrow stuff doesn't appeal to the man in the street'. The councillor was gravely mistaken: the Arts flourish in wartime, as the box-office success of Beecham's New Birmingham Orchestra had shown in 1917.

1940–1

The season started with the sad news of the death of Neville Chamberlain – a broken man since the failure of his efforts to prevent the outbreak of war in 1939. The CBO Committee placed on record its gratitude to him for all that he had done 'to establish on a firm basis orchestral music for the City of Birmingham'.

On the night of Sunday, 25 August 1940, Birmingham's city centre suffered its first major air raid, in which 25 people lost their lives, but there was general agreement that the show must go on. On 30 September 1940, a year to the day after he had returned from New York 'very ill', Heward attended the CBO's Annual Meeting in the Council House; the following day he dined with Gray; a week later he undertook some studio recordings with the BBC Symphony Orchestra, which had been evacuated to Bristol,[6] and on 20 October he conducted the CBO in his first public concert for well over a year, in the Town Hall, now available once again.

The city centre was hit badly between 25 and 30 October, but damage to the Town Hall was not too extensive, and the Sunday Concerts carried on. A correspondent has 'an unforgettable memory of the orchestra playing on Sunday afternoons with bicycle lamps on their music stands, which were switched on as the afternoons got darker – it was impossible to black out the Town Hall windows'.[7] There were further big raids to follow. During the period 19–28 November nearly 800 people were killed and over 2000 injured in the city, and some 20,000 were made homeless. But, despite the difficulties of the Blitz, Heward and the CBO soldiered on; a couple of November concerts had to be postponed when the Town Hall suffered more blast damage, but 22 Sunday Concerts were still presented there during the 1940–1 season. The hall was often bitterly cold and the lighting inadequate, but attendances were good, with 11 concerts over the 1000 mark.

Inevitably the CBO was giving far fewer concerts than it had before the war – the miracle was that it could present any at all. But a modest profit was made[8] and a few out-of-town dates were managed. Heward's diary shows that he was making no concession to his recent illness, undertaking concerts with many orchestras all over the country. On 19 December 1940, an anxious Gerald Forty wrote to him, 'Your account of the last fortnight's peregrinations[9] recalls the hair-raising narration of St Paul. That you have survived to tell the tale is a wonder . . . but I hope that you will not attempt to repeat such an exhausting experience.' Explaining that the CBO was in no position to enter into long-term commitments under wartime conditions, Forty added, 'You are quite right to be looking ahead, and providing against the lean months; but even so, I hope you will not overtax your strength', and he ended his letter with a solemn warning: 'It is better economy to be alive to enjoy half a loaf than to kill yourself in attempting to secure a whole one.' Sadly, Heward gave Forty's wise advice too little heed. In January 1941, Malcolm Sargent and Basil Cameron guested with the CBO, while Heward was working with the Hallé, and his diary looks busier than ever. But there were other occasions when he had to pull out of concerts at the last minute through illness; Boult (twice), Stanton and Raybould stepped in to cover for him.

For some time, Heward had been exploring the possibilities of making recordings with the CBO. In September 1939 he had met some Decca executives in New York; this seems to have come to nothing, but on 15 July 1940, soon after emerging from the sanatorium, he went to London to meet Walter Legge of the Gramophone Company at Pagani's, and discussed plans to undertake 20 recording sessions. On 12 December he met Legge again, and on 21 and 22 December the first recordings were made: Mozart's *Eine kleine Nachtmusik*, Tchaikovsky's *Andante cantabile* and a group of arias sung by the soprano Gwen Catley. These discs form an especially valuable document, for though many of Heward's pre-war players were no longer available to him and he had been back at work with the CBO for only two months, the playing is nimble and stylish, and the performances thoroughly musical.[10]

There was heavy snow in February 1941, when Heward and the CBO returned to the Town Hall to make some operatic recordings with the tenor David Lloyd and a newcomer from Australia, Joan Hammond, making her first orchestral records. The love-duet 'Lovely Maid in the Moonlight' and two Joan Hammond solos – 'They call me Mimi' and 'One fine day' – became instant bestsellers. A fortnight later Constant Lambert (who was making a series of Tchaikovsky recordings for HMV) was the conductor when the full CBO recorded the *Romeo and Juliet* Overture. The story goes that Legge used a hooter before each take, to scare away the starlings, and Frank Downes recalls that one take was spoilt by an air raid siren on the Town Hall roof going off. Legge suppressed the CBO's name on the record labels, but one of the discs did admit to being 'Recorded in the Town Hall, Birmingham'.

An absentee from the podium during the 1940–1 season[11] was Harold Gray. For some time, he had been trying, with no great success, to persuade the CBO Committee to offer him more orchestral concerts and, as Deputy Conductor, he must have felt snubbed when they invited Hely-Hutchinson and Stanton to deputise for the sick Heward. In addition to occasional work with the CBO, Downes played horn from time to time in a 'New Midland Symphony Orchestra' that Gray started up at this time, using a number of CBO regulars, plus other freelance players, with Gwen Berry acting as fixer. It worked mainly out of town, but he remembers that 'It did succeed in passing a BBC audition for Dr Stanton, and we did some broadcasts with Harold from Studio 4, Broad Street'.[12] This inevitably led to tension between Gray and the CBO Committee and in July 1940 they resolved 'to leave in abeyance the appointment of a Deputy Conductor'. Over the months, things went from bad to worse and on 22 March 1941 Gray expressed his frustration to Heward, though in a typically gracious letter:

> I feel I have made rather a sad mess of my efforts to help you to understand the way things have gone over the past 12 months or so. However, on two points you must allow me to insist: One, that I honestly do not, nor ever will associate you in any way with the action taken by the CBO committee. That

> you were not acquainted with all the moves that went on whilst you were in the sanatorium I readily admit – nor was it right that you should have been worried by them. Two, I want to repeat that I count it a tremendous privilege to have worked so closely with you over the last 10 years: had I the opportunity of study with any great conductor, I would not choose otherwise.

On the night of 9–10 April 1941, 250 German bombers launched a massive air raid, causing widespread destruction in the city centre, in which there were over 1100 casualties. The Prime Minister, Winston Churchill, visited Birmingham to view the damage and encourage the people. The Theatre Royal in New Street (where the CBO's very first concert had taken place in September 1920) was badly damaged, and the Empire and Prince of Wales Theatres were destroyed. One regular concert-goer remembers seeing the façade of 'The Prince' still standing, as her bus made its precarious way along Broad Street to the last concert of the winter season, but the interior was a total wreck. 'However,' she adds, 'we got to our seats on the ground floor of a crowded Town Hall on time.'

Neville Chamberlain's daughter Dorothy, wife of Alderman Stephen Lloyd, remembered that 'We lived near the city centre and were told that the safest place to shelter was under the stone staircase. Our cairn terrier Hamish was always the first to hear the whine of the falling devices – he was our own personal early bomb warning system.'[13]

1941–2

For the first time, a series of summer concerts was presented in the Town Hall; there was clearly a demand for concerts throughout the year, and the longer days made it feasible to hold them in the evenings. The first was planned for 26 June, but from mid-May onwards Heward was unwell again and still too ill by 24 June to take part in a recording session of Franck's *Symphonic Variations*, with Myra Hess as soloist. Basil Cameron took his place, and on the same day they accompanied Isobel Baillie – her Handel aria was advertised as 'Art Thou Troubled by the City of Birmingham Orchestra'. These were to prove the last of Legge's planned 'twenty sessions', and there would be no more recording until 1945. Boult, Stanton and Raybould took over the summer Popular Concerts,[14] there was another 'Family Party' and Heward returned to conduct the last of the six-concert series, on 31 July, at which the soloist was Cyril Smith.

He opened the winter season on Sunday, 5 October, but had to take three concerts off in November in order to go into the specialist chest clinic at Birmingham's Queen Elizabeth Hospital for X-rays and cystoscopy.[15] At the end of September he had received a kindly letter from Malcolm Sargent, urging him to make an appointment to visit Lord Horder at his Harley Street consulting rooms. Horder (the leading TB specialist of the day) had cured Sargent, and both men were concerned about Heward's illness. From Heward's diary it seems that Horder did indeed see him, but his condition may already have been too far advanced for effective treatment.

Though far from well,[16] Heward was able to conduct most of the Sunday Concerts up to mid-January 1942 and occasional concerts thereafter (Lenore Heward's diary records, on 22 February, 'splendid concert and bumper house'[17] and, on 15 March, 'packed house') but his increasingly untidy diary reveals that, despite his fragile health and dreadful wartime travelling conditions, he was still undertaking a punishing schedule of concerts with other orchestras, and that many of his absences from Birmingham were due not to illness but to his other commitments. In the early months of 1942, Lambert, Warwick Braithwaite and Cameron (no fewer than six times) filled in for Heward (at his expense), often when he was working with the Hallé, who were showing more than a passing interest in him. He had a contract in Birmingham, but now that the BBC Orchestra had folded and the CBO was working only on Sundays, it had become something of a liability to him.

The BBC's microphones were present when Sammons returned on 19 April 1942 to play the Delius Concerto with Heward, but in mid-May he was back in the Queen Elizabeth Hospital for an operation; a further diary reference to Horder suggests that he may have supervised the surgery, which was followed by a period of recuperation. Meanwhile, the CBO continued to do its bit for the war effort: on 17 May 1942 it played at a special Norwegian Independence Day concert in the London Coliseum, in the presence of King Haakon; earlier in the season the orchestra had been in Birmingham Town Hall for a big patriotic 'Pageant of the Allies', organised by the Ministry of Information.

1942–3

The success of the previous year's experiment encouraged the CBO to undertake an extended series of eight summer Popular Concerts on Thursday evenings in June and July, under guest conductors. In the early hours of 28 July there was another substantial air raid, in retaliation for Bomber Command's massive incendiary raids on Hamburg. It brought down the ceilings in the Hewards' Harborne Road home and was followed by further Blitzes on the nights of 29 and 30 July, but they were to be the last of any consequence.[18] Gradually the balance of the war was shifting in the Allies' favour, and when Montgomery's Eighth Army finally routed Rommel's Afrika Korps at El Alamein in November 1942, ultimate victory seemed assured.

From the summer of 1942, Norris Stanley replaced Cave, who had served as the CBO's Leader with great distinction since 1933. Stanley was Birmingham born and taught; he 'played the Beethoven Violin Concerto with orchestra at the age of 15, and even at that period he displayed an astonishingly able command of his instrument'. At 17 he joined the orchestra of the Beecham Opera, before enrolling for service during the 1914–18 war. A founder member of the CBO, he was at the back desk of first violins in the Elgar concert on 10 November 1920, but in the mid-1920s he became Leader-Director of the salon orchestra at Pattison's Restaurant in New Street. He had a prodigious memory and could play virtually any light-music selection by heart. In addition to leading Gray's New Midland Orchestra, he had played a Mozart Concerto with the 'Emergency' Orchestra two years before; Heward showed his confidence in him by inviting him to play Lalo's *Symphonie Espagnole*.[19] Like most of the other players of the day, he had also been closely involved in the cinema orchestras.

Did Heward know that time was running short from him? In an interview with Lyndon Jenkins, CBO violist Herbert Lumby recalled a touching aside concerning his little daughter Karen, then two years old: 'I shan't live to see my little girl grow up.' His 1942–3 programmes certainly seem to have a certain valedictory feel to them. Myra Hess (now a DBE) was the soloist at the first on 4 October (broadcast by the BBC). On the following day, a member of the orchestra sent him a letter, grammatically insecure but written straight from the heart:

> Dear Mr Heward – As yesterday's concert was my last with the CBO, and there was too much of a crush to see you, hence this letter. I cannot allow this opportunity of telling you how much, (and also in what manner) playing under you has had for me, pass without comment. As one who has concerned himself for the past seven years with the uplifting of the status of professional musicians, it has been a thrill and an enlightenment, and, humbly, an added incentive to know what music really means. Thank you, Mr Heward. I trust your health will be maintained so that hundreds of musicians and thousands of people can absorb to the same degree everything it has been my fortune to experience. Yours sincerely, Charles Kahn.

From this season, the CBO started once more to supply small groups of players to the Education Committee for concerts in Birmingham schools. 'Each school received an annual visit from a string quartet and a woodwind quartet and from a small balanced orchestra of about 20 players. That this scheme did not operate satisfactorily was due to the fact that, until 1944, the orchestra was composed of part-time players who had a considerable number of engagements elsewhere.'[20]

Heinz Unger ('Late Conductor Leningrad Symphony Orchestra')[21] conducted Brahms's First Symphony on 11 October, when Heward was supposed to be conducting a Harold Holt concert in London's Albert Hall (Queen's Hall having been destroyed some months earlier), but his diary reads 'Albert H busted. Home to Brum.' He was ill again that week, but conducted the Sunday Concert on the 18th before travelling north for the first in an extended series of weekly studio recordings with the BBC Northern Orchestra. Maurice Johnstone records that this engagement 'was intended to assist him through a semi-convalescent stage to complete recovery', but seeing that he was routinely rehearsing and recording three separate programmes for them each week, plus the rigours of wartime commuting, this does seem a trifle naïve. Johnstone does, however, give us a rounded picture of Leslie Heward in the autumn of 1942:

> Heward knew that at this time he was expected, instructed even, to conserve his energy. But it was characteristic of the man that he was incapable of sparing himself in the preparation and performance of music . . . The temporal quality of his existence was emphasised by the simple enjoyment of life. Wearing the famous cap, informal but sedate, he would taxi to the studios with his overcoat pockets bulging with chocolate, apples and other sorts of refreshment. Often he would bring flowers, regardless of their wartime cost, to the secretaries who typed his letters . . . And throughout the bitter fight against sickness his sense of humour, refined, subtle, occasionally cynical, occasionally impish, never deserted him.[22]

Heward's chosen life-style did little to improve his health. Perhaps, like his friend Philip Heseltine/Peter Warlock, he was two very different people – the intensely serious artist and the convivial drinking companion. The schizophrenic Warlock had taken his own life; in Heward's case the term 'death-wish' might seem overdramatic, but despite his protracted hospitalisation and surgery, he persisted in smoking like a chimney and drinking to excess. According to one of the CBO players, 'one of Leslie's New Year resolutions made in Eli's pub was that he would drink no more doubles – in future they would be trebles!'[23] His family and friends accepted any tendency to overindulgence as a natural response to the debilitating pain of his illness. He was always excellent company, generous to a fault, but he was his own man, and though there were warm tributes in plenty after his death, one gets the impression that nobody actually 'knew' Leslie Heward very well.

On Boxing Day 1942, in response to an invitation to take over the Hallé Orchestra, Heward finally wrote his letter of resignation, to take effect from the end of the season. On New Year's Day 1943, Gerald Forty sent a handwritten reply: 'Dear Leslie – The meaning of "Amen" is "so let it be" – but, like Macbeth, "I could not say 'Amen' – 'Amen' stuck in my throat" – for it is with extreme reluctance and sorrow that I accept the finality of your decision . . . I cannot at the moment say more than that the prospect of your leaving is one which I envisage with deep regret – personally and officially.' The Committee passed a resolution 'That Mr Leslie Heward's resignation be accepted with regret and that the best thanks of the Committee be accorded him for his twelve years[24] of distinguished service during which the artistic standard of the orchestra had been raised and its prestige enhanced.' On 14 February, Heward conducted a Sunday Concert, which included Sibelius's *Tapiola* and Beethoven's Fifth Symphony, but nobody realised that it would be his last CBO concert. We learn from his wife Lenore's diary that he was 'very whacked after concert; goes to bed early', and a fortnight later, on Monday, 1 March, 'Leslie turns up unexpectedly to lunch. Looks very ill, and is. Try to persuade him to stay the week and rest in bed whilst I'm here. No good. Duty beckons.'

On the morning of Sunday, 7 March, though clearly far from well, Heward took the rehearsal for the afternoon concert,[25] but then became too ill to carry on; Shephard telephoned Stanton, who came in and took over. Heward went back into the Queen Elizabeth Hospital in Edgbaston, and guest conductors took over his programmes, but it soon became apparent that he would be unable to work again.

A week later, Gray (now Music Adviser to Western Command) was travelling on military business from Chester to South Wales, and took a detour to visit Heward, now back at his Harborne Road home.[26] He found him looking thin and pale, but still able to chat about future plans and to give him a cheery wave as he left. 'I told him I was on my way to Cardiff. "Hold on," he said, "I'll come with you!" Next day,' Harold recalled, 'I read in the paper that Leslie had died during the night.'

On Friday, 11 June 1943, a Memorial Concert, broadcast by the BBC, was given to a packed Town Hall ('every seat was occupied and could, one heard, have been filled twice over') with Sir Adrian Boult and Dame Myra Hess, who had officiated at his Tenth Anniversary Benefit Concert in 1940. A number of former CBO players augmented the orchestra to present what Eric Blom described as 'a programme of the sort he would have loved: a Handel Concerto Grosso, Beethoven's G major Piano Concerto and the first Brahms Symphony'.

Blom's 'Memorial Volume', together with countless obituaries in local and national newspapers, and in musical periodicals, speak movingly of the sense of loss felt by the whole musical profession – a feeling of 'what might have been', tempered with gratitude for what Heward's friend Cecil Gray summed up as 'an example of that rarest combination in the world, a fine artist who was also a lovely personality', or, as Harold Gray put it, 'the kind of man people responded to naturally; the orchestra felt that he was a friend'.[27]

For the CBO, in particular, Leslie Heward's untimely death marked the end of an era. There was to be no going back, but it still remained to be seen who would guide the orchestra forward into its next phase.

11

George Weldon – Going for broke

Having lost its conductor so tragically, the CBO Committee suffered two further blows in rapid succession. First, Professor Ernest de Selincourt, a loyal supporter of the CBO since its inception, died, only a few days after Leslie Heward;[1] then it found itself faced with the resignation of its long-serving, ever-dependable Secretary A. H. Shephard, a stalwart of Birmingham's orchestral life since before the Great War. A tremendous worker, 'his geniality always equalled his competence'[2] and Frank Forty remembers that 'he knew exactly at which public houses any orchestral players in the Midlands could be located, if needed at short notice as an emergency replacement'. He was presented with a silver salver, and in his place, Ulric C. Brunner, an experienced musical administrator,[3] was appointed Secretary and Librarian, at a salary of £500.

1943–4

For a major symphony orchestra to appoint a new principal conductor these days can take, seemingly, for ever, but in those far-off wartime years there were many experienced musicians eager to find a post. Having known since the beginning of the year that Heward would not be with them for the 1943–4 season, the Committee employed the last few Sunday Concerts and the Summer Series to try out possible candidates. Committee Minutes gloss over the selection process, but we may assume that those under consideration would have included Cameron and Julian Clifford[4] (both of whom had been used extensively in Heward's absence) and perhaps Braithwaite, Unger or Harrison. Gray (who conducted one of the summer concerts) must surely have been considered, despite recent tensions, but there were some new horses in the field too.

Maurice Miles, Gideon Fagan, Boyd Neel and Richard Austin were each given a Summer Concert, but the three who emerged as the front-runners were Neel, Muir Mathieson and George Weldon. Neel was making a name as a baroque specialist, while the Scot, Muir Mathieson, was the leading conductor in the rapidly expanding world of commercial cinema.

George Weldon had undertaken his trial concert as early as Sunday, 4 April 1943. Hely-Hutchinson, who attended this concert, was none too impressed,[5] but Eric Blom reviewed it warmly, remarking that Birmingham would be 'very lucky to secure Mr Weldon'. Weldon was later told in confidence by a member of the Committee that Blom's very public support was, in fact, nearly his undoing, since they resented being told by a music critic whom they should engage.[6] They even agreed to offer the position to Neel, but then had second thoughts and at a further meeting, a day or two later, decided to invite Weldon to conduct the 1943–4 Sunday Series.[7]

George Anthony Thomas Weldon was born in Chichester on 5 June 1908,[8] and although not coming from a musical family, he took to the piano very readily as a boy. He was lame from birth, with one leg shorter than the other, which restricted his mobility and gave him considerable pain from time to time throughout his life. At Sherborne School,[9] where he still wore leg-irons, he was 'excused games', so he concentrated his very considerable energies more and more on music, and (in a school with no great musical tradition) enjoyed the spotlight as a recital pianist and accompanist. 'At Sherborne I distinguished myself by doing nothing in particular . . . I am frequently asked why I took up conducting, to which I usually reply, "I was no good at anything else" – and this has a strong element of truth in it, since I was never more than a competent instrumentalist!'[10]

He was being unduly modest, for he won the school's Holliday Music Prize in 1925, then 'went to the Royal College of Music as quickly as a Southern Railway train would carry him'.[11] There he found himself in the conducting class, under Malcolm Sargent and Aylmer Buesst, his fellow-students including Gray and Mathieson. In 1929–30, all three conducted the RCM's Second Orchestra regularly, with Weldon and Gray being singled out by Sargent for special responsibilities. Weldon gained further experience working with semi-professional ensembles, and from 1937–9 he was assistant to Julius Harrison at the Hastings Municipal Orchestra,[12] standing in for him for some time during his illness. When war broke out, the Hastings Orchestra folded, but 'George Weldon and his Orchestra' kept orchestral music alive in the town, with a series of Sunday concerts, although it was right in the front line during the Battle of Britain. He also toured extensively with the LSO, and had a season as Musical Director of the International Ballet.

For the first time in his life, George Weldon now found himself in sole musical charge of a professional symphony orchestra. He was not yet Musical Director of the CBO, and his appointment was initially for one season only, but to all intents and purposes he was now in command, and his first task was to plan the 1943–4 Sunday Series, due to start on 3 October. From the City Orchestra's offices at No. 161 Corporation Street, Brunner issued details of the forthcoming programmes in the form of a large postcard, the concerts listed on one side and space on the other for an address, a stamp and the booking details (ticket prices ranging from 5/- in the Lower Gallery down to 1/6d behind the orchestra). Two of these cards were issued each season, before and after Christmas, and were known as the 'First Card' and 'Second Card'.

The first concert opened appropriately with Walton's *Spitfire Prelude and Fugue*, followed by Vaughan Williams, Tchaikovsky and Dvořák – the kind of music that Weldon did exceptionally well. W. S. A. Taylor, writing in the *News*, was bang on target: 'He is what might be called a dramatic conductor. I believe that a totally deaf person, unable to see more in action of him than his face, could tell exactly what type of music was being played by his expression alone. He gets results, too; the standard of playing was high. Birmingham is going to like Mr Weldon.'[13]

Weldon revived Heward's 'Family Concert' idea, with Cunningham, Stanton and Hely-Hutchinson playing the two Bach Concertos for three keyboards and strings,[14] and besides the redoubtable Mark Hambourg (with his reputation for breaking piano strings), other 'First Card' pianists included Kathleen Long, Irene Kohler, Moiseiwitsch, Cyril Smith and Kendall Taylor, who remembers playing 'many times with George Weldon and the Birmingham Orchestra. He got himself quickly in tune with whatever concerto was playing, and was an excellent accompanist.'[15] On Armistice Day (a doubly moving occasion in wartime) Cunningham and the City Choir gave a performance of *The Dream of Gerontius* 'which was generally agreed to be of a standard never excelled in the Choir's history'.[16] The soloists – hard to better in Elgar at that time – were Astra Desmond, Heddle Nash and Roy Henderson.

Lady pianists featured strongly in Weldon's 'Second Card': Myra Hess, Phyllis Sellick, Shulamith Shafir, Moura Lympany playing Khachaturian and Eileen Joyce in the Shostakovich Concerto for Piano, Trumpet and Strings. Denis Matthews (on leave from the RAF) finally made his CBO début in Beethoven No. 2.[17] Weldon's programmes continued to be as adventurous as was advisable on a single rehearsal, with an orchestra 62 strong, whose membership still varied somewhat from week to week as the result of the exigencies of war. Violinist Stan Murphy recalled, 'Most of us worked in munitions factories and George Weldon had to get permission from our bosses for us to get time off to play.'[18]

Critical and popular reaction to Weldon was very positive[19] and by March 1944 the CBO Committee was sufficiently impressed with his musical and administrative abilities to invite him to conduct a further series of six Thursday evening Summer Concerts. The season finished with a concert in aid of the Leslie Heward Memorial Fund, Weldon conducting and Moiseiwitsch the soloist.

In launching the City of Birmingham Orchestra in 1920, Appleby Matthews had stated categorically, 'Complete success is represented by a *permanent* Orchestra which is *self-supporting*.' Thus far that goal had not been attained. Weldon must have been delighted to discover, therefore, that even before he conducted the first CBO concert of the 1943–4 season, Brunner had submitted to Forty a Memorandum concerning the practicalities of establishing a permanent orchestra.[20] Although not yet appointed Musical Director, he lost no time in lobbying the Committee in support of Brunner's well-thought-out scheme, but he already knew that he would have to drop some of the existing players, whose performance was not up to scratch. After a broadcast concert on Sunday, 9 January, in which Beethoven's notoriously tricky Fourth Symphony had been the main work, Weldon expressed the hope that Eric Blom 'will have a crack at the 1st violins, they deserve it. I wonder how many had looked at the part beforehand? I am determined to raise the standard if I can.'[21]

The war was still grinding on, and the choice of available players limited. As early as January 1944, we find the names of some of his current players appearing in his desk diary, perhaps being scrutinised with an eye to the future. In April, at Byng Kenrick's behest, Hely-Hutchinson wrote to the *Post*, setting out the advantages to the city of a full-time orchestra, and by 18 May we find Weldon writing to Mrs Coats, 'You will be glad to hear that we had a very successful Elgar, last Thurs. & a full house (due to Louis Kentner).[22] I am getting on quite well about players for the permanent orch. although it is by no means an easy job. It seems fairly certain Ernest Element will return, and several others. Applications are coming in very well & so far things look satisfactory. And now we must get on with the business arrangements also.'

In local political circles, these arrangements had, in fact, been progressing well towards the establishment, at long last, of a permanent full-time orchestra for the city. Brunner's figures postulated an annual expenditure of £34,600, of which the CBO hoped to raise £20,100, leaving a deficit of £14,500. On Tuesday, 2 May 1944, the City Council authorised an annual grant of £7000 for a period of five years from 1 September 1944, and (largely due of the work of its Chairman, Sir Wilfrid Martineau) the Education Committee agreed to find the balance of £7500, in return for which the CBO was to make itself available for education work for fifty days each year.

In the summer of 1944 Hely-Hutchinson left Birmingham University for London, to succeed Arthur Bliss as the BBC's Director of Music; he was succeeded as Professor by Jack Westrup. In a farewell letter to Mrs Coats he wrote warmly of Weldon's work with the CBO, ending, 'Anyhow, with him and Brunner where they are, and the orchestra on a permanent basis, it is a mathematical calculation that in about three years – short of unforeseen accidents – the whole show will be on top of the world. I wish I could be here to see it, but as it is I shall have to cheer loudly from my metropolitan fastness. How delighted Leslie and Joe[23] would have been!'

From Weldon's desk diary we learn that, during the first half of 1944, the CBO was still giving only a weekly Sunday programme, plus an occasional 'out-of-town' concert, but he remained in Birmingham throughout the period, interviewing, auditioning, meeting politicians and other influential people. On a personal level, there is a reminder of the discomfort he constantly suffered from his 'gammy leg' – regular Tuesday morning visits to the chiropodist, never less than monthly and sometimes fortnightly. But neither his physical limitations nor his standing as CBO Conductor could exempt him from a weekly 'Fire Watch' duty.[24] Nevertheless, things were gradually returning to a semblance of normality and, at the end of February, Weldon notes 'MLO return to Birmingham Studio'. Now renamed the BBC Midland Light Orchestra, this body would no longer share a conductor with the City Orchestra, as it had pre-war, and once the CBO also introduced permanent contracts in the autumn of 1944 there would be no further sharing of musicians either. Even so, the City Orchestra had every reason to be grateful to the BBC for its friendly co-operation, especially over the previous decade, which had seen it through a critical phase in its history.

On 26 June, after a good deal of wheeling and dealing over his contract, the CBO Executive Committee finally approved the appointment of George Weldon as Musical Director and Conductor, at an annual salary of £2000. Unfortunately, Brunner's health was giving increasing cause for concern, and John Maude, who had been Legge's assistant (both at ENSA[25] and EMI) joined the CBO staff in June as Assistant Secretary, with special responsibility for 'Outside Engagements'. Later that year, an Education Officer was added to the staff to deal exclusively with the enormous amount of additional work resulting from the CBO's fifty days of schools work each year.

On the two days following 'D-Day' (6 June), Weldon held further auditions for the 'permanent orchestra', and the following week he saw Ernest Element and persuaded him to join. Ruth Gipps remembers that he decided to retain Norris Stanley as Leader, because he had been leading even before Weldon had started in 1943. 'So we had the strange position of seeing Norris Stanley as No. 1, Ernest Element as No. 2 and Dorothy Hemming as No. 3, although we all knew that Ernie should have been leading, Dorothy No. 2 and Norris No. 3!'[26] Final decisions were made and invitations to the successful candidates sent out. The new full-time CBO was in business.

1944–5

Sadly, in August 1944 Ulric Brunner's rapidly failing health finally led to his resignation. Although in the post for only a short time, he had made a sterling contribution to the CBO at a critical moment in its history. He was replaced by Major Denzil G. Walker, at one time aide-de-camp to the Viceroy of India, but recently invalided out of the Army.

September opened with three and a half days of rehearsal at Digbeth Institute, giving Weldon and his new orchestra the chance to get accustomed to playing together and to build up some core repertoire. On one of the rehearsal days, the Lord Mayor provided a Civic Reception for the players – a nice gesture, especially in wartime. This was followed by the very first concert by the full-time orchestra, surprisingly not in Birmingham but in Stafford, on Tuesday, 5 October 1944; it was repeated in Birmingham Town Hall two days later. Despite the short notice, Maude had done his job well and the orchestra's diary was already full to bursting with promotions in Birmingham and around the Midlands, plus a number of ENSA engagements[27] and some bookings by choral societies.[28] All these activities add up to a recipe for a busy orchestra – 97 working days in three months. The extra travelling involved taking on, for the first time, a full-time 'roadie', Arthur Knight, who had played principal horn in the City Police Band, joining the CBO for Sunday Concerts from 1920. The City Orchestra bandwagon was really starting to roll, at long last!

The new pattern of Birmingham concert giving retained the traditional Sunday Series, but Weldon introduced a new Thursday Series, which would remain the backbone of the City Orchestra's winter season Birmingham promotions until the diversification of the 1980s. Pricing was identical for both (the top of the range now increased to 6/- and serial tickets being available). For the first time the orchestra had a logo – very 1940-ish, with a black roundel on to which the letters CBO were superimposed in white (the 'CB' lying within the 'O').

The season included the warmly received première of a Symphony in F minor by the CBO's young second oboist, Ruth Gipps; in the same concert she played the Glazunov Piano Concerto. However, the most substantial work in this category was undoubtedly the Walton Symphony, which Heward had given with such success in 1938; its blend of orchestral brilliance and bitter-sweet lyricism suited Weldon's gifts exactly, and it rapidly became a repertoire work for the CBO. Once again, the composer was in the audience, and Alan Fitton of the *Mail* wrote that 'The orchestra was superb. George Weldon drove them to the limit, but they responded to every beat. No wonder they were given an ovation at the close. When Mr Walton appeared on the platform there was the nearest thing to cheering that a Birmingham audience can manage.'[29]

During the 1944–5 season, Weldon and the CBO alone undertook no fewer than 183 concerts, plus 49 pre-rehearsal sessions on other days, and 49 recording sessions for Columbia. Little wonder that one Committee member (who evidently knew his *Elijah*) said of Weldon that 'he neither slumbers nor sleeps'!

The recording sessions were the natural outcome of the appointment to the CBO staff of ex-EMI boffin John Maude. At its meeting on 26 March 1945, the CBO Committee assented to enter into an agreement with Columbia to undertake 'not less than six sessions in any one year'. In fact, the first of these sessions had taken place in Dudley Town Hall[30] on that very day, and there were to be 15 days of recording sessions during the 1945–6 season. Much of the recording repertoire allotted by Legge to Weldon and the CBO was fairly light in character, and recording quality is variable, but the discs demonstrate what excellent work Weldon had been doing in the few months of the permanent orchestra's existence.

In the summer of 1945, George Weldon introduced a week of summer Promenade Concerts, advertised on the sides of buses and trams. The six concerts (Monday, 30 July to Saturday, 4 August) built on the success of the 1943 and 1944 Summer Series, with popular repertoire barely distinguishable from his winter programmes – every one of the soloists, for example, had performed with the CBO in the Town Hall recently. An instant success with the public, these modestly priced[31] 'CBO Proms' grew to a two-week season the following year and by 1947 had assumed the three-week format that they were to occupy for so many years. A space was even provided on the reverse of the printed programme for autograph hunters, who were charged 1/- in aid of the CBO's newly established Benevolent Fund. Weldon's cousin, who lived near Bristol, told the author that when the CBO played at the Colston Hall, dozens of programmes would be brought into the conductor's room at the end of the concert for signing. Since both were called George Weldon, they used to share the task!

Although hostilities between the nations had now ceased (Tuesday, 8 May was

VE Day, followed by VJ Day on Tuesday, 14 August), the CBO's ex-army Secretary, Major Walker, had been fighting a battle of a different kind with the Musicians' Union, which had recently negotiated substantial wage increases with the Hallé and Liverpool Philharmonic, and now sought a 100% rise for the CBO players. Walker held out strongly and, faced with the very real likelihood of extinction, the Union eventually climbed down. The increase would have meant another £7000 a year on the salary bill, which was in fact the City Council's total grant to the orchestra at that time, apart from the Education Committee's subvention of £7500, which was fully allocated. The CBO's accounts for 1944–5 (its first season on a 'full-time' basis) showed a deficit of £1200, but, by and large, there was general agreement that Weldon and his permanent orchestra had got away to an excellent start.

12

Peace and productivity

Post-war euphoria found the CBO in good shape to meet a growing appetite for classical music. As young people were being demobbed, or released from work in munitions factories, they were looking for evening entertainment of all sorts. The ballrooms and the theatres were full, and so was the Town Hall. At the cinema the punters paid to see the stars, and whether its top people liked it or not (and some of them were certainly uneasy about it) Birmingham had its own star, and his name was George Weldon. One might have thought that his lameness would have militated against his achieving pop idol status, but the concert-goers scarcely even noticed it. With his excellent baton technique, a carnation in his buttonhole and a slightly theatrical but highly effective manner on the rostrum,[1] Weldon certainly had charisma. Groups of young people (young ladies in particular) would queue for hours to sit on the unreserved front benches of the Orchestra Gallery, partly to watch the players at close quarters, but even more to admire their idol.

Weldon adored fast sports cars, and owned a succession of them throughout his career – Riley, MG Midget, Healey-Silverstone, Armstrong-Siddeley, Atalanta (for whom he test-drove cars) and, long after his Birmingham days, an E-type Jaguar – racing some of them (as 'G. A. T. Weldon') at the Brighton and Lerves Speed Trials, at Brooklands, Goodwood and Silverstone.[2] During his time in Birmingham he drove a Frazer-Nash (with a chain-driven gearbox). Donald Brook noted, 'His formula for dispelling worry is to get a powerful sports model and to let it rip on a good stretch of road.[3] Reputedly, Denis Matthews, booked to play in Birmingham, once politely declined an invitation from Weldon to drive him back to Birmingham after their London concert on the previous evening, but agreed to accept a lift as far as Paddington Station. On arrival at Birmingham Snow Hill after a comfortable train journey, he was surprised to find a grinning George Weldon there already, waiting to drive him the few yards to the Grand Hotel![4]

1945–6

The 25th Anniversary of Appleby Matthews's first CBO concert seems to have passed unnoticed – on 5 September 1945, George Weldon and the orchestra were giving an ENSA concert in Nottingham for Walter Legge. Since Legge had engaged the CBO for a number of ENSA concerts around the Midlands, George Weldon accepted the Presidency of his 'Birmingham Workers' Music Club', which arranged lectures, chamber recitals and symphony concerts. Gerald Moore thought that Walter would have given anything to have been a conductor, 'but after an abortive attempt to rehearse the City of Birmingham Orchestra, he gave up the idea'.[5] Moore may have had the story from the singer Maggie Teyte, who used to recount 'an amusing story (possibly apocryphal) about his attempt one day to conduct in Birmingham, wearing a Russian blouse, "Like Moiseiwitsch. He took up his baton, broke it. Second time he took up the baton. PAM PAM . . . the orchestra walked off." '[6] John Denison's recollection is that that Legge 'threatened to conduct one of the CBO factory concerts at Coventry; he got cold feet on the morning and sent a stand-in to take his place'. Whatever lies behind this story, it has clearly grown in the telling.

Bitterly cold weather ushered in 1946, and the *Mail* critic Alan Fitton sympathised: 'The orchestra played well throughout the concert,[7] though occasionally lacking in assurance. Uneasy was the hand that held the bow. If it was anything like as cold on the platform as it was in the rest of the Town Hall, the wonder is that they could play at all.' Conversely, during a heatwave in July, the success of the previous summer's 'Proms' led to their extension to an 11–concert season, spread over two weeks.

The CBO's principal bassoonist Vaughan Allin was notorious as a practical joker. Eric Blom had gently taken Weldon to task for repeating works too frequently, making some remark to the effect that 'the orchestra ought to be able to play Vaughan Williams's *Fantasia on Greensleeves* backwards, by now'. Seizing the opportunity, Allin wrote out the entire piece backwards and persuaded him to conduct it. Thus it was that the 1946 CBO Proms prospectus announced an unlikely sounding work, somewhat anagrammatically entitled *Enërg Esëlv*, by a composer (said to be of Turkish origin), 'Nila Naguav', who made an impressive appearance at the end, complete with fez and long moustache. Blom cheerfully entered into the spirit of the occasion, referring to 'the Effendi, who was present and repeatedly bowed his acknowledgments of the public's warm reception', and 'Naguav Smailiw, a master whose work the young composer seems to know backwards'.[8]

*

At the Annual Meeting in October, Byng Kenrick was able to present an encouraging report on the full-time orchestra's second complete season, 1945–6, in which nearly 260 concerts had been undertaken, besides a large number of EMI recording sessions. When public subvention was taken into consideration, the accounts had shown a surplus of £2500 on the year. In the *Penguin Music Magazine*, John Waterhouse praised Weldon's work with the CBO, but complained of over-cautious programme building. However, 'The orchestra's education work seems to be working efficiently and fruitfully in school visits and youth concerts. A huge City Orchestra Club flourishes.'[9] This club, started before the war, had been reorganised in September 1945 with Miss Elsie Macklin as its tireless secretary. Wartime camaraderie had broken down much of the old British reserve, and its membership soon built up to the thousand mark.

The education work to which Waterhouse referred formed a vital part of the CBO's income and represented a substantial part of the players' workload. The main thrust of this aspect of the orchestra's work consisted of school visits, involving two groups: a full orchestra ('Section A', generally conducted by Dr Desmond MacMahon) and a string orchestra ('Section B') which visited Junior Schools and was directed by Frederic C. Morris, conductor of the Shrewsbury Orchestral Society. Between them, they covered eight schools a day. On at least one occasion,[10] Weldon conducted 'Section A' visits himself, to ensure that an acceptable standard was maintained. His main contribution, however, was a series of six Youth Concerts (closely modelled on Malcolm Sargent's extremely successful 'Concerts for Schools' in Liverpool) which he conducted in Birmingham Town Hall, in parallel with similar concerts in Wolverhampton Civic Hall. Inevitably, all this education work added to the players' already very heavy workload, but in order to negotiate the huge leap from a freelance band to a permanent salaried orchestra, the CBO's budget had, of necessity, been based on what amounted to a six-day working week.

Weldon's tremendous energy and the professionalism of the players kept things ticking over, but at the expense of those extra rehearsals which alone would have opened the door to better playing. Each session still began with two full days of them, and Weldon would snatch the odd day whenever the busy schedule allowed, but most concerts were rehearsed only on the day.

1946–7

The *Mail* was able to report that on Thursday, 5 September 'the Town Hall was packed . . . for the start of the new season, and hundreds were turned away'. Over at the *Post*, the new initials 'J. F. W.' indicated that Eric Blom had departed for London, and had been replaced by John Waterhouse. Two weeks later, the American composer Samuel Barber conducted ('competently' was Alan Fitton's description) a revival of his First Symphony and the celebrated *Adagio for Strings*, and another eminent visitor was Eugene Goossens, who conducted Bantock's *Hebridean* Symphony.[11]

One can look at Weldon's programmes in two ways. One would be to point out, quite truthfully, that he repeated popular works over and over again, often twice in the same season; the music critics gave him a bad time for it. But one could also look at the number of unfamiliar works that he *did* manage to programme along with the safe crowd-pullers, including the first performances of many pieces by composers who were either members of the orchestra (Ruth Gipps, Vaughan Allin, Mary Chandler and others) or were Midlands based. When one considers the limitations imposed by a double-wind orchestra, the sheer number of concerts undertaken, and the restricted rehearsal time available, what he and the CBO managed to achieve at this time was truly remarkable.

In September 1946, Harold Gray returned to the Town Hall podium, as a guest conductor, for the first time since July 1943. After completing his wartime work for CEMA,[12] Gray had spent the 1945–6 season as Principal Conductor of the Carl Rosa Opera Company, but was now back in Sutton Coldfield and the time seemed ripe for his relationship with the CBO Committee, so strained during 1939–40, to be healed. Weldon was an old chum from Royal College days, so he found himself knocking at an open door. In January 1947, he resuscitated the Sutton Philharmonic Society concerts (using CBO players), was offered a number of CBO concerts in the early months of that year and became Weldon's Assistant Conductor from the 1947–8 season. Harold had a lot of time for Weldon, who he felt 'was exactly the right person for the CBO at that time. He had an excellent stick technique, which was a terrific help, when one thinks of the enormous number of concerts that the orchestra was doing then, and the limited rehearsal time; and of course he was an indefatigable worker.'[13]

The arctic weather of early 1947 posed desperate problems for an orchestra which needed to travel in order to earn its bread. On Wednesday, 5 March, a concert in Derby had to be cancelled due to a blizzard; returning from this abortive outing, the coach ground to a halt on an unlit road and one of the horn players got out to investigate, promptly disappearing up to his waist in a massive snowdrift; he was pulled back in, but minus his wellies, which were never recovered. Fuel shortages and occasional power-cuts led to footnotes in February programmes, stating that 'This is an "Emergency" programme printed by hand, due to the existing fuel crisis'; after one of them, the *Gazette* carried a photo showing musicians playing with the use of bicycle-lamps, as had happened occasionally during the early days of the war.

On 11 March 1947, Victor Hely-Hutchinson died, following a severe bout of pneumonia brought about mainly through overwork and an attack of 'flu during that terrible winter. He was only 45 – almost the same age as his great friend Leslie Heward had been at his death four years previously – and although he had by then moved away from the city, his passing represented yet another tragic loss to Birmingham's musical life. Jack Westrup, who had succeeded him as Professor of Music at Birmingham University, moved on to Oxford and was in turn succeeded (both at the university and on the CBO Committee) by Anthony Lewis, who had earned considerable respect as the first Director of Music of the BBC's Third Programme.

John Waterhouse put his foot in it by referring in the *Post* to some 'drunken' playing by the CBSO's trombone section, for which he received an outraged letter from the formidable (and teetotal) principal Harold Greensmith, and had to apologise; but his good opinion of Weldon was steadily growing: 'To hear under Mr Weldon a performance of Elgar's *Falstaff* (whose regular establishment in our repertoire is a most welcome feature) is to be convinced that he is among the finest conductors of our age.'[14] It is interesting to compare Waterhouse's assessment of Birmingham's musical life at this time, in the burgeoning confidence of post-war Britain, with the situation that would obtain some 45 years later, after the opening of the city's superb new Symphony Hall: 'We have had plenty of good and varied fare set before us. But in retrospect one fact emerges very clearly: the city has been offered a great deal more music than it can digest; more, anyway, than it is willing or able or can afford to swallow.'[15] In April 1947, conscious of some criticism from the élite, but also of his immense 'grass roots' popularity, George Weldon spoke his mind to the members of Birmingham Rotary Club: 'We run run some popular concerts. The object is not entirely financial but to create a new audience that can be gradually led up the musical garden path until it arrives at the top. The question of audiences is a very sore one. The City Orchestra is not a philanthropic society and we are dependent on public support to maintain an orchestra at good salaries and a proper size. I hate to say it, but the orchestra is actually the smallest symphony orchestra in the country. We are not as large as other orchestras, but we should be. That will undoubtedly come in the end.'[16]

Denzil Walker, who had accompanied Weldon to the luncheon, estimated that the cost of enlarging the orchestra to 75 players would be between £8000 and £10,000 a year.

In five concerts in the Sunday Series (between 20 April and 18 May),

Weldon and the CBO played all nine Beethoven Symphonies, in order. Anthony Lewis provided an impressive printed introduction, ending, 'To anyone who, in these uncertain times, is tempted to lose faith in humanity, I recommend the nine symphonies of Beethoven. Written under equally difficult conditions, when the future must have seemed even less secure, they are a triumphant testimony of the power of man to create beauty out of strife, and to rise above the wreckage of war to unparalleled heights of artistic achievement.'

On 23 June and 24 June 1947, Weldon and the CBO undertook what were to be their last recording sessions for EMI: Grieg's *Peer Gynt* Suite No. 2 and music by Edward German. Both at ENSA and EMI, Walter Legge had played an important rôle in providing useful work and exposure for the CBO, but now he had other fish to fry – his new and splendid Philharmonia Orchestra, in particular. In any case, he had always been a hard man to work for, quite prepared to break written agreements if necessary. Some letters that survive show Denzil Walker desperately trying to keep the CBO's recording contract alive in the face of Legge's procrastination, with his letters sometimes going unanswered for six months or more: '4 July 1947. My dear Denzil – I have now had a chance of reading through those letters. Unfortunately they came at a period when I was in Germany. I left actually on the first day of the year and got back late in January. The decisions made subsequent to the letters settle the points which at that time remained unanswered.' It was the final brush-off. It would be nearly 20 years before Birmingham's orchestra would enter a commercial recording studio again[17] and 23 before it would record again for EMI.

The 1947 Proms were extended by yet another week to reach the exhausting total of 19 concerts, all played by the CBO and all within the space of 22 days (Saturday to Saturday, only the Sundays free). At the first of them, the irrepressible 'Ronnie' Allin provided once again what the surprisingly tolerant John Waterhouse described as 'an agreeable diversion', enlivening the end of the *1812* Overture by discharging his double-barrelled shotgun (loaded, presumably, with blank cartridges). Harold Gray averred that Allin had a special case made to accommodate all the component parts of one bassoon and one shotgun, and that when commuting to Birmingham from his East Anglian cottage, he would often 'bag' a rabbit, or a brace of pheasants, conceal them in a hedge and recover them *en route* home, after the concert.

1947–8

There was talk at this time of abandoning the City of Birmingham Orchestra's Friendly Society status and turning it into a Limited Company, but the idea was dropped; it would be another 40 years before that aim would see fulfilment. One change was effected, however: Major Walker was in future to be known not as General Secretary but as General Manager and Secretary. The change of title recognised the steadily increasing importance not only of Walker's own rôle but of the Society's professional administrative staff in general. Furthermore, the establishment of an Orchestral Employers' Association at this time opened the way for national wage negotiations within the profession.

On 11 September, Weldon opened the Thursday Series with a splendid concert in which the brilliant young violinist Ida Haendel played the Mendelssohn Concerto and the CBO played Holst's *Planets* Suite, complete. A month later, tribute was paid to Ralph Vaughan Williams on his 75th birthday with a concert which included *The Lark Ascending*, the *49th Parallel* Prelude and the Fifth Symphony. A week later, it was the turn of Harold Gray to celebrate the marriage of Princess Elizabeth and Prince Philip, earlier that day, with Mendelssohn's *Wedding March* and other festive music.

It was, indeed, a time of celebrations. On 17 November, the City Orchestra had the honour to be invited to present a concert promoted by the BBC, and broadcast live from the Town Hall,[18] to open its own Silver Jubilee Festival. The conductor (Sir Adrian Boult) and the soloist (Paul Beard) had close links both with the CBO and with the BBC's own Symphony Orchestra. Gerald Forty was invited to give the Interval Talk, reviewing the long (and, by and large, happy) association between the two bodies.

A work new to Birmingham was Walton's Viola Concerto,[19] with the CBO's principal Gilbert Shufflebotham as soloist. John Waterhouse was full of praise in the *Post* ('Expression was sensitive and beautiful, intonation impeccable') but cellist Gwen Berry noted in her diary: 'I like Gilbert so much and do wish I could like his playing more, but no, I think it's very poor. Poor style, peculiar tone quality and shaky intonation. Can't understand Waterhouse, who states he has impeccable intonation. Personally I think it's very peccable.' In December 1947, G. D. Cunningham conducted the CBO and the City Choir in two memorable performances of *Messiah*, with Isobel Baillie and Kathleen Ferrier amongst the soloists.

In many ways, life in Britain in the late 1940s was tougher than it had been during the War. Many things were still available only on ration, but in August 1948 the Board of Trade agreed to provide symphony orchestras with a supply of vouchers[20] which could be exchanged for clothing coupons. Players had to specify what they needed them for; Gwen Berry, for example, duly signed a slip stating that 'having received 16 clothing coupons for the purchase of one black two-piece suit and 3 pairs silk stockings; the articles purchased will be for my own use in connection with my employment'.

Change was in the air. From January 1948, ticket prices were increased, now ranging from 2/- up to 7/6d. A month later, at George Weldon's personal request and after no little debate, the CBO changed the name it had borne for nearly twenty years, and became the CBSO by adding the word 'Symphony' to its title. John Waterhouse (a literary man) felt that 'the new title, like the old, is quite respectable. I happen to prefer the old, but merely because it seems to me to have a more distinctive and dignified euphony, and because I find the adjectival "Symphony" an even more tiresome and meaningless convention than "Philharmonic".'[21]

On Monday, 23 February 1948, Weldon and the CBSO gave their first full-dress symphony concert in London's Albert Hall. Between four and five thousand people braved deep snow for a mixed programme in which tried and tested crowd-pullers – the Grieg Piano Concerto, with the enormously popular Eileen Joyce as soloist,[22] and the *Trumpet Voluntary* – were framed by Rimsky-Korsakov's *Cortège des Nobles*, a Handel Organ Concerto and the Walton Symphony, which proved the undoubted triumph of the evening, *The Times* describing it as 'a superlatively fine performance . . . Mr George Weldon has obviously made it his own. He maintained its tension, kept the counterpoint clear, and brought out the organic unity . . . the "malizia" of the *scherzo* is the more sinister for being light-fingered and so makes a further contrast with the grandeur of the finale.'[23] In the *Birmingham Post*, Eric Blom found it a nostalgic experience to hear the orchestra again, after a couple of years away from Birmingham; he liked what he heard, and was careful to get the new title right.

March 1948 brought some encouragement on the financial front, too, CBSO programmes proclaiming that the orchestra was now 'in association with the Arts Council of Great Britain'. A month later, Sir Adrian Boult gave his services to conduct a special concert in aid of the orchestra's Welfare and Benevolent Fund; in due course this became a regular annual event.

In April 1948, Weldon was invited by the British Council to replace, at short notice, the indisposed Malcolm Sargent at an Anglo-Turkish Music Festival in Ankara. Gwen Berry reported his return, 'bursting with energy and high spirits' and much entertained by his experiences with the somewhat undisciplined Turkish orchestra. 'He, by the aid of an interpreter, said to the Piccolo that he was not in tune. The man replied that he had put it somewhere and it had got cold. George replied he didn't care *where* he put it, as long as it kept warm. Whereupon the whole orchestra arose and told him what to do with it.' But CBO players could sometimes prove unreliable, too, in those post-war days; Denzil Walker was present when Weldon conducted Tchaikovsky's *Romeo and Juliet* during which an inexperienced young player essayed the tricky syncopated cymbal part, and succeeded in getting the two plates so perfectly aligned one with the other that a vacuum set in; they stuck together, and they stayed together.

In May, Elisabeth Schumann was the distinguished soloist at a special concert in the Town Hall in aid of International Student Relief, singing '*Deh vieni*' and '*Voi, che sapete*'.[24] On the musical front, things were looking good, but despite all the concert giving it was still hard to make ends meet; the accounts for the 1947–8 season showed a slight deficit of £400. Attendances were still very variable, and at the end of the Last Night of the CBSO Proms, at which he shared the conducting with Gray, Weldon announced that from the beginning of the 1948–9 season, 'Thursday concerts will in future contain at least one rarely-heard, new or contemporary work; alternate Tuesdays will be devoted to the music of one composer and alternate Sundays are chiefly to be concerts of light classical or ballet music. It would be foolish to predict how this scheme will work, but the orchestra cannot exist on empty houses, and if lack of public initiative causes the idea to fail, the flicker of hope for music in Birmingham, at last burning more brightly, will be burned out indeed.'[25]

13

Unlucky for some

In August 1948, Birmingham's musical world was deeply saddened to hear of the death of the much-loved conductor of the City of Birmingham Choir, Dr G. D. Cunningham, City Organist since 1924. Only a month before, he had given his 900th Wednesday lunch-time recital on the Town Hall organ, and when his CBO appearances and his recitals in the Great Hall of the University, the Oratory and elsewhere are taken into consideration, he must have played over a thousand times in the city. He was succeeded in the post by Dr George Thalben-Ball of the Temple Church. George Weldon added the conductorship of the City Choir to his already onerous CBSO duties, with Dr Ruth Gipps as Chorus Master.

1948–9

In September the CBSO visited Sheffield for a five-concert Prom Season which was to become an annual event, Weldon regularly sharing the conducting with Herman Lindars, the wealthy steel magnate who underwrote the series; unfortunately his high opinion of his own musical gifts does not seem to have been shared by the players. In Birmingham, Weldon launched his new-style Thursday Series with Vaughan Williams's powerful Sixth Symphony; later, he programmed John Veale's Second Symphony[1] and Arthur Bliss conducted the first performance of his *Adam Zero* Suite. And yet the myth persists that Weldon's programmes were stodgy and unenterprising.

Harold Gray was given a few orchestral concerts, but his main task at this time was to conduct the CBSO's Schools Concerts, at locations all around the city. Frank Downes remembers 'one cold frosty morning in the winter of 1950, arriving at a school in the city to play in a school hall packed with children sitting on the floor'. To begin, Gray asked the various principals to play a few bars each, to demonstrate the different instruments. Despite cold fingers, Norris Stanley was required to demonstrate double-stopping. ' "Now, what did that sound like?" said Harold to our young audience. "Hands up!" and Harold pointed to a young lad near the front. "Awful, Sir," came the innocent reply.'[2]

Playing standards were still rather variable, and changes of personnel not infrequent.[3] As 1949 began, Alan Fitton, music critic of the *Birmingham Mail* since 1943, proposed a New Year resolution for the CBSO's players: 'The Strings: never to fall below that full, rich tone which they produce from time to time and which, at its best, would satisfy the most fastidious conductor or composer. Brass: never to play too loudly, but to remember that its power must be proportionate to the other sections of the orchestra. Woodwind: never to allow pitch to be suspect.' For Weldon he suggested the avoidance of over-dramatised climaxes in Tchaikovsky and Dvořák, and 'the introduction of more seldom-heard works'; John Waterhouse was still pursuing his crusade along similar lines.

January 1949 found the CBSO and its Principal Conductor undertaking their longest excursion to date, to Edinburgh's Usher Hall, where Weldon conducted his admired account of Elgar's Second Symphony,[4] and later, they undertook another outing to the Royal Albert Hall, this time with Elgar's No. 1 as their principal offering. In the *Mail*, Alan Fitton summarised the critical response. Once again, Eric Blom had given a very upbeat assessment of the visitors' efforts, but most of the London papers had been patronising: '*The Times* is charming in its ingenuous condescension. For an opening gambit, the following would be hard to beat: "Such is the pride shown by communities nowadays in the prowess of their respective orchestras that several of the larger ones are sent to the Albert Hall from time to time in order that London should know what they are good for." ' But Fitton also quoted the *Telegraph*, with a reference to the Elgar Symphony, 'whose difficulties were overcome very creditably', and the *News Chronicle* ('Their high standard of playing confirmed a previous impression that they are a most capable orchestra').

A decision had been taken in 1948 to bring the Society's financial year, which since 1920 had run from September to September, into line with general practice, starting in April. This had the added advantage that budgeting became possible before too many commitments were entered into for the ensuing season. The Society's 1948–9 accounts covered, therefore, only seven months, but still showed a deficit of £650. Musicians' pay still lagged well behind industrial rates, and protracted negotiations with the Musicians' Union had resulted in two wage increases, but box-office revenue found it hard to keep up with increased costs.

Part of the problem was that Weldon's slightly more adventurous Thursday programmes were not selling well. Artistically, Waterhouse noted some definite successes; in March 1949 he devoted one entire notice to Ruth Gipps's Piano Concerto, given its best performance at a Thursday concert and 'very much the best large-scale work of hers so far heard in Birmingham . . . admirably laid out for the keyboard and admirably lucid and effective in orchestration'. However, many of what he called the 'Thursday novelties' proved to be 'a mere trivial token of a policy on which one had set high hopes'. The difficulties of attracting an audience for unfamiliar programmes proved no barrier to Wolverhampton's Council, who engaged the CBSO to present an attractive three-day Contemporary Music Festival in June 1949, in which Weldon brought together many of the 20th-century works he had been programming in Birmingham during the season.

The summer of 1949 saw an ongoing correspondence in the *Post* about the CBSO – its financial problems, its overwork and its repertoire. John Waterhouse pasted up all these letters into a six-foot-long 'snake'[5] and then wrote a series of well-argued articles urging a new approach. But most CBSO concerts continued to be popular in character. The July–August issue of *Play On* includes an amusing cartoon by 'Rus' (violinist Albert Russell) showing George Weldon, Norris Stanley and Denzil Walker in Spanish bullfighting costumes – the reference is to the *Carmen* Suite, played at a Sunday concert. The 1949 Proms offered 'several innovations – a fountain which is most refreshing to look at, and to add to the gaiety, George presented Norris with an egg after the "Carnival of the Animals" last Saturday!'[6]

1949–50

The summer of 1949 saw the deaths of two men who had been closely involved in the birth of the City Orchestra: its first conductor, Appleby Matthews, and his deputy, Richard Wassell. Gerald Forty wrote warmly of both in *Play On*, and a Memorial Fund was set up in memory of Matthews. The CBSO's short-lived house-magazine was discontinued at the end of the year, due to the CBSO Committee's need 'to examine every item of expenditure with a view to enforcing economies'. The editor, Dr Gipps, barely disguised her disappointment and disgust at this short-sighted move.

Indeed, the orchestra's finances were once again becoming a major source of concern. During the 1948–9 season, 105,000 tickets had been sold for 89 concerts in Birmingham alone. Good as that might sound, it represented an average attendance of under 60%. The CBSO's total costs were around £80,000, of which the wages bill – for 63 musicians (earning between £10 and £15 a week) and a staff of eleven – ate up about £50,000. Birmingham City Council's grant towards this amounted to £11,000, and the Arts Council contributed a further £9,000. The balance had to be found either from engagement income or from the box office.

Despite these difficulties, Weldon had succeeded in persuading his reluctant Committee to increase the string strength by an eighth viola and cello. But clearly it was felt that something more radical would be necessary if continuing losses were to be stemmed. Faced with a deficit variously estimated between £5000 and £8000, the CBSO Committee reintroduced 'Saturday Pops' (Walter Goehr conducting three of them) and came up with a novel scheme to broaden its audience base: a new series of industrial concerts, billed as *Music You'll Love*.[7] Tickets were not sold to the public, but instead blocks were sent direct to factories and offices for resale to their employees, all the administrative work being carried out from within the CBSO's own office. Despite its slightly cumbersome title, the series caught on quickly. The 2000 available seats for the first concert, in January 1950, sold out within two hours, and the same happened for the second concert on St Valentine's Day. The audience base had indeed been broadened, but the ticket prices had been pitched too low (1/- to 3/6d) and, as a result, the 'take' even with a full house barely covered the costs of the concert, so the financial problems remained.

Another worthwhile experiment, run in parallel with this series, was an Industrial and Commercial Patrons Scheme, aimed at persuading leading local firms to take vouchers for the CBSO's regular promotions, for resale to their employees. It was launched at a Town Hall concert on 20 April 1950, when Byng Kenrick addressed the audience, which already included some 300 extra members as a result of the scheme. By September 1950, 75 firms were subscribing, bringing in around £1000 a year, plus additional ticket sales.

News of the CBSO's successful 1948 Sheffield Proms had evidently reached both Nottingham and Wolverhampton, who engaged Weldon and the orchestra for short September Prom seasons of their own. On 8 January 1950, the CBSO welcomed for the first time one whom it would get to know much better in due course: the conductor of the Bournemouth Municipal Orchestra, Rudolf Schwarz; his programme opened with Schubert's *Rosamunde* Overture and closed with Mendelssohn's *Italian* Symphony.

The customary three-week season of CBSO Proms was the best-attended yet – 3500 up on the 1949 series, to reach an impressive total of 33,079 (the average house in excess of 2000). Had figures anywhere near these been attainable for the winter concerts, the CBSO would have had no further problems, and Weldon (who always considered the CBSO's publicity to be too low-key) had 'A Personal Letter to Promenaders' slipped into all the programmes, encouraging them to support his forthcoming Winter Season.

*

1950–1

On Tuesday, 3 October, the CBSO lost another of its founding fathers, Gerald C. Forty, who had been Chairman of the Executive Sub-Committee from 1931 until early 1950, when he became seriously ill.[8] It somehow seems appropriate that one who had been so intimately associated with Birmingham's musical history should have died on a day when Weldon was conducting the CBSO and the City Choir in Birmingham Town Hall in a special performance of Elgar's great oratorio *The Dream of Gerontius*, fifty years to the day after its première in the same hall. Gerald Forty's first involvement in Birmingham's orchestral music dated back to a meeting convened by Granville Bantock in the Lord Mayor's Parlour to set up what became Beecham's New Birmingham Orchestra, on 4 October 1916, almost exactly 34 years before. From that moment onward, his calm and courteous presence and his wise advice afforded a consistently beneficial influence on Birmingham's orchestral music. His loss would be keenly felt.

At the same time, two other stalwarts, both at the heart of its affairs for many years, resigned their offices: W. Byng Kenrick, the steady and dependable Chairman of the CBO's Management Committee, and (a few months later) the Treasurer, Tom Hamilton Baynes. To replace them, the Committee elected Stephen Lloyd[9] as Chairman of the Management Committee, W. G. A. Russell[10] as Executive Chairman and Arthur Maddison[11] as Honorary Treasurer. An early outcome of the new team was the establishment, in December 1950, of a 'City of Birmingham Orchestral Endowment Fund', which attracted excellent support; by 1952, indeed, its capital was around £8000 and, with covenanted subscriptions, that was expected to rise over a period of years to some £12,000.

At the first Sunday Concert of the new season, Max Rostal broke a string during the Beethoven Violin Concerto; the instantaneous exchange of instruments between Rostal, Norris Stanley and Blyth Major 'had the speed and perfect ease of passes down a first-class forward or three-quarter line'.[12] The third concert in the series was entrusted to Rudolf Schwarz, making his second guest appearance within a year. Weldon exchanged rostra with him, conducting the *Enigma Variations* and Vaughan Williams's *Job* in Bournemouth, quite unaware that, behind his back, Lloyd and Russell were inviting Rudolf Schwarz to take over the CBSO from the autumn of 1951. Once a secret deal had been struck with Schwarz, Bill Russell called Weldon in and suggested to him that 'he might wisely offer his resignation'.[13]

The announcement of Schwarz's appointment was made on 5 December, whilst Weldon and the orchestra were in Cheltenham, at the end of a five-concert tour of South Wales and the West Country. According to a newspaper report, Russell said, ' "Mr Weldon has done sterling work for the CBSO and, indeed, for music generally in Birmingham. His great gifts and tremendous energy have raised the orchestra from an emergency combination set up early in the war to a finely-integrated unit with a wide repertoire and great artistic merits." Interviewed last night at Cheltenham . . . Mr Weldon said he could not, at the moment, speak of his plans.'

Indeed, Weldon had had no time to make any plans for his future at all, and to him all this oratory must have sounded distinctly hollow. There is no doubt that he was genuinely shocked by what he felt to be an underhand way of dealing with this matter. In effect, he had been sacked, and it is probably true to say that neither he nor his career ever fully recovered from the blow, though 'Sir John Barbirolli was understandably furious at the despicable treatment dished out to Weldon and, consequently, made him associate conductor of the Hallé'.[14]

Why would the Committee want to get rid of a conductor who had worked so untiringly for the CBSO since 1943 – one who had personally auditioned and selected the new permanent orchestra in 1944 and had steadily built it into a professional body worthy of the city – a man of enormous charisma, with a big local following, especially of young people, who had often paid for extra players himself and had conducted without fee on many occasions?[15]

The truth is that we have very little evidence on which to draw. After three years of deficits, the orchestra's financial situation was certainly serious, with an anticipated loss of around £8000 and only the CBSO Proms attracting really full houses,[16] and there may have been the feeling that a new face on the podium might stimulate box-office takings.

On the artistic side, there does seem to have been an anti-Weldon lobby. Protracted sniping at CBSO programmes by the music critics of the *Post* and *Mail* (John Waterhouse and Alan Fitton) had, to some extent, rubbed off on to his image in the eyes of Birmingham's musical establishment, represented on the Executive Sub-Committee by Dr Willis Grant (Organist of Birmingham Cathedral and Conductor of Birmingham Bach Society), John Lowe of the BBC and Professor Anthony Lewis of Birmingham University. Lewis exercised considerable musical influence on Committee thinking at this time, but he was a busy man; he was rarely seen at CBSO concerts and was somewhat out of touch with its affairs. At a meeting of the Programme Committee, of which he was Chairman, Lewis suggested that it might be a good idea to do an all-Elgar concert; after an embarrassing pause, it was left to Weldon to explain that he had conducted an extremely popular all-Elgar programme on the previous night.[17]

The CBSO's new Chairman, Councillor Stephen Lloyd, though somewhat reserved in his public manner, was a very strong character (Arthur Maddison, a colleague of some forty years' standing, describes him as 'a man of unshakeable principles')[18] and he may have had some reservations about the way in which Weldon's contract was terminated, but in the autumn of 1950 he was in hospital, having broken his femur whilst on holiday, and Bill Russell was running the orchestra's affairs.

Weldon's final 'official' appearance in the Town Hall was on the Last Night of the Proms, 16 June 1951. Just before the concert, a message arrived to the effect that Arthur Matthews, due to play the *Trumpet Voluntary*, had collapsed at home. Sub-principal Bill Whittaker found himself promoted to solo status, but since three trumpets are needed for the Henry Wood version, Orchestra Attendant Albert Morton was sent off in a taxi with instructions to find another player and bring him back without delay. After an abortive visit to Quinton, and with time running out, he reached Sparkhill, where, according to one newspaper, 'he found Jack Black preparing to blow his trumpet at a Saturday night dance at the Mermaid Hotel'. Dr Gipps recalls that the bass soloist William Parsons 'sang as an encore a negro song, "I'se fired, I'se woefully fired", which reduced a number of people (including George) to laughter. Parsons had no idea of tact!'[19] Ironically, only four days later, the CBSO gave the first of two concerts on consecutive days in London's Royal Festival Hall, just opened to mark the Festival of Britain.[20] Weldon's programmes were built around two of his 'party pieces': *Falstaff* and the Barber Symphony.

It seemed entirely appropriate, for one who had worked so hard to put the CBSO on the musical map, that it was the players themselves who should have provided Weldon with his real Farewell Concert, at the one event of the year over which they had total control – the Benevolent Fund Concert, which took place on Sunday, 7 October 1951. Campoli, an old friend both of the conductor and the orchestra, was the soloist in the Mendelssohn Violin Concerto, and Weldon played out with the *Enigma Variations.* The CBSO staff gave him a handsome commemorative pewter tankard, on the glass bottom of which was engraved 'The Last Drop', over a picture of a man hanging on a gibbet, whose irony will certainly not have been lost upon its recipient. The Lord Mayor gave him a silver cigarette case and ashtray, paid for by gifts from music lovers all around the Midlands, genuinely sorry to see him go. According to one newspaper, 'Traffic was held up outside the building by the crowd that still waited to get a last glimpse of him.'

There can be no doubt that Weldon's extensive 'fan club' was dismayed by his precipitate departure. On behalf of the 400 members of the CBSO Listeners' Club,[21] Elsie Macklin sent him a well-publicised letter saying that they 'might not feel able to transfer their allegiance to any other musician'; in his sensible and dignified reply, he thanked them for their loyalty, but reminded them that their allegiance 'should be to music itself, and not to any mere personality'.

The late Miss Ethel Hatton, who followed George Weldon's career closely and collected all his concert programmes, reckoned that during his seven full seasons in Birmingham, 1944–51, Weldon conducted (in the British Isles alone, and the vast majority with the CBO) 1330 concerts – an average of 190 per season. To this figure must be added concerts with various orchestras overseas,[22] many EMI recording sessions and rehearsal days on which there was no concert. All the leading soloists active in this country at that time – Myra Hess, Campoli, Mark Hambourg, Irene Scharrer, Pouishnoff, Clifford Curzon, Eileen Joyce, Moura Lympany, Cyril Smith and the rest – came to play concertos with the CBSO on a regular basis, often twice or more in a season, and all seem to have found Weldon an ideal collaborator.

That kind of total professionalism represents, of course, only one aspect of the conductor's art. Bill Russell and his Committee clearly felt that the appointment of Rudolf Schwarz represented 'a change to a conductor of higher calibre', and with hindsight, where artistic sensibility is concerned, the broad spectrum of critical opinion would probably support this view; furthermore, 'his appointment was seen by the majority of players as a forward-looking one'.[23] But the punters who occupied the cheap seats on the ground floor of Birmingham Town Hall were to take a good deal of convincing that this change of conductor, for which no one had prepared them in any way, was either necessary, advisable or wise.

14

Rudolf Schwarz – Creativity and crisis

On 11 November 1950, Bill Russell wrote to Stephen Lloyd in Birmingham Accident Hospital, to keep him abreast of developments:

> I am writing to give you the result of my visit to Bournemouth, and to say that it was very satisfactory. Schwarz is a most delightful man, very alert and keen, possessing both ideas and ideals . . . He is 45 years of age and will apply for naturalisation as a British subject as soon as his five years' qualification has elapsed.[1] His contract with Bournemouth was for three years up to February last . . . Schwarz feels rather restricted at Bournemouth, but is obviously so grateful to his employers for having enabled him (as he put it) 'to start life all over again' that he feels bound to give them ample time to find a successor. This fits our time-schedule very well . . . He really welcomed my visit, feeling that it offered a chance such as he was seeking.

Rudolf Schwarz's English was still far from perfect, but it is very clear that the wily Russell, who was hoping to engage someone he regarded as 'a conductor of higher calibre' at a lower salary than the CBSO had been paying Weldon, had more than met his match when it came to wheeling and dealing, and he finally had to agree a salary of £3000, plus £500 expenses – Weldon's remuneration. Schwarz's Swedish wife Greta took one small part in the discussion: 'After he had told me all about it, he said, "Do you think you would be interested?" – and Greta, who was sitting beside me, said "Yes"!'[2]

1951–2

Rudolf Schwarz ('Rudi' to his friends) was born in Vienna on 29 April 1905, had a brilliant student career and was soon well established as an operatic conductor in pre-war Germany, with appointments in Düsseldorf when only 18 and at Karlsruhe in 1927. In 1936, however, his courageous acceptance of the musical directorship of the Jewish Cultural Organisation in Berlin brought him to the attention of the Nazis; he was interned in various concentration camps, ending up in Belsen, from which he was rescued in 1945 more dead than alive.[3] In 1947, whilst recuperating after the war in Sweden, his brother in London spotted and sent to him an advertisement for the vacant conductorship of the Bournemouth Municipal Orchestra. Rudi applied and, somewhat to his surprise, landed the job. When he was shown the enormous list of concerts to be given in his first season, he wanted to know who the other conductors would be. 'You,' the manager told him, 'you are the other conductors.' 'But what if I get ill?' Schwarz wanted to know. 'You will not get ill,' the manager retorted. 'Bournemouth is a very healthy place.'[4] In the event, as he later recalled, 'I conducted 183 concerts in eleven months, but after the first three months I was close to a nervous breakdown.'

Some thirty years later, Rudolf Schwarz recalled his first impressions of Birmingham: 'I received a letter from Adrian [Boult] when the news of my appointment was announced. He congratulated me, and said he was sure I would enjoy Birmingham – "the nicest people, the best water" – and he was absolutely right! I found that Birmingham was *alive* – a city with people who work, and are not just lounging around with bucket and spade on the sea-front!'[5]

To those accustomed to Weldon's programmes, Schwarz's 'First Card' reflected immediately the influence of a very different mind at work. Professor Brian Coghlan observes, 'After the Weldon years, Rudolf Schwarz introduced us to an entirely different, Central European, repertoire – he really "cosmopolitanised" the CBSO.'[6] But he also included much unfamiliar British music. A series of three programmes (29 November, 6 and 13 December) will give a flavour of the whole:

Berlioz	Overture, King Lear
Rubbra	Symphony No. 5
Beethoven	Piano Concerto No. 4 (Myra Hess)
Ravel	La Valse
John Ireland	A London Overture
Mahler	Lieder eines fahrenden Gesellen (Nancy Evans)
Roussel	Symphony No. 3
Mendelssohn	Symphony No. 3 (Scottish)
Malcolm Arnold	Overture, Beckus the Dandipratt
Respighi	Suite No. 1, Ancient Airs and Dances
Bartók	Violin Concerto (Alan Loveday)
Schubert	Symphony No. 9 (Great)

The works by Rubbra, Roussel and Bartók were all new to the CBSO, as were the Mahler songs. Later in the season, as he subsequently recalled, he programmed the *Adagietto* from the Fifth Symphony. 'I tried to introduce Mahler, but I was severely reprimanded . . . we did a little Bruckner, but one had to tread very carefully. Even to introduce a Schumann Symphony[7] was considered very venturesome – his music was not popular.'[8] But in the *Post*,[9] John Waterhouse gave Schwarz's 'First Card' the warmest of welcomes, seeking to reassure the more conservative concert-goers that, despite some unfamiliar names amongst the list of composers, there was nothing to fear in his choice of works, and giving the Programme Committee a warm pat on the back.

Schwarz had made it clear from the outset that he would need and expect more rehearsal time than Weldon had been accustomed to have; one day a week was to be devoted entirely to rehearsal. One might have thought that the musicians would have welcomed the opportunity to learn new repertoire and to prepare it thoroughly, but this does not seem to have been universally the case. Nowadays it seems incredible to us that so basic a requirement should have been considered so revolutionary, but the orchestral players of the post-war generation tended to be conservative both by predisposition and from habit. Schwarz's curious, rather 'sideways' beat was notoriously hard to follow[10] and this can always give rise to the tendency for musicians to say, 'We don't need the extra rehearsal, but perhaps he does!' He also arranged the orchestra differently, with the second violins on his right (as only Boult still did, in those days) and it took time for the players to get accustomed to this. There is, too, no doubt that there was a good deal of residual resentment amongst the players regarding the manner of Weldon's going, and some of this must have rubbed off on to the newcomer.

The extra rehearsal and Schwarz's meticulous care quickly began to bear fruit, but it was inevitable that this new approach to the orchestra's day-to-day work would impact both upon the diary and upon the financial situation, which had not been helped by the closure of the Town Hall during the months of July, August and September 1951 for urgent repair work; the CBSO Proms had been moved earlier, with a resulting drop in attendance. By this time, 'School Visits' had become more complex affairs; the existing symphony orchestra (Section A, with Harold Gray) and string orchestra (Section B, with Dr MacMahon) were augmented by small woodwind and brass groups and by a string quartet; since each group visited four schools, no fewer than twenty could now enjoy a concert on each of these days.

It was not only the players who viewed Rudolf Schwarz's new approach with suspicion; attendances at the Thursday Concerts were still unsatisfactory – worse, if anything, than in Weldon's day. More rehearsals, fewer concerts, smaller audiences – it all added up to a recipe for instant financial disaster. Looking back some forty years, Stephen Lloyd recalled that, when he had become Chairman in 1950, the CBSO was carrying an accumulated deficit of £6000,

> but unfortunately we made a further loss of £2000 that season. We were relying on the Midland Bank, who had covered us up to then, but soon after Rudi was appointed principal conductor, they began to hint that our overdraft must be reduced. The Bournemouth Municipal Orchestra was also in dire financial straits at that time, and Bill Russell came up with the idea that we might form a 'Birmingham-Bournemouth Symphony Orchestra', which would perform mainly in Birmingham between September and April each year, and mainly in Bournemouth during the summer months, with Rudolf Schwarz and Charles Groves as co-conductors. Bill, Denzil Walker and I went off to Bournemouth for discussions with some leading figures there, and the Mayor and Town Clerk of Bournemouth came up here, at our Lord Mayor's invitation, but unfortunately they turned it down flat. Of course, by the time all this had taken place, our overdraft was running around £20,000,[11] and we had a real crisis on our hands.[12]

The Committee's initial response was to announce a desperate measure. It did not feel able to ask its main funders to increase their annual grants (£11,000 from the City Council and £9000 from the Arts Council), but

> The series of annual losses must be stopped and the Management Committee proposed to do this by putting the orchestra from October onwards onto a six months basis. The orchestra will only be in existence from October to March each year. The number of engagements outside Birmingham, which on the whole are very unprofitable, will be greatly reduced and there will be less travelling. Attendances at concerts in Birmingham recently . . . have been especially poor at Thursday concerts, and the number of serial ticket-holders has declined. The Management Committee regrets that it can no longer maintain the CBSO throughout the year. If Birmingham people share that regret, the remedy is in their own hands. They should fill the Town Hall.[13]

What got the CBSO off the hook, initially, was an unexpected change in the political control of Birmingham City Council in May 1952, following R. A. Butler's unpopular Budget. Lloyd went to see Alderman Bradbeer, the new Socialist Leader of the Council, which eventually agreed in July 1952 to grant the CBSO an interest-free loan of £20,000, to be repaid in annual instalments of £2000, over ten years. The CBSO's Treasurer at that time, Arthur Maddison, remembers that 'the loan was supposed to be repaid, of course, although nobody on the Council really thought that it would be. But Stephen Lloyd had made up his mind that we would repay the loan at £2000 a year, and, somehow or other, repay it we did. I think that the most surprised person was probably the City Treasurer.'[14]

With the orchestra's improved financial position helped by some generous private donations, near-disaster had been narrowly averted; there can be no doubt that a reversion to a 'six-month orchestra' would have dealt the CBSO a mortal blow. Times would continue to be hard for many years to come, but, with hindsight, the crisis of April 1952 still looks like the 'life-or-death' one, and it is as well that all those involved kept their nerve and refused to allow the City Orchestra to be snuffed out for purely financial reasons. It would be another thirty years before their long-sightedness would be seen to have paid off fully, and for the CBSO to be seen not just as a great local institution, but as the city's foremost international cultural asset.

While this drama was being played out, partly in the public arena but mostly behind Committee Room doors, Schwarz and his players were quietly getting to know one another and the relationship was beginning to bear fruit. Many of the old familiar soloists still came, and clearly enjoyed working on the great concertos with a musician for whom the Viennese classics were his native air. There were new, or less familiar, faces too: Cherkassky, Tortelier, Franz Osborn, and Boult guested with Elgar No. 2. The *Music You Love* industrial series continued, but no longer with packed houses. Lunch-hour Concerts were presented on the same days, as a sensible economy – these were now attracting over 1000 takers each time. Schwarz's 'Second Card' was rather less adventurous than his first, but he included a lot of Vaughan Williams, Hindemith's *Weber Metamorphosis* and the *Sea Interludes* from *Peter Grimes.* Sir Arnold Bax, Master of the King's Music, was in the audience to hear his own Third Symphony.

In March 1952, Sutton Coldfield Philharmonic Society celebrated its 21st Birthday Concert, Phyllis Sellick playing Falla's *Nights in the Gardens of Spain* and Gray conducting the 'Birmingham Symphony Players' in what must have been a dangerously small-scale version of Sibelius's Seventh Symphony. In July, the CBSO made the first of what would become regular visits to the Cheltenham Festival. In his first season of CBSO Proms, Schwarz did his best to follow the Weldon model, including shortish pieces by locally known composers and plenty of 'pop' concertos, but attendances were still disappointing.

Two other significant changes took place during the season. In January 1952, six additional string players, added a few years before at Weldon's behest but never regarded as a permanent part of the CBSO's establishment, were laid off; and at the height of the crisis, in April 1952, Major Denzil Walker, the orchestra's able and hard-working General Manager since it went full-time in 1944, wrote to Lloyd offering his resignation. He had been taking a certain amount of criticism from the Players' Committee for what they saw as administrative shortcomings,[15] and had been indirectly criticised in the *Birmingham Post* by a prominent member of the Committee. It may well be, though, that Walker had been finding the new management team considerably more demanding to work for than the old. Kenrick and Forty had given him considerable leeway; Lloyd and Russell involved themselves much more closely in the day-to-day control of finance and affairs.

1952–3

From August 1952, the CBSO's new General Manager was Kenneth Matchett, son of the comedian Billy Matchett, who had been an RAF pilot during the war. He came with considerable experience in orchestral administration behind him, most recently as Concert Manager in his native city, Liverpool. The 'grapevine' amongst orchestral managers works pretty well and he must have been sufficiently aware of the situation in Birmingham to realise that he was taking on a tough assignment. Stephen Lloyd guaranteed his salary for one year – he asked for £1250 and got £900, but with a promise held out of a substantial increase if he could effectively modernise the CBSO's administration in that time.

Lloyd, Russell and Matchett knew full well that the orchestra was by no means out of the wood financially. The City Council's £20,000 loan had seen off the greater part of the CBSO's massive overdraft for the time being, but, on virtually every front, the future still looked bleak. Oboist Tony Miller, who joined the orchestra in August 1952, remembers that initially he was given no contract but just engaged from week to week. Somehow, the CBSO had got its affairs into a vicious spiral. At 63, it was by far the smallest of the regional orchestras. To give Schwarz the extra string players that he would so desperately need, if he was to improve the CBSO's slightly tarnished national image, would cost even more money, but the orchestra had been running at a loss for several seasons. Schwarz himself was becoming exhausted by his 150–concert commitment, and the Committee agreed to reduce it to 125. On top of all this, the Musicians' Union was now pressing a national claim for a 20% pay-rise for its members. Whatever the Committee tried, the crisis stubbornly refused to go away.

Lloyd and Russell were well aware that increased subvention of some sort would indeed be needed, and that it would be needed very soon, so they came up with 'Plan A' – a Regional Scheme. People from all around the Midlands regularly attended concerts in the Town Hall, and the orchestra also undertook engagements in many other local towns. It was not unreasonable, therefore, to expect other local authorities to contribute towards the overall cost of running the CBSO. The Lord Mayor of Birmingham sent out invitations to 57 of his fellow-mayors to attend two meetings; the estimate was that £11,000 p.a. might be raised in this way, but between them they only came up with £2371, and even then many of the pledges were hedged about with ifs and buts.[16]

Now there was nothing for it but to invoke 'Plan B' – go back to the City Council and ask for a larger grant. A great deal of lobbying, behind the scenes, succeeded handsomely, and in November 1952 the City Council agreed to a massive increase in the CBSO's grant, from £11,000 to £21,000, and in the Education grant (tied directly to School Concerts) from £9000 to £10,000. They also took the opportunity to transfer future responsibility for CBSO grants from the Education Committee to the General Purposes Committee. In effect, Birmingham had picked up the tab that the other local authorities had declined. In return, the orchestra agreed to more Council representation on its Management Committee,[17] and to undertake a few more Education days. At the same time the Arts Council increased its annual grant to the CBSO to £11,000. The CBSO Society was reorganised, with popular free evening recitals and occasional outings for its members. The crisis was over.

In October 1952, Kenneth Matchett submitted to the Committee two well-prepared and closely argued documents: the first, a scheme for revising the pattern of the CBSO's concert giving in 1953–4, and the second, his 'Proposals concerning increased attendance and membership'. Nothing so radical had been put forward since Appleby Matthews's original proposals of 1920. Matchett was also negotiating on behalf of the CBSO with the Musicians' Union, and in November the players' wage claim went to arbitration before Lord Goodman at the Industrial Court. Predictably, the final increase was about half the amount that the Union had sought, but it was still expected to cost the CBSO £4882 a year; increased hire charges for the Town Hall made the annual increase nearer £6000. As a result, in the spring of 1953, City Council grants for the following season were increased yet again, to £36,000, and following a direct approach from the City Council, the Arts Council agreed to make a substantial increase in its grant for the following season, to £15,000.

By January 1953, the Hallé and Liverpool Orchestras, faced with big losses, had placed their musicians on three months' notice, and Lloyd took no small satisfaction in telling the Press that 'the CBSO is continuing on a permanent basis'; he warned the players, though, that they could not expect regular pay-rises of this magnitude.

Schwarz's 1952–3 programmes were full of interest. The Thursday Series included *The Planets*, Bax's Sixth Symphony, Beethoven's *Choral* Symphony, Bartók's *Concerto for Orchestra*, Vaughan Williams's Fourth Symphony and (for the first time since Boult's celebrated 1929 performance) Mahler's *Das Lied von der Erde*. Highlights of the Sunday Series included Clara Haskil (in Mozart), Magaloff, Cherkassky, Peter Pears (Britten's *Serenade*) and Dennis Brain (Mozart and Gordon Jacob).[18]

Campoli played the work with which he was associated above all others – Lalo's *Symphonie Espagnole* – 'exquisitely. Most soloists in those days only played four movements, but he always insisted on playing all five.' There were plenty of shorter novelties, too, but overall it looked a well-balanced selection and there was really nothing to justify a grumpy letter in the *Post* from a gentleman in Stratford-on-Avon, complaining about the programmes and suggesting that 'the reason why the public will not come is that they have been frightened away'. A lengthy correspondence ensued, mostly from people who claimed to 'know what they liked' but who in reality only liked what they knew. John Waterhouse warmly endorsed Schwarz's programmes and policy, but a good deal of damage was done by the subsequent fuss, at a time when the CBSO could ill afford such unwelcome publicity.

1953 was Coronation Year; the orchestra was involved in celebratory concerts around the Midlands. For the first time since the war, the economy and the whole atmosphere began to feel more buoyant, and Schwarz felt that the time was ripe to approach the Committee about replacing the six string players whose jobs had been axed at the beginning of 1952. Matchett recalls that 'the question was raised in Committee, "Why do you want a larger orchestra? Surely, all you have to do is to ask them to play louder." Rudi chipped in, "Mr Chairman, the reason why we need more string-players is to be able to play more *quietly*, but with quality." ' He was unconsciously echoing Waterhouse's happy phrase: '*Piano* has not, on the whole, been the orchestra's *forte* in the past.'[19] Schwarz might never have got his extra strings but for the generosity of another member of the CBSO Committee, the philanthropist Harry Payne, who was much impressed by the new conductor and provided a series of donations amounting to nearly £11,000, which made it possible to increase the number of players to 71 for the 1953–4 season.[20] As a result, Schwarz re-auditioned all the violinists in April 1953; his confidential notes make depressing reading, with a few complimentary remarks but far too many comments such as 'Out-of-date playing'; 'Completely lifeless'; 'Abominable intonation. Most unsatisfactory'.

Out of town, though, the CBSO was getting some excellent reviews,[21] and Norris Stanley was amongst the 18 orchestral leaders invited to play at the Coronation Service in Westminster Abbey. Ex-CBO musicians were well represented, too: Boult presided and Beard had the somewhat unenviable task of being 'Leader of the Leaders'.

Despite overall optimism, a sour note was struck with the rather public resignation in March 1953 of Kenneth Matchett, after only seven months. Soon after arriving in Birmingham he had produced two long and detailed reports – one suggesting a way forward for the CBSO Society (more recruitment, Members' Evenings, etc.) and the other putting forward a string of imaginative proposals for updating the orchestra's pattern of concert giving (including a new Tuesday Celebrity Series), but with his somewhat abrasive style he soon fell foul of Stephen Lloyd. In December 1952, he was given 'a serious warning' by Lloyd and Russell for 'a grave indiscretion in handing confidential papers to the Press'; in Liverpool, he had been accustomed to taking Press briefings as a routine matter, and had not appreciated that in Birmingham such matters were handled only by the Officers. Matchett was a Manager who actually wanted to manage,[22] and, in Schwarz's view, 'He didn't really get on with Stephen Lloyd, and vice versa. It was a classic case of oil and water!'[23]

By March 1953 matters had come to a head, but there were no substantive grounds for dismissal. At a Management Committee meeting on 16 March, the Committee voted to split Matchett's job ('General Manager and Secretary') into its two separate components, offering him the General Managership, but with a newly appointed Secretary 'occupying the senior administrative position'. He was then called into the meeting and given this news, whereupon he tendered his resignation. It is astonishing to read in the Minutes that, the moment he left the meeting, the Committee changed tack, scrapped the idea of splitting the two posts and agreed to advertise for his successor under the old title, though at a higher salary of £1100–£1250. Matchett's detailed reports were never brought to Committee, but all his major recommendations were adopted over the following couple of years. It was a discreditable episode, and in the long run it was Birmingham's loss, for Matchett went on to become the long-serving, shrewd and highly respected General Manager of the Bournemouth Symphony Orchestra, seeing it safely through some of its darkest and most difficult days.

15

'Ideas and ideals'

After two seasons of high drama and financial crisis, the autumn of 1953 was a time for regrouping and rebuilding. Those qualities in Schwarz which Russell had noted so perceptively – 'very alert and keen, possessing both ideas and ideals' – could now come into their own, as would those later described by Barrie Hall: 'The chief characteristics which distinguish Rudolf Schwarz himself are humility and integrity, and an intellectual asceticism, allied to great personal charm.'[1] This outward charm effectively disguised some deep inner insecurities – notably acute stage-fright, which would drive Rudi to pace up and down in the Artists' Room before a concert, puffing furiously on a cigarette and talking about almost anything in order to take his mind off the matter in hand.

1953–4

The new General Manager was no stranger to the CBSO, for Blyth Major had been for some years its Deputy Leader, in Weldon's day, leaving for South Africa in the Spring of 1951, where he became Deputy Musical Director of the Durban Symphony Orchestra. An experienced musician, Major was for many years Bandmaster of the Coventry Salvation Army Band, and later (during the war, in the course of which he was awarded a DSO for gallantry at Dunkirk) of the Band of the Royal Warwickshire Regiment. Subsequently he directed the City of Coventry Band and led the semi-professional Leicester Symphony Orchestra, so he came to the CBSO in 1953 with advantages shared by no other General Manager and Secretary, before or since: he had administrative experience, conducting experience and – perhaps most important of all – he had himself been a senior member of the orchestra for several years and well understood both its background and its inherent problems.

Following Matchett's proposals to the letter, the main novelties of the

1953–4 season were the Tuesday Celebrity Concerts – a prestige monthly series for which the orchestral players wore tails (a novelty at that time); they commanded higher ticket prices[2] and featured a number of distinguished artists (for example, Gioconda de Vito, Moiseiwitsch, Walter Gieseking), but Schwarz took the chance to couple each with a major orchestral work: *Mathis der Maler*; *Daphnis et Chloë*; Mahler No. 4; *Sinfonia Antartica*. The Russian–American mezzo Jennie Tourel sang Ravel's *Shéhérazade*; the Goossens family (Eugene, Leon, Sidonie) was featured at another concert and the last of the series, featuring the City Choir, was entirely devoted to Britten's music. The composer shared the conducting with David Willcocks, with three soloists closely associated with his music – Jennifer Vyvyan, Anne Wood and Peter Pears – and the CBSO's principal horn James Kirby; the programme included the *Serenade* and the *Spring* Symphony. Gray conducted the Second Symphony (*The Four Temperaments*) by the Danish composer Carl Nielsen, with whose music he was to become so closely associated.

The addition of the Tuesday programmes meant that the CBSO was now providing (at varying degrees of frequency) a wider range of Town Hall concert series than ever before: Tuesday Celebrity; Thursday Symphony; Saturday Popular; Sunday Evening; Lunch-hour; Summer Proms and the industrial *Music You Love* Series. John Waterhouse gave a warm welcome to the additional string players provided through Harry Payne's anonymous bounty: 'They have returned, and lo! they are nine. And, what is far, far more, all of the players are full-timers.'[3]

Performance standards were still inconsistent. Schwarz recalled that 'the orchestra did gradually improve, but some of the playing was still not ideal. Some of the older players, who knew the repertoire pieces very well, were very poor sight-readers.'[4] In April 1954, to stimulate interest within the orchestra, he initiated a two-month exchange visit in which two CBSO viola players changed places with two old acquaintances of his – Inge Möller of the Swedish Radio Orchestra and Kurt Lewin of the Stockholm Symphony Orchestra; an interesting idea which both orchestras seem to have found very rewarding.

During 1953 the CBSO moved its administrative offices from Corporation Street into larger premises at 60 Newhall Street, and another link with the past was broken with the death of the CBO's first Leader, Alex Cohen. At the Annual Meeting, Alderman Bradbeer raised again a matter which had exercised Beecham before World War One, Boult and Heward after it and Weldon after World War Two: 'I think the time has come for this great city to turn its mind to the provision of a building particularly designed for the full appreciation of music.' But, as usual, nothing more was heard of the idea.

*

1954–5

Rudolf Schwarz had no time for avant-garde or experimental music: 'it puts off audiences – once they have left, disappointed, they may not come back.' Nevertheless, at the 1954 Cheltenham Festival he premièred Geoffrey Bush's First Symphony, and first performances were a significant feature of the ensuing Birmingham season. On 23 September, Benjamin Britten was back in the Town Hall to attend the première of the symphonic suite he had recently compiled from his Coronation Year opera *Gloriana*, with Pears, Schwarz and the CBSO. Pears and Britten had been giving a series of recitals in Venice and they drove in relay across Europe in order to get back to Birmingham in time for the rehearsal and concert; Alan Fitton reported that 'the orchestra has rarely played better'.

In October, for the first time since 1929, Sir Thomas Beecham conducted the City Orchestra in what the London critic of the *Scotsman* adjudged 'an evening of distinguished music-making'. Invitations had been issued to 450 people for a Lord Mayor's Reception after the concert, but (depending upon which paper you were reading) Sir Thomas was either 'taken ill', 'tired' or 'collapsed' after the concert, and it had to be called off. Next morning, a photographer snapped him at New Street Station, puffing contentedly on his cigar in a first-class reserved compartment, *en route* for London, a twinkle in his eye, and he was back a week or two later, right as rain, to conduct the CBSO again.

At the beginning of November, the CBSO and the City Choir made their first TV appearance, in a BBC series called *The Conductor Speaks.* Like Heward before him, Schwarz hated talking to audiences, but he agreed to introduce a programme which included a chorus from *Elijah*, a Handel Organ Concerto (with George Thalben-Ball), the Waltzes from *Der Rosenkavalier* and the Choral Dances from *Prince Igor.*

Other highlights of the season included a performance of Edmund Rubbra's Sixth Symphony (three months after its London première) in what the *Mail* described as 'one of the concerts of the season', with Géza Anda as soloist in Brahms's Second Piano Concerto; elsewhere Myra Hess was heard in Beethoven and Robert Casadesus in Beethoven and Ravel. Cellist Gwen Berry especially enjoyed working with Eduard van Beinum – 'a wonderful experience. Such a nice man, and what a conductor! He made a little speech to the orchestra today. There comes occasionally a day when one is glad one is a musician.'

1955 came in with some wretched weather. On one occasion, Gwen found herself trudging through the snow to Digbeth Institute, to rehearse Vaughan Williams's notoriously 'tough' Fourth Symphony with Schwarz, and in nostal-

George Weldon,
in ENSA uniform, 1945.
Photo: Dr Ruth Gipps.

George Weldon and the CBO (Leader: Norris Stanley) with producer Walter Legge, at an EMI recording session in Dudley Town Hall, 1945. *Photo: Sunday Mercury.*

George Weldon
and the CBO in
the Town Hall, c. 1947.
Photo: Geoffrey Hoare.

Part of the crowded Ground Floor at a CBSO Prom, c. 1949. Note the paper sheets provided for the young people to sit on. *Photo: Birmingham Gazette.*

Pianist Denis Matthews and CBSO Leader Norris Stanley, with George Weldon, c. 1949. *Photo: Birmingham Post & Mail.*

Rudolf Schwarz at a Reception in Birmingham Council House, following a CBSO concert.
On the Lord Mayor's right, Greta Schwarz and Bill Russell;
on Schwarz's left, Dorothy and Stephen Lloyd. *Photo: Birmingham Gazette & Despatch.*

Benjamin Britten shakes hands with Norris Stanley after the première
of his *Gloriana Suite* in September 1954, as Rudolf Schwarz and
soloist Peter Pears (left foreground) look on. *Photo: Birmingham Post & Mail.*

Rudolf Schwarz and the CBSO perform before a crowded (but soberly suited) Town Hall audience, c. 1956.
Photo: CBSO Archives.

Stephen Lloyd and Andrzej Panufnik, 1957.
Photo: CBSO Archives.

Andrzej Panufnik conducts a typically minuscule section of the CBSO in the Royal Festival Hall, 1957. *Photo: Keystone.*

Gwen Berry, CBSO cellist and diarist. *Photo: Constantine.*

Hugo Rignold – the expression, the cigarette
and the bowing/fingering demonstration are all typical.
Photo: Paul Chapman.

Benjamin Britten talks to Meredith Davies during rehearsals with the CBSO for the *War Requiem* première in Coventry Cathedral, 1962. Behind the Melos Ensemble (right) are soloists Dietrich Fischer-Dieskau and Peter Pears. *Photo: Erich Auerbach.*

Sir Arthur Bliss with Hugo Rignold, during Lyrita recording sessions in Kingsway Hall, London, January 1966. *Photo: Hans Wild.*

Hugo Rignold, CBSO Leader Felix Kok and composer Egon Wellesz, after the British première of his Fifth Symphony, January 1966. *Photo: CBSO Archives.*

Harold Gray and the CBSO giving a concert for schoolchildren in the Albert Hall, Nottingham, February 1966. The adventurous programme included Sibelius's Fourth Symphony and music from Prokofiev's *Romeo and Juliet*. *Photo: Guardian Journal.*

gic mood: 'My mind went back to the day we did our first rehearsal there, as the CBO, under George Weldon. That was in 1944. We certainly had more fun in those days.'[5] The rehearsal was for one of a series of concerts promoted by the BBC, in which the CBSO played the seven Vaughan Williams Symphonies then published, in order, under Schwarz and Boult, though on 6 February the composer himself conducted the *Sea Symphony*, with Elsie Morrison, Thomas Hemsley and the City Choir. His eyesight was by now failing, and his hearing very limited; at the rehearsal, he said, 'I am simply going to beat four-in-a-bar and leave you ladies and gentlemen to do the rest.' Albert Russell immortalised the occasion in an amusing cartoon, showing the composer as the pilot at the wheel of the SS *CBSO*: 'Full speed ahead! Don't worry about the rocks – we'll cut through 'em!' Oboist Mary Chandler was 'rather surprised that Rusty didn't add an ear-trumpet to his portrait of VW – he certainly used one on this occasion!'[6]

The CBSO's Education programme continued to be heavy going for the players, despite occasional lighter moments. Norris Stanley, who led a string quartet on school visits, recalled a little girl asking him at one of their concerts, 'Please, sir, do you spend all your time playing music, or do you have to work?' On another occasion, he said, 'We are now going to play an air. I hope you children know what an air is?' A bright pupil raised his hand. 'Yes, sir,' he said, 'it's a big rabbit.'[7]

The players led busy lives – there were 101 concerts in Birmingham during the season and 66 out of town, with rehearsal days over and above this. Gwen's diaries confirm the adverse effects of this: 'Queensbridge Road School: Not a good show of Vaughan Williams 4. The fiddles got lost. Not surprising – there wasn't enough time to rehearse.'

On 16 May 1955, Schwarz and the CBSO gave a well-received concert in the Royal Festival Hall, in which Pears was again the soloist in Britten's *Gloriana* Suite and Wilhelm Kempff played Beethoven's First Piano Concerto. Three days later, they left for their first foreign tour,[8] which formed part of a British Week in the Netherlands, set up by Stephen Lloyd following a chance meeting with the British Ambassador during a business trip to Amsterdam. Denis Matthews was the soloist and the entire exercise was described by the *Birmingham Post* as 'a triumph'.

First violinist Harry Van der Lyn (who had escaped from his native Holland in dramatic circumstances during the German invasion) acted as an interpreter when required, and in the course of the tour, which took in such towns as Alkmaar, Utrecht, Hilversum and Arnhem, members of the orchestra were given hospitality in local homes. Oboist Mary Chandler remembers that she and violinist Dorothy Hemming 'stayed one night with two little old ladies, in the attic where they had managed to hide an entire Jewish family for the duration'.[9]

A few months after the tour, the Lord Mayor hosted a Civic Banquet at the Council House for the Burgemeesters of the Dutch cities where the CBSO had played. He also spearheaded a second big Appeal for the City of Birmingham Orchestral Endowment Fund, aimed at increasing its invested capital to the £100,000 mark.[10]

At the instigation of Stephen Lloyd and with the advice and help of Professor Anthony Lewis, the important charitable trust established by the widely travelled collector, philanthropist and benefactor John Feeney[11] initiated what has since become an impressive succession of Feeney Trust Commissions. Lewis and Lloyd had been working on the scheme since early in 1954; having decided to aim high, they must have been gratified by the success of their initial approaches to Sir Arthur Bliss, Michael Tippett, Peter Wishart, Edmund Rubbra, Lennox Berkeley and Alan Rawsthorne, all of whom accepted commissions for major works. Overtures to Vaughan Williams and Britten came to nothing (the one now too old, the other too busy) but it was still an impressive list.

At the 1955 Proms, Colin Ratcliffe, on his first day as Concert Manager, found himself supervising the installation of the large water-tank that always served as a palm-fringed pool in front of the rostrum, and collecting its regular inhabitants, seven fat goldfish, six of which, according to the *Post*, had 'not missed a Prom since 1950'.

1955–6

In the *Post*, John Waterhouse gave the new CBSO Prospectus a warm welcome: 'Beyond a doubt, in the wealth and variety of our fare, we are nowadays far and away the luckiest orchestral public outside London; and no single London orchestra offers programmes to touch ours.' Waterhouse's enthusiasm was well-founded. In a nice gesture to the doyen of British composers, Ralph Vaughan Williams was invited to open the Tuesday Series by conducting the BBC Midland Singers and the CBSO in his *Serenade to Music*, followed immediately by a performance of one of his most powerful scores – the Fourth Symphony, conducted by Schwarz. Matchett's eye-catching title 'Celebrity Concerts' had been dropped from this series, though with Goossens, Malko and Monteux billed as guest conductors, and Rosalyn Tureck, Jennifer Vyvyan and Julius Katchen advertised as soloists, the description would have been amply justified.

The first two Feeney Trust commissions were slotted into this series. Bliss's *Meditations on a Theme by John Blow* had its first performance on 13 December 1955. The première of Michael Tippett's Piano Concerto was announced for 31 January 1956, but after first Clifford Curzon and later Julius Katchen pulled out, it had to be postponed.

Schwarz marked Sibelius's 90th birthday with the Second, Fifth and Seventh Symphonies and several other works; he also conducted the first performances of an orchestral suite from Hugo Wolf 's opera *Der Corregidor* (arranged by Hans Gál), Gál's own Sinfonietta *Meanders* and Gordon Jacob's Trombone Concerto, with the CBSO's principal Denis Wick as soloist. Waterhouse particularly enjoyed André Navarra's account of the Dvořák Cello Concerto ('One listener, at least, will not care if he never hears a greater performance') and the concert conducted by the octogenarian Pierre Monteux in March 1956, which included Beethoven's Second Symphony and *Nuages* and *Fêtes* from Debussy's *Nocturnes.* In Waterhouse's opinion, it afforded 'the finest quality the CBSO has so far been known to provide . . . It was good to know that Mr Schwarz could be there to hear such magnificent results from the ensemble which he has so magnificently developed.'[12] In the *Mail*, too, Alan Fitton was full of praise: 'Age has not wearied him – he is 81 – nor is it likely that the years will condemn . . . It is a long time since Birmingham has had such a concert; both the orchestra and the city were honoured by it.'

Finance remained a matter of concern. One worry was that a condition of the donation of £11,000 which Harry Payne had given the CBSO in 1953 in order to enlarge the playing strength of the orchestra had been that it should be fully allocated within three years. The money had been well spent, but now the Committee was faced with a dilemma: how to maintain the increased strength without the funding to cover it. At the same time, income from BBC broadcasts had been falling off. As a result, Lloyd found himself knocking on the Corporation's door once again in hopes of increased grants. One councillor described the orchestra as 'a white elephant', to which the resident cartoonist Albert Russell responded with a cartoon showing the CBSO White Elephant trudging across the desert, nearly on its knees, a heavy burden on its back, with Rudolf Schwarz as the mahout, perched high on its neck and using some of his favourite rehearsal expressions: 'Courage, my friend! We are nearly there! *Sustain!*'[13]

Membership of the CBSO Society was flourishing, numbering by now some 1300 supporters. During the season, Blyth Major also launched the Midland Youth Orchestra; he conducted it himself, and right up to the present day many of its young and talented members have gone on to become valued players in the CBSO.

In July, Schwarz and the CBSO played to 10,000 people – undoubtedly their largest audience up to that time – at the International Eisteddfod at Llangollen; torrential rain on the roof of the giant marquee nearly drowned the music.

A decade after the war had ended, the reconstruction of the city centre was well under way, not all of it for the better. One example was the demolition of the old Theatre Royal in New Street, where Appleby Matthews had conducted the CBO's first concert in September 1920. It had survived Hitler's bombs, but not Birmingham's planners.

1956–7

In September it was announced that Rudolf Schwarz would be leaving Birmingham at the end of the season in order to succeed Sir Malcolm Sargent as Principal Conductor of the BBC Symphony Orchestra, as Adrian Boult had done, many years before. Press speculation about possible successors included the name of Hugo Rignold.

John Waterhouse was no less enthusiastic about the season's programmes than he had been a year before; but Sir Thomas Beecham had to pull out of the first of his two CBSO concerts at the last moment, due to illness. Schwarz took over the programme, which involved learning Balakirev's First Symphony in a couple of days; he made a considerable success of it. Beecham had expected to be fit enough to conduct his second programme, but had to withdraw from this as well, on the day before the first rehearsal. It fell to Gray, who was left (as Waterhouse observed) 'with far, far the bigger baby to hold': Liszt's huge *Faust* Symphony, never previously performed in the city, in which the orchestra was to be joined by tenor Alexander Young and the men of the City Choir. As Gray later recalled, 'The *Faust* Symphony was just a name to me when I picked up the full score at about four o'clock on the Tuesday afternoon. I took it straight home, went to bed with it and studied it non-stop until about 4 a.m. on the following day, while my wife Jocelyn plied me with cups of strong black coffee!' Beecham had remarked in his letter of apology that 'I am sure that all will go well, despite my absence', and Waterhouse was able to confirm, in his *Post* notice, that 'in view of Mr Gray's colossal task, it most certainly did . . . the effect of the whole is unlikely to be forgotten by those who heard it'.

Artists' fees varied as widely as ever. Beecham's was to have been 220 guineas per concert, Claudio Arrau commanded 250 guineas and Gioconda de Vito 200 guineas. At the lower end of the scale, young Colin Davis netted

20 guineas for a concert which also earned him a rave review for his performance of Sibelius's Seventh Symphony. Another exciting débutant was a 13-year-old Israeli pianist named Daniel Barenboim, and other distinguished visitors included Pierre Fournier, the Soviet artists Vladimir Ashkenazy and Gennadi Rozhdestvensky and Sir Adrian Boult.

The postponed première of the Tippett Piano Concerto took place in Birmingham Town Hall on Tuesday 30 October 1956, with a repeat performance in the Royal Festival Hall. After the disappointment occasioned by Katchen's withdrawal, an approach had been made to Géza Anda, but eventually it was Louis Kentner who was invited to play the work. On 1 February 1956, the composer wrote to the CBSO's General Manager Blyth Major, 'Louis is certainly keen to play the piece', adding, three weeks later, 'really no one could be nicer or more helpful'.[14] The new work had a very mixed reception; Kentner's performance was widely praised, but the orchestral playing came in for some stick[15] and, in general, the critics seem to have been mystified by the work.

My own earliest memory of the CBSO is of attending Schwarz's concert at the Bath Festival on 5 July 1957 – a performance of Beethoven's *Pastoral* Symphony remarkable not only for the gravity and breadth of his interpretation but also for the onset of a real live storm, right on cue. As Ernest Parsons's timpani rolled and the double-basses tore into their scale-passages, we were treated to an equally impressive display of thunder and lightning, with huge hailstones rattling on the tin roof of the Pavilion.

In many ways, the 1950s were the lean years for the CBSO, as they were for many orchestras. Rudolf Schwarz inherited an orchestra which contained a curious mixture of players. On the one hand were the old pros, many of whom had come out of the pre-war cinema and café bands; under Weldon they had built up a big repertoire of popular classics, but many were not amenable to change of any sort. On the other hand were the young players whose musical education had been interrupted by wartime service; they had the enthusiasm, but they lacked both the experience and the technique to play with the warmth of tone that Rudi was asking of them. Schwarz lacked the easygoing consistency that Weldon had provided so ably; Gwen Berry's diaries reveal that he was often moody, even surly at rehearsals – frustrated, doubtless, by the gap between vision and reality. Not all the players appreciated his qualities (the violinist Robert Fleming described him as 'an austere north European scholar')[16] but by and large he earned their deep respect.

Gray got to know Schwarz well, and thought him 'a very talented musician and a very personable, friendly man. I remember his readings of Beethoven and Schubert in particular.'[17] The pianist Phyllis Sellick, too, found him 'a very nice man, and a fine musician. It wasn't always easy to follow his beat, though. I remember that Cyril [Smith] and I played the Lennox Berkeley Two-Piano Concerto with him. At the rehearsal it didn't go too well, but he asked the two of us to stay behind afterwards, to go through some sections again for him. He said, "If I get it right in my head, it will go well tonight." And it did.'[18]

At his best, in some great classical symphony like the *Eroica* or the *Great C major*, Rudi could galvanise the orchestra into a great performance of timeless breadth and beauty, but Stan Smith remembers especially his way with Viennese waltzes: 'Rudi would never ham them up – he just treated them as music; I think I enjoyed playing them with him more than anyone.' Schwarz's technique may have been open to criticism, but not his musicality. Few would have carped at Waterhouse's valedictory remark: 'He is always musician first, conductor second . . . entirely and invariably servant of the music.'

16

Andrzej Panufnik – New thinking

Despite rumours that Hugo Rignold was the prime candidate as Schwarz's successor in Birmingham, he does not seem to have been under serious consideration by the Committee at that stage. In fact there were only two candidates, both of them fugitives from oppressive European regimes, and each had undertaken a trial concert in the first week of December 1956.

George Hurst, of Romanian birth and Russian extraction, chose Beethoven's *Coriolan* Overture and Schubert's *Great C major* Symphony as his visiting card, John Waterhouse adjudging it 'a thoroughly exciting but not notably poetic concert'.

It was Blyth Major who suggested the name of the Polish composer-conductor Andrzej Panufnik; he followed Hurst only five days later with a sensationally successful concert which seems to have bowled everyone over, the *Mail* critic remarking that 'the city hopes it will hear Panufnik again' and Waterhouse summing him up as 'a musician of the first order'. The main work in Panufnik's somewhat unusual programme was Beethoven's Fourth Symphony (still something of a rarity in those days), preceded by a Concerto Grosso by the 18th-century Newcastle organist and composer Charles Avison, Stravinsky's Second Suite and Mozart's early G minor Symphony (No. 25). The decision to appoint the elegant and highly cultivated Pole seems to have been taken more or less on the spot, the announcement being made on 19 January 1957; his interesting, if slightly lightweight, trial programme would prove to be a foretaste of what would follow.

However, even before taking up his new post, Panufnik became embroiled in a monumental row between the CBSO management and its players, all the so-called 'rank-and-file' violinists having been instructed to re-audition for him. Technically this lay within the terms of their contracts, but its timing was all wrong and, as Stan Smith put it later, 'the violins were not (to put it mildly) persuaded of the management's integrity of purpose in this matter'.[1]

Since Blyth Major admitted to the musicians that neither Schwarz nor Panufnik had requested these auditions, they unanimously decided to boycott them, and the other players supported them. As one anonymous *Post* correspondent put it, 're-auditioning is usually a pretext for dismissals'.

This proved an accurate prediction. In April, 16 violinists were placed under notice and, not surprisingly, the resulting furore attracted a great deal of unwelcome publicity. By May, things looked set for a strike, but at the eleventh hour, after all the cliff-hanging, came the breakthrough: 'CBSO to play on – 4 violinists warned'. Nemesis was averted, but it had been a damaging and deeply regrettable incident which was bound to get Panufnik's tenure off to a shaky start and should never have been allowed to occur. It is axiomatic amongst orchestral managers that musicians should take musical decisions and that administrators should take administrative decisions; the rule of thumb was broken in this case, with unfortunate results.

Andrzej Panufnik was born in Warsaw on 24 September 1914, just as the First World War was beginning. His father, Tomasz, was Poland's leading authority on the construction of stringed instruments, which he both made and collected, and his mother, Mathilde Thonnes, was a violinist and composer of British origin. Andrzej was precocious (he wrote his first work at the age of nine) and during the 1930s he studied composition with Sikorski in Warsaw and conducting (mainly with Weingartner) in Vienna, Paris and London. All his works written before 1944 were destroyed in the Warsaw Uprising of that year, though he reconstructed some of them later. After the Second World War he directed the Kraków and Warsaw Philharmonic Orchestras, before deciding to concentrate principally on composition, winning a string of major awards and becoming joint Vice-Chairman (with Arthur Honegger) of the UNESCO International Music Council in Paris.

Panufnik loved his native Poland with an all-consuming passion, but he hated with equal fervour what he always called 'the Stalinist regime', and whilst in Zürich in July 1954, making a recording of his *Sinfonia Rustica* (which had won him the Chopin Prize five years earlier), he and his British-born first wife Scarlett made their escape in dramatic circumstances. In his autobiography *Composing Myself*,[2] Panufnik makes it clear that he took the CBSO position, which would involve his living in the city, mainly to provide himself with a steady income, which would enable him to qualify for British nationality.

*

1957–8

Looking back on his days in Birmingham, in a 1980 interview with Lyndon Jenkins, Panufnik recalled that 'I found the orchestra of a high standard, with a good knowledge of the classical repertoire'. He conducted his first rehearsal as CBSO Conductor on Thursday, 5 September 1957. Gwen Berry observed that 'We don't know quite what to think. His method of going straight through a work, then again with very little to say about it and again to finish it off takes a long time.' As their new conductor became more exacting in his methods, Gwen's diary reflected the players' concern: 'He took trouble with that wretched bit in Weber's *Euryanthe*; but I don't like this business of hearing each desk by itself.' And, a few days later: 'Panufnik made himself a pest in *Euryanthe*, taking cellos alone in that one bit and also, quite unnecessarily, in the *Unfinished*. Felt I was back in Hockie's[3] classes – "Now den, each one alone, I will ferret out de culprit." '

Panufnik had become interested in works by early English composers (Byrd, Avison, Boyce, Stanley) in Poland, before the war, and he introduced a selection of such arrangements at the beginning of the first six Tuesday programmes of the 1957–8 season, adding works later on by Purcell, Arne, Capel Bond, Monteverdi, Barsanti, Tartini, Vivaldi and Scarlatti. One thing that had not occurred to him, however, was that the National Anthem was still played at the beginning of concerts as a matter of course, after which half the orchestra would troop out. This was bound to look faintly absurd,[4] but Panufnik hit on an ingenious solution to the problem: 'I asked Professor Anthony Lewis to write me a special arrangement; he did this in a very beautiful version in the early English style. After the performance I was violently attacked in the Press – "How dare these foreign conductors distort the British National Anthem?" Of course, we were all very much amused, and someone replied in my defence that the arranger was a British composer!'[5]

The inclusion of such works was certainly an interesting idea, in an age when the baroque chamber-orchestra repertoire was still largely unfamiliar, but, as Gray put it many years later, 'People found his programmes a little puzzling; he would regularly start a symphony concert with only thirteen or fourteen people on the platform'.[6] Nevertheless, Panufnik's first season got away to a good start, Alan Fitton of the *Mail* reporting that 'at its close he was accorded an ovation such as has rarely been heard on these occasions. Players as well as audience joined in the applause.' Panufnik's programming was adventurous, including UK premières of *concertante* works by Bloch, Malipiero and Ferenc Farkas. One of his Sunday programmes,[7] built around a 'Dance' theme, is worth quoting in full:

Schubert	German Dances (October 1824)
Bartók	Hungarian Peasant Songs
Mozart	Violin Concerto in E♭ (K.268)
Skalkottas	Five Greek Dances
Debussy–Ravel	Sarabande
Malcolm Arnold	Four Scottish Dances

The season featured a number of eminent pianists. Claudio Arrau (in Chopin), Géza Anda (Mozart and Ravel), Ingrid Haebler (Beethoven) and Rosalyn Tureck (Bach's D minor Concerto, taking, as was her wont, over 28 minutes for a work which generally lasts 23). In March 1958, Gray was again the conductor at a Children's Concert in Leeds Town Hall, when Gwen Berry recorded that 'A wonderful little chap of 11, Michael Roll, played a Mozart Piano Concerto with us today. He'd got it all – technique, musicianship, rhythm, even platform manner.'

Panufnik's contract as Principal Conductor committed him to fewer concerts than Schwarz, and once his appointment was confirmed a decision was taken to employ a second Associate Conductor, to work alongside the long-serving Harold Gray. George Hurst was still being considered and Colin Davis was another candidate, though he withdrew when offered a post with the BBC Scottish Orchestra. Alexander Gibson (then at Sadler's Wells) and Meredith Davies (who had recently left Hereford Cathedral for New College, Oxford) were each given trial concerts in February 1957; both were well reviewed, but it was Davies (then aged 34, and just taking over the City of Birmingham Choir from David Willcocks) who gained the palm. He made his first appearance at a Sunday Concert on 22 September, Gwen Berry noting in her diary, 'I do hope he gets good notices. He is such a good sort and gets results without any fuss.'

Unfortunately none of these developments succeeded in eliciting any great ongoing public interest. The Saturday Series had already been dropped and repeatedly at this time (both in and out of town) Gwen's diary records, 'Very poor house'. At an October Lunch-hour Concert in Birmingham Town Hall, for example, she counted a mere 150 paying customers, 'which means about £7.10.0'. Not surprisingly, this series(which had run intermittently since the 1920s) was dropped in the following season. On top of these purely local concerns, the permanent regional orchestras were facing a demand from the Musicians' Union for a massive £3 all-round wage increase, the MU making the point that orchestral musicians earned less than bricklayers.

Choral engagements formed an important part of the CBSO's income at this time. At the Dee and Clwyd Festival in Corwen, Montgomeryshire, the first two parts of Haydn's *Creation* (sung in Welsh) were followed by Schubert's *Unfinished* Symphony, but its performance was nearly more 'Unfinished' than usual, when all the lights in the hall went out; the orchestra simply kept on playing, to the end of the movement.

Solid, dependable, old-style professionalism of this sort represented, alas, only the obverse side of a coin whose reverse side was old-fashioned playing and a highly conservative attitude. The London orchestras (a good sprinkling of *immigrés* amongst their number) were for the most part 'going great guns', setting new standards of excellence under major European conductors such as Furtwängler, Klemperer, Krips and Karajan. Money apart, one factor which held back comparable progress in most of Britain's regional orchestras during the 1950s was the difficulty experienced by the older players, most of whom had learned their craft under vastly different conditions during the 1930s, in coming to terms with different standards and a new repertoire.

In January 1958, the Norris Stanley affair epitomised the problem. Exactly a year before, whilst Schwarz had still been in post, a special meeting of the Music Advisory Sub-Committee (with Max Rostal in attendance as an expert witness) had agonised over the 61–year-old Stanley's future, trying to weigh his long years of faithful service against the undoubted fact that his playing now seemed very old-fashioned, and that he would fight any kind of innovation within the orchestra tooth and nail. At the time, it had been gently suggested to him that he should take early retirement, but he would have none of it.

Stanley, who had played at a back desk in the CBO when Elgar had conducted the first Symphony Concert in 1920, and had led the orchestra since the latter years of Heward's time, was too old a dog to learn new tricks. Inevitably, Panufnik and he were soon on a collision course, the one wanting to improve the standard of string playing, the other wanting things to remain as they were. According to Panufnik, 'Mr Stanley . . . set about turning the rest of the orchestra against me . . . The atmosphere during rehearsals became unbearable . . . I discovered that the Leader had some extra-musical prejudices against me. He was both anti-Semitic and anti-Communist, and had the mistaken impression that I was a Jew and a committed Marxist, if not actually a Soviet spy!'[8]

Stanley's version would undoubtedly make very different reading; after all, he had worked perfectly amicably with the Jewish Rudolf Schwarz, and no doubt Panufnik's rather 'grand' manner will have had something to do with it, too. In January 1958, Panufnik submitted a list of his grievances against Norris Stanley. He acknowledged his punctuality, reliability, professionalism and experience, but he ruthlessly criticised what he called 'his metallic, "café-style" tone', his poor technique, intonation and musicianship, incorrect sense of style, lack of imagination in solving technical problems and unwillingness to collaborate with the other principals'. In his defence Stanley produced letters of appreciation from Boult and other notables, but eventually he accepted the inevitable (plus a 'golden handshake') and on St Valentine's Day 1958, wrote a letter of resignation to W. G. A. Russell. In the light of all the criticism to which Stanley had been subjected, the CBSO's press statement makes rather hollow reading: 'Mr Stanley's resignation comes because he wants to do some solo work. One or two of the orchestra's other brilliant players may want to move soon. They can command higher salaries elsewhere.'[9]

It was a sad end to a long and distinguished career, and can have done little to improve the atmosphere within the orchestra. The management, having climbed down over its demand that all the violinists be re-auditioned, had then arranged auditions for four players whose work was thought to fall short of the required standard, but was easily outmanœuvred by the Union, which invoked an Interpretations Committee. The wretched business dragged on for months, with nothing to show for it save a deal of aggravation. Not surprisingly, many of the 'old brigade' decided to leave, including Mary Chandler, the CBSO's long-serving and immensely musical principal oboist and principal bassoonist Vaughan Allin. These changes only added to the generally unsettled feeling within the orchestra.

1958–9

The higher prices charged on Tuesdays still discouraged ticket sales, and as a result the series was reduced to just three concerts. Arrau, Menuhin and Casadesus were the stars. Panufnik had wanted to engage the great Hungarian violinist Joseph Szigeti, but his name was not familiar in Birmingham and Blyth Major later told him that 'a businessman on the Committee, comparing Szigeti's modest request to the other soloists' fees, had decided that Szigeti could not be any good, and had insisted that they turn him down'.[10]

The Committee had put pressure upon Panufnik to include some of his own music, and each of these opening concerts included one of his early works.

Feeney Trust commissions of the season were the Second Symphonies of Lennox Berkeley and Alan Rawsthorne, while Meredith Davies was entrusted with novelties by Milhaud, Frank Martin, Peter Wishart and Anthony Lewis. A towering performance of Carl Nielsen's Fifth Symphony earned Gray five curtain-calls and a rave notice from John Waterhouse in the *Post*, and he also produced what Gwen Berry considered 'a magnificent show' with Vaughan Williams's *Tallis Fantasia* and Fifth Symphony, shortly after the death of the old composer had been announced, but Panufnik's own programmes showed every sign of a pulling in of horns by the Committee. Gone was the 'baroquery' and experimentation of his first year, to be replaced by a series of 'Bach, Beethoven, Brahms Nights', inserted into the Thursday Series. These were rather predictable, but they did provide Birmingham with its first complete cycle of the Brandenburg Concertos.

The CBSO's gifted young principal trumpeter Bram Gay gave what seems to have been the first modern performance anywhere of Hummel's engaging Trumpet Concerto, warmly applauded by Waterhouse. The new Leader, the Australian Wilfred Lehmann, who had recently won the prestigious Carl Flesch Prize, proved far more co-operative at rehearsals than his predecessor, and Panufnik and his players found their second season together more congenial than the first, during which (as he wrote later) 'there was not much to laugh about'.

Nevertheless, he decided not to take up the option to renew his contract at the end of the 1958–9 season. There can be little doubt that the requirement to conduct more conservative programmes in the interest of the box office influenced his decision. It is equally true that he had been finding his responsibilities as Principal Conductor arduous, and that he now wanted to concentrate once again on composition. Commissions were starting to come in nicely, but he could not settle down to them. As he explained to Arthur Steele of the *Evening Mail*, 'I have learned one thing. It is impossible to conduct a permanent orchestra and compose at the same time.'[11]

If Gwen Berry is to be believed, Panufnik was put under some pressure to leave: 'we hear that Panuf. has got the sack. Poor man, he hasn't had much luck in this country.' His relationship with the players had not always been ideal, but it takes two to make a disagreement and the CBSO of the late 1950s was a tough assignment for any conductor to take on. And it would certainly be a mistake to think that his two seasons in Birmingham were a total failure. Attendances were no worse than in Weldon's or Schwarz's time, and the reaction both of the audience and of the Press was in general cordial. Oboist Tony Miller 'never felt that Panufnik was really happy conducting; he was a very sensitive person, and his readings of classical music tended to be heavily over-romanticised, with very slow *tempi* and a big *rallentando* at the end of every section'.[12] Nevertheless, at his best he achieved a high standard of playing from an orchestra whose technical skills were still uneven, whilst broadening the scope of the CBSO's repertoire. He bowed out with an all-Mozart concert which characteristically included a totally unfamiliar early Symphony (K.84 in D) and a 'most sensitive and imaginative performance' of the *Sinfonia Concertante*, in which the soloists were Perry Hart and Margaret Major, daughter of the CBSO's hard-working General Manager Blyth Major.

Major himself decided to leave Birmingham at the end of July 1959, to be replaced by Ernest E. Edwards, a former Granada cinema manager who had been for seven years on the staff of the Hallé Orchestra and had recently organised its 3000–mile European tour. Clive Smart, its General Manager at that time, remembers 'Eddie' Edwards as 'a great character and a super personality. He was a first-class Concerts Manager and I was really sorry to lose him, though I was glad that he had achieved a General Managership – he deserved it.'[13]

1959–60

Lloyd and Russell found themselves in a quandary. They had been boosting Meredith Davies's position with the idea that he would ultimately take over the principal rôle, and when Panufnik resigned unexpectedly they did in fact offer it to him. But Davies was still unsure that he was ready to assume a position of such responsibility, and although the majority of the players expressed confidence in him, he asked the Committee to appoint 'an eminent conductor' for the 1959–60 season, with the idea that he should take over thereafter. Meanwhile, he was promoted to Deputy Musical Director, over the head of long-serving Associate Conductor Harold Gray.

A few months earlier, the death had been announced of Dr Eric Blom, CBE, who had done much to encourage the City Orchestra during Heward's tenure, but another figure from the orchestra's past was about to put in a significant reappearance. In his autobiography, Panufnik ended the chapter about his two Birmingham seasons with a nice paradox: 'The Management Committee of the CBSO had some difficulty in finding my successor. The press finally announced that the post of Conductor had been taken over for one year by Sir Adrian Boult, aged seventy, from Mr Andrzej Panufnik, aged forty-five, who had retired!'[14]

Sir Adrian, as Michael Kennedy puts it, 'combined nostalgia and a generous rescue act' by stepping into the breach. He had given up the musical directorship of the LPO two years earlier, but was still in great demand as a guest conductor, so the CBSO post was necessarily something of a token appointment; indeed, in a letter to Waterhouse dated 22 December 1958, Sir Adrian described himself with charming self-deprecation as 'only a carpet-bagger . . . an elderly umbrella to keep, if possible, some of the rain and snow off Meredith Davies, and I gather it is likely that there will be a good deal'. His existing commitments only allowed him to undertake ten concerts in the Birmingham winter season, plus a number of out-of-town engagements.

One of the highlights of Boult's Birmingham programmes was a performance of Mahler's Fourth Symphony, with Joan Sutherland ('in magnificent form', according to Fitton). He also programmed music by Vaughan Williams (who had died the previous year), Walton, Holst, Elgar and the première of Robert Simpson's Violin Concerto, played by its dedicatee Ernest Element.[15] Observing that this was the only public performance that this work has received, Robert Matthew-Walker, a leading authority on Simpson's music, feels that the composer should reconsider his decision to withdraw it. He also mentions, 'The conductor was Sir Adrian Boult, who in the second half of the concert conducted the greatest performance of Brahms's Fourth Symphony I have ever heard.'[16] Despite the relatively small number of his Birmingham appearances, Michael Kennedy could justifiably call it 'a festival of Boult'.

Though he made no public comment at the time, John Waterhouse correctly drew the inference that the Committee was grooming Meredith Davies to take over the CBSO. He admired Davies's work, but felt that he still needed more experience, preferring either Charles Groves or Hugo Rignold, 'two proven and altogether admirable English conductors of the "middle generation" '.[17] Davies shared a concert with Benjamin Britten, who conducted the *Nocturne* (with Peter Pears), Davies taking over the *Spring* Symphony as the result of the composer's arthritis. Britten was sufficiently impressed to offer Davies work with the English Opera Group, and ultimately, of course, to invite him to conduct the first performance of the *War Requiem*, in which the CBSO was to be so closely involved, some three years later.

It was entirely characteristic of Boult that he should have elected to share the conducting of a promotion at the Royal Festival Hall in October 1959 with Davies and Gray (conducting a London concert for the only time, in a CBSO career that spanned nearly fifty years); Albert Russell produced a cartoon entitled 'All along, Down along' which depicted the three of them dressed as jockeys, all riding the same old CBSO 'Grey Mare'. However, a combination of three conductors, two soloists (April Cantelo and Gioconda de Vito) and some 'awkward and uncoordinated' orchestral playing resulted in poor notices.[18]

Winter 'pea-souper' fogs were a major problem in those days before Birmingham was declared a Smokeless Zone, and they could result in tragedy, as Gwen Berry recorded: 'Thursday, 7 January 1960: Morning rehearsal with Sir Adrian, then back home till 6, when I suddenly saw fog! Got to New Inns [Handsworth] with difficulty, and then walked to Town Hall. Arrived about 7.45. Some were playing but many were standing around aghast and silent. Apparently our dear old Rusty [Albert Russell, violinist and cartoonist] had *raced* to get to the T. H. in time. Got on the platform, tuned up, collapsed and died. They put him in our dressing room and I had to go in and get my evening dress. Poor Albert so still.'[19]

Fog was not the only hazard that winter; a fortnight later, Gwen recorded 'the wettest day for 72 years!' Despite widespread flooding, the CBSO got to

Kidderminster but found the Town Hall entirely surrounded by water; the concert was abandoned.

Though it was nearly ten years since he had left the CBSO, George Weldon continued to draw full houses as a guest conductor at CBSO Proms. However, he was unable to drive his 140 mph Jaguar up the newly opened M1[20] to fulfil his first engagement in the 1960 series, having suffered the indignity of being knocked down in the street by a bicycle! Harold Gray took over Weldon's Viennese Night,[21] but Weldon had recovered sufficiently from his bruising to conduct later in this series, which attracted a record 24,500 concert-goers – something in excess of 90% capacity.

The CBSO was now receiving regular invitations to many of the major Festivals. At Cheltenham, Meredith Davies and the orchestra accompanied Ilona Kabos in the première of R. W. Wood's Piano Concerto; a month later, the orchestra made its first appearance at the Edinburgh Festival, playing under John Lanchbery for the Royal Ballet's season there; and in September they were in Worcester for the Three Choirs' Festival, where Zoltán Kodály attended a performance of his *Budavari Te Deum*; Eddie Edwards took the opportunity to invite the octogenarian composer to Birmingham, and it was agreed that the CBSO should give the first British performance of his new Symphony in the 1961–2 season.

But before all this, Sir Adrian had conducted the last Town Hall concert of his 'official' year as Principal Conductor, ending with a Brahms Third of which Waterhouse wrote that 'I have certainly never heard so warmly and fluently lyrical a performance of the work in Birmingham before . . . throughout the symphony the CBSO sounded as good as any orchestra in the country'.[22] He was invited to become the CBSO Society's Vice-President and to address a special meeting in the Art Gallery on 2 June 1960, at which he made an eloquent plea for better accommodation for the orchestra – a properly designed concert hall (such as had been promised to him some 35 years earlier) and better rehearsal facilities – in particular, the opportunity to use the Town Hall, free of charge, on days when it was not otherwise booked. Once again, his pleas fell on deaf ears.

But yet more changes were in the offing. In March 1960, Wilfred Lehmann (whose solo career had predictably taken off since winning the Carl Flesch Prize) left Birmingham[23] and Meyer Stolow replaced him as Leader. Just before this, Davies had announced that he too wished to resign as Deputy Musical Director. If the Committee had still been hoping that he would succeed Sir Adrian, his withdrawal drove them to look further afield for their next chief conductor. John Waterhouse's crystal-gazing of a few months before was soon to prove prophetic.

17

Hugo Rignold – Complete professional

Hugo Rignold, whose appointment to succeed Boult was announced in May 1960,[1] had already made a number of well-received guest appearances with the CBSO, the first as long ago as February 1955. He had appeared several more times in Birmingham during the 1950s, both with the CBSO and with his own Liverpool Philharmonic, always receiving good reviews, and Gwen Berry had noted, on two separate occasions and with evident satisfaction, a rumour that he might become Schwarz's successor. Waterhouse, too, confessed, after Panufnik's appointment had been announced, that Rignold's 'was one of the very first names towards which the secret thoughts of these columns wandered enquiringly. For Mr Rignold is quite certainly one of the very best English conductors under the age of (shall we say?) 55.'[2]

Born in Kingston-upon-Thames on 15 May 1905, Rignold spent his childhood in Canada, where he studied the violin with his father, a viola player and conductor. His mother was an operatic contralto. He gained some orchestral experience, then won the Scholarship of Canada to the Royal Academy of Music in London, where he had a brilliant career as an instrumentalist, taking violin lessons with Hans Wessely, viola with Lionel Tertis, oboe with Leon Goossens and trumpet with John Solomon;[3] he carried off most of the major prizes and then started looking for work.

Life was tough in the 1930s for a freelance violinist in London, but with his outstanding flair and rhythmic drive, he soon found a lucrative niche in the flourishing light-music world, and before long was the lead jazz violinist in the crack Jack Hylton Orchestra, with whom he undertook a number of recordings and European tours. At one time he also had his own ensemble, but he always hankered after the world of classical music and when the war supervened he put both his musical and entrepreneurial gifts to good effect to found the Cairo Symphony Orchestra, whilst serving with the RAF in the Middle East. Initially he played as Leader, but soon decided that he could do as well as the guest conductors they were working with. 'He had always wanted to conduct, since the age of five, but violin playing seemed a more realistic way of earning a living.'[4]

In Cairo, Rignold was spotted by the influential Richard Capell of the *Daily Telegraph*, whose favourable notices earned him a string of guest appearances in 1944 with the Palestine Symphony Orchestra.[5] After demobilisation in 1945, he became principal viola of the newly formed Royal Opera House Orchestra, under Karl Rankl, touring with them to Vienna, Warsaw, Stockholm and Belgium as well as throughout the UK. He was named Principal Guest Conductor of the Liverpool Philharmonic in 1947, succeeding Sir Malcolm Sargent in the senior rôle a year later. His six seasons in Liverpool established him as one of Britain's leading conductors, and during his subsequent appointment as musical director of the Royal Ballet (during the great Margot Fonteyn years) he worked with every major orchestra in the UK, undertaking important tours with the LPO and LSO and guest-conducting throughout Europe, the USA and South Africa. Rignold made some fine recordings with the Royal Opera House Orchestra, including the hitherto-unrecorded suites from Prokofiev's ballet *Cinderella* and a celebrated version of Ravel's *Shéhérazade*, with Maggie Teyte. A pleasant surprise was to discover his daughter Jennifer Gay in the *corps de ballet*; they were delighted to renew their relationship, interrupted following her parents' divorce.

The principal reason why Hugo Rignold was in such demand was not so much his charisma but his total professionalism, reliability and innate musicality. He had showed in Liverpool that he was a top-class orchestra trainer, and that was exactly what was needed now in Birmingham. Weldon had fulfilled a similar rôle in the 1940s, but Rignold ('Riggy', or sometimes 'Uncle Hugo', to the players) brought something extra with him – the technical expertise of an experienced string player, and when one remembers that the five string sections account for two-thirds of an orchestra, that is no mean asset.

Together with his daughter Jennifer – housekeeper, secretary and unpaid publicity agent – Rignold moved in due course into an attractive old house with a large garden in Norfolk Road, Edgbaston.[6] He had a reputation as a disciplinarian, but he undoubtedly had the orchestra on his side from the start. In 1960, relations between the CBSO management and its players were at a fairly low ebb and all Rignold's entrepreneurial skill would be needed to build up confidence. Undoubtedly there was fault on both sides, but the 'violin re-audition' débâcle of 1957, two less-than-satisfactory seasons with Panufnik, the ousting of Norris Stanley and a 'caretaker' year under Boult had left the players feeling distinctly unsettled. Waterhouse's view was that Hugo Rignold was the right man for the job, that Gray was an ideal No. 2 and that two conductors would be better than three. A Gwen Berry diary entry[7] leaves no doubt that the players were pleased with the new appointment: 'Friends' Institute: BBC Recording of Berlioz *Symphonie Fantastique*. Rignold in a happy humour. What a nice soul he is. If only we'd had him instead of Panufnik, how different things might have been.'

1960–1

The task of writing a Foreword for the Annual Prospectus (which cost 2/-) fell to Anthony Lewis, who drew a discreet veil over the demise of the Tuesday Series and picked out a few highlights from the surviving Thursday and Sunday Series. Stravinsky's ballet *Agon* won from John Waterhouse an outstanding review: 'the performance of it was hugely, dazzlingly creditable to all concerned.' Another novelty was Walton's long-awaited Second Symphony. Gray continued his exploration of Nielsen's Symphonies with the *Inextinguishable*.

The decision to abandon the higher-priced Tuesday Series served to enhance the tone of the Thursday Concerts (ten Series A before Christmas and ten Series B in the New Year). Jascha Horenstein made the first of many guest appearances, with Mahler's First Symphony; Rudolf Kempe conducted *Don Juan* and Brahms's Second Symphony and Nicolai Malko returned with the Prokofiev and Shostakovich. Other distinguished visitors included Hess, Katchen, Arrau, Szeryng, Campoli (deputising for Menuhin), Curzon and Leonard Pennario (replacing an indisposed Eileen Joyce). Ticket prices were still extremely modest, ranging from 2/6 behind the orchestra to 9/6 in the front of the Lower Gallery.

In June, Rignold and the CBSO played to an enthusiastic audience of over 5000, standing shoulder to shoulder in Tom Quad, Christ Church, Oxford, in aid of Oxfam; Alan Whitehead, who had replaced Bram Gay as the CBSO's principal trumpet (and is still in the orchestra) played the Haydn Concerto and Rignold's programme ended with Tchaikovsky's *1812*, featuring a real cannon (whose barrel had been cast in that very year) and the bells of Christ Church Cathedral. The *Music You Love* Series continued to draw good houses, as did the three-week series of Summer Proms. Harold Gray was kept busy with his many Choral Societies and with the CBSO's ongoing work for Birmingham Education Committee, which still involved 50 days of work each year. This Education work was lucrative for the orchestra, and it was argued that it was 'building up the audience of the future' but, bearing in mind the highly predictable and repetitive nature of the repertoire, it was soul-destroying for players and conductors alike.

In March 1961 Sir Thomas Beecham died, at the age of 81; British music-making was immeasurably the poorer for his passing. In July, Gwen Berry, whose colourful diary entries have so enlivened these pages, married her old friend and fellow cellist Harry Stanier; a week later, she retired, after some 35 years of loyal service to Birmingham's City Orchestra.

1961–2

Two highlights of Rignold's programmes were Birmingham's first complete hearings of Debussy's orchestral *Images* and of Ravel's *Daphnis et Chloë*. Like Heward and Schwarz before him, Rignold was deeply committed to Sibelius's music, and had a special feeling for the little-played Sixth Symphony, which he programmed in October. He also included Schoenberg's *Verklärte Nacht* and the Walton Violin Concerto, with Alfredo Campoli.

Twenty years on from her début recording sessions in Birmingham with Leslie Heward and the CBO, the great Australian soprano Joan Hammond sang Ravel's *Shéhérazade* and the Liebestod from *Tristan und Isolde* at a Thursday Concert, conducted by her old friend Harold Gray, with whom she had sung *Madam Butterfly* scores of times in Carl Rosa Opera days. At the end of November 1961, John Gardner's Feeney-commissioned *Herrick Cantata* received what *The Times* described as 'a sensitive and telling' first performance from Meredith Davies, Alexander Young, the City Choir and the CBSO, coupling it with Kodály's attractive *Peacock Variations*; a few days later, Rignold conducted the first British performance of the same composer's Symphony.[8]

Standards were improving, but the players were under considerable pressure and sometimes things went wrong. Violinist Stan Smith remembers an altercation between Rignold and the Leader, Meyer Stolow. 'If there was a tricky piece coming up, Hugo would have the orchestral parts taken around with us, and would "nibble" at it at the end of out-of-town rehearsals. On this occasion we were going to play *Verklärte Nacht*, and out came the parts at the end of a rehearsal in Lichfield Cathedral. We'd looked at it once or twice before, but Meyer had been off sick, and he'd never seen the music before. There's a tricky violin solo in the middle, in a horrid key, and Meyer made rather a mess of it; after one or two goes it still wasn't right, and Hugo had a go at him. "Am I the only person who makes mistakes, then?" said Meyer. Hugo was furious! "But you're the Leader," he said, "*You're* the *Leader*!" After the rehearsal they had a terrible row. Next morning, Meyer didn't turn up at rehearsal – apparently Eddie Edwards had them both in his office and told them they had to work together, and that was that. Now, that's what I call a Manager!'

John Lowe of BBC Birmingham, who served on both CBSO Committees, was Artistic Director of the Coventry Cathedral Festival which marked the opening of Basil Spence's impressive new building, in the course of which (as at the Edinburgh Festival) the CBSO accompanied the Royal Ballet under John Lanchbery in the Coventry Theatre. But the orchestra's main involvement was to play for the first performances of Benjamin Britten's *War Requiem*, given in the new Cathedral on 30 May and 1 June 1962. Davies conducted the Festival Choir and the CBSO, with Heather Harper radiantly replacing Britten's intended Russian soprano soloist Galina Vishnevskaya, who had been prevented from travelling by one of the regular 'blips' in East–West relations at that time.[9] The composer conducted the Melos Ensemble, which accompanied the other two soloists, Peter Pears and Dietrich Fischer-Dieskau.

The première, broadcast live, was a great occasion, but at one time it had begun to look as if it might have to be abandoned. The BBC's announcer that evening, Barry Lankester, who also sang in the *ad hoc* Festival Choir, remembers that 'Meredith Davies was not happy with the standard of singing and complained to the authorities.[10] Eventually 16 members of the professional Ambrosian Singers were brought from London to sing as the semichorus and to be "very helpful with the choral entries in this very difficult work".'[11]

To listen to the BBC recording of that first performance is still a moving experience. After a long introduction, there are two minutes of almost total silence[12] before that baleful gong-stroke signifies the beginning of the work, and although one has heard more accurate performances since, the atmosphere throughout is overwhelming. Pears told Paul Jennings that 'At the rehearsals for the first performance Dietrich Fischer-Dieskau was moved to tears'[13] and Heather Harper found that, at the end, 'all around her, people were in tears'. Meredith remembers, 'at the end there was again complete silence; I looked at Ben, who seemed to be in total shock, and eventually we somehow managed to put one foot in front of another and walk off.'

Predictably a major new work of this sort attracted the musical press from near and far (a French paper praised 'le grand orchestre de Birmingham, avec une formidable batterie'). *The Times* reported that 'tonight's performance was was one that will never be forgotten'.[14] Writing in the *Daily Telegraph*, Donald Mitchell was in no doubt that he had witnessed the launch of 'a masterpiece of the first order', even though 'the dubious acoustics of the Cathedral rather clouded what one assumed to be a faithful performance by the chorus and orchestra'.[15] When Davies congratulated Britten on his new work at the end of the première, the reply he received was, 'The idea was good.'[16]

The summer of 1962 saw another protracted wage dispute between the regional symphony orchestras and their players; when it looked like becoming entrenched, at the end of June, the musicians unanimously handed in their notice. On 2 July, Eddie Edwards gave a diplomatically worded statement to the press, and it appeared that the matter might be settled amicably and industrial action avoided. Six days later, everyone was deeply shocked to hear that he had died from a cerebral hæmorrhage, after collapsing on the platform at New Street Station whilst awaiting his train home. He was only 49. In his annual 'Last Night of the Proms' speech, on 28 July, Harold Gray made a special mention of Edwards's contribution to the orchestra, which was quite out of proportion to the relative brevity of his tenure of office. Once again, Gray came to the orchestra's rescue by acting as General Manager until a replacement could be appointed.

1962–3

In what was to be his last Annual Prospectus Foreword in the rôle of Executive Chairman, Bill Russell was able to announce that the City's interest-free loan of £20,000, which had provided a lifeline in the crisis ten years before, 'has now been fully repaid, leaving the orchestra solvent and free of debt'. That this had been achieved (at a steady £2000 p.a.) reflected great credit on Lloyd, Russell, Maddison and the CBSO's professional management team over the previous decade, and did much to enhance the orchestra's standing in the eyes of the City Fathers.

The CBSO's new General Manager, Arthur Baker, came to Birmingham from Bournemouth, where he had been Concert Manager since 1955 and had also organised and conducted a youth orchestra. A Lancastrian, Baker had started his career in orchestral management in 1952 as Concert Assistant to the Liverpool Philharmonic, and in Bournemouth he established a good rapport with his boss, Kenneth Matchett, whose previous managerial experience had included both the Liverpool PO and the CBSO. Matchett was a hard taskmaster, and Baker arrived in Birmingham thoroughly trained in his job. He had no time to sit back and settle in; on his desk he found instructions from Russell to sack two orchestral principals, who would be calling in to see him later that day![17] Further, the wage dispute of June had dragged on, a strike was now threatened[18] and details of the orchestra's second overseas tour (planned for March 1963) had been left incomplete by Edwards at his death.

The first performance of Humphrey Searle's Fourth Symphony in November was something of a *succès de scandale*. Commissioned by the Feeney Trust, conducted by the composer and written in the strict Schoenbergian twelve-tone style fashionable at the time, it received a cautious but not unfriendly reception from the musical Press, though Ernest Bradbury of the *Yorkshire Post* did admit that Searle's music, with its clanging cimbalom and aleatoric *cadenza*, was 'hard on the listener'. That was certainly the view taken by at least some of the Birmingham Town Hall audience, who clearly felt that they had been 'taken for a ride', John Waterhouse reporting 'ripples of discreetly restrained laughter which were almost continuous amongst the audience'.

Meredith Davies revived Britten's *War Requiem* with the City Choir and the CBSO; Waterhouse (who had declined to comment on the Coventry première on account of the cathedral's woolly acoustics) was by now convinced that we had a masterpiece on our hands. Attendance, by and large, remained patchy, but Menuhin and the Torteliers (*père et fils*) drew full houses.

Within the orchestra, Rignold was quietly making his presence felt, especially at auditions, where the rapidly rising standards of orchestral playing in London were slowly being reflected in the specialist music colleges nationwide. In February 1963, John Georgiadis replaced Meyer Stolow to become the youngest Orchestral Leader in the country and at much the same time David Measham was appointed his deputy. Both were short on experience, but Rignold was an astute judge of fiddle playing and he saw in them the kind of brilliance, drive and flair that would be needed to galvanise the CBSO's string playing into something new, vibrant and exciting.

In March 1963, Rignold and the orchestra gave the first performance of Robert Simpson's Third Symphony – another Feeney Trust commission – before flying off on a European Tour, with the young Japanese violinist Hisako Tsuji[19] and the septuagenarian pianist Elly Ney. Organised through the respected Dutch concert agent Johanna Beek (who in turn employed a German sub-agency), it comprised thirteen concerts in German and Swiss cities, including Stuttgart, Munich, the new Beethovenhalle in Bonn, Nürnberg and Basel (where one critic, reviewing the Seventh Symphony, observed that 'Beethoven himself would have been astonished at the playing, so competent and so sure').[20]

Unfortunately the German sub-agents proved to be quite unscrupulous. Rignold and the CBSO were more amused than upset to find themselves billed everywhere as the 'Birmingham Philharmonie, Dirigent: Sir Hugo Rignold', but later matters deteriorated. They arrived in Munich to find the hall double-booked and had to give the concert without rehearsal. On the journey from Offenbach, a freak snowstorm at Ulm and a consequent massive traffic jam on the Autobahn meant that the orchestra's coaches arrived in Friedrichshafen more than two hours after the concert should have started, to find most of their audience still patiently awaiting them. Although they had been travelling for over twelve hours, they piled on to the platform[21] and played a shortened version of the advertised concert before Hugo Rignold decided to call it a day. The German agent later made an issue of this and at the end of the tour suddenly announced that his van, containing all the CBSO instruments, was 'somewhere in Germany' and that if the orchestra wanted them back, it would have to agree to a deduction of DM 2000 from the agreed fee. It was blatant blackmail, but with the CBSO due to play in the Royal Festival Hall on the following day, Baker had little option but to agree.

On 19 August 1963, Gwen Berry noted in her diary, 'Very shocked by death of poor George Weldon in Cape Town.' He had died two days before whilst undertaking a guest season with the Cape Town Municipal Orchestra; he was only 55. Officially Weldon 'died in his sleep', but his old colleague Major Denzil Walker, who since leaving the CBSO had been looking after his diary at the Ibbs & Tillett concert agency, told Lyndon Jenkins that the telegram he received from the Cape Town Orchestra's Orchestral Director read, 'Weldon suicide. Send replacement conductor.' Weldon's close companion over the previous decade, Gerard Prideaux-Lightfoot, asserts that the cause of death was an overdose of painkillers, brought about by severe depression attributable both to a low psychological state and to unremitting pain from his leg.[22]

Since being eased unceremoniously out of his apparently secure position as CBSO conductor in 1951, Weldon had been Sir John Barbirolli's assistant with the Hallé Orchestra, had undertaken a great deal of freelance work in Britain and overseas and had made numerous recordings for EMI, mainly of 'bread-and-butter' orchestral repertoire, with a number of top-class orchestras; but no other principalship came his way. His physical and psychological condition gradually deteriorated and eventually he went downhill and started drinking heavily. His death went unmarked by the CBSO in 1963 – a sad end for a charming, gifted and undoubtedly charismatic conductor who had worked his heart out for them over eight seasons, from 1943 to 1951.

1963–4

There was general satisfaction when it was announced that Rignold's contract had been extended for a further three seasons. Lloyd was still Chairman of the CBSO's Management Committee, but at the end of the 1962–3 season Bill Russell handed over the Chairmanship of the Executive Sub-Committee to A. D. Martineau, who two years earlier had been encouraged by Lloyd both to stand for the City Council and to join the CBSO Management Committee. Denis Martineau's father, Alderman Colonel Sir Wilfrid Martineau, had been a Trustee of the orchestra for many years.[23] Another change was the introduction of a smart new logo for the CBSO, designed by Douglas Clark and featuring an alto clef (whose shape suggested 'B' for Birmingham) superimposed upon a music-stand.

In September, Sir Arthur Bliss's cantata *Mary of Magdala* was performed at the Three Choirs Festival in Worcester, under the composer. This was the first time that a new work commissioned for the CBSO by the Feeney Trust had been given its first performance outside Birmingham; it was repeated in Birmingham in November, and broadcast by the BBC. In October, Rignold and the CBSO launched another Feeney commission, Elizabeth Maconchy's *Serenata Concertante*, with Manoug Parikian.

Rignold had been able to persuade the Committee to enlarge the string strength further, so that the CBSO now numbered 88 players, but inevitably this fact (plus a recent wage rise) spelt financial problems yet again. The CBSO gave more concerts than the Hallé, Liverpool or Bournemouth Orchestras, but received a smaller Arts Council grant (£42,000). Thursday prices now ranged from 10/6 to 3/-, but, as an experiment, three of the twenty concerts in this series were priced higher (12/6 to 3/6). The first of these relied on the pulling-power of Gyorgy Cziffra; the second featured Antal Dorati and the BBC Symphony Orchestra; and the last assumed a good house for Richard Strauss's *Ein Heldenleben*, which received a towering performance[24] by Rignold and an expanded orchestra, with fine solo playing by John Georgiadis. Once again, however, the higher prices put off some concert-goers and the experiment was not repeated.

It seems hard to believe now, but there was an almighty row amongst the good citizens of Cheltenham Spa when the CBSO stopped playing the National Anthem at the beginning of each concert in their Town Hall. In Birmingham the Anthem was now heard only at the first and last concert of each series, but the patriotic Cheltonians were having none of it.

On Monday, 6 January 1964 I joined the CBSO Staff as Concert Manager. On my first morning in the office, Baker introduced me to Gray, who took me for lunch to a wonderful 'Gentlemen Only' lounge at an old Birmingham pub near the Town Hall, frequented by the musical fraternity and known to one and all as 'Eli's'. Sadly, it was demolished before the season was out. Baker believed in throwing his staff in at the deep end, and from my first week I found myself regularly in sole administrative charge at CBSO concerts; this entailed ferrying guest conductors or soloists to out-of-town concerts and being around backstage at rehearsals and concerts to ensure that everything was under control. In February 1964 the Brazilian pianist João Carlos Martins had been engaged to play Beethoven's Third Piano Concerto at a Birmingham Sunday Concert, conducted by Charles Mackerras. It was obvious at rehearsal that he was far from well and it emerged that he had been suffering from appendicitis for some days, but he insisted on going through with the concert. Half-way through the slow movement, he slumped over the keyboard of the Steinway; it was the first and only time that I had to utter the time-honoured call, 'Is there a doctor in the house?'

*

In addition to its Birmingham series (20 Thursdays, ten Sundays, six or seven pairs of *Music You Love* industrial concerts and 16 Summer Proms), the CBSO was promoting in the 1960s a series of six concerts in Cheltenham, four in Kidderminster, three in Dudley and two each in Coventry, Nottingham and the Royal Festival Hall, where Rignold's professionalism and hard work were beginning to bear fruit in much improved London notices. The orchestra also undertook regular engagements for local authorities as far afield as Bristol and Leeds and played for choral societies throughout the Midlands. In June 1964, the CBSO played under Boult in the Royal Shakespeare Theatre at Stratford, to mark the Bard's 400th birthday; the players found the steeply raked stage a nightmare, and the experiment was never repeated.

1964–5

Birmingham was changing, and changing rapidly. Bulldozers cut a series of huge swathes which gradually took shape as a ringway, designed to take the vastly increased levels of traffic around the city centre (at the expense of pedestrians, who now found themselves confined like troglodytes to a series of dreary concrete subways). In 1964, HRH the Duke of Edinburgh opened the new Bull Ring shopping-complex, dominated by the city's most striking post-war landmark, the Rotunda. A year or two later, HM the Queen did the same for what has proved to be the most successful of all Birmingham's new developments up to that time: the extended tunnel sections which completed the orbital Queensway and made it possible for north-south traffic to drive underneath the city centre without clogging its busy streets any further.

The orchestra was changing too and Maggie Cotton remembers that morale was much improved. 'Every fortnight or so, on Friday nights, there was an orchestra party. Everyone was invited; simple affairs – lumps of cheese, loaves of bread, butter in the packet and bring a bottle. The police were regularly called out to quell the noise. Players from the BBC Midland Light Orchestra always came with instruments and improvised jazz was the order of the evening. The ancient swimming-pool in the garden was often the recipient of merry musicians, and the neighbours regularly complained.'[25]

Rignold's programmes included a distinguished reading of *Das Lied von der Erde* (with Marjorie Thomas and Richard Lewis);[26] Violin Concertos by Elgar (Yehudi Menuhin) and Roberto Gerhard (Yfrah Neaman);[27] the *War Requiem*; the *Ritual Dances* from Tippett's *Midsummer Marriage*, and the first Birmingham hearing of the *Rite of Spring*, initiated by John Manduell of BBC Birmingham, who provided the musicians of the BBC Midland Light Orchestra to augment the CBSO.

Pick of the guest conductors was Jascha Horenstein, with *Verklärte Nacht*[28] and a wonderful, glowing account of Brahms's Second Symphony (happily, recorded by the BBC at the Nottingham repeat). Horenstein's platform manner was dour in the extreme, but he certainly achieved results. Christopher Robinson, who had replaced Douglas Guest at Worcester Cathedral, now took over the City of Birmingham Choir from Meredith Davies, who was spending a good deal of his time conducting in Vancouver. Gray still directed the Birmingham Choral Union, which joined forces with the choir of Birmingham School of Music in two memorable performances of the Verdi *Requiem*.

The orchestra was now playing one or two seasons each year for Welsh National Opera, which had no orchestra of its own. In September 1964, Bryan Balkwill conducted *Fidelio*, with Gwyneth Jones, and *Macbeth*, with Pauline Tinsley. Short tours in East Anglia or the Home Counties were not unusual: on one such, in April 1965, the soloist was Campoli, and since he and Rignold had played the standard violin concertos together many times over the years, they would sometimes agree to forgo rehearsal altogether. At one concert, Campoli was sure that he was to play the Max Bruch Concerto, and received a nasty shock when the orchestra started on Mendelssohn, which provides only a bar and a half of accompaniment before the soloist enters.

Every orchestra has its 'off-days' – but then so do music critics. The late Barrie Grayson, at that time writing for the *Evening Mail*, in February 1964 penned a most enthusiastic notice of Lennox Berkeley's Second Symphony (a 1959 Feeney Trust commission) which Gray had revived with considerable success in Birmingham Town Hall: 'It gives an impression of Englishness, combined with a restless energy that admirably fits our times . . . This is music that has a lot to say.' Nine months later, Gray repeated the work at one of his regular Sutton Coldfield Philharmonic Society concerts, for which a section of the CBSO played. Grayson was there again, but the small proscenium stage of Sutton Town Hall was never the most helpful acoustic, and he seems to have forgotten that he had heard it before: 'This is an arid work that says practically nothing rather unpleasantly. Dissonance is used without any noticeable artistic reason. Despite brilliant orchestral skill, it gave no pleasure.'[29]

The end of the 1964 also saw the retirement of John F. Waterhouse, music critic of the *Birmingham Post* since 1946 and a tireless (though by no means uncritical) supporter of the CBSO. In addition to his perceptive notices, covering an immense range of music, he had penned no fewer than 756 weekly 'World of Music' articles, always well-informed, sometimes provocative, often humorous. He left a gap that was going to be hard to fill.

18

Discord and Harmony

At the beginning of 1965, Kenneth W. Dommett succeeded John Waterhouse as music critic of the *Birmingham Post*. He had for a number of years been a lecturer at the Extra-Mural Department of Birmingham University, with a wide range of specialist musical interests. There were changes within the orchestra, too. Timpanist Ernest Parsons left the CBSO in May 1965, having played since 1920. 'Ernie' was not so much a musician as an institution; he had not only played drums and other percussion instruments but also made them, in partnership with his brother Albert. Time had to some extent passed him by, and Rignold (who had a highly developed sense of rhythm) found his playing less than satisfactory in challenging modern repertoire.[1]

A far younger leaver was John Georgiadis, who went to lead the London Symphony Orchestra, followed there, shortly after, by his desk partner David Measham; during their short time in Birmingham they contributed greatly to the drive and attack of the string playing. His replacement was Felix Kok, who brought with him a wealth of orchestral experience unequalled by any other CBSO Leader at the time of his appointment. Born in South Africa, Felix had gained experience in the Boyd Neel Orchestra before joining the Blech String Quarter; after returning to the Boyd Neel as Co-Leader, he went to the Philharmonia, in its great days, playing under Klemperer, Karajan, Furtwängler, Cantelli and many other great conductors of the post-war period. He then became Leader at Bournemouth (where he got to know Arthur Baker) under Constantin Silvestri, before returning briefly to London to take up a senior position in the BBC Symphony Orchestra. He was also a Professor at the Royal College of Music. Denis Martineau remembers Felix's arrival on the scene in 1965 as 'perhaps the real start of orchestra and management beginning to work together – he was especially good at pouring oil on troubled waters'.[2]

*

1965–6

The orchestra's pattern of work has always been to some extent seasonal, built around a main winter series and a summer programme, with May, June and September the most difficult months for the management to fill. The opening of the 1965–6 season was typical for the period: eight days of work for the Three Choirs Festival in Gloucester; five for the BBC at Garretts Green School; Tchaikovsky Nights with Rignold in Dudley and Leamington; a Birmingham Festival of Entertainments concert with Gray and three solid weeks during which two-thirds of the orchestra played for the Welsh National Opera in Cardiff, whilst the remainder undertook School Visits with either Gray or Dr Christopher Edmunds. It kept the diary full and brought in much-needed revenue but it had little to do with what a symphony orchestra should be doing; in the face of such schedules, player morale tended to plummet again.

Like every Principal Conductor before or since, Rignold was anxious to improve the standard of orchestral playing, and especially of string playing. In his Liverpool days he had been through a major re-audition crisis not dissimilar to the CBSO's, and both he and Arthur Baker were anxious to avoid a similar furore. The leader and section principals were consulted, decisions were taken to move certain players to different positions within the orchestra, and the players concerned were then informed.

One of those affected was Wilfrid Pook, a first violinist since 1953, who was now required to move to the second violin section. A violinist's contract did not specify which section he would play in, and the standard contract allowed the management to place players wherever they wished; Baker maintained that the decision to move some of them had been taken in order to maintain internal balance. But although the 1957 problems had pre-dated both Rignold's and Baker's day, plenty of the musicians remembered very well that Pook had indeed been one of the four violinists who had been instructed to re-audition at that time, precisely because their playing *had* been called into question. Furthermore, the players claimed that this had happened again – buttonholed by Pook in an unguarded moment, Rignold had referred to his 'holding on to notes too long'. They invoked a local agreement, entered into at the time of the earlier problems, according to which he should have been 'entitled to eight weeks in which to remember any alleged inadequacies in his playing'.[3]

The situation was further complicated by the fact that Pook was also the Musicians' Union Steward. The first day on which he was scheduled to play as a second violinist was a BBC recording before an invited audience at Solihull Civic Hall on Sunday, 12 December. Following a series of orchestra meetings over the previous week, the players decreed that unless Pook played as a first violin on that day, nobody else would take part. The management felt unable to retract what it saw as a legitimate instruction, and they all walked out.

'The Wilfred Pook Affair' was the first and thus far the only occasion on which the CBSO players have gone on strike, and from the safe distance of thirty years it still does not really look like a striking matter. If Rignold had undermined the management's case by his indiscreet remarks to Mr Pook, it was equally true that the Union's own position had been weakened by the fact that several of its members had asked (through the Leader, Felix Kok) to have Pook moved;[4] Philip Boothroyd, local Secretary of the Musicians' Union, had also overstepped the mark in telling the *Birmingham Post* that 'No player has ever been transferred to an inferior position against his will'; the existing members of the second violin section were understandably irritated by the implied slur.

Returning, somewhat shaken, to the CBSO Office on the Monday morning, my spirits were considerably lifted to receive a telephone call from Richard Butt of the BBC (faced on the previous evening with an invited audience but no orchestra) saying 'Good morning – when can we find another date to record yesterday's concert?' That kind of cheerful common sense prevailed generally and following a long meeting between Martineau, Baker and two Union officials, the players were rehearsing again by the Monday afternoon for a Christmas concert in Kidderminster, with Gray. Pook was persuaded to accept suspension on full pay until the matter was resolved, and Lord Goodman (Chairman of the Arts Council) was invited to arbitrate in the dispute.[5] Arnold Goodman's judgement was that neither party had behaved wisely, that Pook should move to the second violin section forthwith and that he should be offered a first violin vacancy when next one arose. On both sides honour was felt to have been satisfied, but as usual there had been no winners and the principal loser had been the orchestra's reputation. Many newspapers which would never have bothered to review a CBSO concert were happy enough to print lurid banner headlines about its industrial problems; the *Evening Standard*'s effort was 'Pook's Pique'.

So much for the Discord – what of the Harmony? The German collective noun for an ensemble of flutes, oboes, clarinets, bassoons and horns is *Harmonie*, and no better antidote to the recent unhappiness could have been found than the Birmingham International Wind Competition, during which over a hundred young and outstandingly gifted players of those five instruments came together in Birmingham Town Hall, between 17 and 25 May 1966, to take part in one of the most exciting and stimulating exercises ever promoted by the CBSO. The Jury, chaired by Sir Adrian Boult, with John Manduell as his deputy, was of exceptional quality and included Nadia Boulanger, William Glock, John

Cruft and a string of eminent British wind players such as Leon Goossens and Archie Camden. The prizes offered were generous, and the take-up of candidates gratifying in its number, geographical spread[6] and quality. Each instrumental class included names that are now well known internationally in the profession.

For the opening stage of the Competition, Malcolm Arnold was commissioned to write five unaccompanied *Fantasies* – one for each instrument and all extremely challenging. The order of play had been predetermined by ballot and, in the oboe section, the first name to come out of the hat had been that of the young Frenchman Maurice Bourgue, who played Arnold's piece note-perfect, with exquisite tone and from memory. The impact on the other competitors was dramatic, and from then on it became a thrilling contest. In Stage II each competitor was given the chance to play a concerto with a section of the CBSO (Rignold and Gray sharing the conducting) before the best five in each class were selected to go forward to the finals, with Bourgue finally sharing First Prize with a young Irish flautist called James Galway.[7] At the Prizewinners' Concert on 25 May, broadcast live, the CBSO seemed to play as never before, inspired by the atmosphere of the occasion (and perhaps 'showing off' a little to their international visitors). Major competitions of this sort were far rarer in the 1960s than they are today and it seems a pity that the experiment was never repeated.[8]

In January 1966, Rignold and the CBSO made their first long-playing disc, for the Lyrita label, in London's Kingsway Hall: Bliss's *Music for Strings* and *Meditations on a Theme by John Blow*. Sir Arthur was present throughout the sessions and expressed himself delighted. The Thursday Series had opened with a splendid occasion – the British professional première of the Symphony No. 5 by the distinguished Austrian composer and musicologist Egon Wellesz, given in his presence on his 80th birthday and broadcast live. The work itself, Rignold's reading of it and the orchestra's playing created a considerable impression both with the public and the press; Noël Goodwin remarked that 'the performance had a splendid eloquence that made an immediate impact'.[9]

As a Centenary tribute, all seven Sibelius Symphonies were programmed during the season, though a special Centenary Concert on 9 December was somewhat overshadowed by the industrial ferment going on at the time; a week later, Colin Davis encountered an orchestra still in deep shock, and his concert was chiefly memorable for some beautiful singing from the great Viennese soprano Irmgard Seefried in orchestral songs by Mahler and Hindemith. Strauss's *Also sprach Zarathustra*, repeated at the Royal Festival Hall, drew warm praise from that doyen of music critics, Neville Cardus.[10]

As ever, financial anxieties loomed large: there was a Government pay freeze in force, local authorities were feeling the pinch and (for the first time) the City Council actually cut the annual grant, from £35,000 to £30,000. Eventually, conditional upon internal economies and increased ticket prices, the Council was persuaded to increase its subvention to £66,000, with a £10,000 guarantee; the Arts Council provided £54,000, with an £11,500 guarantee; other local authorities chipped in £4500 and engagement income amounted to some £13,000. These increased grants brought the CBSO at last more or less in line with its fellow regional symphony orchestras, but all of them found it hard to recruit good young players.

In the mid-1960s, choral societies could still afford to engage a professional symphony orchestra; *Gerontius* was favourite – there were no fewer than 12 performances involving the CBSO during the two seasons 1964–6. Good Friday saw the first of many annual performances of Bach's *St Matthew Passion*, given uncut, in English and on what one might now consider an exaggerated scale, the City Choir and Choral Union joining forces and conducted in alternate years by Gray and Robinson, who also employed the orchestra at the Worcester Three Choirs Festival in September 1966.

The CBSO was still undertaking regular seasons for Welsh National Opera, whose May season at Cardiff's New Theatre included John Moody's memorable productions of Rossini's *Moses* (with Pauline Tinsley) and a double bill consisting of Puccini's *Il Tabarro* (Marie Collier superb as Giorgetta) and the première of Grace Williams's clever and hugely entertaining one-acter *The Parlour*, the veteran Edith Coates memorable as Grandmama. The Birmingham Proms celebrated their 21st Birthday season; a cartoon in the *Evening Mail* showed a CBSO percussionist playing his triangle part on a large key. Narrating Prokofiev's *Peter and the Wolf*, the glamorous Diana Rigg caused a few flutters amongst the younger male members of both audience and orchestra, and a 'Hugo Rignold' rose was named – buds were given to the musicians and to every member of the opening night audience.

1966–7

In his Foreword to the Annual Prospectus, Denis Martineau skilfully made a virtue of necessity: 'The *Music You Love* concerts, which have been held on Tuesdays, have become increasingly popular. To meet the popular demand, therefore, this series will be repeated on Wednesdays. To make this possible, the Sunday Series, in which public interest has been declining, is not included in this season's programmes.' The truth was that public interest in the industrial series had also been declining, to the extent that it had been reduced in 1964–5 from its traditional two-night formula to a series of one-night stands;

with only half the number of concerts on offer, it was hardly surprising if the *average* attendance had increased. Another new development was the introduction of the 'Junior CBSO', open to under-18s, who, for an annual subscription of 10/-, could buy tickets for CBSO concerts in most parts of the house for only 2/6d. In its first year, the scheme attracted 750 members, while membership of the CBSO Society itself was approaching the 2000 mark.

The season opened with two weeks of opera in Llandudno, a week at the Three Choirs Festival in Worcester and three days recording for a D'Oyly Carte film of *The Mikado*; following the drama of the one-day stoppage, balanced by the stimulus of the Wind Competition, things seemed pretty much back to normal. At the Cheltenham Festival, Hugo Rignold conducted the first British professional performance of Egon Wellesz's Sixth Symphony, the composer and the Austrian Ambassador attending a repeat performance which opened the orchestra's Birmingham season and was then taken to the Festival Hall, where Dommett enjoyed 'playing of a mellowness and sensitivity that seldom engages my ear in A39 of the Lower Gallery'.[11] The great Romanian conductor Constantin Silvestri introduced Tchaikovsy's *Manfred* Symphony to the city; Alfred Wallenstein conducted the *Symphonie Fantastique*; Walter Susskind brought Shostakovich's Symphony No. 12 and Ida Haendel gave a memorable performance of the same composer's First Violin Concerto.

The pianist Kendall Taylor played many times with Rignold, remembering him as 'a very capable conductor with an excellent technique; perhaps, though, one could detect a little lack of warmth in his accompaniments to romantic works like the Schumann or Rachmaninov Concertos'.[12] There was, to be sure, a certain coolness of approach in Rignold's conducting; precision was all, the stick demanding,[13] but one should never forget that he was Moiseiwitsch's chosen accompanist for gramophone recordings of some of the very concertos Taylor mentioned.

Standards were undoubtedly improving, even if the process was a slow one. Stan Smith feels that 'a lot of the pressure for improvement was coming from within the orchestra itself, not just from the management'.[14] In the course of a distinguished season, all five Beethoven Piano Concertos were included – Hans Richter-Haaser's superb interpretation of No. 4 stands out in the memory – and another highlight was Karel Ančerl's account of Dvořák's D major Symphony, 'ravishingly revealed'.[15] Nadia Boulanger introduced some attractive works by her sister Lili and a memorable performance of the Fauré *Requiem*. In February 1967, Gray conducted the Birmingham première of Carl Nielsen's Sixth Symphony (*Sinfonia semplice*), in Dommett's view, 'the best performance of it that I ever recall hearing. And that does not exclude recorded performances.'[16]

A *Birmingham Post* correspondent complained of the conservatism of the (admittedly popularist) CBSO Proms, claiming that they contained 15 works by Tchaikovsky and none at all by Italian composers. Baker must have enjoyed writing his reply: 'I make it 12 works by Tchaikovsky and not 15 (we count *Romeo and Juliet* as one work only) – and I always thought that Rossini, Ponchielli and Respighi were Italian composers.' At the Cheltenham Festival, Rignold and the CBSO played the Richard Rodney Bennett Symphony and gave the première of Robert Simpson's Piano Concerto, written for its soloist John Ogdon. Simpson was at odds with some of the music critics and barred them all from the afternoon rehearsal; for whatever reason, the work was panned by several.

Rignold conducted three concerts at the Bexhill Festival, the fourth being directed by Harold Gray. After the last, the Mayor rose from his seat, taking conductor and orchestra by surprise, and launched into a long, rambling speech, in the course of which he mentioned 'Mr Rumbold' but said that he had 'especially enjoyed Mr Gray's concert', while the orchestra stood there trying unsuccessfully to control its mirth and Rignold visibly fumed. Rignold's name appeared in many forms: 'Rignold', 'Rheingold' and 'Gingold' were popular – even 'Hugh Rignodl'.

1967–8

With the retirement in the summer of 1967 of cellist Harry Stanier, the last direct link was broken with Appleby Matthews's original CBO of 1920. Harry (who had married Gwen Berry after the death of his first wife) had played in the first Symphony Concert under Elgar and had later spent many years as a distinguished section principal; Gwen noted in her diary that they were invited 'as honoured guests to hear the opening concert of the new CBO season. Sitting in the Lower Gallery again, all amongst the VIPs. Never seen so many gold chains all together. We sat behind two long rows of Mayors from neighbouring towns who support the orchestra – a positive Stud of Mayors!' And with that characteristically light-hearted comment, the frequent extracts from Gwen Berry's delightful and informative diary which have so enlivened this book come to an end, she and Harry both having retired from the CBSO. Professor Anthony Lewis moved on to the Royal Academy of Music; his place was taken by Ivor Keys, from the University of Nottingham.

There was a new series-within-a-series, 'Masterpieces of the Twentieth Century', featuring such works as the Alban Berg Violin Concerto (Ralph Holmes), Sibelius's Seventh Symphony, Holst's *Planets* and Stravinsky's *Rite of Spring* (the orchestra considerably more confident than on its first appearance); but, in the *Post*, Kenneth Dommett, who had been complaining only a year before of 'the serious lack of great 20th-century music', disappointingly used his article on the new prospectus[17] to damn the new development with faint praise. Dommett's case was well argued, but the style of his piece seemed unnecessarily critical, and some of his expressions ('Some of the programmes do not look as if they have been designed so much as thrown together . . . I do not notice any of the obvious ineptitude that characterised a few of last year's programmes') caused a lot of resentment in the CBSO office at the time. Baker entered the lists and a lively correspondence ensued; it was almost reminiscent of the situation between Boult and Sheldon in the 1920s. In his end-of-year piece, Dommett was far more helpful, urging greater public support for the CBSO.[18]

Rudolf Schwarz introduced Bruckner's Third Symphony and Harold Gray conducted Act I of *Die Walküre*, 'with a sure grasp of the structure of the music'[19] – and a strong cast: Sylvia Fisher and Charles Craig as Sieglinde and Siegmund and Michael Langdon as a menacing Hunding. Heather Harper sang Strauss's *Four Last Songs* exquisitely; Hans Richter-Haaser was back with Brahms's Second Piano Concerto, Wilhelm Kempff with the Beethoven No. 3 and Clifford Curzon with No. 4; Ida Haendel played the Sibelius Violin Concerto and Paul Tortelier the Schumann Cello Concerto. The growing prestige of the CBSO was making it easier to attract international guest conductors. Jascha Horenstein returned with Beethoven (all of whose symphonies were played during the season), Kodály and Brahms; Antal Dorati made his first appearance with a shattering account of Mahler's Sixth Symphony.

The CBSO's annual performance of Bach's *St Matthew Passion* (conducted on this occasion by Harold Gray) was accident-prone, too. On the rehearsal day one of the soloists arrived somewhat tiddly and seemed very uncertain of his notes; the Evangelist, Ian Partridge, spent every available minute coaching him in his part. Early on Good Friday, Ian telephoned me, in a whisper, having lost his voice; it was too late to find a substitute, and Peter Bamber (who had only expected to sing the tenor arias) undertook the additional rôle with considerable distinction. To cap it all, the soprano soloist, Eileen Poulter, had an attack of giddiness during her first aria and had to sit down for a while. Apart from that, everything went just fine.

Equipped at long last with its very own instrument van,[20] the CBSO undertook in May 1968 its third and most ambitious European tour to date, entirely behind the Iron Curtain: East Germany, Poland and Czechoslovakia. In those pre-telex, pre-fax days, setting up a tour of this sort[21] called for great skill and patience on the part of Baker and the CBSO's experienced tour agent Adolph Borsdorf; in the event it proved to be one of the most successful the orchestra has ever undertaken.

British planes were not given access to East Berlin's Tegel Airport at that time so they flew into West Berlin's Tempelhof and were kept waiting for ages in the menacing atmosphere of 'Checkpoint Charlie'. The three concerts in East Germany went well and after paying homage to Bach's tomb in Leipzig the orchestra went on by train to the ancient Polish capital, Poznan (where Rignold and the CBSO were joined by Heather Harper for Britten's *Les Illuminations*) and thence to Warsaw, where two splendid concerts in the Philharmonic Hall were the undoubted highlights of the tour.

The 13th of May very nearly proved unlucky, as the CBSO headed southwards towards Czechoslovakia in three coaches, followed by Arthur Baker's car, with Hugo and Jennifer Rignold. These were the exciting days of the 'Prague Spring', when Prime Minister Dubček was guiding his countrymen towards what was hoped would be a lasting measure of independence from Soviet domination, and international tension was running high. As we sped through Silesia we became aware of hundreds of tanks massed in the forests near the Polish–Czech border,[22] but when we finally arrived at the Cieszyn border-crossing, there was no sign of Baker or the Rignolds. Eventually they showed up, having been stopped, searched, 'taken to a soundproof room and questioned extensively for two hours before being released after their identities were established'.[23] Jennifer Rignold remembers, 'they took our passports away – it was distinctly worrying'.

After this cliffhanger, our last few days, based in Janáček's beloved Brno, were a wholly delightful relaxation. Any anxiety the orchestra might have had about playing Dvořák No. 8 to the Moravians proved totally unfounded, for the audience gave it a tremendous reception. Jen recalls that the conductor of the Brno Philharmonic, Jiři Waldhans, 'commented to Daddy, "I was *sooorrprrised* – it was *real* Dvořák!" ' Shortly afterwards, the tanks which we had seen in the foothills of the Carpathians rolled into Czechoslovakia. The 'Prague Spring' was over, and the Russian Winter had recommenced.

The 1968 tour proved to be the climax of Rignold's eight seasons in Birmingham. In the autumn of 1967, the Committee had sensed that, his major contribution to the orchestra notwithstanding, the time was drawing near when they should be looking for another principal conductor – one who could take the CBSO up a league – and instead of offering him another three-year contract they only offered him one further year. Denis Martineau remembers that Rignold 'took the huff' and decided to resign, in order (as the press release put it) 'to give himself more time to work with other orchestras, in Britain and overseas'.

Rignold's contribution to the CBSO had been crucial. He had introduced many excellent young players, had achieved far tighter discipline in the now much-enlarged string sections and a new professionalism throughout, reflected in quicker sight-reading, more exacting intonation and a wider dynamic range. Although his relations with the players had not been uniformly cordial, they had a great deal of respect for him, as did the CBSO's long-serving Associate Conductor Harold Gray, who recalled him as 'once again, the right man at the right time, just as Weldon had been after the war. It needed someone who was thoroughly professional, and that's exactly what Hugo was.'[24] Dommett, too, wrote warmly of Rignold's contribution to the CBSO: 'He has raised its standards and set it on an even keel. He has won the esteem of visiting artists and the respect of everyone who has come into contact with him.'

Rignold was deeply touched when the players spontaneously stood as he came on to the Town Hall platform for his final concert as Principal Conductor, at a CBSO Prom on 18 July 1968. After a magnificent account of Berlioz's *Symphonie Fantastique*,[25] which ended the concert, the audience gave him a standing ovation – a rarity in Birmingham and a heartfelt tribute to a distinguished conductor, a fine musician and a charming man, who had done so much to raise the standard of orchestral music in the city. A month later, he was elected 'Conductor of the Year' by the Composers' Guild of Great Britain, to mark his outstanding work with the CBSO in promoting and performing the music of living British composers. It was a fitting and well-deserved honour, and rather gave the lie to Dommett's long standing criticisms of the CBSO's programme policy.

It was entirely characteristic of Alderman Stephen Lloyd that when he too decided to retire as Chairman of the CBSO Management Committee during the season, it was achieved with the minimum fuss and publicity; he was replaced by Councillor A. D. Martineau, who now chaired both committees, something that had not happened since 1931. Lloyd would continue to serve and be an influential force on the Committee for many years to come, but his strong Chairmanship over the previous eighteen years had been absolutely crucial to the success – often to the very existence – of the orchestra. He was a very private person who led (despite physical disabilities which would have deterred most men) a tremendously public-spirited life. His style was to lead forcefully, but from the rear, and his shrewd lobbying both of business people and of politicians extracted the CBSO from many a financial scrape. His was going to be a hard act to follow.

*

1968–9

The old Triennial Festivals were generally reckoned to have had their origins in a week of Handel oratorios given in St Philip's Church (now the Anglican Cathedral) in 1768, and the City Council agreed to mark its bicentenary by underwriting what it was hoped would be the first of many new-style Festivals. The Festival Committee included strong CBSO representation in Councillors Denis Martineau and George Jonas, Professor Anthony Lewis and the orchestra's General Manager, Arthur Baker.

The ambitious and expensive celebration that resulted included contributions from many international artists: Isaac Stern played the Brahms Violin Concerto in a CBSO concert which also included the première of Richard Rodney Bennett's Feeney-commissioned Piano Concerto, played by Stephen Bishop, and Mstislav Rostropovich played the recently discovered Haydn C major Concerto and the Cello Symphony which Benjamin Britten had written for him five years before. Both these concertos were conducted by Rignold, but it was Sir Adrian Boult who opened the Festival, with a fine account of *The Dream of Gerontius* featuring the City Choir, who also performed Handel's *Utrecht Te Deum* and Beethoven's *Choral* Symphony with the CBSO under Christopher Robinson.

In February 1969, the Austrian conductor Henry Krips had charge of a CBSO concert in the Victoria Hall, Hanley, at which the soloist was Shura Cherkassky. They had not worked together before, so we warned Krips that Shura could prove elusive in a work such as Rachmaninov's Second Piano Concerto. Rehearsal went smoothly and Henry made it clear that he thought we had exaggerated the problems, but in the stunning performance, every tempo was different.

Hugo Rignold's rather late decision not to renew his contract left the Committee without a principal conductor for the 1968–9 season, but it gave them plenty of time to try out possible candidates. The field was narrowed sharply by the impact of their choice for the first Thursday Concert – a young Frenchman called Louis Frémaux, who came with a strong recommendation from David Blenkinsop, Concert Manager of the Bournemouth Symphony Orchestra, with whom he had been doing some excellent work. On 3 October he had a distinguished soloist in Nathan Milstein (his 700 guinea fee a CBSO record at that time) but it was Frémaux's elegant and intensely musical conducting that caught the eye of the players, press and public alike. There were other candidates in the field, of course: Walter Susskind followed Frémaux with two fine concerts; the intensely musical and knowledgeable Norman Del Mar undoubtedly had his supporters too, and other names were discussed as well. But Denis Martineau (who had gone down to Bournemouth with Kok and Baker earlier in the year to watch Louis Frémaux at work making recordings with the BSO) remembers that 'I was determined to have him, though against some opposition from some members of the Management Committee who felt that we should have another British conductor'.[26] Since Frémaux's trial concerts, in many people's minds it had been a one-horse race, and there was general satisfaction when it was announced that he was to become the CBSO's new Principal Conductor from the autumn of 1969.

Rignold had agreed to do a number of concerts during the season, and he did indeed give the first performance of Egon Wellesz's Seventh Symphony in November 1968,[27] the concert including an incomparable performance of the Brahms D minor Concerto by Hans Richter-Haaser, but in January 1969 Rignold was taken seriously ill and he had to cancel all his engagements for some months. Jascha Horenstein and Antal Dorati both returned during the 1968–9 season. Horenstein conducted 'an exhilarating performance'[28] of Bruckner's Fourth Symphony, repeating the concert on the following day in the Royal Festival Hall. The CBSO's other Festival Hall concert was in the safe hands of the distinguished German conductor Ferdinand Leitner:[29] an all-Beethoven programme[30] which called forth probably the most consistently disciplined playing that the orchestra had produced up to that time. In August, the CBSO was in the Albert Hall for a Henry Wood Prom; Walter Susskind conducted Schubert's *Tragic* and Tchaikovsky's Fifth Symphony, and Stephen Bishop repeated the Richard Rodney Bennett Piano Concerto.[31] These London concerts rounded off a good season, and, with Frémaux poised to take over the reins, they augured well for the future.

19

Louis Frémaux: 'A wrist second to none'

Crystal-gazing in the *Post*, when the imminent departure of Hugo Rignold was announced, Kenneth Dommett hoped that his successor would be 'someone young and personable, someone with his feet firmly planted in the 20th century, but someone who will impress himself upon the programmes and leave his imprint on orchestral policy'. Louis Frémaux was just such a person. Born at Aire-sur-Lys in the Pas de Calais, in the extreme north of France, on 13 August 1921, his studies at Valenciennes Conservatoire were interrupted by the war. Just turned 18 at its outbreak, he worked with the French Resistance,[1] subsequently serving in Vietnam as an officer in the French Foreign Legion, being twice awarded the Croix de Guerre for gallantry.

At the age of 27, Frémaux resumed his studies, this time at the Paris Conservatoire, though he remembers that he found it difficult: 'it was a crazy life – teaching to live, and studying as well.' He worked with Louis Fourestier and Jacques Chaillez, gaining a *premier prix* for conducting in 1952. Then he had a lucky break: he was due to conduct the Fauré *Requiem* at the Conservatoire, but the sudden death of the Principal, Claude Delvaincourt, turned the event into a Memorial Concert, attended by all the leading musicians and critics in Paris. Engagements followed rapidly, but just as his career seemed about to take off, he was reconscripted into the Légion to serve in Algeria. However, in 1956 he was demobilised as a result of the personal intervention of Prince Rainier of Monaco, and took over the Monte Carlo Orchestra.

Even before this, Frémaux had established himself with several French recording companies as the result of some stylish discs of 17th-century music. In Monte Carlo, his reputation grew rapidly, as did that of his orchestra, and soon they were producing a string of first-class recordings for Erato and other companies, mainly of French repertoire. By the time he took over the CBSO, he had over thirty recordings to his credit and had been awarded no fewer than eight Grands Prix du Disque.[2] After nine successful seasons in Monte

Carlo, Frémaux freelanced for a while. Then, in the late 1960s, the French government began to set up a series of high-profile orchestras, of which the first two were L'Orchestre de Paris and L'Orchestre Philharmonique Rhône-Alpes, based in Lyon, which Frémaux was invited to take over in 1968. He guest-conducted regularly in Bournemouth, where, according to Kenneth Matchett, he would have been invited to fill the vacancy left by the untimely death of Constantin Silvestri (who had recommended him to the BSO), had not the CBSO got in first with its bid. Fortunately, Frémaux's contract in Lyon gave him sufficient flexibility to accept the principalship in Birmingham whilst still making regular visits to France.

1969–70

Harold Gray remembered the Frémaux years in Birmingham with considerable affection: 'The word that I always connect with Louis is "flair", combined with the results of that rigorous *solfège* training that musicians in France still went through in those days. He had a rather fastidious outlook on music which could pull you up and really make you think about the music he was conducting.'[3]

CBSO Chairman Denis Martineau had high hopes of Frémaux: 'When Rignold left, I knew that we simply had to get the best man we possibly could, regardless of expense. I felt that in Louis we had found a man who would build up the orchestra; he would build up our audience, especially with young people; he would attract recording companies; he would get us regular overseas trips; and within two years he would be bringing in far more than any increase in salary would cost us.'[4] His optimism was not misplaced. The programme for Frémaux's first concert had been shrewdly chosen, drawing virtually all the London critics either to Birmingham Town Hall or to its repeat in the Royal Festival Hall on the following evening. Guitar Concertos by Vivaldi and Castelnuovo-Tedesco, played by John Williams, were framed by Britten's *Young Person's Guide* and the second suite from Ravel's *Daphnis et Chloë*, but the centrepiece of the programme was the British première of Henri Dutilleux's *Cinq Métaboles.*[5] The critics were ecstatic, Felix Aprahamian writing, 'great days ahead for the CBSO with Frémaux . . . *Métaboles* left no doubt that Birmingham had secured a wrist second to none.'[6]

1969–70 was celebrated as the CBSO's Jubilee Season,[7] and in the week during which Louis Frémaux undertook his first rehearsals as Principal Conductor, the orchestra was also involved in an hilarious concert directed by Fritz Spiegl, including such unexpected items as a Concerto ('in the C&A Modes') for Two Tuning-Forks and Orchestra; a Do-It-Yourself Concerto for Handyman and Orchestra; the *Thunder and Greased Lightning Polka;* and a

Concerto for Harpic-cord and Orchestra. The Birmingham-based commercial station ATV also got in on the Jubilee with a televised concert from Coventry Cathedral in which, *inter alia*, the entertainer Dudley Moore joined Frémaux and the orchestra in a poetic account of the slow movement from Mozart's C major Concerto, K.467.

Arthur Baker had succeeded in engaging some fine artists for the Jubilee Season. A week after Frémaux's opening night triumph, Elisabeth Schwarzkopf joined them for operatic arias by Verdi and Puccini,[8] and shortly afterwards the great Russian pianist Emil Gilels played Beethoven's G major Concerto, with Rignold. Hans Richter-Haaser gave a magisterial account of the C minor, as did Clifford Curzon of the *Emperor*, with Boult. Gina Bachauer played the Grieg Concerto in the course of a programme in which Harold Gray gave a fine interpretation of Nielsen's Symphony No. 1 in G minor, thus completing his extended cycle of the six Nielsen symphonies – the first British conductor to achieve this. Other distinguished guests included Ciccolini, Tortelier, Leonid Kogan, Igor Oistrakh, Shura Cherkassky (in a typically mercurial account of Strauss's curious *Burleske*) and the conductor Paul Kletzki. Frémaux's contemporary British offerings included Richard Rodney Bennett's Second Symphony ('an excellently rehearsed performance', according to *The Times*) and two premières: Kenneth Leighton's Third Piano Concerto (a Feeney commission) and *Catena*, by the young American composer Richard Henninger, winner of the CBSO's Jubilee Competition for a short orchestral work.

The season saw another development of far-reaching significance. CBSO players had presented concerts in Birmingham schools intermittently since the 1930s and regularly since 1945. Now the Education Committee could no longer afford to employ the orchestra and this work ceased abruptly. Initially there were a number of concerns, among them, the loss of income from this source[9] and that young people would no longer have contact with the CBSO. In the event, it soon became clear that the gains far outweighed any apparent losses. 'Schools Days' had proved artistically stultifying and consequently none too well played. It was a happy accident that the arrival of Louis Frémaux should have occurred at the very moment when conditions made it possible for the players to work together at last solely as a symphony orchestra. Undramatic as it may have seemed at the time, this was a turning point in the orchestra's history.

Increased availability meant that, away from Birmingham Town Hall, the Jubilee Season found the CBSO busier than ever. The gradual improvement in Britain's roads, with Birmingham increasingly taking on the rôle of the spider in the middle of a web of motorways, gave the orchestra certain practical and financial advantages over the other regional symphony orchestras. In particular, it was perfectly possible for the CBSO to undertake a concert in London and still return by coach to Birmingham before midnight (the witching hour at which overtime became payable). This meant that Baker could offer very competitive quotations to an impresario such as Victor Hochhauser, who promoted regular Sunday night 'pops' in the Royal Albert Hall. During the season, the CBSO appeared in London no fewer than 19 times, in addition to four concerts in the Greater London area. The London dates included the RAF Anniversary Concert (in the Festival Hall) and the Gandhi Centenary Concert (in the Albert Hall, attended by HRH the Prince of Wales), in which it was conducted by Zubin Mehta and Menuhin played the Beethoven Violin Concerto. Under Frémaux, the orchestra gave two concerts at the Swansea Festival, which included a memorable performance of the Dvořák Cello Concerto by Jacqueline du Pré.

However, most out-of-town dates continued to be within easy reach of Birmingham. In Bedworth, near Coventry, one councillor found an unusual reason for voting against the town's annual support for the CBSO: 'It calls itself a Symphony Orchestra, but in its last concert here there were no symphonies.'[10] A regular employer of the CBSO was Eastern Authorities' Orchestral Association. In May 1970 it promoted two superb Viennese Concerts, directed by Willi Boskovsky, who succeeded in triumphing over the unpromising surroundings of some dreary cinemas in Colchester and Slough.

In April 1970 the expression 'one-night stand' took on a totally new meaning for Frémaux and the CBSO, who flew to Amsterdam one Tuesday morning, gave a concert in Rotterdam's handsome new De Doelen concert hall that evening, presented a different programme on the Wednesday evening and immediately flew back to their own beds that night. Dommett used the visit to reproach Birmingham City Council over its inertia with regard to a new concert hall; the headline ran 'Could Birmingham ever possess a hall so fair?'[11] More acutely, the Rotterdam excursion brought home to everyone the yawning gulf that existed between civic funding for orchestras on the continent and in this country. The CBSO was receiving £50,000 from Birmingham City Council and £75,000 (plus a £12,000 guarantee) from the Arts Council. Rotterdam, on the other hand (like Birmingham, a 'second city'), subsidised its Philharmonic Orchestra to the tune of £300,000 a year, to which the Dutch government added a further £90,000.

June 1970 saw the CBSO recording for EMI, for the first time since 1947. Wisely, Frémaux suggested that since the experience would be new to many of the players, the orchestra's first two projects should be in the rôle of accompanist; the first (which he conducted himself) was with the Birmingham-born pop-star-turned-opera-singer David Hughes and the second, a few days later, with Cyril Smith and Phyllis Sellick. Gray had conducted their first three-handed concert following Cyril Smith's tragic stroke in Russia, but it was Malcolm Arnold who was invited to conduct this recording, which included the Concerto he had written for them.[12]

As an additional footnote to the Jubilee, the CBSO Management Committee invited the present author to write a brief history of the orchestra up to 1970; its final paragraph included the following:

> It would be nice to say, 'and they all lived happily ever after'. But if the Jubilee Season has seen exciting new developments it has also seen the gravest financial crisis for many years, a crisis by no means resolved as this history goes to press . . . The report of Professor Peacock's committee[13] throws the problems of Britain's regional orchestras into relief on a national plane, but for long-term solutions one looks in vain at present, as one does for signs of the desperately needed and long-promised new concert hall, though the Leader of Birmingham's City Council went on record in August 1970 with a firm promise of one 'within the next five years'. But, financial considerations apart, the CBSO embarks on its second half-century in splendid heart, with young conductors, many young players and more young people in its audience than at any time in its history – a recent survey at a packed Thursday Concert showed that 45% of the audience were under twenty-five![14]

The reference to 'young conductors' arose out of the appointment in July 1970 of an additional Staff Conductor to work alongside Frémaux and Gray. Maurice Handford was a musician of considerable experience; after twelve years as principal horn in the Hallé Orchestra, he had succeeded Weldon as Barbirolli's assistant[15] and later became the orchestra's associate conductor. He held appointments in Canada and Romania and conducted the First Orchestra at the Royal Academy of Music. In 1967 he had been awarded one of two Arnold Bax Memorial Medals for conducting, the other going to Claudio Abbado. At the same time, the young Leader of the BBC Midland Light Orchestra, John Bradbury, was appointed Co-Leader of the CBSO, partly working alongside the experienced Felix Kok but also leading a number of concerts in his own right. All this represented a move towards greater flexibility and professionalism. A new Midland Authorities' Orchestral Association, too, got away to a more encouraging start than its ill-starred forerunner, Stephen Lloyd's 'Plan A' of 1952, and several local authorities[16] promised financial support.

Louis Frémaux backed the idea of a new hall strongly, hinting that he might not renew his contract unless it went ahead, and in December 1970 a scheme was indeed launched. Two years before, in reply to a series of questions from the *Birmingham Post*,[17] Arthur Baker had provided a well-argued case for a properly designed, purpose-built concert hall for the city, on the Bingley Hall site in Broad Street. Now, at the Endowment Fund's expense, the John Madin Design Group produced an excellently thought-out preliminary design,[18] based on the premise that the CBSO would itself manage the new hall; the City Council seemed poised for action, when yet another financial crisis put a stop to the idea. Denis Martineau is philosophical about that now: 'It probably wouldn't have been half as good as Symphony Hall.'[19] We can also be eternally grateful to the City Council that it decided to turn down a well-meant offer from the local commercial television company ATV to provide a multi-purpose exhibition-cum-concert hall, without cost to the local authority. Multi-purpose buildings rarely make successful concert halls.

1970–1

Overall, then, the CBSO was setting out on it second half-century in good heart and (in all respects other than the purely financial) in good shape. A Registered Friendly Society with over 2000 members who paid an annual subscription of £1, its President was Birmingham's Lord Mayor, its Vice-President Sir Adrian Boult and its Trustees Alderman Stephen Lloyd and Councillor Denis Martineau. The latter also chaired both its decision-making fora. John Cruft, Music Director of the Arts Council, was a member of the Management Committee *ex officio* and its meetings were also attended by Baker, who ran a tight ship with a none-too-numerous and hard-working staff in rather cramped quarters.

During the early 1970s, the pattern of the CBSO's concert giving in the Town Hall consisted of a main winter series of 24 Thursday Concerts; seven 'Saturday Gala Pops' which started after Christmas; six Wednesday Concerts during the spring; a three-week series of 15 Proms in July; a Christmas Carol Concert in late December; a performance of the *St Matthew Passion* on Good Friday; and the orchestra's own Benevolent Fund Concert. Out of town, the CBSO regularly promoted concerts in Cheltenham, Kidderminster, Dudley and at the Royal Festival Hall and undertook a wide range of engagements for local authorities and choral societies around the Midlands and farther afield. After its summer holiday, the orchestra generally plunged straight into the Three Choirs' Festival, which in 1970 took place in Hereford.

In a personal memorandum of his Birmingham years dating from 1989, Louis Frémaux noted that one of the main reasons for the CBSO's success in the early 1970s 'was the fact that we recruited better and better young principals. It was not easy, with numerous auditions, periods of trials, testing both the talent and the personality of each candidate before offering them a position.'

He and Baker knew, too, that if standards were to go on rising, detailed sectional rehearsals would be essential. In September 1970, before the Birmingham season started, they blocked off three days of rehearsal sessions, many of them sectional. Felix Kok remembers that 'Louis's beat was less precise than Hugo's had been, but he was a very hard worker, and he would do things over and over again.'[20]

The Birmingham season opened with a Fiftieth Anniversary Concert, including Mozart's Symphony No. 33 in B♭, Bach's Two-Violin Concerto (Kok and Bradbury) and Holst's *The Planets*, Gerald Larner observing encouragingly in the *Guardian* that 'the CBSO demonstrated, quite simply, that there is no better British orchestra outside London, and that it is an invaluable asset to life in Birmingham and in the West Midlands'.[21] At a reception in the Council House, the Lord Mayor launched a £150,000 Appeal on behalf of the Endowment Fund, strongly backed by the CBSO's Vice President, Sir Adrian Boult, who also conducted the orchestra in Elgar programmes during the season, in Birmingham and Worcester. At a repeat in the Royal Festival Hall on the following day, the Bach was replaced by Ravel's *Shéhérazade*, gloriously sung by Victoria de los Angeles. The ethereal voices in *The Planets* were ladies from the City Choir. Other choirs were employed, too; a week earlier, Birmingham University had provided the chorus for Berlioz's Symphony *Roméo et Juliette* and on another occasion Beethoven's C major Mass was sung by Worcester Festival Choral Society, under Maurice Handford, as part of the orchestra's celebration of the composer's bicentenary. It was becoming increasingly obvious that if the CBSO wanted to programme substantial choral works, it would at some stage need to form its own chorus.

Ida Haendel was heard in Bartók, Shura Cherkassky in Prokofiev and Wilhelm Kempff in Schumann. Jascha Horenstein returned with two programmes (Mozart, Mahler and Schumann; Bruckner and Wagner); Jiři Waldhans (of the Brno Philharmonic) conducted Dvořák's trilogy of Overtures, *Nature, Life and Love* (never before heard complete in Birmingham) and Brahms's Third Symphony; and, in January 1971, a young Estonian conductor making his British début created a considerable impression in an all-Russian programme; his name was Neeme Järvi. In April, Frémaux and the orchestra recorded their first purely orchestral LP for EMI, in the resonant acoustics of the Great Hall of the University of Birmingham. This all-Massenet disc proved to be a real winner, 'bright with colour and full of kinetic energy'[22] and in one format or another it has rarely been out of the record catalogues since.

In the same spring, the CBSO took part in two curious events in East Anglia. One was simply unfortunate: a performance of Tchaikovsky's First Piano Concerto in Thaxted Church, conducted by Handford, in which the soloist underwent a catastrophic succession of memory lapses, with disastrous results. The other was simply unusual: in Great Yarmouth, Antony Hopkins masterminded and conducted in the Hippodrome Circus an intriguing performance 'in the round' called *Othello/Otello* (a comparison between Shakespeare's and Verdi's masterpieces) with Paul Rogers and Ronald Dowd in the respective title rôles.

Othello concerns a power struggle, and a minor one was going on back in Birmingham. As in many societies like the CBSO, elections to the Management Committee generally went through on the nod ('four nominations to fill four vacancies') but during the run-up to the Annual Meeting in June 1971, eight unfamiliar names appeared on the ballot-papers representing what the *Post* described as a 'No Name Group' of CBSO Society members, which was unhappy with the status quo. Two – its spokesmen Ivan Geffen (a Walsall solicitor) and John Patrick (band leader and a local officer of the Musicians Union) – were actually elected, replacing two long-serving members of the Committee: retired journalist Leslie Duckworth and solicitor George Jonas (though both were soon co-opted back into office). The dissident group's declared aims were: 'to see the committee more responsive to the interests of orchestra members, more regular children's concerts, more concerts by the orchestra in Birmingham and the region, better facilities for audience and orchestra at concerts, and more risk-taking enterprises with distinguished visiting soloists and conductors.'[23] The group had concluded that the existing committee was 'rather out of touch'. Dommett wrote a thoughtful article which, while sympathising with many of the group's declared aims, fell far short of whole-hearted support for it. Some at least of the ground swell was political, linked to the views of one section of the players; London orchestras were by now managing their own affairs, and moves were afoot nationwide to extend this development to the regions. The seeds of future internal problems had been sown, but they would not come to full flower for another seven years.

1971–2

Since Louis Frémaux had taken over the helm, the CBSO's Birmingham attendances had been rising steadily, from 67% in 1968–9 to 83% in 1970–1. In September 1971 this encouraged the City Council to resurrect the prospect of a new concert hall. It was agreed in principle that it should be built on the Bingley Hall site adjoining the new Repertory Theatre in Broad Street, and the City Architect was instructed to prepare estimates.

The artistic success of the 1968 celebrations marking the bicentenary of Birmingham's historic Musical Festivals encouraged the Council to promote another in the autumn of 1971, which opened with a performance of Mendelssohn's *Elijah* (125 years on from its first performance in the same hall). The Festival commissioned an oratorio from John Joubert: *The Raising of Lazarus*, given its first performance by Janet Baker, Ronald Dowd, the City Choir and the CBSO under Maurice Handford, and the Feeney Trust commissioned John McCabe to write his Second Symphony, which Frèmaux and the CBSO premièred and later recorded together with his song-cycle *Notturni ed Alba*, beautifully sung by Jill Gomez; this disc subsequently received both an MTA and a Koussevitzky Award. The CBSO's work for EMI also included a disc of Offenbach Overtures, music by Malcolm Arnold (conducted by the composer) and the Saint-Saëns Organ Symphony, which remained a best-seller for years and did much to popularise this work.[24]

May 1972 saw another major tour of Eastern Europe, with both CBSO conductors and soloist John Lill. Supported by the British Council and the Endowment Fund, the tour was arranged by the impresario Victor Hochhauser, who had always specialised in popular repertoire. Dommett felt that, by comparison with Rignold's 1968 tour, the programmes seemed 'a trifle unadventurous',[25] but the venues were considerably more prestigious, taking in the capitals of Romania, Yugoslavia, Hungary and Slovakia. The Bucharest concert took place in what Louis Frémaux describes as 'a very disappointing hall' in the Palace of the Republic, clearly designed for President Ceaucescu to address the party faithful; in the back of the each seat was a minuscule loudspeaker, through which the sound of the CBSO reached us as though from some ancient television set – an orchestra apparently consisting of piccolos and squeaky violins! After that, matters improved as the party went on first to Belgrade, where the British Ambassador entertained the orchestra right royally at the Residence, and then to Budapest for two concerts: Frémaux's in the Erkel Theatre and Handford's in the splendid Franz Liszt Academy of Music.

Orchestral tours on which nothing goes wrong exist only in a concert manager's imagination. The CBSO's recently appointed American timpanist James Strebing was travelling on an International Travel Document in place of a passport. Attempting to enter Romania from Yugoslavia, late at night, the customs officer on duty refused to accept the ITD. Strebing, principal oboist Richard Weigall (who spoke German, our only common language) and the author spent a few anxious hours in no man's land in the early hours, until the problem was resolved. The rail journey from Romania to Hungary involved boarding one of those great Trans-European expresses which comprise rolling-stock from many different countries. When it pulled into Arad station, the first problem was to identify the CBSO's reserved coaches; then nearly a hundred people, with instruments and baggage, had to embark. Long before

Hugo Rignold and a group of players in front
of the Palace of Culture, Warsaw, during the 1968 tour.
On Rignold's left, percussionist Maggie Cotton and Felix Kok.
Photo: Alan T. Foreman.

Louis Frémaux with Dudley Moore, who played a movement from a Mozart Piano Concerto in the course of an ITV programme from Coventry Cathedral, marking the CBSO's Jubilee in 1970.
Photo: Simon Livingstone Studios.

Chairman Denis Martineau presents a painting (held by General Manager Arthur Baker) to Harold Gray on the Last Night of the 1970 Proms, marking his 40 years of service to the CBSO.
Photo: Birmingham Post & Mail.

Maurice Handford, in characteristic pose; the first violins are led by John Bradbury, with Barrie Moore, Stanley Smith and Philip Head. *Photo: Birmingham Post & Mail.*

First Night of the CBSO Proms, July 1972 (conducted by Maurice Handford) – an interesting visual experiment, designed by the author, which proved too expensive to repeat. *Photo: Simon Livingstone Studios.*

London début of the CBSO Chorus – with the CBSO under Louis Frémaux in the Royal Festival Hall, February 1974. *Photo: Constantine.*

A playback during recordings of Walton's *Gloria* in Birmingham Town Hall, September 1976 – left to right: Louis Frémaux; Barbara Robotham; EMI Producer David Mottley; Anthony Rolfe-Johnson; Brian Rayner Cook; Chorus Master Gordon Clinton. *Photo: EMI.*

Hot work at the Harold Gray Farewell Concert in the Town Hall, July 1979, marking the end of Gray's fifty-year association with the CBSO. *Photo: Alan Wood.*

The CBSO makes its first appearance in Vienna's Musikverein, during the 1980 tour conducted by Christopher Seaman. *Photo: the author.*

Simon Rattle's first concert as Music Director of the CBSO was for BBC TV – Tippett's *Concerto for Double String Orchestra. Photo: BBC.*

CBSO Proms, 1982 – a view from the top of the organ-case. The Town Hall stewards traditionally provided acrostic banners on the Last Night of the season. *Photo: Alan Wood.*

Simon Rattle in ebullient mood, on the same occasion.
Photo: Alan Wood.

Chorus Master Simon Halsey with Rattle and the CBSO Chorus, during EMI sessions for Britten's *War Requiem*, 1983. *Photo: Alan Wood.*

In September 1984, Stephen Lloyd decided to retire from the Management Committee after 34 years, 18 of them as Chairman. He and his wife Dorothy are seen with the photo of the CBSO in the Philharmonie, Berlin, signed by all its former conductors then living. *Photo: Alan Wood.*

all were aboard, the train started to move. Frantic shouting won a brief reprieve, but, with two or three still waiting to get on, it moved off yet again and this time it was clearly not going to stop. While orchestra manager John Lackland was hauled in through a carriage window, the Romanian agent (who had been largely inert throughout the tour) sprinted the length of the platform to rescue and throw on board a box of camera equipment belonging to the tour photographer, Dennis Constantine.[26] Two fine concerts in Bratislava's beautiful white-and-gold Reduta Hall led on to Eastern Slovakia, uncomfortably close to the Russian border, for the final concert of the tour; a packed and enthusiastic audience awaited the CBSO at the Košice Festival, where it was learned that (for political not musical reasons) Mravinsky and the Leningrad Philharmonic had played to an almost empty house the night before.

While Birmingham Town Hall was undergoing the third and final stage of its most radical refit since the 1920s, the 1972 Proms took place in the Birmingham Theatre (now the Hippodrome) in Hurst Street. A highlight of the series, making sensible use of the availability of a proper stage with sophisticated lighting, was an evening in which Handford conducted exciting performances of Walton's *Façade* and Stravinsky's *Soldier's Tale*. Narrators Fenella Fielding and Michael Flanders were joined in the Stravinsky by Edward Petherbridge as the Soldier and Robert Eddison as a memorable Devil.

1972–3

The restructuring of Birmingham Town Hall had involved alterations to platform access, a reduction in the number of Lower Gallery seats and an enlarged performing space. These certainly improved its visual and musical[27] aspects considerably, but a few months later Arthur Baker was complaining that 'because of cost there has been no improvement in acoustics. We still have the same woolly sound.'[28] In point of fact, the new platform configuration *did* result in some incidental improvement, in sound quality, internal balance and reduced extraneous noise, but no one dared mention these things, for fear of undermining the possibility that, one day, Birmingham's orchestra would have the fine hall it deserved. One of those who had worked hard towards that end, Kenneth Dommett, stepped down as music critic of the *Post* in October 1972, and was succeeded by John Falding.

The highlight of the Three Choirs Festival in Worcester Cathedral was a Vaughan Williams Centenary Concert, including a performance of the *Sea Symphony* under Boult. The CBSO's Birmingham season also included three Vaughan Williams symphonies: Nos. 4 (Handford), 5 (Boult) and 6 (Frémaux) and some enterprising French repertoire which included Messiaen's *Et exspecto resurrectionem mortuorum*, Debussy's *Jeux*[29] and two unfamiliar works for piano and orchestra – Franck's *Les Djinns* and Vincent D'Indy's *Symphonie Montagnarde*, both played by Aldo Ciccolini.

November 1972 saw an influx of Russian artists for CBSO concerts in Cheltenham and Birmingham, which formed part of a government-sponsored cultural exchange, resulting in protests from Ukrainian Jews and the Birmingham Women's Campaign for Soviet Jewry; they had a point to make, but in the end all passed off smoothly. The young conductor was Yuri Temirkanov, making his British début; the star soloist, Emil Gilels, had to withdraw through illness, but since his replacement was David Oistrakh, there was no complaint. Other visitors included Jean Fournet, Kurt Sanderling, Paul Tortelier, Christian Ferras, Igor Oistrakh, Henryk Szeryng, Alfred Brendel (making his first appearance in the city), John Lill, John Ogdon, Hans Richter-Haaser and Lili Kraus. The season included two symphonies by Bruckner, Maurice Handford conducting the Seventh and Uri Segal the rarely heard First, replacing Jascha Horenstein (who was already gravely ill and died only four days after this concert, on 2 April 1973). Sadly, Horenstein's was not the only death: the tenor David Hughes, soloist at the Civic Concert which opened the season, died of a heart attack soon afterwards. The orchestra's popular principal flautist Tony Moroney collapsed and died on his own front doorstep on the day of the first Thursday Concert, and the funeral of principal horn player John Johnson took place on the day of the last concert on the series. However, even with these tragedies and resulting substitutions, it remained an outstandingly interesting and successful season.

On 27 October 1972, the CBSO went north to play *Belshazzar's Feast* for the Huddersfield Choral Society. Sir William Walton was sitting in one of the Town Hall boxes but unfortunately he was talking to his neighbour and failed to notice the conductor, Bryan Balkwill, indicating that he should take a bow at the end of the performance. The Mayor, sitting in an adjacent box, assumed that it was he who was being indicated, rose and accepted the audience's applause with evident satisfaction, to the vast amusement of the orchestra.[30] A few weeks later, the CBSO was back in Huddersfield for a performance of *Messiah* in which one of the soloists was a young soprano named Kiri Te Kanawa, recently arrived from New Zealand, who 'revealed a voice of charm and strength, if at times her diction seemed strange'.[31]

Behind the scenes, the power struggle emerged into the open once again. The Committee was proposing to amend the Constitution at the Annual Meeting so that the Society would cease to be a Friendly Society and assume Company status. Geffen's group raised objections and the names of six more of its members were put forward. At the Benevolent Fund Concert in June, leaflets were distributed to members of the audience, but since these were produced (without the Society's permission) on official CBSO paper, a furious row broke out. In the upshot, none of the new nominees was elected, but the Committee decided to drop for the time being the idea of altering the Constitution.

Nevertheless, the resulting publicity brought the Committee under fire from another of its regular critics, Councillor Charles Collett, who criticised both the idea of a new concert hall and the CBSO's appointment of a part-time Publicity Officer, Elizabeth Laverack,[32] suggesting that her annual salary of £1500 was a waste of public funds. He received little support. Martineau had felt able to claim in his 1972 Annual Report that the previous season had been 'from an artistic point of view, perhaps the most successful the CBSO has ever had'; and Frémaux remembers, 'They were playing so well; if we came back to a piece we had done two or three years before, when I first came, I was amazed that immediately it was better than before.'[33]

Apart from some concerts for Lina Lalandi's English Bach Festival in Oxford and London, 'popular classics' dominated the CBSO's summer programmes. In addition to three weeks of Birmingham Proms, the orchestra regularly undertook a week of Proms in Cheltenham and Solihull, and similar lightweight programmes in Bristol and Malvern, along with *al fresco* concerts for the GLC in London parks. Handford conducted open-air concerts in Bury St Edmunds and at Woburn Abbey, but at the latter, someone had miscalculated; it was still broad daylight when Handel's *Royal Fireworks Music* was reached (which rather spoilt the visual effects) and the impressive-looking cannons in Tchaikovsky's *1812* Overture went off some time after the orchestra had finished the piece.

20

'The best French orchestra in the world'

The *bon mot* above is attributed to Simon Rattle – an off-the-cuff comment to a reporter, on his appointment as Louis Frémaux's successor in 1980; it was prefaced with a cautionary 'Possibly', and was undoubtedly based more on the CBSO recordings he had heard than on first-hand experience in the concert hall. Nevertheless, the remark was characteristically shrewd, and it was not just about Frémaux's admittedly authoritative handling of French music, and the way in which the CBSO played it. Lyndon Jenkins put his finger on it, talking about Frémaux's Beethoven performances. 'The trouble was that the kind of sound he habitually drew from an orchestra was not of the right weight to support the imposing though unaffected structures he was wanting to build; and much the same could be said for his Brahms . . . But give him a Romantic symphony – Dvořák's Eighth, the *Spring* of Schumann, Tchaikovsky's *Pathétique* or *Manfred* – and you had the complete conductor.'[1]

1973–4

The distinctive Frémaux/CBSO sound regularly attracted enthusiastic reviews from London critics. Edward Greenfield noted, 'Under Frémaux they combine a purity of intonation which metropolitan orchestras might envy with a fluid and spontaneous style of phrasing that is a tribute to his care in rehearsal.'[2]

Andrew Davis conducted a memorable account of Elgar's First Symphony at the Three Choirs' Festival in Hereford, and made his first Birmingham appearance with the CBSO a few weeks later. The season saw no premières, but included Dutilleux's Second Symphony ('a totally committed performance')[3] and Tippett's *Concerto for Orchestra*. Both were conducted by Frémaux, a great admirer of Britten's music; a memorable feature of the series was a concert marking that composer's sixtieth birthday, on 22 November 1973, which opened appropriately with the *Hymn to St Cecilia* (Christopher

Robinson and Worcester Cathedral Choir) and included the *Frank Bridge Variations*. Frémaux was steadily expanding the orchestra's range and repertoire. The strings needed to be on their mettle again for Bartók's *Divertimento* and an attractive *Sinfonietta for Two String Orchestras* by the Polish composer Kazimierz Serocki; he also programmed Roussel's Suite in F, Debussy's *Ibéria* and Satie's jazzy *Parade*, in which CBSO Concert Assistant Betty Milne found herself playing the typewriter as an official member of the orchestra.[4]

Apart from an exciting performance by Frémaux and the City Choir of Beethoven's *Choral* Symphony, imaginatively preceded by excerpts from *Fidelio*, the season was dominated by concerts inspired by Goethe and Byron. Harold Gray was invited to mark his 70th birthday by reliving a past triumph – the celebrated occasion in September 1956 when Beecham had fallen sick and he had stepped into the breach, not only to rescue a performance of Liszt's *Faust* Symphony but to make an outstanding success of it, as he now succeeded in doing once again. There was widespread satisfaction when he was awarded the OBE in the 1974 Queen's Birthday Honours.

Frémaux marked the 150th anniversary of Byron's death by coupling Tchaikovsky's *Manfred* Symphony with Berlioz's *Harold in Italy*. Berlioz also provided what proved to be the true highlight of the 1973–4 season: *La Damnation de Faust*, performed in Birmingham on 31 January 1974 and in the Royal Festival Hall on the following evening. Anne Howells was touchingly lyrical a Marguerite, Pierre Thau menacingly authoritative as Mephistopheles and Frémaux and his orchestra on excellent form, but what made the two evenings really special was that they marked the début of a completely new body: the CBSO Chorus.

From his first season in Birmingham, Frémaux had been pressing Baker and, through him, the Committee, to establish a chorus which would be under the CBSO's full control and would not only perform to an exemplary standard the great repertoire of oratorios, cantatas, masses and Passions but could also be available for those works such as Beethoven's Ninth, Liszt's *Faust* Symphony, Holst's *Planets* and Debussy's *Nocturnes*, for which a chorus is needed only at the end of a mainly orchestral work. When Frémaux met Gordon Clinton, Principal of Birmingham School of Music, he knew that he had found the man to train his new choir. Clinton had himself been a distinguished baritone, whose career had been given a considerable boost by the support of Beecham. In earlier years he had sung with Alfred Deller in Margaret Field-Hyde's Golden Age Singers, Britain's first professional madrigal group; he was also a fine teacher of singing. Frémaux was quite clear what he was looking for: 'Standards will be high – they must be.'[5] And Clinton too was absolutely clear about what was needed: 'When choosing the Chorus, we looked for good voices that would blend to a texture we had in our imagination. The voices must then belong to people who had personality projection and musical appreciation.'[6] The new choir was to be young and fresh-sounding, so an upper age limit of 45 was set. Frémaux, Clinton and Baker auditioned over 250 hopefuls, talking to each one as well as hearing them sing; about 120 were accepted, and, on 3 October 1973, the CBSO Chorus came together for its first rehearsal. Wisely, Gordon Clinton started it by passing around copies of Bach's *St John Passion;* the chorus's first task was to sight-read its magnificent closing chorale, and a very exciting sound it made.

By March 1974, the CBSO's finances had reached a low ebb. A year before, when the deficit had been less than £1500, Baker had warned the Society's members that the orchestra had virtually no financial reserves, and received less subsidy than any comparable orchestra.[7] By the end of the financial year 1973–4 the deficit had mushroomed to £17,500, with wage negotiations in train which threatened to increase it still further. Representatives of the CBSO were summoned to meet its funding bodies and were told in no uncertain terms to trim budgets or face catastrophe. Ticket prices were increased and efforts made to economise wherever possible, but in Baker's view, the CBSO was faced with 'the most serious financial position for years'.

At this juncture, Councillor A. D. Martineau decided to step down from the Chairmanship of the Society. Undoubtedly he would have preferred to have handed on to his successor a healthier-looking balance sheet, but orchestras should be measured not by their financial but by their musical assets, and in this regard Denis Martineau could look back with justifiable pride on what had been achieved during his term of office. He was succeeded by his Deputy, George Jonas, who had been fulfilling an increasingly significant rôle in the Society's affairs during recent seasons. At 46, he was certainly the CBSO's youngest-ever Chairman, but he had a wealth of professional and political experience, including nine years as a City Councillor during the 1960s, and had been a member of both CBSO Committees since 1966.

As usual, the season ended with three well-attended weeks of CBSO Proms in Birmingham Town Hall. When a pianist had to withdraw from one, through illness, the concert-agents Ibbs & Tillett recommended a promising young Japanese artist called Mitsuko Uchida, who gave a stunning performance of Rachmaninov's *Paganini Rhapsody.* Her fee was just £75.

1974–5

The enormous success of the CBSO's recording of Saint-Saëns's Organ Symphony (described by John Falding of the *Birmingham Post*, as 'one of the best the CBSO has ever made')[8] gave rise to a succession of concert performances of the work, up and down the country, often linked to opportunities for Louis Frémaux to sign copies of the disc. EMI had latched on to his winning ways with French music, and recording sessions became a regular feature.

The members of the CBSO Chorus had a taste of recording conditions when they joined the orchestra briefly at its Berlioz sessions in EMI's Abbey Road Studios; their first real test, however, came with Berlioz's *Grande Messe des Morts*, recorded in quadraphonic sound in the Great Hall, in April 1975. To stand in the listening room, with a huge monitor-speaker in each corner, when the chorus, orchestra and four brass groups were recording the 'Tuba mirum' was an unforgettable experience, and not surprisingly the resulting discs received rave reviews. In *Hi-Fi News & Record Review*, John Crabbe called it 'a strikingly beautiful and deeply moving performance: the sort to revive one's faith in fine music-making. What excellent players the CBSO have become under Frémaux, and what a splendid chorus they have.'

In 1974, the CBSO's official establishment was 89 players, consisting of 60 strings and 29 others; the breakdown between males and females was 64 to 25.[9] Despite rampant inflation nation-wide, and local financial gloom, attendances were soaring – especially in Cheltenham, where CBSO promotions consistently sold out. But Birmingham Town Hall still came in for a good deal of criticism, wittily encapsulated in Peter Herman's prize-winning entry in a Musical Limerick Competition promoted by the orchestra's house-magazine *Music Stand:*

> The Town Hall in Brum would be nice
> If you wanted a warehouse for ice;
> And because of the echo
> The sound is *non secco*,
> So you tend to hear everything twice.[10]

The odds against lightning striking twice in the same place are reputedly long, but the CBSO experienced the musical equivalent at the opening concert of the 1974–5 season. Frémaux was to conduct the first half of the programme, including the Beethoven Violin Concerto with soloist Kyung-Wha Chung, and in the second half Boult agreed to conduct Brahms's First Symphony, the main work in his first concerts as conductor of Birmingham's City Orchestra just 50 years before. In the event, Sir Adrian had to go to hospital with back trouble, and M. Frémaux asked that he might take over the symphony as a personal tribute to the 85-year-old conductor. However, he was himself struck down with a serious kidney infection, and (as on so many occasions in the past) Gray stepped into the breach, conducted the whole concert (broadcast live) and made a considerable success of it. The soprano Jessye Norman sang a memorable performance of Wagner's *Wesendonck Lieder* and the great Czech artist Josef Suk gave the first British performance of Martinů's recently rediscovered First Violin Concerto, long thought lost. Indeed, violinists and Violin Concertos from Eastern Europe were a strong feature of the season: Igor Oistrakh played Szymanowski's First and his illustrious father David was to have played Prokofiev's First, but he died on 24 October 1975, only a fortnight before the concert. Oistrakh's distinguished pupil Stoika Milanova took his place, dedicating her performance to his memory.[11]

Double-glazing of the tall windows on either side of Birmingham Town Hall, carried out during the most recent refit, had reduced extraneous noise interference considerably. Nevertheless, on Thursday, 21 November 1974, while Louis Frémaux and the CBSO were playing Dvořák's Eighth Symphony, a dull thud could be heard, followed a few minutes later by another which made the windows rattle, and then the sound of police sirens. It was the night of the infamous 'Birmingham Pub Bombings', in which 21 died and 162 were injured. A few days later, Frémaux was due to conduct the Fauré *Requiem*, to mark the 50th anniversary of the composer's death; chorus bass Mike Cox remembers that, in the circumstances, the performance took on a specially moving quality. A few weeks later, Frémaux, the members of the CBSO and soloist John Lill gave their services for a Gala Performance in aid of the dependants of the bomb victims.

Undoubtedly the musical highlight of the 1974–5 season was a Beethoven Festival, promoted by the CBSO in Birmingham Town Hall between 10 and 17 April 1975. It was built with great care by Baker and Frémaux around the Dresden-born pianist Hans Richter-Haaser, who had in recent seasons become a frequent and much-admired visitor to Birmingham. In five concerts, at the beginning and end of the Festival, Frémaux included six of the symphonies and Richter-Haaser played the five Piano Concertos and the *Choral Fantasia*. In the middle came two contrasting concerts: one a towering performance of the *Missa Solemnis*[12] and the other a marathon of a recital in which Richter-Haaser played four sets of Variations, culminating in the mighty *Diabelli* set. The bluff, leonine figure of Hans Richter-Haaser dominated the week's music-making. It seemed to many almost as if Beethoven himself was there, creating his music afresh for them; but Frémaux, the orchestra and chorus played a tremendous part, too. Max Loppert wrote of the *Missa Solemnis*, 'it proved to be the most keenly played, sung and listened-to account of the work I have heard in a long time, in which each listener seemed to be thrown with lightning force on and back to the music – its physical impact, its meaning, its might – in a way seldom possible in the Festival Hall.'[13] John Falding of the *Birmingham*

Post summed up the Festival as 'one of the finest musical events in the city within living memory', and Arthur Steele of the *Evening Mail* wrote, 'This week has proved a triumph.'[14]

The myth that Frémaux 'was only good in French music' is one that seems to have spread after he left the CBSO; certainly it owes something to EMI's tendency to employ him mainly in his native repertoire. In fact, his Birmingham programmes faithfully reflected not only the breadth and eclecticism of his taste but also his skilful and fastidious approach to music of widely differing styles, including that of the great Austro-German classical and Romantic repertoire. BBC Producer Richard Butt remembers that 'whatever Louis conducted, it always seemed to have a certain delight and excitement about it. I loved working with him.'[15]

1975–6

September saw the CBSO back at the Henry Wood Proms, after a long absence. EMI must have been delighted with the choice of main works, all of which they had recorded: the Bizet Symphony, Saint-Saëns's Organ Symphony and John McCabe's *Notturni ed Alba*.

In October, more than two years after its abortive attempt to amend the constitution, the Management Committee felt sufficiently secure to call an Extraordinary General Meeting at which the members voted overwhelmingly to become a non-profit-distributing Limited Company, known as CBSO Society Ltd. Any advantages that Friendly Society status might once have carried with it had long since evaporated, and financial survival was the name of the game. The annual cost of running the orchestra was by now approaching half a million pounds. It received from Birmingham City Council and West Midlands County Council £30,000 less than its opposite numbers in Manchester or Liverpool got from their local authorities, but the Committee had only a limited range of options open to it in order to bridge the gap. The Endowment Fund helped wherever it could – a replacement for the orchestra's much-travelled instrument van, for example, now nearly eight years old. Ticket prices had gone up and could perhaps be increased again; there was some scope, too, for attendance at Birmingham promotions to be built up, but these two solutions seemed likely to cancel one another out. It was becoming increasingly evident that the CBSO needed to address, at last, those two new-fangled concepts: marketing and sponsorship.

The Birmingham Marketing Project had been started during the 1974–5 season, with Arts Council funding and encouragement, and with Peter Cox as its Director. It provided, for the first time, a forum where the CBSO could meet Birmingham's other principal arts organisations with the object of finding a common purpose, identifying the potential audience and targeting it more precisely. First fruit of the project was a research document, *A strategy for marketing the arts in Birmingham*,[16] based on a series of audience surveys which revealed, for example, that 77% of those quizzed who lived in the city had heard of the CBSO, and that 15% had attended a CBSO concert; for those living in the wider West Midlands conurbation, the equivalent figures were 61% and 9%, which really seemed quite encouraging. The first tangible outcome of this 'strategy' was 'Basil' – Birmingham Arts Shop – which opened in City Arcade in October 1974; it has survived various crises and still fulfils a useful rôle in the city centre, mainly as one of several computerised ticket outlets.

Another obvious line of approach open to the CBSO was sponsorship for the vast and wealthy business community which made the West Midlands conurbation 'tick'. First to come in were Imperial Metal Industries (IMI), which still supports the CBSO to this day, and the national jewellery chain H. Samuel Ltd, followed soon afterwards by the Midlands' own commercial radio station BRMB, which started broadcasting selected concerts, and promoting occasional CBSO concerts itself. CBSO Chairman George Jonas reacted enthusiastically to this influx of funding from the private sector, whilst sounding a note of caution: 'I really welcome it, though it is not a substitute for public money, and never could be.' IMI's £6000 sponsorship was linked to a series of five Frémaux/CBSO concerts (one in Leeds, two in the Royal Festival Hall and two in Birmingham broadcast by the BBC), each of which included one of the season's two new Feeney Trust commissions. The two programmes were of outstanding interest and are well worth quoting in full:

Dukas	Fanfare et Poème Dansé: La Péri
Nicola LeFanu	Columbia Falls
Richard Strauss	Don Quixote (Paul Tortelier)
Debussy	Cantata, La Damoiselle Élue
R. R. Bennett	Violin Concerto (Ralph Holmes)
Walton	Belshazzar's Feast

'H. Samuel Family Music' (four concerts, mainly in the CBSO's Saturday Series, masterminded by Elizabeth Laverack's Arts Appreciation Agency) was aimed at a predominantly young audience, and, with this in mind, the orchestra engaged the American conductor Robert Mandell, Musical Director of the Haymarket Theatre, Leicester, who had arranged a successful series of 'Family

Proms' in July 1974. He had been for a while Leonard Bernstein's assistant in New York, and although his rather brash approach did not go down too well with some of the players, it certainly proved effective in drawing in a whole new audience, at a time when the pattern of the CBSO's 'popular' programmes had become somewhat fossilised.

Frémaux opened the Thursday Series sonorously with a selection of *Canzone* by Giovanni Gabrieli, using the additional brass players called for in *The Rite of Spring*, the main work in the concert; not even Martha Argerich, though, could persuade one that Chopin's First Piano Concerto 'sat' happily in that programme. Overall, the 1975–6 programmes did perhaps look a trifle bland, but the CBSO Chorus contributed first-class performances of some widely differing works: *Belshazzar's Feast;* Poulenc's *Gloria;* Beethoven's *Choral* Symphony. Frémaux followed the previous season's much-praised performance of Mahler's Third Symphony with a really exciting reading of the *Resurrection* Symphony, a score quite new to Birmingham, eliciting tremendous popular enthusiasm. His doomladen Ninth Symphony was given a deeply felt performance, too, under Handford; he had received news earlier that day of the death of his mother, but insisted on going through with what must have been for him a deeply harrowing experience.

There was a good deal of sadness in Birmingham on learning of the deaths both of Hugo Rignold and of Norris Stanley, the orchestra's Leader from 1941 to 1958. On the plus side, however, on 23 May 1975, a 21-year-old conductor with tousled hair and winning ways called Simon Rattle (winner of the Bournemouth Symphony Orchestra's John Player Competition in Portsmouth just a year before) conducted the Birmingham orchestra for the first time in what was (for him, even at that time) a rather unlikely looking Beethoven programme: *Leonora No. 3*, the *Emperor* Concerto (Cyprien Katsaris) and the Fourth Symphony. As Nicholas Kenyon wrote, 'The concert went well, and Rattle now remembers it as a surprisingly positive experience in view of its being a programme he should never have agreed to conduct. Others recall that he was worried by the orchestra and found them a little stand-offish, but that the actual performance was a success.'[17] It was evidently considered sufficiently successful for Rattle to be engaged to conduct two out-of-town concerts in the following season.

1976–7

At the Three Choirs Festival, which took place that year in Hereford Cathedral, Roy Massey conducted *Gerontius* for the first time: 'Like most of his fellows, Massey is not, I think, naturally at home with a professional orchestra. But something, divine spirit or demon, propelled him and his Gerontius, David Johnston, into giving the most moving performance that I ever heard.'[18]

A feature of the season was a nine-concert Beethoven Cycle which the CBSO undertook for Tony Burley of Eastern Authorities' Orchestral Association in Hemel Hempstead, Luton, Watford, Dunstable and St Albans; Frémaux and Meredith Davies shared the conducting of all nine symphonies and Malcolm Binns played the five Piano Concertos. The season included some unusual features, too – a Liberal Party Concert in the Royal Albert Hall (Frémaux, Menuhin, Heather Harper) at which party leader Jeremy Thorpe took the baton for the National Anthem; two concerts conducted by Victor Borge, and an all-Tchaikovsky CBSO Benevolent Fund Concert at which Tortelier played the *Rococo Variations* and conducted *Romeo and Juliet* and an exciting (if decidedly eccentric) account of the Fifth Symphony.

IMI felt sufficiently encouraged by the reception for its 1975–6 series to support four more CBSO concerts in the following season. H. Samuel Ltd did not renew its sponsorship, but others came in to take its place: Midland Bank, Lucas Industries, GKN and the Harry Payne Trust, mostly supporting a new and exciting series of BRMB-broadcast Saturday morning 'Young People's Concerts', conducted once again by Robert Mandell. Some idea of the impact of these may be gleaned from 9-year-old Alison Lever of Streetly; her spelling may have been cavalier, but her enthusiasm could not be questioned: 'Last Saturday I went to a CBSO concert for young people in Birmingham town hall. CBSO stands for City of Birmingham Sinforny Orchestra. It was very nice and I enjoyed it very mich. In the orchestra some people were playing violins. In on piece of music they were playing piccicato. Piccicato is when you pluck the strings of the violin with your fingers. I have just started to play the violin and I am playing it piccicato. The conductor was telling us about Orcestrashin . . . We took our granny to the concert she enjoyed it very much and we were sad when the concert finished. Love from Alison.'[19]

James Galway, joint winner of the CBSO's International Wind Competition ten years before and by now an international star, gave the first performance and London première of the latest Feeney Trust commission: a flute concerto called *Mandala ki Raga Sangeet* ('A Circle of Raga Music') by the Anglo-Indian violinist and composer John Mayer. The recent death of Shostakovich was marked by the first hearing in Birmingham of his Fifteenth (and last) Symphony, and Frémaux also revived two major Berlioz scores: *Harold in Italy* (CBSO principal viola John Brearley the expressive soloist) and *The Damnation of Faust*, with which he had launched the CBSO Chorus; Thau was again a superb Mephistopheles, with Sandra Browne as Marguerite, Kenneth Bowen as Faust and John Rawnsley as Brander. Mahler featured again (a fine account of *Das Lied von der Erde*, with Yvonne Minton and Ernst Haefliger) and it was no surprise to find Frémaux turning his hand very effectively to Wagner, with what Lyndon Jenkins described as 'a splendidly successful' account of the First Act of *Die Walküre* (Lorna Haywood, Heribert Steinbach and Gwynne Howell, repeated at the Norfolk and Norwich Triennial Festival).[20] When Richard Lewis sang Britten's *Nocturne* it was widely known that the composer was already gravely ill, and he died on the day of the Leeds repeat (4 December 1976), which took on the nature of a memorial concert. Louis Frémaux was much affected by Lord Britten's death; he played his arrangement of Purcell's *Chacony* at a couple of concerts in his memory, and (although they had never met) took time out to attend his funeral in Aldeburgh Parish Church.

A Walton 75th Birthday Concert included the Violin Concerto (Gyorgy Pauk) and the First Symphony. Otherwise, the Thursday programmes were on the safe side – an attempt to counter faltering attendances in the past couple of seasons. There were several more EMI recordings: Poulenc, Lalo, Ibert; and during the summer, when the Queen's Silver Jubilee was celebrated with a nation-wide Festival in which the orchestra and chorus duly played their part, EMI invited Frémaux to make two records of music by Sir William Walton, including the 1953 *Coronation Te Deum*, the two Coronation Marches and the hitherto-unrecorded *Gloria*, eliciting a letter from the composer, thanking Frémaux for 'the splendid results'.

The old Management Committee was now called the Council of Management and the former Executive Committee was now the Committee of Management, but there were no significant changes within them.

21

All change

'Where did it first go wrong?' – so muses the dying Alexander the Great, in the Prologue to Terence Rattigan's play *Adventure Story*.[1] It is a question which has to be addressed, as we approach the most dramatic season in the orchestra's 75-year history to date – a season which was marked by the sudden and unforeseen departure both of its Principal Conductor and of its General Manager, but one which saw, too, a remarkable resurgence of popular support for the CBSO, at a Beethoven Festival which looked at one time as though it might never take place.

Louis Frémaux had involved himself in every aspect of musical direction; he has records of attending over 900 auditions of orchestral players, and as many again of hopefuls for the CBSO Chorus. He was deeply committed to his position in Birmingham, though of course he conducted other orchestras as well. He had given up his Lyon post after only three years, because he felt that orchestral music in France was going nowhere, and now he was looking forward to taking over the Sydney Symphony Orchestra in 1979, in addition to the CBSO. He pointed out to the *Birmingham Post*, 'As it is winter in Australia when it is summer here, I shall be able to do both jobs.' No hint there that he was thinking of leaving Birmingham; he was proud of the orchestra's musical achievements, but he was aware too that player–management relations were growing increasingly uneasy, and he was unhappy about the high level of political activity within the orchestra. As he observed to Felix Kok, 'The kitchen is bad, but the *cuisine* is good.'

The times they were a-changing. In his 1989 memorandum, Frémaux remarked, 'We must remember the political situation of the seventies: disruption, conflict, strikes, unions wanting to run the country, no sponsorship, grants not sufficient and poor salaries.' One worrying aspect was the regularity with which key CBSO players were leaving for London, which offered not only higher salaries but many more opportunities for freelance work. But there was also dissatisfaction at home. Denis Martineau's hopes in 1969 that Frémaux would build up the audience, attract recording companies and get regular overseas trips had been fulfilled in considerable measure, but the orchestra had not been abroad since 1972, appearances at the more important British Festivals were still rarities and some at least of the orchestra's out-of-town engagements continued to be either in unsatisfactory halls or with choral conductors of limited accomplishment. Repertoire, too, which had been expanding fast during Frémaux's first five seasons in the direction of Messiaen, Dutilleux and other 'interesting' composers, was now tending towards stagnation. To take one example only, in seven seasons, between 1972 and 1978, Frémaux conducted 23 public performances of the Saint-Saëns Organ Symphony – good for record sales and for the box office, maybe, but certainly not for player-satisfaction.

1977–8

As the season opened, there was no indication of trouble ahead – indeed, it began with a moment of near-farce. During the Three Choirs Festival, Frémaux conducted Mahler's *Das Lied von der Erde* in Gloucester Cathedral, with Janet Baker and John Mitchinson as soloists – a memorable performance, though deficient in one detail. At the rehearsal, the London player engaged to play the brief but important mandolin solo started to behave strangely, wandering around on the platform and making loud comments. Frémaux recalls that the CBSO's harpist, Robert Johnston, told him, 'Louis, he is drunk!' Dame Janet sat there, apparently, totally impassive. Percussionist Maggie Cotton remembers, 'At the evening concert, we had to post sentries on either side of the platform, to keep him off!'[2]

On Saturday, 24 September, Sir Adrian Boult directed the CBSO for the very last time, when, at the age of 88, he gave his services to conduct the first half of a special concert in Worcester Cathedral in aid of the Elgar Foundation's Birthplace Appeal. Helped on to the platform, he sat to conduct the Prelude to *The Kingdom*[3] and the Cello Concerto, with Paul Tortelier. The atmosphere was electric, and became more so when Tortelier broke a string during the *finale* of the concerto; seizing the nearest orchestral cello, he finished the work on that. In many ways, the concert marked the close of an era.

The musical press found it hard to raise much enthusiasm for the Thursday Series; the programmes seemed unremarkable. Many top-class artists were engaged, but all too often their contributions were of predictable repertoire. On a lighter note, the CBSO/BRMB Radio Concerts for Young People were now in the hands of flautist and extrovert Atarah Ben-Tovim; again these proved popular and successful.

Arthur Baker kept a tight rein on the CBSO's artistic policies. Within sixteen years as CBSO General Manager behind him he felt that he was well qualified to exercise such control; the CBSO of 1978 was a bigger and enormously better band than that of 1962, and no one could deny that Baker had played a significant rôle in that transformation. To achieve his ends, he was perfectly prepared to 'fight his corner'. George Jonas and the Management Committee undoubtedly respected him, but perhaps, towards the end, they did not entirely trust him. He had made friends, but enemies too. Internal politics are rife within every orchestra, but within the profession, the CBSO of the Sixties and Seventies had a special reputation in that respect; many players just want to get on with rehearsals and concerts, but there will always be activists seeking to improve working conditions, and theirs tend to be the voices most readily heard. Gradually, Baker's battles with the players began to marginalise him. Ultimately that spelt trouble for him and, because they were inseparably linked in many people's minds, for Frémaux as well.

The problem came to a head, without warning, on Wednesday, 8 February 1978, during rehearsals at Carrs Lane Church for a Birmingham concert and BBC recording. At the beginning of the season the front desks of the viola section had sported a full complement: a principal, a co-principal and two sub-principals. The section principal and the 'No. 4' player left for the Royal Opera House and, as luck would have it, the acting principal was away sick on this day, leaving the only other remaining sub-principal leading the section.

From Frémaux's point of view, this could not have happened at a worse time. In the second of the Tippett *Ritual Dances (The waters in winter)*, where the violas represent the fish being chased by the otter, they have a notoriously difficult, high-lying passage, so he was relieved when the Orchestra Manager, Tony Evans, told him that he had been able to engage the CBSO's recently departed sub-principal, Andrew Sippings (who had played the work before) as a freelance player, to sit on the front desk for this programme.

Most people would probably agree that this was a common-sense solution to an exceptionally difficult musical situation, but the violist who would normally have 'sat up' on the front desk objected to it, on the basis that players who were not members of the CBSO always sat at the back of the section. During the break in the morning rehearsal, Paul Smith, Chairman of the Players' Committee, asked Frémaux whether he insisted on having Andrew Sippings on the front desk, which he confirmed. An Orchestra Meeting was held during the lunch-break, at which a resolution was passed unanimously that, unless Sippings moved to the back of the viola section, the orchestra would not play. As Louis Frémaux says, 'It all happened so quickly. I felt that to say who should play at a particular desk was a musical decision, which only I could take. If the performance not up to scratch, I would be the one to take the blame, not the orchestra. I was very unhappy about it, and I felt let down by the management, who would not support me over it.'[4]

In the afternoon, Frémaux resumed rehearsals, but now with Sippings sitting at the back of the section, as instructed by the orchestra's shop steward. It was humiliating for Frémaux; in a memorandum made at the time he noted that he had seen trouble of this sort coming, and had issued warnings on three occasions[5] that it needed to be defused, but that nothing had been done. Against his better judgement, he agreed to conduct the Tippett concert and the BBC sessions, and gave his services to conduct the CBSO Benevolent Fund concert on the following day. He was then away from Birmingham for a couple of week, returning on Wednesday, 1 March, straight into the next crisis.

The performances of Britten's *War Requiem* at the beginning of March, in Birmingham and the Royal Festival Hall, were of exceptional importance to the CBSO. Not only had the orchestra taken part in the première but it had now been invited to make for EMI, at the end of June, the only other recording of the work besides Britten's own. Again the concerts were bedevilled by sickness, compounding the existing shortage of front-desk players. Frémaux noted that 'I could not envisage a recording on the standard of these performances and I asked EMI to consider bringing in an outside chamber orchestra', thus sparking off another row with the players, and another climb-down by the management. Understandably, he felt that his authority as musical director was being eroded to an unacceptable degree.

Each of these incidents, while in itself a storm in a teacup, was symptomatic of a malaise that went far deeper, targeted not primarily against Frémaux but Baker. For some time, the Players' Committee had been quietly putting together a dossier of what it saw as damning evidence against him. Paul Smith, its Chairman at that time, 'felt that he was accepting the "easy" dates that came his way rather than going out to look for more prestigious work for the orchestra. We discovered that he had turned down some good opportunities, including a Bruckner Festival in Linz, apparently because Louis wasn't free at that time. Arthur had become Louis's agent, which we thought was a bad move, and we felt that he was tending to manage Louis rather than the orchestra; we had a long meeting with George Jonas and Arthur Maddison about it, but in the end the Management Committee agreed to it.'[6]

Sadly, Baker is no longer here to put his point of view, which might be very different. On Thursday, 9 March 1978, the players held a meeting at which they passed a vote of no confidence in his management. On the following day, Jonas, Maddison and Baker (none of whom seems to have had any inkling of what was going on) had a routine meeting with the members of the Players' Committee. Jonas remembers it well: 'Nothing was said, though the atmosphere was certainly frosty. Then, after the meeting had ended, Paul handed me a letter setting out the wording of the orchestra's vote of no confidence in Baker, together with a large dossier of background material. I met the whole orchestra, and heard their objections; eventually I was able to persuade them to withdraw their resolution, on condition that I put their complaints to Arthur Baker. Arthur Maddison and I met with him and put the whole matter before him, but it soon became clear that the point had been reached at which his position was no longer tenable.'

After further discussion and consultation of lawyers, Baker offered his resignation on 16 March, and it was accepted. The parting of the ways was said to be 'without acrimony', but, beyond that, Baker maintained a dignified silence, to the frustration of the Press.

The effect upon Frémaux was immediate. In an interview with Judith Jackson of the *Sunday Times*, some five years before,[7] he had said, 'Ten years is a long time to stay with an orchestra, and some do not need the same conductor for too long. But you can tell when it is time to go.' After the unhappy 'viola' episode in February, Frémaux had already decided that that time had come; he would not renew his contract when it expired. 'The Union wanted to manage the orchestra. Some of them wanted a revolution, and that's what they achieved.'

Unquestionably, the least disruptive outcome would have been if Frémaux had elected to see out his contract, but not to renew it. However, following so soon on the *War Requiem* problem, the sudden 'sacking' (Frémaux's word) of Baker (which he still considers quite unjustified) precipitated a startling decision: he would resign as well. 'I felt that it was impossible for me to carry out my duties as Musical Director any longer. To me, it seemed better to go than to stay.'[8] So, on 12 March (even before Baker had finally bowed to the pressure on him) Louis Frémaux sent a letter to George Jonas, asking to be released from his contract with immediate effect. He was not willing to conduct the orchestra again in any circumstances. Jonas, sensing everything crumbling around him, implored him to reconsider his decision, giving him a few days to think it over. Neither the officers nor the players seem to have foreseen this turn of events.[9] On 18 March, Jonas and Maddison[10] held another meeting with Frémaux, emphasising that if he left the CBSO in the lurch, he could neither expect to work for it again, nor any other British orchestra to engage him as its principal conductor. Frémaux, however, was adamant and, on that unhappy note, the most distinguished phase in the CBSO's musical history thus far came to an abrupt end. The CBSO's officers proved as good as their word; he has never conducted the Orchestra again, and perhaps now he never will, though the warmth of his reception by the Symphony Hall audience at a superb NYO concert in April 1995 showed that his continued absence from the podium has been Birmingham's loss.

To say that news of the twin resignations caused a sensation would be an understatement. As soon as the story broke, journalists from all over Britain were on the telephone to the CBSO, wanting to know more, but they learned little. Jonas issued a brief factual statement, and neither Baker nor Frémaux was available for comment; ranks were closed and nothing more was forthcoming. There were angry leading articles in the *Post* and a few attempts elsewhere to embroider the story, but gradually it died, for lack of oxygen.[11]

In Birmingham, the classic trial of strength had taken place between Stephen Lloyd and Kenneth Matchett in 1952. The idea of having a General Manager who might actually 'manage' was still too novel to be taken on board at that time, but as both orchestra and administration became more professional over the ensuing quarter of a century, the balance of power gradually changed, so that during the 1960s and 1970s, working closely first with Rignold and later with Frémaux, Baker was able to exercise an increasingly potent influence on the orchestra's artistic policy. Like Matchett, he was combative, and he crossed swords with the Committee and the players. He knew almost by heart the wording of the standard contract which governed the musician's working conditions. Battler he may have been, but the suggestion that he ran the CBSO entirely *ex cathedra* for some fifteen years does not hold water; had it been so, it would surely have suggested criminal negligence on the part of the Society's officers. Minutes suggest that he kept the Committee well informed about what was going on in the office – he needed their support, and they needed his. As for his dealings with the players, both sides could be abrasive, but a year before the crisis broke, long-serving violinist Stanley Smith had struck a sensible balance: 'We are not perfect; neither are the management. Both sides have a job to do. Both sides can be bloody-minded. Both sides can be surprisingly accommodating. Such is life.'[12]

Baker's domestic life was stormy, with two broken marriages during his Birmingham years, but he was a man of considerable charm and also a first-class manager who not only made a tremendous contribution to the CBSO's progress but prepared the way for the giant leap that was to follow so soon after his departure. An able pianist, with some conducting experience, he was a discerning musician, with a critical ear.[13]

There were, of course, recriminations. Public money was involved, and since Frémaux would have to be replaced by other conductors, there was some talk of suing him for the balance of his contract but, wisely, this idea was dropped.

Felix Kok, who remembers the whole incident as 'a miserable business', also found himself briefly drawn in. His contract with the CBSO required him to lead for only half the concerts, but when Co-Leader John Bradbury announced his intention to leave, the Players' Committee insisted that Kok should in future lead full-time; as a result, the Musicians' Union instructed its members to boycott auditions for a new Co-Leader. At one stage in the drama, Frémaux, Baker and Kok were all consulting the same London solicitor.[14]

The story broke on Monday, 13 March 1978. The immediate problem was to replace Frémaux, who was supposed to be rehearsing a greatly enlarged orchestra on the following two days for a Birmingham concert on the Thursday. The Japanese conductor Michi Inoue took over a slightly changed programme. Mercifully, this was the last Thursday Concert of the season; Frémaux had only one or two CBSO dates booked in the immediate future, and it was not too difficult to find replacement conductors for these.

The really worrying problem looming was another six-concert Beethoven Festival, already announced for the beginning of May with Frémaux as conductor, and selling well on the strength of the success of its forerunner. Where the first Festival had been built around the five Piano Concertos, the principal element in this second one was the cycle of nine Symphonies. Baker had agreed to remain in post (nominally at least) until July 1978, and he worked hard to replace Frémaux where necessary. It was a tall order to find, at such short notice, not only a conductor who would be capable of giving authoritative performances of a complete Beethoven cycle, but one who was available for what amounted to three weeks: three days of rehearsals at the end of April, and the Festival itself, 4–11 May. The redoubtable Howard Hartog of Ingpen & Williams came up with a name: the senior Swiss conductor Erich Schmid, a Schoenberg pupil who had had charge for many years of the Tonhalle Orchestra, Zürich, and later of the Radio Orchestra, Beromünster. He had worked extensively with the BBC Symphony and BBC Northern Orchestras, but was quite unknown in Birmingham; however, he was free and Hartog was convinced that he could and would make a success of the Festival. It seemed a tremendous risk, but eventually the decision was taken to go ahead.

Since its fine Beethoven concerts with Ferdinand Leitner, ten years before, the CBSO had not really worked with a conductor of the 'old school' Central European tradition. From the opening bars of the Seventh Symphony, with which Schmid began his first rehearsal, it was apparent to the orchestra that his complete familiarity with and understanding of Beethoven's scores would ensure performances of great humanity, combined with intellectual rigour; and from the first concert, it became apparent to the audience too that something exciting was happening. As the Festival gathered momentum, word got around, the few empty seats filled up and the corporate sigh of relief was almost audible. The performances attracted enthusiastic reviews and the audience – desperate for good news – took Erich Schmid to its heart. One outcome was that a group of concert-goers got together spontaneously and raised enough, by voluntary donations, to make presentations on the last night of the Festival – an engraved silver box for the conductor, an orchid for his wife Martha and red and white roses for each performer and for every member of the audience. In the *Mail*, Arthur Steele gave a graphic description of the scene: 'It was roses, roses – and carnations – all the way . . . the audience stood, cheered and applauded through the most emotional demonstration I have ever seen in this hall . . . after the mighty climax of the Ninth Symphony had brought this remarkable Festival to a close. With champagne from the management came the news that Erich Schmid will be back with us next season. And yet more cheers!'[15] Long-serving CBSO bass player Charles Wall (who lists the festival amongst the two or three musical highlights of his career) sums it up as 'the right conductor at the right time.'[16]

At the end of June Erich Schmid was back, 'By special request', to conduct the four Brahms symphonies, and Harold Gray shared the direction of the CBSO Proms with Atarah Ben-Tovim and seven guest conductors; highlights included a performance in costume of *The Mikado*, with Marilyn Hill-Smith, Peter Pratt and an experienced cast conducted by Michael Moores.

So ended a season of high drama. In the May 1978 issue of *Music Stand*, George Jonas expressed the Society's sense of regret at losing the services of Louis Frémaux and Arthur Baker, and thanked them for all that they had done for the CBSO. 'In the long term, the search for a new conductor has begun. It may take a little time to find the right person.' It was to take longer than he expected.

1978–9

1978 saw a number of other changes. Arthur Maddison became Deputy Chairman; Richard Hartshorn took his place as Treasurer, with Tom Walls as his Deputy. One thing which had emerged strongly from the crises of 1978 was that the quality of communication between players and management was simply not good enough and Jonas was determined to improve it. For a number of years, two player representatives had served on the large Council of Management, but never on the far smaller Committee of Management, where the majority of important decisions were taken. Now all the Council members were grouped together (though the officers continued to meet regularly with the General Manager) and this automatically brought the player representatives[17] into the heart of the decision-making process.

In July, before the new season began, the final phase of platform alterations was carried out in Birmingham Town Hall,[18] and the CBSO moved its administrative offices from Newhall Street to more spacious accommodation in the Birmingham and Midland Institute building in Margaret Street. At last there was space for a Board Room where the various committees could meet; the CBSO Music Library, too, was transferred from a poky little room behind the Town Hall organ into a more suitable space. The post of General Manager was advertised, and from a shortlist of four, Edward Smith was appointed from the beginning of the 1978–9 season, with the author (Acting General Manager, during the interregnum) as his Deputy.[19] Ed Smith had valuable experience behind him with the Royal Liverpool Philharmonic, first as Concert Manager and later as Assistant General Manager.

All these changes helped to reinforce the feeling of 'all things new'. An editorial in the September 1978 issue of *Music Stand* caught this sense of optimism: 'It has been a difficult year, but that is behind us now and we are eagerly looking forward to an exciting season, for which advance bookings are already looking very encouraging.' Ticket prices were rising, but in order to offer patrons a more flexible deal, the weekly Thursday Series had now been arranged in such a way that they could either book for all 26 concerts or for one of two fortnightly 'half-series' of 13 concerts.

Predictably, the Thursday Series was not too adventurous, though the knowledge that the CBSO was in the market for a principal conductor made the season an unusually interesting one for talent spotters. Edward Downes opened the Thursday Series with *The Rite of Spring* and conducted two other concerts in the series, including Mahler's Sixth Symphony. Vernon Handley was also allocated three concerts, including two premières: Christopher Brown's *Triptych* (a Feeney Trust commission) and John Joubert's *Déploration for Orchestra* (a BBC commission).[20] As promised, Schmid was back with four programmes (including a Schubert 150th Anniversary Concert); David Atherton, Yuri Temirkanov, Moshe Atzmon and Gaetano Delogu took on two concerts each and other conductors included Volker Wangenheim, Brian Wright, Michi Inoue, Owain Arwel Hughes and Lawrence Foster, who included a Feeney Trust commission: John Tavener's *Palintropos*, with Stephen Bishop-Kovacevich.

A great deal of interest centred upon the concert allocated to Simon Rattle, still a month short of his 24th birthday. His first appearance with the CBSO, in Oxford, had been reasonably successful, and his follow-up concerts with the orchestra in Cheltenham and Newcastle were exceptionally happy affairs, including an exciting account of Shostakovich's Tenth Symphony, but 14

December 1978 was the first time the CBSO audience had seen him at work. Typically, there was no overture – just two great and very different masterpieces. In the first half of the concert, John Lill played Brahms's D minor Piano Concerto; in the second, Rattle, conducted Nielsen's Fourth Symphony – the *Inextinguishable*. He had only a day's rehearsal with the orchestra, but the performance was electric and the Town Hall responded to it with great enthusiasm.

Ed Smith had known and worked with Rattle throughout his time in Liverpool. Even whilst still at school, Rattle had played as an 'extra' percussionist in the Liverpool Philharmonic from time to time, and one of Smith's responsibilities had been the administration of its offshoot, the Merseyside Youth Orchestra, whose conductor Rattle had become in 1973, at the age of 18. Looking back, he feels that 'there was a distinct element of luck – things happening at the right time. It was quite by chance that I came here in 1978 from Liverpool, having known Simon since he was fifteen or sixteen and having worked with him there in the Youth Orchestra, at the very moment when the CBSO was looking for a new conductor. Simon was still an unknown quantity to most people, but not, of course, to me. I pushed very hard to have him appointed. Perhaps another General Manager would not have done.'[21] Rattle had made no secret of the fact that he wanted the CBSO position. Smith was convinced that he was the right man for Birmingham, and Rattle's London agent (Martin Campbell-White of Harold Holt Ltd) concurred, but they still had to convince everyone else.

For the first time, the members of the orchestra had a substantial input into the choice of their next conductor. In addition to Felix Kok and others serving on the Selection Committee, a poll was taken of players' opinions, which carried some weight in its deliberations. Jonas and Smith made it their business to go to see and hear many conductors at work. The former had attended two of Rattle's Liverpool concerts, summing them up as 'a total disaster', but he was brought around after hearing Rattle conduct Mozart's *Così fan tutte* with Glyndebourne Touring Opera and the Bournemouth Sinfonietta.

So the decision was taken to appoint Simon Rattle, with the slightly cumbersome title Principal Conductor and Artistic Adviser. It was known that he would not be available to take up the post until the 1980–1 season, but that seemed a relatively small price to pay in order to secure the services of someone who was already attracting a good deal of media attention, and who so evidently combined youth, energy, ideas and exceptional talent. A press conference was called for Monday, 2 July to announce the appointment and to introduce the CBSO's Conductor-Designate.[22] Some of Rattle's off-the-cuff remarks about establishing 'a sense of musical adventure' gave rise to an alarmist report in the *Post*, implying that the CBSO was about to jettison all music written before 1900; a letter from Smith to the editor allayed any such fears. Rattle subsequently remarked that he would expect to do at least one *avant-garde* piece each season, but he emphasised that the CBSO's programmes would continue to be as wide-ranging as ever: 'Louis Frémaux brought the orchestra up to a great height, and if it does not go on getting better, the only person to blame is me!'

Birmingham was changing yet again. Joseph Hansom's classical Town Hall, designed in 1834 to tower over its surroundings, now found itself dwarfed by high-rise buildings typical of the Seventies and Eighties. The recently opened National Exhibition Centre was attracting new business to the city, reflected in a CBSO 'Motor Show' concert conducted by Marcus Dods, built around the theme Entente Cordiale and sponsored by Peugeot.

In November 1978, the CBSO Chorus and the orchestra performed Britten's *War Requiem* in Chester Cathedral, conducted by Meredith Davies, who was in charge again a month later when the orchestra was engaged by the Royal Choral Society to play the same work in the Royal Albert Hall with an exceptionally distinguished team of soloists: Felicity Palmer, Peter Pears and John Shirley-Quirk. In April 1979 the chorus was back there for the BBC's Sir Adrian Boult 90th Birthday Concert, and soon afterwards they sang in *Gerontius* at the Malvern Festival, with the RPO under Yehudi Menuhin. That a choir only five years old should attract invitations of this sort was a tribute to its first chorus master, Gordon Clinton, whose health had been uncertain for some time, leading him to step down at this stage.

Bridging the gap between the end of the winter series and the July Proms was a perennial problem. The orchestra could easily become bored, and playing standards drop commensurately. Building on the success of the Beethoven Festival of 1975 and 1978, and generously sponsored by TI (Tube Investments Ltd), a Spring Festival of Russian Music was promoted in Birmingham Town Hall in May 1979, with the Finnish conductor Okko Kamu at the helm. The programmes were designed to be user-friendly and an excellent standard was achieved, but public response was somewhat disappointing.

July 1979 saw the retirement of Cyril Read, the CBSO's longest-serving member, who had joined the orchestra when it went full-time under George Weldon in 1944, and had been allowed to stay on long after normal retirement age. It was with a mixture of sadness and gratitude, too, that Birmingham bade farewell at the Last Night of the Proms to Harold Gray, OBE – retiring at last, fifty years after he had first conducted the City of Birmingham Orchestra.[23] Regular concert-goers, given an opportunity to contribute to a Presentation Fund, demonstrated by their generosity their great affection for this lovable and warm-hearted musician, enabling George Jonas to present Mr

Gray with a fine painting by Russell Flint. The players gave him a complete recording of Wagner's *Ring* cycle, so dear to his heart, and there were other handsome gifts, from the CBSO staff and the Incorporated Society of Musicians. It was typical of the man, too, that he should have wanted to express his affection for the players by giving something to *them* – appropriately enough, a handsome wooden conductor's music-stand, specially made by Dr A. D. Wardle, a member of the CBSO Society. The CBSO was immensely fortunate in having Harold Gray, OBE, as its loyal and ever-available Associate Conductor for the best part of half a century. If a conductor missed his train or was taken ill at short notice, the message was always the same – 'Give Harold a ring and ask him if he can come straight in'; and no matter what score he found on the stand when he got there, he would soon be at work so that precious rehearsal time was not lost, whether or not at the end of the day he conducted the concert itself. The Council of Management resolved to appoint him Conductor Emeritus, for life.

1979–80

There was widespread satisfaction, too, when Erich Schmid was appointed Principal Guest Conductor (a title new to the orchestra) for three seasons, from September 1979. With Rattle's appointment from the following year, the question of the orchestra's future musical direction was resolved and now in the public domain, so Smith and Council of Management[24] could concentrate all their efforts on streamlining the Society's financial and administrative infrastructure, improving player-management relations and planning for the 1980s.

It was Schmid who opened the season, with Mahler's Fifth Symphony, following it, two days later, with a performance of Mendelssohn's *Elijah*, with Benjamin Luxon in the title rôle, followed by the Brahms Violin Concerto (with Ida Haendel) and Beethoven's *Missa Solemnis*, with which the Thursday Series closed. Predictably, Rattle's one concert of the season attracted a great deal of excitement; never afraid to take risks, he chose one of his now-celebrated calling-cards – Deryck Cooke's completion of Mahler's unfinished Tenth Symphony. It posed immense technical problems for the orchestra, not all of which were solved as successfully as they would be at the symphony's next airing three years later, but it still made an extremely powerful impact on public and players alike.

Christopher Seaman was the conductor during a short but decidedly successful European tour, comprising three concerts in Yugoslavia (Belgrade,[25] Zagreb and Ljubljana) and two in Austria (Linz and Vienna). Highspot of the Yugoslavian leg of the tour was a splendid account of Shostakovich's Tenth

Symphony in Zagreb, but there were anxieties, too, since President Tito was known to be gravely ill at that time and his demise would undoubtedly have led to cancellations; in the event, he died a few days later. As in 1972, the tour soloist was John Lill. Britten's *Young Person's Guide* featured in every concert – doubly appropriate, since the Austrian concerts were promoted by Jeunesses Musicales. The programmes included Elgar's First Symphony – new to both cities. Linz's modernistic Brucknerhaus looked more impressive than it sounded, but in Vienna's justly famous Grosse Musikvereinsaal there could be no such complaints, and it proved an undoubted triumph, with Seaman having to lead Felix Kok off the platform after the tenth curtain-call. Lyndon Jenkins wrote, 'What an evening, and what a superb conclusion to a highly successful tour.'[26]

Before the season proper had begun, the orchestra was back in the studio for EMI, recording three works by Sir Arthur Bliss, with Vernon Handley conducting. Bliss's music for *Christopher Colombus* also featured in an interesting record of film-music by British composers, sponsored by Lucas Industries, to which Marcus Dods brought his considerable experience and his great expertise, and later in the season Handley made another disc, with tenor Robert Tear: orchestral songs by Elgar, George Butterworth's fine cycle *Love blows as the wind blows*[27] and the first recording of Vaughan Williams's *On Wenlock Edge*, with its orchestral accompaniment.

For the first time, the CBSO Chorus joined forces with the City of Birmingham Choir and the CBSO conducted by Norman Del Mar to present *The Dream of Gerontius* in the Royal Albert Hall, on behalf of the Elgar Foundation, with Dame Janet Baker, Kenneth Bowen and Michael Rippon as soloists. Tragically, the CBSO Chorus's newly appointed chorus master, Dr Richard Greening of Lichfield Cathedral, died suddenly following a heart attack, after taking only two rehearsals; Gordon Clinton returned to mind the shop, but he was far from well, and he was eventually succeeded by Nicholas Cleobury.[28]

Out of town, Harry Blech conducted a Brahms cycle for Eastern Authorities' Orchestral Association. In Birmingham, another TI-sponsored Spring Festival was built around the diverse talents of 'The Chung Family' – violinist Kyung-Wha, cellist Myung-Wha and conductor-pianist Myung-Whun; as with the Russian Festival, though, the programmes did not quite succeed in seizing the popular imagination. In a conscious effort to reduce the burden on the orchestra, the CBSO Proms in July were reduced to twelve concerts only, one of which was presented by a visiting orchestra.

Support from sponsors was building steadily under the guidance of the CBSO's Deputy Chairman[29] Arthur Maddison and Marketing Manger Julianna Szekely, who devised an attractive promotional brochure entitled *We're*

Making Overtures. In point of fact, overtures would be appearing less and less frequently in the CBSO's programmes, since Simon Rattle preferred to dispense with hors d'œuvres and to plunge straight into the main course; the idea was good, though, and it indicated a new willingness on the part of the CBSO's bosses to go out and win fresh support from Birmingham's largely untapped industrial and commercial base.

22

Simon Rattle – Making music an adventure

The autumn of 1980 was an eventful time for the CBSO's newly appointed principal conductor. In September, he had married the American soprano Elise Ross and they had moved into a house in Islington; for some time, though, he had promised himself that this was to be a sabbatical year from conducting, during which he would go to Oxford to read English Literature and Philosophy, and to 'catch up on some of the education I missed out on in my teens, when I was music-mad'.[1] He saw it through cheerfully, often turning up at Birmingham rehearsals with a bunch of scores and a well-thumbed copy of James Joyce's *Ulysses.*

Simon Rattle was born in Liverpool on 19 January 1955 into a musical household. His father Denis enjoyed playing jazz piano and his mother Pauline had run a music-shop in Dover. Simon's father bought him a drum-kit when he was four; he had soon battered it to death, but it was a clear pointer to the future, and as a six-year-old he started lessons with the Liverpool Philharmonic's principal percussionist John Ward. Simon's sister Susan (nine years his senior) brought home records and scores for him from the library – Bartók, Schoenberg, Tippett, Walton; before long 'he could sit and read a score, just as other children would read a comic'.[2]

What Simon called his 'road to Damascus' experience came at the age of 11, when he heard George Hurst conduct Mahler's Second Symphony. A year later (by now an accomplished pianist) he was Liverpool Youth Music Committee's Student of the Year, and in April 1970 (aged 15) he got together an orchestra, 70-strong, to give a charity concert which (of course) he conducted. He played piano and percussion on a National Youth Orchestra course led by Pierre Boulez and, a year later, went on a scholarship to the Royal Academy of Music, where he became increasingly certain that he wanted to conduct. A student performance of that same Mahler symphony in December

1973 brought his name to the attention of London's musical world, and his spectacular success in the John Player Competition in Portsmouth a year later provided him with a two-year contract to work with the Bournemouth orchestra. Neither this nor his subsequent associateship with the Liverpool orchestra was an entirely happy experience, though with the BBC Scottish Symphony Orchestra he rapidly established a good working relationship. It was all valuable experience.

Local apprehension about the new appointment stemmed partly from Rattle's declared penchant for contemporary music and partly from a sense of disbelief that this tousle-haired youth could be ready to assume such a major responsibility. As the season opened he was 25, going on 26. He would have been the last to make the comparison, of course, but the fact remains that, at that age, Mozart had nearly 400 compositions behind him, and Schubert had written a comparable number of incomparable songs. Prodigious talent is not confined to creative artists, of course – Yehudi Menuhin's wonderful 1932 recordings of Elgar's Violin Concerto was made at the age of 16, with the 75-year-old composer on the rostrum. The word 'conductor', though, seems to conjure up a more senior image – Monteux, Toscanini, Furtwängler, Stokowski or Sir Adrian Boult (with whom young Mr Rattle had shared the rostrum at a London Philharmonic concert in February 1977, the one just turned 22, the other almost exactly four times his age). Was it reasonable to expect a conductor of 25 to direct and control 80 or 90 professional musicians? Could one so relatively inexperienced really possess the interpretative maturity to move an audience, or the personality to enable him to handle those public relations responsibilities that were by that time the inevitable lot of the principal conductor of a major symphony orchestra?

1980–1

Unlike any other phase of the CBSO's history, some aspects of the period 1980–7 have already been dealt with exhaustively in print. In his interesting and well-researched book *Simon Rattle – The Making of a Conductor*,[3] Nicholas Kenyon approached those seven seasons from the standpoint of one young man's impact on Birmingham's orchestra and audience, and of theirs on him. 1980–1 was designated as the CBSO's Diamond Jubilee Season. In a foreword to the celebratory Year Book,[4] Norman St John-Stevas, MP (the Minister for the Arts) wrote perceptively,

> When Sir Edward Elgar stepped on to the podium on that November night sixty years ago to conduct a programme of his own works, he established an orchestral tradition that has continued to the present day. The CBSO has

> consistently championed the work of British composers and has been quick to recognise native musical talent. This was true in 1924 when the young Dr Adrian Boult was appointed the orchestra's Chief Conductor, and it is just as true today. In sixty years' time, the appointment of the remarkably talented Simon Rattle as the CBSO's Principal Conductor and Artistic Adviser will be looked upon as a milestone of equally significant importance.

Kenneth Loveland, too, caught (with uncanny prescience, and more penetratingly than any other writer then) the spirit of what Rattle and Smith were driving at:

> In the end, it's about communication . . . He'll make mistakes (Beecham littered the floor with them) and will often be ahead of his audience (Wood was, frequently) but, again like Beecham and Wood,[5] he'll make music an adventure, because he is a communicator . . . The sordid, the violent, the false are all around. We need an antidote to them, an alternative to the sleazy. The orchestra's rôle is to provide that antidote and that alternative. But it has to be positive . . . a force which takes quality out into the marketplace and says 'Try me'. And in Birmingham I detect a spirit which suggests that music is going over to just that attacking rôle.

The Diamond Jubilee Season was marked by a number of other major developments. Although there were now over 20 firms supporting the orchestra financially, a loss of well over £10,000 on the previous year's trading had led to severe restraints. The CBSO Society's long-running house-magazine *Music Stand*, for example, was downgraded to a duplicated news-sheet, despite a very modest saving in cost; members already received little enough for their subscriptions, and the recent establishment of a small but entirely autonomous Concert-goers' Association gave a clear indication that the Society was not fulfilling the expectations of all its members.

On a more positive note, the pattern of the orchestra's Birmingham concerts was completely rethought. Thursday Concerts were now augmented by a Tuesday Series,[6] the two operating in alternate weeks. By extending the winter season from mid-September to early May, patrons were offered the chance of booking for 16 concerts in a single series, or for 32 in both. Predictably, there were some grumbles from Thursday subscribers, but faced with offers of not less than 25% savings, many new ones were attracted to this Tuesday Series. A Saturday Family Series of seven concerts ran from January to May, now with a 7 p.m. start in order to avoid late finishes. The 12 concerts that comprised the 1981 CBSO Proms, too, included some 'heavier' symphonies than usual – Mahler Nos. 1 (Handford) and 4 (Gibson and the SNO); Brahms No. 1 (Seaman) and Sibelius No. 2 (Rattle).

*

CBSO Marketing Manager Julianna Szekely, who had worked with American orchestras, came up with a fresh approach to selling the Birmingham series: out went the old Annual Prospectus, of which a few thousand booklets had traditionally been printed and sold, and in came smart new two-colour broadsheets – 100,000 were printed and given away free. Designers Sean O'Farrell and Keith Grady of Triad Graphics devised a different corporate logo (still in use today), and a slogan for the season – Musically Yours. These changes certainly presented an exciting new image of the CBSO.

In August 1980, Norman Del Mar was the conductor for some Vaughan Williams recordings, with the CBSO Chorus.[7] Simon Rattle's Oxford term did not start until mid-October, enabling him to conduct the first four concerts of the season, but his very first performance as Principal Conductor of the CBSO was on 8 September, in front of television cameras at the BBC's Pebble Mill Studios, directing Tippett's *Concerto for Double String Orchestra*. Restricted rehearsal time and an unhelpful acoustic placed an upper limit on what could be achieved, but undeniably the performance had 'great capabilities'. Immediately afterwards, six days of intensive and detailed work provided a very necessary opportunity for Rattle and the orchestra to get to know one another better.

His declared intention was that 'every concert should be an event', and so it proved. Nevertheless, the first concert of the Diamond Jubilee season, on Thursday, 18 September, opened less than auspiciously. The work advertised to begin this IMI-sponsored programme was Janáček's *Sinfonietta*, but a special arrangement of the National Anthem was commissioned, using all Janáčak's extra trumpets. Doubtless some splendid fanfares were expected, but the audience, which had stood respectfully expecting 'God save the Queen', found itself quite unable to recognise the famous melody, and sat down again. No sooner had it done so than fragments of the tune became discernible and again some rose to their feet, amid laughter which must have been audible to those tuned in to the BBC relay. Not surprisingly, the ensuing Janáček took a while to settle down, and it was not until Sibelius's Fifth Symphony, after the interval, that it became clear that something new and exciting was happening.

A day or two later, the audience in Leeds Town Hall was, if anything, even more enthusiastic, when the CBSO and Chorus performed Szymanowski's hauntingly beautiful *Stabat Mater*, followed by the work which had proved so seminal in Rattle's career to date: Mahler's *Resurrection* Symphony, conducted without the score. On the way out, Ernest Bradbury (of the *Yorkshire Post*) was heard to remark. 'That man is a genius!' At a repeat in the Royal Festival Hall, the London critics too were extremely positive, and the concert even attracted an enthusiastic review by a visiting critic from Berlin[8] – a foretaste of what would follow, much later.

Smith and Rattle had taken a conscious decision to concentrate initially on works that Simon knew well. There were bound to be exceptions, however, and Rattle recalls that 'apart from the BBC Symphony, we were the first British orchestra to play a note of Boulez's music'.[9] His *Rituel in memoriam Bruno Maderna* was handled with great authority, excitingly played and remarkably well received. Rattle's ensuing programmes included Stravinsky, Elgar, Ravel and Britten's *Frank Bridge Variations.* He worked hard on the Britten – first with the string principals alone, then section by section and finally with them all together – and it was as well that he did, for its first performance (in Grantham Parish Church) had to be given without rehearsal *in situ*, the CBSO's instrument van having broken down *en route.*[10]

On 18 November, in the Royal Albert Hall, Rattle conducted his only date during his 'sabbatical', at the Royal Concert (attended by HRH Princess Alexandra), the programme including a highly idiomatic version of Tchaikovsky's B♭ minor Concerto by the eminent Russian pianist Emil Gilels. The CBSO's Diamond Jubilee Concert on 13 November, entrusted to Sir Charles Groves and attended by HRH the Duke of Gloucester, featured the season's Feeney Trust commission – Roger Marsh's *Still (as far as may be)* – and two of the works which Elgar had conducted at the CBO's first symphony concert sixty years before, almost to the day: his Cello Concerto (Tortelier) and the Second Symphony. Rattle, up from Oxford for the concert and the subsequent reception, was free to give a TV interview to the BBC's *Midlands Today* programme, which, after fifteen years, makes intriguing reading:

> I intend to stay as long as they'll have me – certainly I think I will have to be kicked out forcibly! I really want to build up a relationship . . . and this can only be done with time. I think people are beginning to realise that there's a flourishing musical life outside London . . . I feel that it's in the provinces that you can make some real music. We have a marvellous orchestra, one that wants to get better, something I hope we will be able to match with anything in England . . . the orchestra is younger than it may at first seem. We did a little census and discovered that there were 41 people under the age of 30 – and, for the first time in my life, there's a substantial number of people who are actually younger than I am, which is a relief! We want to expand the repertoire at both ends – to play more early music, more recent music, a wide spectrum of repertoire.

Rattle's second group of concerts led off on Thursday, 8 January 1981 with Janáček's *Glagolitic Mass*, for which the distinguished Czech choral conductor Antonín Tučapsky was brought in to help the CBSO Chorus master the Old Slavonic text. The work was also recorded for EMI.[11] Erich Schmid, in his second season as Principal Guest Conductor, included Bruckner's Seventh Symphony, Dvořák's F major Symphony and his own orchestration of Debussy's *Six Epigraphes Antiques*, besides a distinguished programme comprising Mozart's *Masonic Funeral Music*, Berg's Violin Concerto (Gyorgy Pauk) and the Brahms *Requiem*.

Distinguished performances by cellist Lynn Harrell and pianist Vladimir Ashkenazy notwithstanding, the 1980–1 season was chiefly notable for its guest conductors, who included Okko Kamu, Kurt Sanderling, Rudolf Barshai, James Conlon (an outstanding all-Ravel programme) Andrzej Panufnik and Rudolf Schwarz, with a spacious reading of Schubert's *Great C major* Symphony. Returning at the end of March, his Oxford term over, Rattle included Kurt Weill's *Seven Deadly Sins* (starring his wife, Elise Ross) and Stravinsky's *Petrushka*. The standard of orchestral playing was rising steadily, reflected in increasingly enthusiastic press comment. June saw the CBSO in Worcester for a 'Royal Elgar Concert', conducted by Donald Hunt and attended by HRH the Prince of Wales, who had earlier unveiled the new statue of the composer outside the Cathedral; but, in many ways, the outstanding event of spring 1981 was Messiaen's enormous oratorio *La Transfiguration de nôtre Seigneur Jésus Christ*, promoted by the City Choir and conducted by Christopher Robinson, with Peter Donohoe and a number of CBSO soloists.

During the season, a sad note was struck by news of the death of Hans Richter-Haaser, a regular and much-loved soloist between 1967 and 1978 and the guiding light of the CBSO's first Beethoven Festival in 1975. But, overall, though Simon Rattle's University commitments limited his availability, it proved to be a gratifying season. The Thursday Series averaged 96% attendance, and even the new Tuesday Series achieved 81%. The CBSO Proms and the Saturday Family Series (seven concerts, promoted between January and May) both averaged 90%. Lyndon Jenkins summed it up as 'the orchestra's most completely satisfactory season for years';[12] 'the successful matching of artists to music has frequently been miraculous.'[13] The auguries looked good.

1981–2

The slogan for the season was 'Good News', and, happily, there was plenty to be had. In 1980–1, about half the available seats had been sold to subscribers, and since only two-thirds of the seats in Birmingham Town Hall offered any kind of acceptable listening conditions, demand for subscription tickets was increasing rapidly. And the season opened with further good news: an announcement that Rattle had agreed to extend his CBSO contract to 1986 –

an encouraging vote of confidence at so early a stage in the relationship. He had also accepted a position as Principal Guest Conductor of Giulini's Los Angeles Philharmonic, whilst retaining his relationship with the Rotterdam Philharmonic and the Philharmonia Orchestra.

Under the headline 'Fanfare', a leading article in the *Birmingham Post*[14] warmly welcomed Rattle's extended contract. He was good news to outside promoters, too: his name on a poster undoubtedly sold tickets. There was a limit on his availability, of course, but it was only right and proper that he should also conduct at least once in every venue where the CBSO was still self-promoting against a grant; for example, a stylish programme, using only half the orchestra, on the minuscule platform of Kidderminster Town Hall.[15] Another out-of-town highlight of Rattle's second season as Director of 'South Bank Summer Music' was a concert performance at the Royal Festival Hall of Gershwin's *Porgy and Bess*, with Willard White and Laverne Williams in the title rôles and the CBSO Chorus in sparkling form. The Birmingham repeat was televised by ATV with great success.

It was a measure of the orchestra's growing prestige that, for the first time, it was invited to present two Henry Wood Proms, Simon Rattle and Erich Schmid conducting one each. It was Schmid's final season as Principal Guest Conductor. Recalling the dramatic circumstances of his first appearances in Birmingham four years before, it seemed appropriate that his final Thursday Concert, on 29 April 1982, should have ended on a triumphant note with Beethoven's *Choral* Symphony, with the combined forces of the CBSO Chorus and the City Choir. Harold Gray, who had seen so many conductors come and go in Birmingham, described Erich Schmid as 'a person whom the orchestra clearly respects, to whom the audience respond and who has kept things on an even keel here by continually presenting us with scholarly performances of the great classical repertoire.'[16]

During this season, the CBSO boasted two eminent principal guest conductors at the same time, for the Estonian Neeme Järvi, who had now made his home in the West, accepted a three-year appointment from September 1981. It would be hard to think of two conductors more different in their approach to music than Rattle and Järvi, but both have immense charisma and the instinctive ability to communicate with orchestras and audiences alike. Järvi conducted the CBSO's first recording for the Chandos label: Weber's three *concertante* works for clarinet and orchestra, with Janet Hilton as soloist. For EMI, Rattle recorded Liszt's First and Saint-Saëns's Second Piano Concertos, with Cécile Ousset, and an interesting disc of early works by Benjamin Britten, with pianists Peter Donohoe and Philip Fowke: the *Scottish Ballad, Young*

Apollo, Canadian Carnival and the exquisite *Four French Songs*, written at the age of fifteen, and wonderfully sung by Jill Gomez.

September 1981 witnessed the first CBSO performances of a work which would assume considerable importance for Simon Rattle and the CBSO: Messiaen's *Turangalîla* Symphony, with soloist Peter Donohoe. The piercing high trumpet notes and the enormous volume generated during some of the climaxes caused no great problems in the lofty spaces of Birmingham Town Hall, but in some of the smaller venues the sound sometimes reached the pain threshold – notably in Cheltenham Town Hall, where a few elderly patrons walked out in protest, and others were observed switching off their hearing-aids.

Rattle's programmes featured a number of his favourite solo artists – Ida Haendel, Alfred Brendel, Imogen Cooper, Heinz Holliger, Alfreda Hodgson, John Mitchinson. There were memorable performances of Sibelius's Fourth and Sixth Symphones, Mahler's First (with Elise Ross in Berg's *Wozzeck* Fragments) and Britten's *War Requiem*.

On a sweltering Sunday afternoon in June, Alan Fearon and the CBSO were in the pit of the newly refurbished Birmingham Hippodrome to play Carl Davis's brilliantly devised score (full of Haydn, Beethoven, Cherubini and other composers of the French Revolution period, in addition to his own music) for Abel Gance's wonderful 1927 five-hour silent film *Napoleon*. The theatre even offered a special 'Napoleon Supper'; all in all, quite an experience. Rattle conducted the Last Night of the CBSO Proms, including Grainger's suite *In a Nutshell* and Malcolm Arnold's *Grand Grand Overture* (CBSO office-staff on vacuum-cleaners and floor-polishers).

Chairman George Jonas summed it all up as 'A wonderful year, artistically . . . a standard of playing higher than I can ever remember'. Attendances were booming and audiences ever more enthusiastic, but no amount of apparent success could disguise the fact that Britain was in the middle of a nation-wide economic recession; and when the 'full house' signs are out, the only way to increase revenue is to bump up ticket prices to what may seem an unacceptable level. Despite increased grant aid,[17] the deficit on the season amounted to £38,642.

January saw the death of W. G. A. Russell, Chairman of the City of Birmingham Choir from 1937 to 1944, of the CBSO's Executive Committee from 1950 to 1963 and a member of the Management Committee until 1972. Whilst it was unquestionably Stephen Lloyd who had called the shots during the 1950s, Russell had also made a considerable contribution in his own right. Another long-serving supporter, Harold Burnett, MBE, retired from the Council of Management after 32 years' service; but some 'old soldiers' just seemed to keep going on and on: in March, Sir George Thalben-Ball reached a remarkable milestone – his 900th lunch-time organ recital in Birmingham Town Hall.[18]

1982–3

'Three Cheers for the CBSO's Subscription Series! Hear! Hear!' was the eye-catching slogan which launched the subscription brochure, reinforced with the chance of winning a Horizon holiday voucher worth £400 – a far cry from those days in the 1950s when publicity seemed to be regarded as something dangerously down-market.

October saw an important European Tour, given with financial help from the Endowment Fund. The eight venues included The Hague; the De Doelen Hall in Rotterdam; the Concertgebouw in Amsterdam; the circular Tonhalle in Düsseldorf; Bratislava's elegant white-and-gold Reduta and the Konzerthaus in Vienna.

In his end-of-year review of the best new LPs of 1982, Edward Greenfield picked out all three of Simon Rattle's initial EMI/CBSO recordings for special mention: Janáček's *Glagolitic Mass;* Cécile Ousset playing Liszt and Saint-Saëns and the early Britten disc.[19]

Whilst the CBSO had been working on Gershwin's *Porgy and Bess* in the autumn of 1981, Central Independent Television had produced a documentary. The title (*Porgy, Bess and Simon Rattle*) was clumsy, but it was skilfully compiled and well received. A leading article in the *Birmingham Evening Mail* observed that 'the splendid hour-long Central TV film about the CBSO was a welcome contribution to the education of the world south of Watford . . . The city and the orchestra are very fortunate to have such an exciting, charismatic figure as Simon Rattle as Principal Conductor. He is young, enthusiastic, exceptionally talented, and quite clearly dedicated to the development and improvement of the CBSO for some years ahead.'[20]

Simon Rattle used the forum of the TV documentary to criticise the City Council for dragging its feet over what he still saw as its inadequate financial support for the orchestra, and to emphasise once again the urgent need for a new concert hall. His remark that 'In some ways the town may not deserve the orchestra' predictably raised a few eyebrows in political circles and Jonas (who had himself been pressing hard for a new hall in the columns of the *Post*) had to smooth some ruffled feathers. However, in December Councillor Bernard Zissman confirmed the city's firm intention to build a hall – a decision was forecast within six months. Those who felt that it all sounded terribly familiar could perhaps be forgiven their scepticism, but, happily, this time they were to be proved wrong.

Another television programme (this time for the BBC) featured Kurt Weill's *Seven Deadly Sins*, which EMI also recorded; Rattle's high-profile rating was affirmed by the use of his picture on the cover of the April 1983 issue of Britain's oldest-established specialist record magazine, *Gramophone.* In February 1983, EMI's *War Requiem* project, originally planned five years before for Frémaux, finally came to fruition, with Rattle in charge. Soloists were Elisabeth Söderström, Robert Tear and Thomas Allen, with the boys of Christ Church Choir, Oxford, and the CBSO Chorus, now under its new chorus master Simon Halsey (son of the distinguished choral trainer Louis Halsey and Director of Music at the University of Warwick.) In May, Tear and Allen were back in Birmingham to record two Vaughan Williams song cycles – *On Wenlock Edge* and *Songs of Travel* – with financial help from the VW Trust. In June, Simon Rattle repeated the *War Requiem* memorably (though with a different team of soloists) in Bury St. Edmunds Cathedral, and a few days later made another EMI recording with Cécile Ousset – this time of Rachmaninov.[21]

In December, Simon Rattle and the CBSO had the honour of presenting the inaugural concert in the splendid Royal Hall, Nottingham. On the face of it, the choice of Haydn's *Representation of Chaos* to open the programme might seem to have been tempting providence, but despite one or two back-stage problems all went well. The other major event of the season took place in the Arts Centre of the University of Warwick, where, at the beginning of May, Rattle and the CBSO marked the 25th anniversary of the death of Jean Sibelius by playing all seven of his symphonies on three consecutive evenings.[22] The series generated an enormous public response, on the strength of which EMI agreed to start recording the complete Sibelius cycle during the following season. A Stravinsky Centenary Concert included the *Symphonies of Wind Instruments*, *Apollo* and *Petrushka*, with the *Circus Polka* as a jolly encore. Oliver Knussen's Third Symphony was another novelty.[23]

Undoubtedly the most overwhelming concert of the season was a coupling of Britten's deeply felt *Sinfonia da Requiem* with Mahler's Tenth and last symphony. The atmosphere of the evening – already electric – was further heightened by news of the death, at his home in Ischia, of Sir William Walton; Rattle opened the concert with the movingly simple 'Touch her soft lips and part' (from *Henry V*) as a tribute to his memory. Earlier, Neeme Järvi had opened the season with Mahler's Third Symphony, and other guest conductors included David Atherton, Mariss Jansons, Paavo Berglund and Rudolf Barshai. In May 1983, the CBSO played for the first symphony concert to be presented in the new 12,000–seat Arena at Birmingham's National Exhibition Centre;

Maurice Handford conducted a 'pop' programme, with John Ogdon as soloist in the Grieg Piano Concerto.

The CBSO Proms included Vaughan Williams's *Sea Symphony* (Christopher Seaman and the CBSO Chorus) and Vivaldi's *Four Seasons* (played and directed by Iona Brown). Once again Rattle conducted the Last Night, but this time with less success. The Viennese composer-performer H. K. Gruber's iconoclastic (and somewhat overlong) *Frankenstein!!* might just have worked in one of the winter programmes, but it did not go down at all well with the Last Night audience – still the most conservative that Birmingham could offer.

In February 1983, the musical world was saddened to learn of the death of that doyen of British conductors, Sir Adrian Boult, CH.[24] The CBSO's Conductor Emeritus Harold Gray (himself in his 80th year), who had worked as Boult's amanuensis in Birmingham in the 1920s, wrote in *Music Stand*: 'Complete integrity was the keynote to his character. He was unostentatious, never allowing his own personality to obtrude between the music and his audience. A true musician, revealing superb judgement and timing, perception and insight.'

1983–4

No CBSO season had ever opened remotely like this. A week of rehearsals, then a series of three concerts in the Royal Festival Hall marking Rattle's final year as Director of 'South Bank Summer Music', the seven Sibelius symphonies again providing the main fare, with Jessye Norman (in songs by Strauss and Ravel) and Ida Haendel (playing the Sibelius Concerto) adding spice to the programmes. Next, a revival of the programme consisting of the *Sinfonia de Requiem* and Mahler's Tenth, now even more impressive in the lofty spaces of Gloucester Cathedral and then taken on tour to Newcastle City Hall and on to the Edinburgh Festival, where Shura Cherkassky joined Rattle and the orchestra for a second concert. Then a Henry Wood Prom with Donohoe and finally a week of intensive sessions for a series of BBC TV programmes directed by Barrie Gavin: *The Year 1911*, majoring on Mahler's Tenth and Sibelius's Fourth Symphonies but also including an eclectic selection of music, ranging as widely as Webern's *Five Orchestral Pieces* and Irving Berlin's *Alexander's Ragtime Band*. And all this before the Birmingham season had even begun.

In the *Financial Times*, Andrew Clements wrote of the Sibelius cycle. 'It was a splendid, inspiriting experience . . . The CBSO produced playing of a refinement and coherence that has not been bettered and only rarely approached by other British orchestras this year; the strings especially were exceptional in their smoothness and dynamic range,'[25] while *The Times* (reviewing a concert by one of the London orchestras) noted, 'No orchestra can be envied the task of playing a note of Sibelius so soon after the CBSO's provocative and regenerating South Bank cycle under Simon Rattle.'[26]

The Birmingham season was full of interest, too (Gerald Larner expressing an opinion in the *Guardian* that 'If I had to buy a subscription for just one orchestra, it would be for the CBSO') but, as it opened, the Rattles were expecting their first child and Simon had made it clear that, in these circumstances, the old theatrical adage 'The show must go on' would not apply; so when Sacha Rattle finally put in an appearance on Friday, 30 September, his former teacher John Carewe took over the next few concerts, which included, as it happened, the first British concert performance of a work by Benjamin Britten: *An Occasional Overture*, commissioned by the BBC in 1946 to mark the opening of the Third Programme, but never publicly performed in this country.

Rattle returned in time to perform (and to record for EMI) Mahler's early cantata *Das klagende Lied* (in its complete three-movement form) and the World Première of another Britten novelty: *An American Overture*, commissioned by Arthur Rodzinski and the Cleveland Orchestra in 1941 but overtaken by the composer's wartime return to Britain, and never performed. Both these early concert overtures were committed to disc for EMI in May 1984. Other Rattle highlights included Nielsen's Fourth Symphony (with which he had introduced himself to the CBSO audience five years before); Berg's *Lulu* Suite; Mahler's Sixth Symphony (described by Felix Aprahamian as a 'triumph') and a real 'Simon Special':

Delius	Walk to the Paradise Garden
Elgar	Violin Concerto (Ida Haendel)
Grainger	A Lincolnshire Posy
Ravel (orch. Grainger)	La Vallée des Cloches
Grainger	Suite, In a Nutshell

The CBSO Chorus's Tenth Anniversary Concert was devoted to a performance of *The Dream of Gerontius* (with Dame Janet Baker and Willard White amongst the soloists) which featured, too, in Jim Berrow's Central TV Elgar documentary *Hope and Glory*. In November, the Chorus was invited by Düsseldorf's Städtischer Musikverein to supply the semi-chorus for three performances of *Gerontius*, conducted in the Tonhalle by Sir Charles Groves,[27] while the orchestra undertook a five-concert 'Klubhaus Konzerte' tour of Switzerland, with Principal Guest Conductor Neeme Järvi and violin soloist Dmitri Sitkovetsky. Järvi contracted a virus infection; he looked terrible but braved it out, as some excellent press notices confirmed. The weather was dire, but by the time the party reached Bern for the final concert of the tour the sun was shining brightly, encouraging some to visit the celebrated Bear-Pit, where the animals that give the city its name are kept fat on carrots thrown to them by visitors. Instead of a carrot, however, General Manager Edward Smith accidentally threw one of his gloves; a bear chewed it thoughtfully, but soon found that he preferred carrots.

The 1983–4 season was Järvi's last with the orchestra. Looking back on his three years with the CBSO, Simon Rattle says, 'In many ways, Neeme reminded me of John Pritchard, who was the conductor in Liverpool during my formative years; both had an unobtrusive, near-perfect technique, but both seemed to be subject to the mood of the day.' Tying the sanguine Järvi down to plan a programme and stick to it was always something of a problem. 'At one planning meeting, he said, "I think I'd really like to do a Beethoven cycle"; then he thought about it for a moment, turned to me, and said, "or maybe a Tubin cycle".'[28]

More inducements were being offered to subscribers; for example, a new 'Top Deck Rover' was introduced – a flexible arrangement for booking heavily discounted seats in the Upper Gallery, which had generally proved harder to sell. Flexibility was also the keynote in an offer to 'mix' and match' tickets for a minimum of 10 concerts from the Tuesday or Thursday Series, at a saving of up to 15%. Around this time, too, the Society introduced its new 'Minim Club'; children attending their first CBSO concert got a chance to meet the conductor, soloist and members of the orchestra, plus a badge and a certificate. There was a big initial response to the scheme and soon the club had over 600 members, of whom Sacha Rattle (then aged five months) was unquestionably the youngest.

Individual programmes for CBSO promotions were discontinued and smart new 'programme-books' introduced, covering eight concerts to a book and selling for £1.50. This represented a big saving for regular subscribers, but a swingeing increase for the casual concert-goer. Sponsorship was on the up-and-up, netting a record £121,472. During the early 1980s, commercial radio companies had a legal obligation to spend 2% of their revenue on live music; as a result, very large sums of money were coming in to the CBSO from BRMB Radio, and a new audience was reached through concerts for young people, senior citizens and others who might never previously have thought of attending a symphony concert or of listening to one on the radio.

Reviewing 1983, the critic of the *Financial Times* noted, 'Perhaps the most gratifying experience was the emergence of the City of Birmingham Symphony

Orchestra under Simon Rattle as a band of international stature, putting most of its rivals to shame.'[29] As Edward Smith points out, 'We were fortunate that we were able to expand our out-of-town work through the arrival "in our patch" during the early Eighties of three really excellent new halls: Nottingham's Royal Hall, Derngate in Northampton and the Arts Centre at the University of Warwick, which soon became EMI's favoured recording venue. St David's Hall in Cardiff, too, is a quick trip down the motorway, and it rapidly became another important addition to our out-of-town range.[30] At the very time when we were beginning to lose some of our traditional choral dates, these fine new venues were coming on stream, with new series, new budgets and new approaches.'[31]

During the financial year 1983–4 the total cost of running the Society's activities was £1.75m, the item called 'Maintenance of Orchestra' alone topping the £1m mark for the first time. The Arts Council and West Midlands County Council contributed over £700,000 towards this, and Birmingham's grant was boosted to over £100,000 as the result of a one-off grant of £60,000, designed to enable the CBSO to write off its accumulated deficit. Average attendance for Birmingham promotions reached the record figure of 96% and through its own activities the CBSO was able to raise £928,000 (an increase of £170,000 on the previous year).

All in all, things were looking up, but behind the scenes there were some very real anxieties about how the orchestra's recent exciting progress could be maintained and built upon, in the context of continuing low salaries and the loss of key players to London orchestras. A radical new approach was called for. The idea of the Development Plan was born.

23

The Development Plan

The Arts Council's report 'The Glory of the Garden' (published in March 1984) caused alarm and despondency in London and some optimism amongst the regional orchestras, but it produced little in the end. The proposal to move a London orchestra to the East Midlands, lock, stock and barrel, was never a starter, but any suggestion of this sort served to emphasise once again the importance of the CBSO's Development Plan. Its gestation period was extended, complex and (at this stage, at all events) conducted in strict confidence; we shall encounter it again later.

1984–5

Simon Rattle's customary start-of-season period of intensive rehearsal was followed by a Henry Wood Prom and EMI recordings of Nielsen's Fourth Symphony, with *Pan and Syrinx* as an attractive make-weight. Then off to Europe for two concerts of major importance: to Paris, for the Festival d'Automne at the Châtelet, and to the Berlin Festival, to play for the first time in the impressive modern Philharmonie. The Paris programme (which included Xenakis's *Synaphai*) attracted good reviews for orchestra and conductor ('ce compatriote des Beatles . . . un nouveau grand') but the bold move of playing Brahms/Schoenberg and Sibelius to a largely uncomprehending Parisian audience did not entirely pay off. Predictably, the Berliners were far more receptive to these works, prefaced this time by the first continental performance of Britten's *American Overture*. The concert was cheered to the echo, and even when Rattle felt (after countless curtain-calls) that he must finally take Felix Kok and the orchestra off the platform, he had to return again, on his own, to acknowledge the continuing applause.

Beneath the headline *'Eine phänomenale Begabung'* ('A phenomenal talent'), Albrecht Dümling of *Der Tagesspiegel* described 'this brilliant début': 'Orchestras of greater renown, directed by conductors of greater fame, have played during the Berlin Festival this year, but none of these concerts equalled the performance of the City of Birmingham Symphony Orchestra, under its young principal conductor Simon Rattle.'

It was just 150 years since Joseph Hansom's Town Hall had been opened. Following the retirement of Sir George Thalben-Ball,[1] the brilliant 25-year-old Thomas Trotter was appointed City Organist, completing, alongside the two Simons – Rattle and Halsey – an astonishingly young team in charge of Birmingham's musical life. Trotter's first task was to engage the London firm of Manders to overhaul the Hill organ, to his specification. The original Town Hall organ was installed by Birmingham General Hospital, so it was appropriate that it should have benefited from the first of a series of annual charity concerts organised by Ken Maslen to support its work by purchasing much-needed new equipment.

The Birmingham season had opened with a Feeney Trust commission:[2] a work for oboe d'amore (Peter Walden), guitar (John Williams) and orchestra by the Japanese composer Toru Takemitsu, entitled *Vers l'arc-en-ciel, Palma*. Takemitsu's was not the only rainbow-inspired work in the season – indeed, the cover design of the broadsheet was based on *The Rainbow Snake*, by the Danish composer Erik Nørby, which Maurice Handford included in an October concert. One of the CBSO's former principal conductors, Andrzej Panufnik, returned with his *Sinfonia Sacra*; Michael Schønwandt included Hindemith's symphony *Mathis der Maler*; Bryden Thomas programmed Harrison Birtwistle's *Triumph of Time*; Martin Turnovsky conducted Martinů's Concerto for Two String Orchestras, Piano and Timpani and Simon Preston directed a performance of Monteverdi's 1610 *Vespers*, with the CBSO Chorus and the Parley of Instruments. Both in Cheltenham Town Hall (now handsomely repainted) and in Birmingham, further highlights of the season were two Erich Schmid Farewell Concerts, featuring Bruckner's mighty Ninth Symphony. The prolonged standing ovation which greeted its final performance could have left Professor Schmid in no doubt of the warm affection in which he was held by an ever-grateful Birmingham audience.

Rattle's wide-ranging programmes included Walton's First Symphony and Mahler's Seventh, and two major scores by Ravel, in consecutive weeks: a complete *Daphnis et Chloë* and a concert performance of *L'enfant et les sortilèges*, with Elise Ross in the title rôle. Two enterprising TV documentaries were made: the BBC's *Young Apollo* dealt with some of Benjamin Britten's earliest works, including the première of a hitherto-unperformed *Humoresque*, written at Gresham's School, Holt, at the age of fifteen. Percy Grainger was the subject of an ITV programme – *The Noble Savage* – which included extracts from his extraordinary score for the ballet *The Warriors.*

The musical press was becoming increasingly alert to the CBSO's development. In his end-of-year summary in the *Financial Times*, Andrew Clements picked out two orchestras for special mention: 'The Philharmonia (under some conductors) and the City of Birmingham Symphony Orchestra (consistently) remain the most refined of home-based bands; the CBSO manages to maintain an admirable level of freshness and excitement for its London appearances.'[3]

At the end of the winter season, Rattle and the orchestra were off on their first visit to Italy, including concerts in Florence, Rome, Bologna and Birmingham's twin city Milan. The concert in La Scala, especially, received excellent notices, but Edward Smith's feeling is that 'it was an ill-fated tour. Nothing was right about it: some of the venues were unsatisfactory, and the repertoire was difficult for those audiences.'[4]

At the Annual General Meeting in September 1984, it was announced that Stephen Lloyd had decided to retire from the Council of Management, after 34 years, 18 of them as Chairman. On behalf of the Society, George Jonas presented him with a framed photo of Simon Rattle and the orchestra playing in the Philharmonie, Berlin, the mount signed by all previous principal conductors of the orchestra still living: Schwarz, Panufnik, Frémaux and Rattle, plus the CBSO's Conductor Emeritus, Harold Gray. Lloyd continued, however, to chair the Endowment Fund. Changed circumstances meant that the long-running 'split dates' in the very small Town Halls of Kidderminster and Sutton Coldfield no longer made commercial sense; already reduced from four to two concerts a year, they were dropped altogether at the end of the season.[5] Another landmark was the CBSO Chorus's first *a capella* concert – 'The Bach Connection' – conducted by Simon Halsey in St Mary's Church, Warwick; the Chorus also took part in a performance of Mahler's *Resurrection* Symphony, with which Simon Rattle opened the CBSO Proms.

The season saw the launch of the CBSO's enterprising 'Adopt-a-Player' scheme: individual members of the orchestra worked with pupils in seven local schools, finally all coming together to a CBSO rehearsal and concert in the Town Hall. There was encouraging news, too, about plans for Birmingham's International Convention Centre and the concert hall which was to form such a significant part of it.

Simon Rattle and the entire CBSO team were joint recipients of the prestigious 'Midlander of the Year' award, made annually by the brewers Bass, Mitchells & Butlers. Compact discs, which had made their first appearance a couple of years previously, were now catching on fast; the CBSO's first CD transfers were Britten's *War Requiem* (EMI) and the Weber Clarinet Concertos (Chandos). In the American magazine *High Fidelity*,[6] Rattle did some crystal-gazing: 'I'd hope that I'll be with the CBSO for a long, long time yet. I'd hope that I could bring them to a level where it would be ludicrous for me to leave.' It was by no means the first time he had talked like this, and it should have been required reading for those London-based musical gurus who kept affirming that Rattle was only waiting for the right vacancy to crop up before he upped and moved on to one of the 'international' orchestras.

1985–6

With five extremely successful CBSO seasons behind him, Rattle now took on a new supporting team: the Finn Okko Kamu ('a magnificent spontaneous conductor whom I admire tremendously')[7] replaced Neeme Järvi as Principal Guest Conductor, with responsibility for fifteen concerts a year; Iona Brown, who took up the newly created post of Guest Director, was allocated ten concerts. Both appointments were for three years, and both were aimed especially at building and refining the string playing.[8] Kamu had led the Helsinki Opera House orchestra before becoming an internationally recognised conductor, and Brown[9] had led the Academy of St Martin in the Fields for some years before taking over its musical direction from Neville Marriner. Rattle too entered into a new contract, committing him to the CBSO up to August 1989; there was a built-in option which could extend it by a further two years to August 1991, by which time the new concert hall should be a reality, but it was made very clear that this extension would depend on the implementation of the promised Development Plan, whose advance planning was still at a comparatively early stage.

A televised Henry Wood Prom included Mahler's *Das Lied von der Erde* (with Jessye Norman and Jon Vickers). A few days later, Simon Rattle and the CBSO were in the Arts Centre at the University of Warwick to record a fascinating selection of music for a BBC television documentary entitled *East meets West*, including excerpts from Holst's oriental suite *Beni Mora*: Koechlin's *Les Bandars-log* Nielsen's *Aladdin* and even *In a Persian Market* by Birmingham's own Albert Ketèlbey.[10]

A week later, they were back again for an EMI recording of Bartók's Concerto for Two Pianos and Percussion[11] with the Labèques. Other recordings included Messiaen's *Turangalîla* and Mahler's Second Symphony (with Arleen Auger, Dame Janet Baker and the CBSO Chorus). The Messiaen and Mahler (played on consecutive evenings at the Brighton Festival) produced some of the most exciting playing to date. At a Bath Festival concert, Olivier Messiaen himself turned up, unannounced, to attend a performance of *Turangalîla*, in the radiant acoustic of Wells Cathedral.[12] But it was not only the performance of vast romantic symphonies that concerned Simon Rattle at the time:

> I can't stress too highly how the stylistic battles of the Seventies and Eighties have marked out my whole generation of conductors; even now, a great swathe of music is more in flux than it's ever been. What people felt about the performance of classical music fifteen years ago has been turned almost on its head by the impact of the Early Music movement, but very few of the symphony orchestras have really taken this on board. There was a time, during my early years in Birmingham, when I began to realise that I was painting myself into a corner. My view of this music had changed; I had one leg on the boat and one on the pier, and as the boat moved steadily further and further away from the pier, I had to choose which way to jump – or, at best, split my trousers! It was really a matter of us learning together – being a kind of laboratory. I was quite used to being an evangelist for 20th-century music; now it was our approach to *classical* music that started to become more radical, but it's been really impressive to see the open-mindedness with which the players have been willing to take new techniques on board. I remember the first time we started working together in this new way, in January 1986. I chose Haydn's Symphony No. 70 specifically, as it has a lot of baroque references. I remember wondering how Felix [Kok, the Leader, who had worked with all the major post-war conductors – Karajan, Klemperer, Böhm, Kempe, Cantelli] would take it, to the extent where I didn't do what I would do now, which would be to call the section-leaders together and say, "Look, this is what I'm trying to do. Bear with me – I need your help." Instead, I just went straight in with it; and one of the things that I shall love Felix forever for was his immediate interest and total co-operation in this new approach.[13]

September 1985 saw the opening of the new 500-seat Adrian Boult Hall, purpose-built to serve as a rehearsal room for the CBSO and the Chorus, and as a concert hall for Birmingham School of Music. At the same time, the orchestra moved its administration into offices adjoining the new hall, greatly enhancing contact between staff and players and providing a valuable link with the School of Music, with which it would now share a building. Unfortunately, neither the hall nor the offices have proved entirely suitable. Since 1985, orchestra and staff have grown and, ten years on, there are plans afoot for a much-needed CBSO Centre.

West Midlands County Council was abolished and Birmingham City Council took over responsibility for the CBSO's local authority funding, agreeing to write off the Society's accumulated deficit of nearly £37,000. Demand for Tuesday, Thursday and Saturday winter concerts was now so heavy that a new monthly Wednesday Series was introduced, with a helpful development grant from the Arts Council of £13,400. 'Selling' the CBSO was becoming an increasingly important matter. However laudatory the press, it was vital that the message should get through not only to the punters but to local authorities and sponsors. Around twenty of the winter-series concerts each season were now underwritten, but as the recession started to bite deeper, commercial sponsorship became increasingly hard to secure. On a more encouraging note, though, the Society entered into an arrangement with the LSO whereby Rattle and the CBSO would present several concerts each season in its Barbican series. The Birmingham season included Alfred Brendel's towering performances of Beethoven's Fourth and Brahms's First Piano Concertos; in February 1986 the CBSO repeated them with him in Paris's Théâtre des Champs-Élysées. As Simon Rattle remembers, 'The other highlight was to be able to work with Brendel . . . and to be able to do what he asked instead of *nearly* being able to do it, which was always our experience before!'[14]

Elgar's Second Symphony opened the season; in the *Listener*, Meredith Oakes (who heard the live broadcast) found it 'proof that Rattle can deliver great performances, not just brilliant ones'. Maria Ewing and Willard White were the soloists in Bartók's *Duke Bluebeard's Castle* and Dame Janet Baker headed the cast in *Gerontius* at the Edward Boyle Memorial Concert, attended by HRH the Duchess of Kent. One Rattle programme is worth quoting in full, both for its originality and for its satisfying symmetry:

Beethoven	Overture, Leonora No. 1
Sibelius	Symphony No. 3
Beethoven	Overture, Leonora No. 2
Sibelius	Symphony No. 7
Beethoven	Overture, Leonora No. 3

'That was one of the wilder ideas . . . there are five towering masterpieces in this programme and although it's not particularly long, I can assure you that it feels like conducting two and a half Mahler symphonies.'[15]

Sir Charles Groves conducted six beautifully paced performances of Brahms's Third Symphony.[16] These were exciting times – thrilling concerts, stunning reviews. But in his book *In the Orchestra*,[17] one of Britain's musical elder statesmen, the clarinettist Jack Brymer, shrewdly picked up some negative aspects, too: 'All this looks and certainly feels like success, and I am sure the members are very happy to be on the crest of a wave. However, a glance at [recent] annual reports indicates it is all being done . . . without the sort of prosperity which guarantees long-term loyalty from even the most devoted members.' The Society's turnover in the financial year 1985–6 had reached the £2¼m mark, with a deficit of £32,000 covered by Arts Council guarantee.

Ahead, though, lay the Great Unknown. Faced with these concerns, and in the midst of all this activity, the CBSO's Development Plan had quietly been taking shape.

As long ago as 1982[18] Simon Rattle had laid great stress on the need for salaries to be increased and working conditions to be improved. 'We needed to pay people more: an orchestra isn't a charity, and our rank-and-file strings were earning less than Birmingham bus-drivers . . . it was clear to me what a difference just having one or two really good people in important positions in the orchestra made: perhaps a system of co-principals could help to lift the thing on to a new plane. The players needed to work less hard, not to do absolutely every date.'[19]

The starting-point of the Development Plan was that 'the CBSO and the City of Birmingham together provide a uniquely fertile ground in which to cultivate an orchestra of great international prestige under the direction of a distinguished British conductor'. Its avowed object was to turn the CBSO 'from a very good British regional orchestra into one of the highest international calibre which would *consistently* challenge the standards set by the world's greatest orchestras. Such an orchestra would be to British musical life what the Royal Shakespeare Company is to British theatre – a national and international cultural institution which happened to be based in the regions rather than in London.' It stressed the absolute primacy of retaining the services of Simon Rattle beyond the term of his existing three-year contract, which would involve fulfilling certain conditions:

1. A new concert hall for the CBSO in Birmingham;
2. The enlargement of the string sections and the employment of additional experienced string principals;
3. Improved pay and conditions for the orchestral musicians so as, first, to attract the best possible talent to Birmingham, and then to retain it rather than have the CBSO used as a stepping-stone;
4. The ability to undertake adventurous and enterprising tours and projects and explore new fields of contemporary music.

Intensive and persistent lobbying by the CBSO, long-sightedness on the part of the city's politicians, some adroit manipulation by its chief executive Tom Caulcott[20] and substantial subvention from the EEC had seen to it that plans for the International Convention Centre were going ahead,with its second largest space a custom-built 2200–seat hall whose acoustics and interior design were to be overseen (at Rattle's urgent behest) by Artec of New York, 'whose track-record of success is unmatched'.

Condition 2 was certain to be controversial, since it involved the appointment of eleven more players, bringing the orchestra's theoretical establishment up to 101.[21] These additions were to include 'a new senior string player in each of the five string sections', the front-desk players in each section generally playing alternately, though for recordings, tours or major concerts both would play. The incumbent section principals might see the new arrivals as a threat to their prestige, but the Plan also offered them a substantial amount of time off.

Condition 3 was a logical extension of this; to attract tip-top London players to the new co-principal positions, the salaries offered would have to be enhanced. It was therefore essential that *all* the musicians receive a higher level of remuneration, linked to a much more flexible working week, which would offer them more time for practice, for teaching, for other musical activities and for themselves and their families.

On 2 May 1986, the Development Plan was submitted in outline form to the Arts Council and the City Council, with an application for substantial funding from each body. Smith and Rattle were then invited to present their case to the Arts Council's music panel – a sufficiently unusual procedure in itself to reinforce the feeling that everyone involved knew that they were dealing with a matter of considerable national importance.[22]

1986–7

It must have given Birmingham's Lord Mayor, Councillor Denis Martineau, great pleasure to host a Civic Luncheon in October for Jacques Delors, President of the European Commission, who had just laid the foundation stone of the ICC, which was to incorporate the city's new concert hall. At the same time, the CBSO's administration was extensively rethought, Edward Smith being redesignated Chief Executive.

Recording sessions dominated the season. One important new EMI project was to record many of the major Stravinsky ballets, starting with *Petrushka*, which was coupled with the Symphony in Three Movements. In addition, the final Sibelius symphonies were recorded – Nos 4, 5 and 6, plus the Violin Concerto (with Nigel Kennedy). Other exciting projects included Elgar's *Dream of Gerontius* (Baker, Mitchinson, Shirley-Quirk and the Chorus) and, for Chandos, Shostakovich's powerful Symphony No. 13 (*Babi Yar*), with Okko Kamu and a large chorus of men drawn from the CBSO Chorus, the City Choir and Warwick University. Simon Halsey and the CBSO Chorus also made their first recording for Conifer: music by Elgar and Holst.

More television documentaries took shape, too, featuring Berlioz, Robin Holloway and Luciano Berio's *Sinfonia*, which also featured in two concerts at the Edinburgh Festival. The CBSO's long-serving principal bassoonist,

Andrew Barnell, had reason to regret the fact that he and his wife owned identical suitcases. She arrived at her local Oxfam Shop to discover that her case contained a tail-suit; he, for the concert, with a caseful of baby-clothes and ladies' underwear.

There was sadness at news of the death of Maurice Handford, aged only 58, CBSO staff conductor 1970–4, and a regular visitor since, and at the death of the CBSO's first chorus master, Gordon Clinton, at the age of 75; a few days later, his widow Phyllis died also; at a Memorial Concert in St Paul's Church, Simon Halsey conducted the CBSO Chorus, with his deputy Peter King at the organ, in a moving performance of Fauré's *Requiem*. Another who died during in the season was Paul Beard, who had led the old CBSO with such distinction under Appleby Matthews, Boult and Heward for ten years from 1922, before going to London, where he was chiefly remembered as the autocratic but highly respected Leader of the BBC Symphony Orchestra.

Okko Kamu included Tchaikovsky's First Symphony and Iona Brown was soloist and director in Bach and Mozart. Maxim Shostakovich conducted his father's *Leningrad* Symphony (a Birmingham première), Mark Elder conducted Berlioz's *Roméo and Juliette*, Eduardo Mata directed Falla's ballet *The Three-Cornered Hat* and the young English conductor Sian Edwards introduced Tippett's Fourth Symphony to Birmingham. A City Choir concert featured Michael Berkeley's highly-charged *Or shall we die?* Paul Griffiths of *The Times* was bowled over by Rattle's first Birmingham performance of Beethoven's Ninth Symphony: 'a performance . . . so utterly candid it was a benediction.'

Over the Easter holidays, the CBSO Chorus undertook its first overseas trip, to the USA. Simon Halsey, Chairman Mike Cox and his committee raised sponsorship from Central Television and set up the tour, in partnership with the CBSO administration. In San Francisco they joined forces with the resident Symphony Orchestra and its chorus for four performances of Beethoven's *Choral* Symphony under Wolfgang Sawallisch, then went north to present four concerts (Sacramento, Portland, Seattle, Vancouver) mainly of *a capella* music. In June, Rattle and the orchestra undertook their first tour of Japan, sponsored by Jaguar Cars. The nine concerts (including five in different halls in Tokyo) were adjudged a big success – after the first, in Matsudo, Rattle, players and members of staff were amazed to find themselves mobbed by Japanese schoolgirls clamouring for autographs.

Soon after their return, on Sunday, 21 June 1987, a new and exciting venture, started by CBSO cellists Simon Clugston and Ulrich Heinen – Birmingham Contemporary Music Group – was launched in the Adrian Boult Hall, with financial help from West Midlands Arts, the Endowment Fund and other trusts. Simon Rattle became its Artistic Adviser and Peter Donohoe its Musical Director, for the first couple of seasons, during which it was experimenting with repertoire and finding out which players 'fitted in' best.

In July 1987, the Prince and Princess of Wales attended a special televised concert marking the tenth anniversary of Birmingham's National Exhibition Centre. Simon Rattle, who had been awarded the CBE in the New Year's Honours,[23] conducted a popular programme which included Borodin's *Polovtsian Dances* (with the CBSO Chorus and the Seattle Symphony Chorale) and Ravel's *Bolero*, featuring an astonishing laser show. 1987 also saw the publication of Nicholas Kenyon's book *Simon Rattle – The Making of a Conductor.*

Predictably, anything as revolutionary as the Development Plan was certain to receive a mixed press, and it could not be kept under wraps for ever. When the story finally broke in the *Observer*, in October 1986, there was talk in the media of a 'Super-Orchestra' and some understandable comments from London bands (all of which received far less subsidy than their opposite numbers in the regions) along the lines of 'Who do they think they are, then?' Nor were managements of the other regional orchestras any too happy to learn that the CBSO, for so many years a party to national negotiations on wages and working conditions with the Musicians' Union, would now be going it alone. But, quizzed by Terry Grimley of the *Birmingham Post* at a Press Conference, Rattle played down the 'hype' with great skill: 'We basically want a bit more to enable us to do more of what we are doing already, to enable the players to be paid better and to give us more rehearsal time. I will believe it all when it actually happens.'

Whatever anyone said publicly, many influential people were saying privately that the Plan was well thought out and presented, that the charismatic Mr Rattle and his orchestra might just be able to pull off this coup, and that, in so doing, they would be injecting much-needed new life into Britain's somewhat stagnant orchestral life. The proof was in the pudding: in a *Financial Times* review of the musical scene during 1986, Andrew Clements observed that 'there is no doubt the concerts the CBSO have brought to London with Simon Rattle have been of a quality that only the Philharmonia on its highest current form could have matched.[24]

The timetable appended to the Plan had envisaged full implementation by October 1987, but it was March before funding could be secured from the City Council and the Arts Council, along with confirmation of Rattle's extended contract. The period between September and December 1986 had been allocated for 'Advertising and auditioning for new players and opening of negotiations with the orchestra', but this always looked like wishful thinking; the Plan would stand or fall on those negotiations and any question of boosting the CBSO's establishment would have to await until they had been completed.

Michael Buckley, the CBSO's General Manager, was singularly well-qualified to lead the complex negotiations, for he could see the players' point of view as well as the management's. He had joined as a violinist in 1967 and for a while served as Chairman of the Players' Committee. Later he joined the staff as Orchestra Manager, being promoted to Assistant Chief Executive in 1987 and General Manager (Personnel and Touring) in 1989. Over a period of several weeks he and Rattle discussed the Plan with the players, in groups of about ten at a time, culminating in a plenary meeting in the Library Theatre in Paradise Place.

1987–8

The CBSO Development Plan was accepted by the Musicians' Union on 14 January 1988, and by the orchestra's own players two weeks later, though only by a very small margin. Advertisements were placed for a string of new positions, attracting over 600 applicants, roughly half of whom were called for audition. Buckley remembers that at one time there were 40 trialists playing, in virtually every section of the orchestra, but gradually sheep were separated from goats, and the new appointments began to come on stream; the standard was extremely high and the average age extremely low.[25]

The season began with a week of rehearsals, for part of which the strings were coached by the Russian violinist Victor Liberman, Leader of the Concertgebouw Orchestra, while the wind players worked with Rattle; with such detailed work, it was small wonder that the standard of playing quickly improved. There were two Henry Wood Proms, the first featuring Mahler's First Symphony and the second the versatile Swedish soprano Elisabeth Söderström, in *Songs of the Auvergne* and Sibelius's exquisite *Luonnotar*. Then off to Europe again, for concerts in Finland, Belgium, Luxembourg and Germany. Smith remembers especially the second of the Helsinki concerts: 'The Festival laid on coaches to take the whole orchestra out to Ainola [Sibelius's home] after our rehearsal; there was a wonderful atmosphere, and after that it seemed just right to go back to the Finlandia Hall and play the composer's last three symphonies to the Finns.'[26] Writing in the *Helsingin Sanomat*, Professor Erik Tawaststjerna wrote, 'the supreme triumph of this evening of symphonies, in my opinion, was the performance of No. 7.'

Concerts in Ghent and Esch (attended by the Grand Duchess, for whom the Luxembourgian National Anthem was duly performed) were followed by two in the splendid Alte Oper in Frankfurt, including the Sibelius programme, several critics remarking favourably on the 'near-inaudible *pianissimi*' which were becoming something of a hallmark of Rattle/CBSO performances. The final concert of the tour, in the Philharmonie, formed part of the 1987 Berlin Festival, of which a special feature was music by *emigré* composers. Invited to suggest a work, Rattle immediately thought of his old friend Berthold Goldschmidt, who, as a Jew, had been hounded out of pre-war Germany by the Nazis. 'Simon rang me to ask if I had written a short orchestral piece which he and the orchestra could include in their programme. I said, "Yes – the *Ciaconna Sinfonica*." "Do you have a tape?" "Yes, I do." "Good, I'll come right over and listen to it." He listened to the tape; then he said, "That's exactly the piece to open the programme." '[27] The conductor, the orchestra and especially the composer received a tremendous ovation after the Goldschmidt – Berliners atoning, perhaps, for the crimes of their forebears.

Back in the UK, they played for the televised finals of the Leeds International Piano Competition, earning warm accolades for their sensitive accompaniments. Next on the itinerary was Nottingham's Royal Hall, for another daring project: the four Brahms Symphonies (not generally regarded as Rattle repertoire at that time) in two days; they were subsequently repeated in Birmingham, and followed by the UK première of *Harmonium*, by the Californian composer John Adams. The concert on 3 December 1987 in which Dame Janet Baker gave exquisite performances of Mahler's *Rückert Lieder* and Brahms's *Alto Rhapsody* was her last with the CBSO prior to her retirement.

In *Gramophone*, Michael Kennedy gave Simon Rattle's EMI recording of Mahler's Symphony No. 2 a rave review, and in *The Times*, Paul Griffiths commented that 'Even among the crowding peaks of Simon Rattle's achievements with the City of Birmingham Symphony Orchestra, their new recording of Mahler's *Resurrection* Symphony is something outstanding. And it is very much "their" success, a joint effort, not merely because the playing is so wonderful but also, and more importantly, because Rattle's tempos are felt and breathed by everyone concerned.'[28]

EMI recording sessions were dominated by Stravinsky (including *The Firebird* and *The Rite of Spring*), together with music of the Second Viennese School: Schoenberg's *Five Pieces, op. 16*; Webern's *Six Pieces, op. 6* and Berg's *Lulu Suite* (with Arleen Auger). Concert highlights included Mahler's Ninth Symphony, and his *Four Last Songs* (Maria Ewing); two concert performances of Oliver Knussen's opera *Where the Wild Things Are*, conducted by the composer; the final scene from *Die Walküre* (Phyllis Cannan and Willard White) and the British and London premières of Henri Dutilleux's Violin Concerto, played quite superbly by Isaac Stern. The sudden death of another great violinist, Henryk Szeryng, in March 1988, was a sad blow, Gyorgy Pauk replacing him admirably in the Berg Concerto.

At Easter 1988, the CBSO undertook its longest and most ambitious overseas tour to date, this time to the USA – a 15-concert coast-to-coast affair, planned in association with Frank Salomon and made possible by sponsorship from Merrill Lynch & Co. Inc, Republic New York Corporation and the Endowment Fund. The first seven concerts were given on the West Coast, including four in Los Angeles (where CBSO players Mark Goodchild and Cathy Hamer decided to get married, and were given a splendid wedding-cake by the LA Philharmonic) and one in San Francisco; the remaining eight took place on the East Coast, including the Kennedy Center (Washington, DC); Carnegie Hall and Lincoln Center (New York); and Symphony Hall, Boston (where CBSO cellist Ian Ludford raised a substantial sum for Birmingham Children's Hospice by competing in the Boston Marathon). The *New York Post* spoke of 'an outstanding Carnegie Hall concert (how exciting to see the "Sold Out" signs up there)' and *Newsday* added, 'A thrilling evening of music. If you haven't heard them yet, beg, borrow or steal a ticket.'

Immediately after this tour, Rattle took a long-planned six-month sabbatical. For the players, though, there was one more big project in store. The CBSO Proms had by now given way to a brief 'Summer Season', but on this occasion it was preceded by two complete cycles of Beethoven symphonies, conducted by Walter Weller, played in Birmingham and Northampton and subsequently recorded (extremely successfully) for Chandos, with the help of sponsorship from Glynwed. In an interview with Sir Simon, in February 1995, I asked him whether he agreed that, especially during his early years in Birmingham, the orchestra had played a good deal better for him than it generally had for guest conductors? 'Yes, and it's something I've really had to work on. I found it very noticeable that they adapted by far the best to those conductors who told them exactly what they wanted, and insisting on getting it. One of the great joys of working with Walter Weller was that he was absolutely precise about what to do and how to do it. His approach to Beethoven is very different from my own, of course, but I came to his concerts with enormous pleasure and enjoyment – his account of Beethoven No. 7 was, I think, the most exciting I've ever heard.'

By the summer of 1988, with the first phase of its Development Plan beginning to come on stream and funding in place to make that possible, the CBSO had reached the point where, in the view of many highly qualified musicians, the sky was the limit. The main limiting factor remaining was Birmingham Town Hall.

24

Symphony Hall

'Everybody knows that no other conductor and orchestra in the country are consistently, year after year, delivering work of this quality. But as long as it continues to happen, we may as well keep on saying so.' Robert Maycock's remark[1] stemmed from a Rattle/CBSO performance of Shostakovich's Fifth Symphony at the Barbican, but it was in no way exceptional; the *Yorkshire Post*, for example, had no hesitation in stating that 'The orchestra is without doubt the finest in the country',[2] and, in Birmingham, 'Average attendances at Town Hall concerts have now crept up another percentage point to 98%, and a waiting list has had to be introduced for subscriptions. Ed Smith identifies the capacity of the Town Hall – 1750 – as the main factor holding back the orchestra at the moment.'[3]

1988–9

Walter Weller's recorded cycle of Beethoven symphonies (including a novelty: Brian Newbould's reconstruction of the unfinished Tenth) was completed in September. His first task was to finish the incomplete recording of No. 8, but Chandos producer Brian Couzens and his engineer son Ralph needed to check that the sound quality would match, so after the first take, the July and September versions were played back on parallel machines. Not only did they match, but, after several minutes, the two performances were still perfectly in sync – a *tour de force* on Weller's part. When issued, it promptly became Edward Greenfield's top choice: 'Altogether an outstanding set, easily outshining the other recent Beethoven cycles from the international brigade.'[4] The EMI recording of Mahler's *Resurrection* Symphony also received its final, thrilling accolade, when it was declared (by vote of all the *Gramophone* reviewers) the 1988 'Record of the Year'[5] – the most prestigious hi-fi award that the UK can offer, and a tremendous achievement by any standards. If anyone still had lingering doubts about what had been achieved in Birmingham since 1980, they must now have been finally laid to rest.

Rattle's sabbatical coincided with a season in which the CBSO had no principal guest conductor,[6] so the early part of the season was the responsibility of guest conductors. Paavo Berglund, allocated nine concerts in October (in Birmingham and elsewhere), was taken ill; Rattle stretched a point and agreed to take over one of his programmes.

Twentieth-century music so dominated the CBSO's 1988–9 programmes that even Ed Smith was slightly apprehensive about whether the Birmingham public would support them, so a special 'New Music' brochure was produced, listing works by Gorecki (the British professional première of his now-famous Third Symphony),[7] Messiaen, Elliott Carter, John Adams, Jonathan Lloyd, Franz Schmidt, Schoenberg, Britten, Boulez, Michael Torke, Alexander Goehr, Heinz Holliger, Zimmermann and Tippett. Other highlights included a *Carmina Burana* programme (Philip Pickett directing the mediæval originals and Okko Kamu conducting Carl Orff's version) and Birmingham's first hearing of Bruckner's Eighth Symphony, under Yoel Levi.

Birmingham's musicians are quick to respond to national and international disasters. In December, members of the Chorus and Orchestra under Simon Halsey raised over £5000 in aid of victims of the Armenian earthquake, performing the Fauré *Requiem* in Birmingham Cathedral; carol-singing and *ad hoc* Viennese music after the Christmas and New Year concerts raised a further £3000 for the Lockerbie Disaster Fund.

The end of 1988 saw the retirement of Felix Kok, after 23 years as Leader; at a special Farewell Concert in Birmingham Town Hall, he played the big violin solo in Strauss's tone poem *Ein Heldenleben*.[8] CBSO Society members contributed generously to a fund, as a result of which George Jonas was able to present Felix with some splendid hi-fi equipment and a complete set of the CBSO's compact discs. In an interview with Christopher Morley, he contrasted the CBSO of the 1960s and the 1980s: 'so many players used the orchestra as a means of passing through on their way to London. Now things are very different. People are leaving London and coming here, where the working conditions are so much better.'[9] The CBSO's new Leader, Peter Thomas, had led the BBC Welsh SO and had later been Joint Leader of the Philharmonia Orchestra, where he had worked with Rattle on many occasions.

Shortly after Felix's retirement came news of the death of Arthur Baker, the CBSO's General Manager from 1962 to 1978, following a heart attack; he was only 62, and, since leaving Birmingham in dramatic circumstances, at the time of Louis Frémaux's precipitate departure, he had first run a concert agency and later started his own computer-typesetting business.

In January 1989, Rattle returned from his sabbatical, and instantly everything moved up a gear. Revivals of the Brahms–Schoenberg Piano Quartet and Janáček's *Glagolitic Mass* in the Royal Festival Hall had Andrew Clements writing, 'Once again the CBSO has set a standard of excellence for its London counterparts to match as and when they can in 1989.'[10] The platform of Birmingham Town Hall is too small to accommodate the huge forces required for *Gurrelieder*, of which Rattle and the CBSO gave two wonderful performances in the Royal Festival Hall as part of a Schoenberg festival: 'The Reluctant Revolutionary'. An unusual première took place in the Town Hall on 2 February, when the original version of Benjamin Britten's *Sinfonia da Requiem*, whose manuscript Simon Rattle had located and inspected during the CBSO's tour of Japan in June 1987, was given its first performance, revealing many interesting differences from the published version.[11]

In March, Rattle directed two wonderful concert performances of *The Marriage of Figaro*, with Arleen Auger, Helen Field and Elise Ross in the female leading rôles; after their performance in the Arts Centre of the University of Warwick, Rattle and the cast celebrated the first Comic Relief Day by taking their final curtain-call wearing not red roses, but red *noses*. Later that month, conductor and orchestra were at Wembley Studios to record Pat Doyle's stylish sound-track for Kenneth Branagh's film *Henry V*. The same weekend, the CBSO Chorus flew to Belgium to take part in three performances of its 'party piece' – Mahler's Second Symphony – in Ghent, Antwerp and Brussels, with the Royal Flanders Philharmonic under Günther Neuhold. As Simon Halsey recalls, 'it was on this occasion that they sang it for the first time from memory, and they made a tremendous impression; it established the chorus as a major European force.'[12]

In April, Rattle and the CBSO were back in Paris, for two performances of Mahler's Seventh Symphony at the Théâtre du Châtelet. Michael Kennedy heard it in Birmingham and described it as 'one of the greatest Mahler performances I have ever heard . . . When the CBSO plays like this it has no rival in the land.'[13] In May, Sir Michael Tippett attended a mini-festival of his music in Birmingham,[14] in the course of which Christopher Robinson celebrated 25 very distinguished years as conductor of the City of Birmingham Choir with two splendid performances of *The Mask of Time*.[15]

The Spring Bank Holiday weekend found the CBSO back at the Brighton and Bath Festivals – this time with an all-Berlioz programme. Having performed the *Symphonie Fantastique, Lélio* and *La Damnation de Faust*[16] on Saturday, Sunday and Monday, with tremendous success, Simon Rattle responded to a desperate *cri de cœur* from the LPO to take over yet another Berlioz *Faust* at its Tuesday concert, from an indisposed Lorin Maazel.

In June, Leader Peter Thomas forsook his bow in favour of a baton to conduct Mendelssohn's incidental music for *A Midsummer Night's Dream*, with scenes from the play entertainingly enacted by a cast which included Leslie Crowther as Bottom. During the 'play-within-a-play', producer Nick Fogg even roped in Peter to play the part of Wall, revealing hitherto unimagined thespian abilities. And Rafael Frühbeck de Burgos conducted a performance of *Elijah* 'of a quality of which Mendelssohn can only have dreamed when he conceived the oratorio nearly 150 years ago for this very hall . . . a happy, triumphant way to celebrate Birmingham's centenary.'[17] With help from the Arts Council's well-established Contemporary Music Network, Birmingham Contemporary Music Group and Birmingham Jazz got together to start 'The Series'.

1989–90

The CBSO's steady improvement was not attributable to Simon Rattle alone. Looking back, he picks out some of those whose detailed work, often with quite small groups, has been of enormous value to the orchestra: 'Iona Brown, Viktor Liberman, Heinz Holliger and, later on, early music specialists like Nicholas Kraemer, Frans Brüggen, Nicholas McGegan – they've all been at various times part of this essential process of growth that we've been going through; what they achieved not only had its immediate effect but it had the effect of spreading vitamins throughout the whole orchestra.'[18] Simon Halsey echoes this: 'Each time we've seen a development in the Orchestra, we've tried to match it in the Chorus. For a long time now we've been working with internationally recognised choral specialists like John Eliot Gardiner, Robert Shaw and Eric Ericsson. It's gratifying to know that all three seem keen to work with us again, too.'[19]

On the Broad Street site, the International Convention Centre was still taking shape, and now the area in front of it, re-designated Centenary Square, began to be developed as well.[20] One of the first areas to be improved was the dreary space beneath the Central Library (which HRH the Prince of Wales had earlier described as looking 'more suitable for burning books than for storing them'). Renamed 'The Forum' and improbably adorned with pillars and Roman-style statuary, this area, which adjoins the CBSO offices and the Adrian Boult Hall, now houses a variety of shops and fast-food restaurants.

The season opened with four concerts at the Edinburgh Festival – a rare honour for any orchestra. Rattle's programmes were wide-ranging, starting with Haydn's *Creation*,[21] then Webern, Boulez, Debussy and Strauss (Heinz Holliger superb in the Oboe Concerto); then the UK première of Takemitsu's *Gemeaux* coupled with Brahms's Fourth Symphony, and finally another 'Rattle Special':

John Adams	A Short Ride in a Fast Machine
Christopher Rouse	The Infernal Machine (UK première)
Gershwin	Piano Concerto (Peter Donohoe)
Gershwin	Rhapsody in Blue (Peter Donohoe)
Bernstein	Prelude, Fugue and Riffs

October saw the CBSO's first encounter with the music of Mark Anthony Turnage – a Feeney-commissioned work which would become one of its calling cards: *Three Screaming Popes*, inspired by Francis Bacon's famous paintings. Turnage's appointment as Radcliffe Composer in Association was to prove extremely fruitful, as Simon Rattle recalls: 'As it became more and more important to us that 20th-century music should be well represented in a living way, so the idea of a composer living with us became more and more important too. At the beginning, we weren't quite sure how it would work out, but Mark soon got to know the individual members of the Orchestra – and, later on, the Chorus too – and they seemed to warm to his music from the start.'

Demonstrating exquisite sensitivity (unlike his older brother Sacha), Eliot Rattle put in an appearance on Sunday, 22 October, one of the few Free Days in an exceptionally busy period, so this time his father was able to be present for the birth without missing any CBSO concerts. At the end of November 1989, he and the orchestra were off on another big European tour, with help from the CBSO's Corporate Sponsors, Merrill Lynch: two concerts in Vienna, four in Switzerland and Liechtenstein, one in Frankfurt and then back to Paris again for two concerts in the Salle Pleyel.[22] It was a tremendous success, with reviews to match, repertoire including Mahler's Sixth Symphony[23] and *The Rite of Spring*, with Gidon Kremer the soloist in Sofia Gubaidulina's Violin Concerto *Offertorium* (which had received its UK première, in Birmingham, shortly before the tour). On their return to Birmingham, Mahler's Sixth was recorded for EMI; the Seventh Symphony was also recorded – live, at the Snape Maltings. By this time, the Mahler style came very naturally to the players, as Esa Pekka Salonen's reading of the Third Symphony demonstrated; Rattle's Bruckner No. 7 drew some wonderful playing, too; they were far more stretched by Roger Norrington's unconventional but exciting account of Beethoven's *Eroica*.

*

As 1990 came in, the music critics looked back and saw one bright spot above all others: 'It was the decade when . . . Simon Rattle and the CBSO went on and on providing a glorious contrary to a stagnant orchestral world.'[24] 'The focus of interest in British orchestral life has switched from London to the Midlands.'[25] Consumer research prepared at this time on behalf of the CBSO[26] concluded that 63% of the population of the West Midlands had heard of the orchestra, 15% claimed to have attended a CBSO concert, half of those within the last six months. These figures were certainly encouraging, and there was understandable satisfaction, too, when Rattle agreed to extend his contract until 1994.

Every now and again an orchestra welcomes something new and unexpected. In April 1990 it found itself at the NEC Arena, surrounded by 'media hype' and playing in front of some 10,000 fans, for 'Luciano Pavarotti in Concert'. Then more EMI sessions – Ravel, this time: the Piano Concertos (Cécile Ousset), orchestral works and *Shéhérazade*, thrillingly sung by Maria Ewing. Works by Britten and Bartók followed during the summer, and honours were picked up for earlier recordings – a 'Best Orchestra' award from *Hi-Fi & Music* magazine, and, in France, a bunch of Grands Prix du Disque.

July saw Rattle, the CBSO and Chorus off to Spain for performances of Beethoven's *Choral* Symphony in Madrid and Granada, the latter unforgettable, played late at night under the stars in the Alhambra Palace. A week later, he conducted what would be the very last 'Last Night' of the CBSO's summer season – the thinking that lay behind this was that the patriotic flag-waving of yesteryear held less appeal for the younger audiences of the 1990s, but it seemed a pity, nevertheless.

A client of the Arts Council (as the CBSO has been for nearly 50 years) expects from time to time to go through the process of being vetted by an expert panel, as a check on the use to which it puts the Council's very considerable public subvention. The Appraisal Report produced in the autumn of 1989 proved to be a disappointingly low-key affair, only one member of the assessment panel having any experience of orchestral administration. Ed Smith looks on it as 'an opportunity wasted'.

In preparation for the challenges of the 1990s, which would see the opening of Birmingham's new concert hall, the CBSO's office administration was rethought, with the creation of several new posts, some of which had uncomfortably long titles: Desmond Graham was brought in as General Manager (Concerts & Administration), Mike Buckley became General Manager (Personnel & Touring), Kate Walker joined the staff as Audience Development Manager and the author was given the all-embracing title of Special Projects

Manager.[27] But the CBSO's new high-profile status provided challenges for the musicians, too. One sign of the times was the appointment of a specialist Medical Adviser, to address problems which can arise so readily from playing an instrument; another was a special 'CBSO Chair', designed by the School of Furniture at Birmingham Polytechnic to help combat back-strain, especially for string players.

1990–1

In September, the *Post* produced a special supplement marking the tenth anniversary of Simon Rattle's appointment. Christopher Morley admitted to earlier doubts: 'We wiseacres who shook our blinkered heads when Rattle's appointment was first announced could never have envisaged the healthy state which now prevails, both within the CBSO and on its wider cultural stage, the City of Birmingham itself.'[28] The orchestral team was further strengthened by the appointment of Lyn Fletcher as Associate Leader. Now styled Music Director, and the recipient of Birmingham Civic Society's Gold Medal, Rattle and his family moved from London to Birmingham. In August, he took two characteristically original programmes to the Henry Wood Proms: who else would start a concert with Brahms's Fourth Symphony, followed by Debussy's *Clarinet Rhapsody* and then John Adams's *Harmonium*? Edward Seckerson asked 'What is it about Rattle and the CBSO that sets them apart?' and supplied his own answer: 'In three words – preparation, imagination, revelation.'[29] Max Loppert felt almost diffident about 'proclaiming the supremely musical exhilarations of Rattle–CBSO concerts; but after such a one as this, how can a responsible reviewer do otherwise?'[30]

At the invitation of Chorus Director Simon Halsey (now Artistic Director of the Salisbury Festival), Rattle, Chorus and Orchestra performed Beethoven's Ninth Symphony in the Cathedral, repeating the exercise at the CBSO's 70th Anniversary Concert in Birmingham Town Hall[31] and at the South Bank's 'Brave New Worlds' Festival, where it was the CBSO Chorus that captured Meirion Bowen's attention: 'singing entirely from memory, [they] were staggeringly disciplined and made every word tell . . . It was music-making to leave one starry eyed.'[32]

Exciting piano-playing was another feature. Maurizio Pollini was the soloist at a second concert in the Festival, Peter Donohoe recorded Gershwin and Bartók Concertos for EMI and Rattle and the CBSO were invited back to Leeds for the finals of the International Piano Competition, won by Artur Pizarro. Later in the season, the five Beethoven Piano Concertos were recorded for Chandos, with John Lill and Walter Weller. Walton's First Symphony was thrillingly performed and subsequently recorded,[33] but the highspot of the first half of the Birmingham season took place in October, when Rattle and the orchestra performed Nicholas Maw's remarkable *Odyssey* – the longest continuous span of orchestral music ever written. It proved a totally absorbing experience, and because Rattle had made the extension of his EMI contract conditional on a recording, it was captured for posterity. Nevertheless, as the composer wrote to Ed Smith, 'Even if we were not to have the recording, this performance would stay with me for the rest of my life.'[34]

'It was the year when the dream became reality.'[35] Ed Smith noted, 'In 1987, I marked in the Orchestra's Planning Diary the date of Sunday, 13 January 1991 as the date for our first rehearsal in the hall.' And on that very day, by arrangement with hall director, Andrew Jowett, and in conditions of considerable secrecy, Simon Rattle and the CBSO held their first experimental rehearsals in Symphony Hall, as Birmingham's wonderful new concert hall was now known.[36] A series of 'Open Evenings' gave the chance for regular subscribers to choose their preferred seats, and finally, on 15 April, the Opening Concerts took place, in which two sold-out houses[37] enjoyed magnificent performances of two Diaghilev ballets: Stravinsky's *Firebird* and Ravel's *Daphnis et Chloë*, plus a champagne reception for each audience.

Artec chief Russell Johnson explained to the *Sunday Telegraph* the philosophy behind Symphony Hall's acoustic design, which aimed to emulate the best features of great 19th-century halls such as the Concertgebouw or the Musikverein: 'Think small. Conserve the sound energy of the music by restricting the size of the audience – by shrinking the floor area.'[38] His assistant Nick Edwards explained to *Music Stand* readers that the sound was variable by the use of huge reverberation chambers, sliding acoustic panels and the raising and lowering of the canopy over the platform. 'A tremendous amount of work has gone into ensuring that you hear the music, the whole music and nothing but the music. That means a silent air-conditioning system: the design standard for unwanted noise has been Total Inaudibility.'[39] In Mike Buckley's view,

> Symphony Hall has probably had an even bigger effect on the orchestra's playing than the Development Plan. When we first moved in, it was a bit like a pea rattling around in a pod – the sound was so different from what they'd become accustomed to in the Town Hall, and it took a while to get used to this wonderful new acoustic. They soon rose to the occasion, of course; the string sound is so much *bigger* nowadays – we simply can't rehearse satisfactorily in the Adrian Boult Hall any more, because the strings produce so much volume, and a lot of that is due to playing regularly in Symphony Hall. They can go and play now in the Festival Hall or the

Musikverein with confidence and pride in their own performance – that's very much down to Symphony Hall.[40]

Simon Rattle's exploration of the Mahler symphonies had arrived at No. 9, Paul Griffiths stressing 'the extraordinary playing of the City of Birmingham Symphony Orchestra – one simply cannot get used to being bowled over by it.'[41] The CBSO's Far East Tour (sponsored by Jaguar and the Sumitomo Corporation) included three concerts at the Hong Kong Festival and eight in Japan. For percussionist Maggie Cotton, Rattle's performance of Mahler's Ninth in Tokyo's Suntory Hall was an overwhelming experience: 'I found myself on my feet for my last entry with tears in my eyes and my heart thumping. The audience knew that something extraordinary was happening and remained silent for a full half-minute before the applause broke.'[42]

March 1991 saw the launch of an important new initiative: 'Towards the Millennium'. 'As long ago as 1986, while sitting in a traffic jam, Vyner[43] and Rattle dreamed up the idea of celebrating the arts of the century in its last ten years – one year devoted to each decade.'[44] This multi-media event, stylishly promoted, was tailor-made to suit the conductor's extraordinary gifts as a programme builder, but it was also (in Hugh Canning's happy phrase) 'a test of Rattle's trust in his audiences'. The 1991 festival covered the period 1900–10 – a decade of profound change, reflected in programmes which embraced Schoenberg and Stravinsky, Elgar and Mahler, Suk's *Asrael* and Ives's *Unanswered Question*. The concerts were presented in London as well as Birmingham – Cardiff would get involved later, too.

Ever alert to the possibility of attracting extra funding to enhance the CBSO's growth, the management applied to the Arts Council for an Incentive Funding Award. The assessor, Pat Abrahams, liked what she saw and recommended an award of £230,000, spread over four years, mainly to help with office computerisation, the recording of live concerts and the appointment of a Community Development Officer. But making ends meet throughout the year grew no easier; the CBSO's Arts Council grant for 1990–1 was still the smallest of any regional orchestra.[45]

The CBSO's much-loved Conductor Emeritus, Harold Gray, OBE, died peacefully on Easter Sunday, aged 87. There was sadness, of course, but the main emotion was one of gratitude for what he had contributed to the orchestra: 'He conducted all the Nielsen symphonies, and all but one of the Sibelius symphonies, many times, and he became increasingly identified with the CBSO Proms, over which he presided like a sort of amiable uncle. We shall all miss

Harold tremendously: a fine musician, a lovely man and a dear friend. In accepting his Honorary Degree from the Open University, ten years ago, he said, "I owe far more to Birmingham than ever it does to me." That debt (if debt there ever was) was amply repaid.'[46]

April saw the orchestra in Lyon and Paris and, on Thursday, 16 May, Walter Weller was back to conduct Beethoven's *Missa Solemnis*, at the CBSO's last concert in Birmingham Town Hall; everyone received a 'Town Hall-shaped' souvenir brochure, and at the end there was a presentation to hall manager Betty Milne.

In the spring of 1991 came the announcement that HRH the Prince Edward CVO had agreed to become Patron of the CBSO and the Chorus. On Wednesday, 12 June, HM the Queen officially opened Symphony Hall. She looked in on Simon Rattle's rehearsal for that evening's televised gala performance of Mahler's Second Symphony, commenting, 'This is a marvellous place – you can feel a kind of wrap-around warmth.' Turnage's BBC-commissioned *Momentum* and the Mahler might have seemed a good programme to show off the hall and the performers, but it was certainly not the 'cup of tea' of the far-from-capacity invited VIP audience. The wonderful Sunday repeat, before a paying public, proved just how much the orchestra's ever-appreciative following could contribute to the success of a performance. By now, everyone at the CBSO knew that they had a world-class concert hall to play in. They knew too, though, that the advent of Symphony Hall would generate its own set of problems.

Rattle with a group of players, *en route* for Italy, May 1985.
Photo: Alan Wood.

Simon Rattle receives from Jeremy Isaacs the Gramophone Record Award 1988, for the CBSO's EMI recording of Mahler's Symphony No. 2. *Photo: Doug McKenzie.*

Simon Rattle, George Jonas and Erich Schmid in the Town Hall foyer, 1979. *Photo: City of Birmingham.*

Neeme Järvi outside the Town Hall, 1981. *Photo: Alan Wood.*

Okko Kamu recording Shostakovich's Symphony No. 13 (*Babi Yar*) for Chandos with the CBSO (Leader: Felix Kok) and a men's chorus, in the Great Hall of the University of Birmingham, 1987 *Photo: Alan Wood.*

Walter Weller, Edward Smith and Chandos Producer Brian Couzens, during recording sessions for the Beethoven Symphony cycle, 1988. *Photo: Alan Wood.*

Sir Michael Tippett with Meirion Bowen and City Choir conductor Christopher Robinson, during rehearsals for *The Mask of Time*, 1989. *Photo: Alan Wood.*

Mark Elder. *Photo: Alan Wood.*

Leader Peter Thomas, with Simon Rattle, in the Adrian Boult Hall, 1989.
Photo: Birmingham Post & Mail.

'Blame *him*!' – Simon Rattle with EMI Producer David Murray, 1991.
Photo: Alan Wood.

Simon Rattle enjoys a joke with HM the Queen, during her visit to open Symphony Hall and the ICC, June 1991. *Photo: City of Birmingham.*

The CBSO's Royal Patron HRH the Prince Edward meets Symphony Hall Director Andrew Jowett, CBSO Chief Executive Edward Smith and Mr & Mrs George Jonas in Symphony Hall, January 1992. *Photo: Alan Wood.*

Chorus Director Simon Halsey with Radcliffe Composer in Association Mark Anthony Turnage and accompanist Peter King, during CBSO Chorus rehearsals for *Leaving*, 1992. *Photo: Alan Wood.*

Typical of the orchestra's lively programme of education projects, CBSO horn-player John Logan duets with Rebecca Thomas at an Erdington school, 1992. *Photo: Birmingham Post & Mail.*

Nathalie Wheen, Simon Rattle and composer Hans Werner Henze
at a public rehearsal in Symphony Hall, 1993.
Photo: Birmingham Post & Mail.

Simon Rattle with acoustic designer Russell Johnson at the CBSO's Open Day
in Symphony Hall, March 1993. *Photo: Alan Wood.*

'A concert hall that any city in the world would be proud to own'
– Sir Simon Rattle and the CBSO at work.
Photo: Alan Wood.

25

Towards the Millennium

'At last', wrote Simon Rattle, 'we have a concert hall that any city in the world would be proud to own.'[1] But with the move from the Town Hall to Symphony Hall the goalposts, too, had moved. First, there would be another 500 seats to fill each night; second, the hall rental was enormously greater; third, as this prestigious new venue was added routinely to touring itineraries, the CBSO, which up to now had promoted virtually all Birmingham's symphony concerts, found itself competing with major international orchestras; and finally, the city's resources, which had been stretched so far in building the ICC (and would be stretched still farther in promoting its own programme of concerts in Symphony Hall) might not be able to maintain an adequate level of support for the CBSO.

1991–2

The 'honeymoon period' for Symphony Hall could only be expected to last for the first full season, so it was essential that this be well attended. In the event, public response was overwhelming: a record 4357 subscribers necessitated taking on a Subscriptions Officer to deal with bookings and set up a computerised system. Corporate Membership was introduced, offering package deals (from 'Emerald' to 'Diamond') at various levels of benefit, depending on the subscription selected.

In September, the CBSO Chorus took part in a performance of Beethoven's Ninth Symphony in Symphony Hall, with Kurt Masur and the Leipzig Gewandhaus Orchestra. Birmingham Contemporary Music Group (BCMG) continued to provide imaginative and well-prepared concerts, mostly in the Adrian Boult Hall, and now there were other satellite groups as well: Peter Thomas's 'Birmingham Ensemble' (presenting chamber concerts in the Town

Hall), several string quartets and 'Prince of Wales Brass'. In February 1992 the Radcliffe Trust agreed to extend Mark Anthony Turnage's appointment, which was proving mutually fruitful, by a year to December 1993. *Three Screaming Popes* (now recorded as the first EMI 'single' CD) was included in the repertoire for a CBSO tour in September 1991, retracing the ground of past triumphs: Helsinki, Paris, Berlin.

Rattle, Chorus and Orchestra started the season with Janáček's *Sinfonietta*, coupled with *A Child of Our Time*, and shortly afterwards Sir Michael Tippett himself conducted a recording of the work for Collins Classics in Symphony Hall, which would now become the CBSO's favoured recording venue. Cycles of the Beethoven Piano Concertos were played by Alfred Brendel there and at the Barbican (the *Emperor* boldly coupled with Turnage's *Momentum* and Henze's Seventh Symphony). Looking back, Simon Rattle says, 'Working so regularly with Alfred over the years really brought enormous rewards. To start with, it was hard for the orchestra to respond with everything he wanted them to do. But when we did those Beethoven cycles with him, he told me that in a couple of the concertos he thought he'd never heard such beautiful orchestral playing; and of course that was all the more touching for knowing that Alfred only says what he believes.'[2]

But even taking into consideration the many fine guest artists, it was the musical content itself which was especially remarkable during a season which included Strauss's *Alpine* Symphony, Schoenberg's *Variations*, a magnificent Wagner programme (Lawrence Foster), Walton's Cello Concerto (Lynn Harrell – also recorded), Prokofiev's Third, Fifth and Sixth Symphonies, unfamiliar stage music by Kurt Weill and no fewer than three world premières: Robin Holloway's *The Spacious Firmament*, Turnage's *Leaving*[3] and Gerard McBurney's stunning reconstruction of Shostakovich's theatre piece *Hypothetically Murdered*, conducted (and later recorded for United) by Mark Elder. 'Towards the Millennium' reached the second decade of the century, 1911–20, offering a fascinating spread of music, all tailor-made for Rattle: Ives, Szymanowski, Stravinsky, Ravel, Berg's *Three Pieces*, Nielsen's *Sinfonia Espansiva* (the performance dedicated to the memory of Harold Gray), Elgar's *Falstaff*[4] and (with Elise Ross and the BCMG) Schoenberg's seminal *Pierrot Lunaire*. Rattle included two great Debussy scores – *Jeux* and *Images* – Max Loppert especially enjoying the latter in Symphony Hall: 'Already, after nearly a year's residence, the gain in the players' responsiveness and spontaneity of detail is a cause for simple amazement . . . the corporate achievement of these Birmingham Debussyans is now marvellous to behold.'[5]

Birmingham, designated 'UK City of Music 1992', was the centre of a year-long 'Sounds Like Birmingham' Festival. In January 1992, it hosted the

Association of British Orchestras' Conference at the Hyatt Hotel; delegates attended a CBSO concert, after which Simon Rattle was presented with the ABO Award, marking his outstanding contribution to British music. In June, about 70,000 people attended a splendid free concert conducted by Bramwell Tovey in Cannon Hill Park, marking the first National Music Day.

Not everything went smoothly, however. The Cheltenham series, which had run continuously since 1945, was threatened with extinction when the local authority withdrew its support; local enthusiasts – and later, Gulf Oil – came to the rescue, but the number of CBSO concerts was reduced from ten to five. Then, in April 1992, due to continuing world-wide recession and the consequent dearth of sponsorship, a major USA tour had to be cut back from three to two weeks.[6] What survived, however, was of tip-top quality. Both in Boston's Symphony Hall and in New York's recently refurbished Carnegie Hall, Rattle presented a highly imaginative 'mini-Millennium' festival of three programmes – one each for the years 1911, 1912 and 1913.

The final concert, in Washington DC, marked the end of George Jonas's Chairmanship of the CBSO Society; his tenure had been long and eventful, seeing the Orchestra through the crisis of 1978, on past the appointment of Simon Rattle and into the great days of the 1980s. There was a strong team of officers[7] and now Symphony Hall was a reality, so, at the end of the season, Jonas felt that the time was ripe to hand on the reins of office to a new Chairman, Arthur Knapp,[8] who was elected by the Board of Directors from within its own number. Another who retired at this time was Paul Dudding, after a remarkable 37 years' service, initially as a horn player but for the last 16 years as the orchestra's Librarian: Ann Tennant was appointed Education Manager, to develop the CBSO's increasingly important work in this field. Rosemary Harby, lynch-pin of the CBSO office and long-serving Personal Assistant to both Edward Smith and Simon Rattle, became in addition Company Secretary. Richard York came from the Barbican Centre to replace Desmond Graham; as Deputy Chief Executive, an important part of his remit was to roll forward the Society's recently introduced Business Plan.

EMI recordings included Prokofiev's Fifth Symphony and *Scythian Suite*; with the help of £30,000 from Birmingham International Airport, Mahler's First Symphony was also recorded live, in Symphony Hall.[9] But, as in Rattle's first season, it is a series of wonderful performances of Mahler's Tenth Symphony which remain most indelibly in the memory.

There was much concern when the CBSO's former Leader Felix Kok was very seriously injured in a railway accident in Portugal, where he had been guest-leading an orchestra for a while; his one-time colleague Philip Head organised a massive collection to buy him a specially adapted car. In the December 1991 issue of *Music Stand*, Stephen Lloyd contributed an obituary of Sir Andrzej Panufnik, Principal Conductor of the CBSO, 1957–9, but soon afterwards, on Saturday, 1 February 1992, Lloyd himself died. This book, dedicated to the memory of Stephen and his wife Dorothy, affords many glimpses of this most private of men, who nevertheless exercised so powerful an influence on the fortunes of the CBSO over so many years. At a Memorial Service for him, in a packed Birmingham Cathedral, two aspects emerged which have perhaps been insufficiently stressed. The first was his astounding industry,[10] the second his sheer raw courage in the face of physical disabilities which would have crushed many people.[11] The CBSO Society owes him an unpayable debt of gratitude.

1992–3

Following so soon on the heels of Boston, New York and Washington, the 'European Festivals Tour' in August 1992 served to reinforce the international standing of Simon Rattle, the CBSO and the Chorus. After two concerts in the Schleswig Holstein Festival, the orchestra proceeded (via Munich's impressive Gasteig) to Salzburg. Many members of the Chorus (which undertook separate concerts in Ingolstadt and Munich) attended the Orchestra's first Salzburg concert (Turnage and Mahler's Tenth), then joined them at the second in the *Glagolitic Mass*, which was sung, amazingly, without the book. Mike Buckley says, 'I think that tour was a turning point in the improving relationship between the amateur singers of the Chorus and the professional players of the Orchestra; they take a real pride in each other's work now.'[12]

Ed Smith noted, with no small satisfaction, that the CBSO had 'the proud distinction of being one of the very few orchestras in the world to have played at least once at every major international music festival during the last five years'. Sometimes Europe came to Birmingham instead of vice versa: in October 1992, Prime Minister John Major invited his opposite numbers to a Euro-Summit at the ICC; the necessary security resulted in endless queues for a CBSO concert, and a late start.

At the beginning of the season, the team was strengthened once again with the appointment as Principal Guest Conductor of Mark Elder, CBE; his programmes included Ives's *Washington's Birthday*, Holst's *The Planets* and a delectable Viennese Night. Again there was much of musical interest, including Ligeti's *Atmosphères* under Michael Gielen, and the Brahms *Requiem* under the doyen of American choral conductors, Robert Shaw,[13] but the highlight was undoubtedly Rattle's cycle of the Nielsen Symphonies, promoted in London and Birmingham with European Arts Festival funding, as part of the

'Tender is the North' Festival. This superb cycle (which one must hope will one day be recorded) also gave rise to two BBC television programmes.

In January 1993, Pierre Boulez spent two and a half weeks with the CBSO, the BCMG and students of Birmingham Conservatoire; the musicians found the experience of working with him on Webern, Stravinsky, Bartók and Debussy immensely stimulating. Remarkably, at the second Symphony Hall concert, Boulez's own *Notations I-IV*[14] had to be encored and, in the *Daily Telegraph*, Geoffrey Norris described the Festival Hall performance as 'an evening which made one glad to be alive'. European mainstream contemporary music loomed large over the season; BCMG worked with Karlheinz Stockhausen in Cannon Hill Park and Hans Werner Henze took part in 'Open Sessions' in Symphony Hall, attending EMI recordings of his *Barcarola* and Seventh Symphony.

'Towards the Millennium' arrived at the Twenties, with the usual fascinating juxtapositions: Varèse and Gershwin; early Britten and late Ravel; Sibelius's last symphony and Shostakovich's first; Berg's *Wozzeck Fragments*; Bartók's complete *Miraculous Mandarin*, Szymanowski's *Stabat Mater* and *Litany*. December saw the last of eight annual concerts given in aid of the General Hospital: 'in all, over £50,000 was raised, to buy essential equipment for the hospital.'[15]

The CBSO's first Open Day in Symphony Hall, on 13 March 1993, included free concerts, acoustic demonstrations and a CBSO Chorus Sing-along and was, if anything, *too* successful – it was overrun, and the best estimate was that 12,000 people attended. Rattle also talked to Christopher Morley about the Society's plans for a new rehearsal hall and administrative centre: 'We need it. This orchestra is a real strapping teenager; we're going through clothes at an alarming rate, and we can't patch them up much longer.'[16]

But however successful the orchestra might appear to be in local terms, there were still financial concerns, as the result of Government cut-backs and a major crisis affecting the London orchestras, which seemed likely to spill over into the regions. In Norman Lebrecht's opinion, only three orchestras could count themselves safe: the LSO, the Hallé and the CBSO, which 'with a new hall, young audience, charismatic conductor and crafty management, has lit a beacon of renewal that central and local authorities will not dare extinguish'.[17] It was shrewdly expressed, though what he described as 'crafty' was simply *good* management.

There were further changes within the CBSO team, too. Julianna Szekely, who had arrived on the day Louis Frémaux had resigned and had played a crucial rôle in boosting the orchestra's profile, left to concentrate on her young family.[18] Another who had played an important part in the process of growth and development, Financial Controller Graham Escott, decided to take early retirement, and in July 1993 the author also retired, after nearly 30 years in various senior management posts, mainly in order to concentrate on writing this book. Principal second violinist Jeremy Ballard had already left the CBSO; now principal oboist Richard Weigall also departed in order to freelance, after 23 years of very distinguished service.

1993–4

Birmingham Contemporary Music Group was gaining in stature year by year; its very successful 'Sound Investment' scheme allowed patrons to buy Sound Units costing £100 each, making them part-commissioners of a new work, with various associated privileges. BCMG's innovative programme 'The Series' was honoured with the 1993 Prudential Award for Music and the Royal Philharmonic Society's Chamber Ensemble Award.

For the CBSO, it was a season of tours: in September to Western Europe and in May 1994 farther east, including Warsaw, Budapest, Athens, Leipzig and three concerts in Vienna's superb Musikverein. Independently, the Chorus visited Flanders again, for Mahler's *Resurrection* Symphony under Stefan Soltesz, and Rotterdam for his Eighth Symphony under James Conlon.

Simon Rattle agreed to extend his contract as Music Director to 1996, with an option to prolong it on a rolling basis. This made him the orchestra's longest-serving conductor, but his high profile stretched well beyond Birmingham's boundaries; he was declared *Gramophone* Artist of the Year and accepted yet another honorary degree, from the University of Leeds, using his acceptance speech (at the International Piano Competition) to express his concerns for the future of instrumental music in this country: 'Although Music is part of the National Curriculum, not a week passes but I receive anguished letters from parents, education authorities, schools, music teachers, saying "We're sorry, we can no longer afford to teach musical instruments. We've had to sack our peripatetic teachers" . . . Without the scholarships bestowed on me by Liverpool, I would not have been able to afford the teaching I had, which was such a life-saver for me. Now, of course, I want all children to have the opportunities that I had.'[19] When he received the prestigious Montblanc de la Culture Private Vision Award, Rattle allocated his prize money to the CBSO's education projects.

> We came relatively late to serious educational work – indeed, it came about very largely at the insistence of the players themselves – but it's every bit as important as anything else we do and it has developed the members of the orchestra as people in many different ways. Maggie Cotton was doing tremendous work with deaf kids, for instance, long before we started the

> Adopt-a-Player scheme.[20] The scheme became something really important to us and now, of course, everybody's doing it. But what we've refused to say is, 'Now this will bring children in, and put more bums on seats' – because it won't. Once again, what we're trying to do is to spread vitamins. If we're not in the business of changing people's lives, then I don't know what business we *are* in.[21]

The Arts Council was in crisis at this time, losing its Chairman, Secretary General and several Council members within a matter of weeks; Ed Smith reported, 'The stark fact is that . . . its grant has not kept pace with the rising costs of continuing to deliver a first-class orchestra.'[22] Arthur Knapp goes further: in his opinion, the Arts Council has never paid more than lip service to its support for the CBSO's Development Plan and this has led directly to the financial problems the Orchestra is still facing. Once again, however, the city came to the rescue, with an additional grant of £250,000, spread over 1993–4 and 1994–5, to tide the Society over its immediate cash-flow problems, but local authorities were themselves facing long-term financial difficulties and the future seemed as uncertain as ever. As the CBSO's Finance Director, Richard Hartshorn, remarks, 'It seems to be the nature of the Arts in this country that we have financial crises, but they're really a matter of perspective. When you look at a graph showing the cost of running the orchestra over the past seventy-five years (see p. 242), the remarkable thing is not just the enormous increase in the figures in real terms (which mirrors the artistic quality of the orchestra), but that income and expenditure regularly cancel each other out. It was ever thus. There are no shareholders to be paid – salaries and fees account for the bulk of our costs and we need to ensure that our income – from the box office, from engagements and grants – balances our outgoings. In the late Eighties we did manage to accumulate some modest reserves – a small cushion – but the City Council simply said "You don't need it, so we won't give you any extra this year – we'll try to make it up to you next year." '[23]

If Simon Rattle was preparing an opera for Glyndebourne, there was generally a valuable spin-off of one or two concert performances beforehand. In October 1993 it was *Don Giovanni*, semi-staged with a wonderful cast, led by Thomas Allen as the Don and Willard White as Leporello. Rattle describes it as 'One of the great experiences of the past year. We had just eight rehearsals – God! Hardly enough time to play the piece through twice! – but it was amazing to see the speed with which they absorbed it; in effect, they were saying "OK – we know what to do; this is our language; we know how to listen; we know what it is to make a performance with singers: we know what the style is" – so exciting!'[24]

Other Rattle highlights included Liszt's *Faust* Symphony; Bruckner's two greatest symphonies (Nos. 7 and 9); the final Turnage commission: *Drowned Out*;[25] Maurizio Pollini in Mozart's C minor Concerto, K. 491; Phyllis Bryn-Julson in Schoenberg's powerful *Erwartung*; Tippett's Fourth Symphony and, of course, 'Towards the Milennium', which now reached the Thirties – wonderfully inventive programme building again, along these lines:

Hindemith	Symphony, Mathis der Maler
Bartók	Piano Concerto No. 2 (András Schiff)
Roy Harris	Symphony No. 3
Copland	Suite, Billy the Kid
Varèse	Ionisation
Berg	Violin Concerto (Gidon Kremer)
Shostakovich	Symphony No. 4

There was, indeed, a good deal of American music during the season. John Adams conducted works by Ives, and choruses from his opera *The Death of Klinghoffer*; Richard Stolzman played the John Corigliano Clarinet Concerto and Mark Elder introduced and conducted Charles Ives's Second Symphony.

In February 1994, when he conducted two hugely impressive performances[26] of Mahler's vast Eighth Symphony, Elder's extensive operatic experience proved invaluable. At what he calls 'the end of the journey' – Mater Gloriosa's brief but beautiful solo – he sited soprano soloist Susan Chilcot in the doorway of one of Symphony Hall's great reverberation chambers, high above the platform. 'I climbed up a sort of fire-ladder, to see for myself, and asked them to open the hydraulic doors. From there you have a complete command of the house, but you're elevated away from all the other performers. The music is marked to be sung very quietly, but we found that if Sue stood in the doorway and the doors slid silently open, it created a magical effect in that wonderful hall. For the final *Chorus Mysticus* we placed the brass bands high up, on either side – it helped to bring the work to a really grand climax.'[27]

On Saturday, 11 June 1994 it was announced that HM the Queen had awarded Simon Rattle (already a CBE) a knighthood in her Birthday Honours. Characteristically, 'Sir Simon said he was "shell-shocked" by the honour, which he said was earned by his musicians. "Although I can see that an investiture for over 100 musicians would be a trifle unwieldy, it would still be fully deserved." '[28]

Many Birmingham concert-goers were saddened to learn of the death, on

30 January 1994, at the age of 88, of Rudolf Schwarz, CBE, the CBSO's Principal Conductor, 1951–7. In 1955 he had taken the orchestra on its first overseas tour, to Holland, and had always followed its progress and development with keen interest.

In June 1994, the Orchestra's Benevolent Fund celebrated its Jubilee with a Grand Prize Draw, raising nearly £7000 towards this worthwhile cause. Edward Smith made a presentation to Christopher Robinson, who had conducted the CBSO at City Choir concerts (and on countless other occasions) for over 30 years. In the summer of 1994, too, Arthur Maddison decided to retire from the Board of Directors, after no fewer than 42 years, first as Treasurer and later as Deputy Chairman. Of his many quiet but sterling contributions to the Society, perhaps none was more important than his work in attracting commercial sponsorship.

1994–5

Schoenberg's *Gurrelieder* was unthinkable in Birmingham Town Hall, but it was heaven-sent for Symphony Hall, as Sir Simon Rattle's September performances showed, Rita Hunter and John Mitchinson heading the cast.

In October, Martha Argerich (Prokofiev) and Gidon Kremer (Elgar) accompanied Rattle and the orchestra on another big Japanese tour. Violinist David Gregory was intrigued by one concert hall, 'on the seventh floor, with a garden behind the stage (sliding screens reveal the picture window) and a green neon waterfall at the entrance'. By now, the musicians were hardened travellers, accustomed to local food, but Mike Buckley confirmed that 'fish-eye salad and raw sea-slug can be more than a little off-putting for those with a typical Anglo-Saxon constitution'.[29]

On its return, the CBSO and the Orchestra of the Age of Enlightenment shared the programme for the Royal Concert at the Barbican, attended by HRH Princess Margaret; Rattle conducted both orchestras, cunningly prefacing Tippett's *Fantasia Concertante* (CBSO) with the Corelli Concerto Grosso (OAE) on which it was based. In Birmingham, he was the dedicatee of a Feeney première – Sofia Gubaidulina's *Zeitgestalten* – giving what Christopher Morley described as an 'extraordinarily assured' performance; Anne-Sophie Mutter offered an extremely lush view of the Beethoven Violin Concerto in the same concert. A week later, Rattle's gifted young protégé, Daniel Harding, conducted Alfred Schnittke's Viola Concerto, with Yuri Bashmet as the authoritative soloist.

In January 1995, Mark Elder rounded off his final season as Principal Guest Conductor with three splendid programmes, including Puccini's one-acter *Il Tabarro*, Strauss's *Symphonia Domestica* and Rachmaninov's *The Bells.* The last of these formed part of the CBSO Chorus's 21st Anniversary Concert, on 19 January, in which Chorus Director Simon Halsey shared the rostrum. Shortly afterwards the Chorus was renamed the City of Birmingham Symphony Chorus, as he explained: 'The term "Symphony Chorus" is much more readily understood overseas. In 1995, for example, we're doing *A Child of Our Time* in Vienna, Beethoven's Ninth in Frankfurt and three performances of Britten's *War Requiem* in Leipzig, with Kurt Masur and the Leipzig Gewandhaus Orchestra.'[30]

Rattle's view of the Chorus is that 'they're extraordinary. Over the past few years, the standard has risen so far and so rapidly; I think that the process has been very similar to what the Orchestra has been through, and it's been due, in very great part, to the work of Simon Halsey.' The Symphony Chorus now has its own Manager (Justin Lee) and Secretary, and over 200 singers on its books, including a record 32 tenors. May 1995 also saw the début of the City of Birmingham Symphony Youth Chorus, established partly because the CBSO needs a top-class children's choir several times a year for the repertoire it undertakes, and secondly as an antidote to the worrying decline of singing in schools, nation-wide.

On 16 January, Norman Lebrecht, in the *Telegraph*, raised the hoary old 'Life stops at Watford' message for Rattle: 'The obvious move for him would be London – and that is a challenge he has so far ducked . . . London is a nettle he simply has to grasp.' His answer came three days later, at the reception that followed the Chorus's 21st Anniversary Concert: Sir Simon (40 that very day) had extended his CBSO contract to 1998, with an option to renew it beyond then.

In March 1995, 'Towards the Millennium' arrived at the Forties. War and Peace were juxtaposed in consecutive Rattle programmes: one featured works linked to the Holocaust, beginning with a powerful *Study for Strings* by Pavel Haas (composed and first performed at the concentration camp in Terezín); then Schoenberg's *A Survivor from Warsaw*, narrated with blazing intensity by Benjamin Luxon; and finally Tippett's great oratorio, *A Child of Our Time*, in which the Symphony Chorus was joined by the Wiener Singakademie; a memorable evening, if a somewhat disquieting one. The following concert featured three more wartime works, this time permeated with hope for the future – Copland's *Appalachian Spring*; the closing scene from Strauss's last opera *Capriccio* (Felicity Lott) and Vaughan Williams's Fifth Symphony (not what one might think of as Rattle repertoire, but beautifully paced).

During the season, the CBSO recorded for a wider range of labels than ever before: Hyperion (Piano Concertos by Scharwenka and Emil Sauer, played by Stephen Hough); Clavès (Cherubini Overtures, with Lawrence Foster);

Decca (works by Aaron Jay Kernis, with Hugh Wolff, and works by Bertholdt Goldschmidt) and, of course, plenty of Rattle/EMI sessions, including Violin Concertos by Szymanowski, played by Thomas Zehetmair.

At the beginning of 1995, the Scottish composer Judith Weir accepted a three-year appointment as the CBSO's Fairbairn[31] Composer in Association. Sir Simon says, 'Mark Turnage did a fantastic job in the four years he worked with us, writing and rewriting and getting involved in some superb projects with young people. Judith is one of the most important composers working in Britain today, but she's a very different kind of person – a theatre person, through and through – and we'll have to work together to find what will work best for us all.'

It was also in January that the CBSO Centre Development Campaign was launched, with the intention of raising £5m, a substantial part hopefully from the National Lottery Fund; Sir Michael Checkland (now Deputy Chairman of the CBSO) sent a personal letter to all Society members, outlining an ambitious but exciting plan to convert a derelict factory on the corner of Berkley Street and Holliday Street (4 minutes' walk from Symphony Hall) into a new home for the Orchestra, the Chorus and their associated organisations, including a purpose-built rehearsal hall, studios, an instrument store, music library and administrative offices; the initial response was encouraging. In Sir Simon's opinion, 'It was a tragedy that we couldn't make Symphony Hall our proper home in 1991 – in that respect it was a great opportunity lost. We desperately need somewhere, though, and soon; the playing and administrative parts of the orchestra are really separate entities at present. The CBSO Centre will help to put us together.'

When Adrian Boult received his Honorary Doctorate of Music from the University of Birmingham, just before leaving the city in 1930 to become Director of Music at the BBC, the Public Orator remarked, 'his translation to this exalted sphere only proves the profound truth that what Birmingham played and listened to a year ago, the nation will play and enjoy tomorrow.' What was true of the Boult era has proved even truer of the Rattle years. The CBSO's Birthday Concert on Friday, 10 November, 75 years to the day after Elgar conducted the first CBO Symphony Concert in Birmingham Town Hall, seems certain to be a splendid affair, featuring Sir Simon, the Orchestra, Chorus and distinguished soloists in a typically arresting programme: Vaughan Williams's *Serenade to Music*, the first performances of commissioned works by John Adams and Oliver Knussen and Beethoven's Ninth Symphony.

The CBSO remains as active and as high-powered as ever. As these final pages were being written, the Orchestra was approaching the end of yet another successful European tour, which included three programmes of Forties repertoire in Vienna ('rapturously received', according to CBSO Chairman Arthur Knapp), and also involved the Symphony Chorus. Advance plans for the 1995–6 season reveal plenty of goodies, too – Sir Simon conducts his first complete Beethoven Symphony cycle and (believe it or not) an all-Tchaikovsky programme. Rozhdestvensky conducts Tchaikovsky too (*Manfred*) and Robert Shaw returns with the Verdi *Requiem*.

It is certainly no longer true that the CBSO only plays at its best for Sir Simon. No one who attended Pierre Boulez's concerts, who was present when Elder conducted Strauss's *Symphonia Domestica*, or has heard Weller's recorded Beethoven Symphony cycle, could subscribe to that idea for an instant. Yet, as Edward Smith observes, 'Inevitably, after such a long and fruitful association, the CBSO is almost totally identified in the popular imagination with the name of Simon Rattle. One of the biggest challenges we face now is to get major Festival engagements or overseas tours for the orchestra with other conductors.' In the coming season there are plans for a series of seven performance-led London Weekend Television documentaries for Channel 4 about music in the 20th century, and in June 1996 the orchestra will be in Paris for eight performances of Janáček's opera *Jenufa*, at the Châtelet. These will be with Rattle at the helm, though the CBSO will also be playing in Saarbrücken under Marek Janowski.

In 1992, asked about his ongoing multi-media 'Towards the Millennium' Festival, Rattle gazed deep into the crystal ball: 'By the year 2000 we shall be presenting a programme of work that has yet to be written, composed, performed or shown, and we shall be debating issues that have not yet appeared on the cultural agenda.'[32] Whether that prospect excites you or alarms you, all one can say is that, up to now, audience reaction to the festival has been consistently positive. In March 1996, it reaches the radical Fifties – late Stravinsky, Shostakovich, Messiaen, Stockhausen, tempered with Bernstein, and it is a safe bet that, with his flair and charisma, Rattle will pull it off yet again. As he says, 'It's not just myself and the CBSO that have changed over these past fifteen years; the whole orchestral scene has been changing too. When we did Boulez's *Rituel*, just after I arrived in 1980, we were the first British orchestra apart from the BBC Symphony to play a note of his music, and mainstream European contemporary orchestral music simply wasn't being played over here. That's undoubtedly changed now, and it's good that we've been able to make our contribution.'

But Sir Simon concedes that the expansion of the CBSO's repertoire in certain directions has had its down-side as well; as he says, 'We've realised that there's a lot of catching up to do on repertoire. In the early days, you paid the price for having a very young conductor; not only did I not conduct some repertoire, but you'd better be damned grateful that I didn't!' Many standard orchestral works, which the orchestra would once have taken in its stride, now pose considerable difficulties, especially for young players.

> I remember that when Walter Weller did all the Beethoven symphonies with the orchestra, one outstandingly gifted young violinist said to me, 'You know, Simon, four or five of those pieces I'd never seen in my life!' One of the things I did here early on was to concentrate specifically on certain pieces – the *Eroica*, for example, which has kept coming back into our repertoire. And it's been very interesting to see how it's changed – not just how my interpretation has altered, over a dozen years or more, but how differently the Orchestra *expects* to play it now.
>
> There's something about Beethoven which is a crucible for everything in contemporary music. I believe in total immersion; one of the things we learned from doing the Sibelius cycle is how one symphony affects another, and this year will see my first complete Beethoven cycle. Over the years, the CBSO and I have done an enormous amount of Mozart and Haydn together, and I think that now we've reached the stage where we have something to say together about Beethoven as well. The music will always challenge you, of course; as Samuel Beckett says, 'Ever fail, try again, fail better'.
>
> Orchestras can only go up or down. Obviously we have to be able to play a wide swathe of music successfully, but what we have attempted to do over the years is to carve out an area in which we were expert. There was no sense in pretending that the CBSO was the Berlin Philharmonic, but what is interesting now is that there are a number of areas where our orchestra can see the Berlin Philharmonic well away. Now it's a matter of building on that foundation. We have to find a way in which the Orchestra will feel as completely at home in a Schumann symphony, say, as they do in a Stravinsky ballet. But it's getting harder, not easier. They still play well out of their skin, but now sheer will-power has much less part to play; we're having to deal in areas of culture and thought and expectations, and it's hard for an orchestra to keep pushing away at these very high levels of attainment.
>
> The goalposts have moved, and so they should. I'm very aware that the Orchestra's association with me brings both benefits and debits; they are too closely associated with me, not only in the public's mind but in their own. Now it's up to me to try to find other people who can really help them to reach beyond the point we've arrived at together so far; but it's still very hard to attract the type of conductors the Orchestra most needs. The Cleveland Orchestra, for example, doesn't find it easy to attract the guest conductors they would like to work with, and it's the same problem all over the world – by and large, orchestras have got very much better than their conductors. Here, the players need to work at regular intervals with conductors who will ask for more from them than I can. But I know the kind of demand that *I* am in, and here we're talking about people on another level.[33]

The City's budget for 1995–6 envisages an expenditure of nearly a billion pounds, of which the CBSO will receive approximately one thousandth. Over the past 75 years, Birmingham City Council has consistently kept faith with the city's orchestra; sometimes its annual subvention has not kept pace with ever-rising costs but its support has always been there. It must be gratified, now, to see that long-term confidence vindicated and a quantifiable return on its investment; the CBSO is the city's cultural flagship, adding glitter to Birmingham's name around the world on disc, on radio and TV and through a series of highly prestigious overseas tours. For a city which has not always been good at banging its own drum, it is something to be really proud of.

Orchestral music is a growth area: a recent joint Arts Council/BBC report shows that, nation-wide, attendance at symphony concerts has increased by 70% since 1979. But Sir Simon is realistic, too:

> We don't necessarily have the right to exist and to be supported, *per se*. It's our duty to spread the good news, and bring in the people. We have to demonstrate that we're flexible – willing to change as we go. Our audience has really stuck with us through an enormous range of music. They've been incredibly loyal, despite the financial hardships of the last few years. We're working in a city full of people from all sorts of different backgrounds; for instance, we're finding that there's an audience which is interested in what we can offer, but unwilling to come out at night. It's been fascinating, too, to discover that there's a correlation between the audience for jazz and for contemporary music. I think we're beginning to see the orchestra no longer as something monolithic, but as a body with many different responsibilities. In addition to the Orchestra and the Chorus, we already have the BCMG, the Birmingham Ensemble, Prince of Wales Brass and several other chamber groups operating as satellites of the CBSO; the Youth Chorus is just one other aspect of this proliferation, of course, and these are all ways in which we're trying to make a model for what this strange animal – the symphony orchestra – really is. Nobody really has the answer to that question yet, but we have to try to find one.

Will Sir Simon still be in Birmingham in the year 2000? The *Birmingham Post* recently quoted him: 'You know how much this orchestra and this city mean to me – it is so much the centre of what I am as an artist.'[34] There was both sadness and dismay when it was announced in February 1995 that he and Elise had separated and were seeking a divorce – sadness, because they had been married on the very day that Simon had taken up his CBSO appointment, and they appeared to have managed their respective professional and family lives so happily and successfully, Sacha and Eliot both being born during that time; and dismay, lest future uncertainties in one half of Sir Simon's life might lead to parallel uncertainties in the other. What is certain is that everyone wishes them both well.

If the time does come for Sir Simon to leave, it goes without saying that his will be a hard act to follow. As this book clearly shows, the past 75 years have been a steady *crescendo*, but no earlier period can compare in brilliance with the Rattle years. Despite the media hype, though, the CBSO is not and never has been a one-man band. Behind the pages of this history are many unsung heroes and heroines – members of the Orchestra and Chorus, officers, Board members, administrative staff of one kind and another – currently some 350; and beyond them, the countless people who support the CBSO's concerts and make it all possible.

If any one man's contribution has been undervalued in this book, that man is Edward Smith, Chief Executive since 1978. His management style is unobtrusive but it is also strikingly imaginative and enormously effective. He pushed and pushed for Rattle's appointment, for the Development Plan, for Symphony Hall (whose name he suggested) and for virtually every innovation that Birmingham has enjoyed over the past 15 years or more. He has a thoroughly professional management team behind him and, despite a financial climate as uncertain as ever, the outlook remains fine. In Birmingham, the name of the game continues to be Excellence.

In recent years Sir Simon Rattle and the whole organisation have received many well-deserved awards. He has always been quick to share the honours he receives with everyone else, so, assuming that he is still in Birmingham as the Millennium draws to a close (and he is currently under contract until 1998) there will be one additional cause for celebration, which may well have slipped his mind. As long ago as 1989, he won a Chivas Regal Millennium Award as 'a musician with the potential to achieve greatness by the year 2000'. His prize – a cask of 12-year-old Scotch whisky – was presented on one condition only: in order to mature fully, it must remain at the distillery until the year 1999. Cheers!

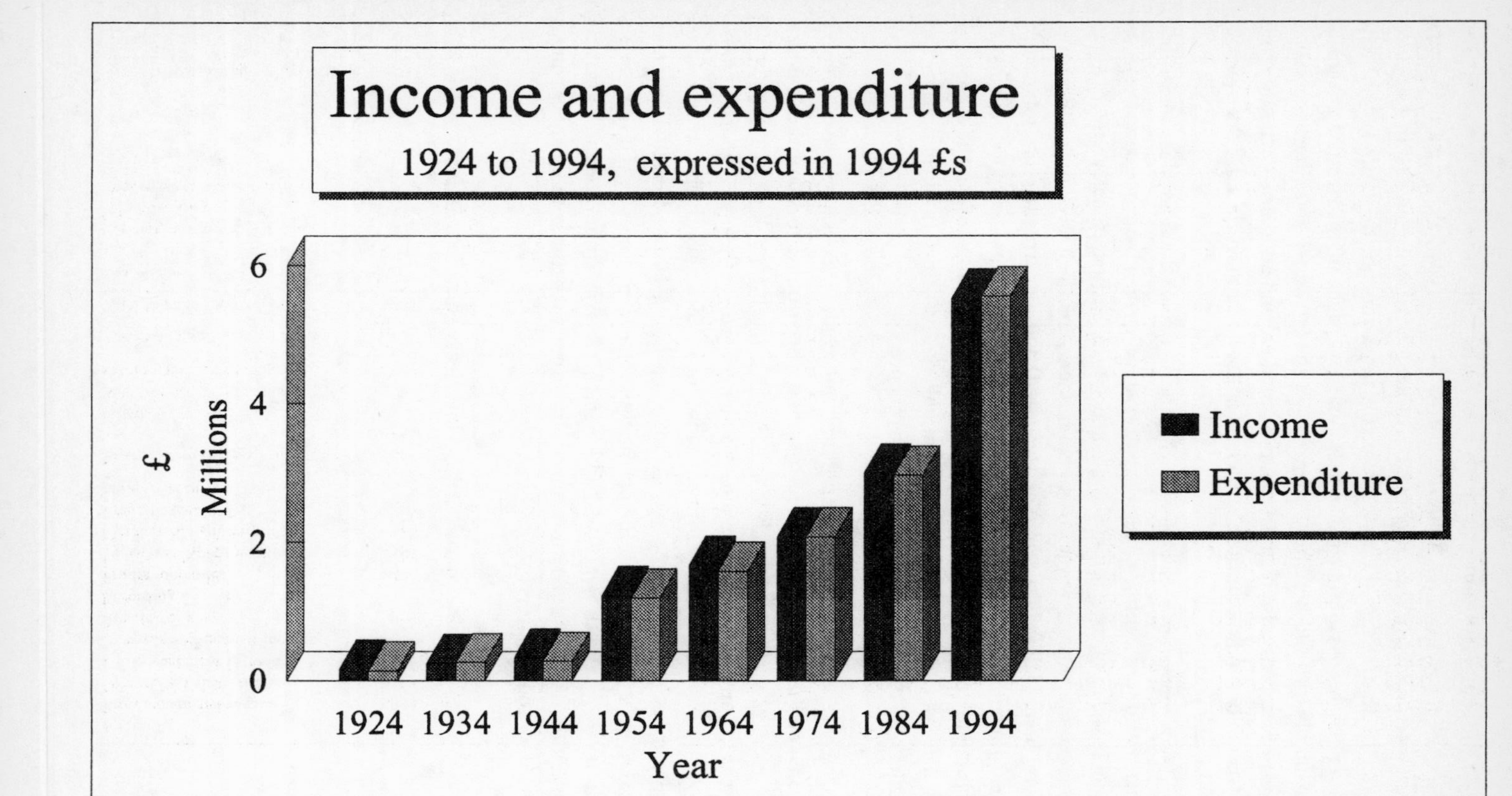
Income and expenditure
1924 to 1994, expressed in 1994 £s
£
Millions
6
4
2
0
1924 1934 1944 1954 1964 1974 1984 1994
Year
Income
Expenditure

INCOME AND EXPENDITURE, 1924–1994

Year	1924		1934		1944		1954		1964		1974		1984		1994	
	£	%	£	%	£	%	£	%	£	%	£	%	£	%	£	%
Income																
Birmingham ticket sales	3,393	46.9	3,334	38.3	7,893	48.9	16,569	18.7	16,062	10.0	47,742	12.2	222,542	12.2	1,236,450	22.4
Other UK ticket sales	-	-	-	-	-	-	7,048	8.0	6,108	3.8	17,276	4.4	102,773	5.6	89,493	1.6
UK engagement income	1,346	18.6	2,512	28.9	3,269	20.2	20,502	23.2	47,831	29.7	73,282	18.8	306,844	16.8	775,243	14.0
Overseas engagement income	-	-	-	-	-	-	-	-	-	-	-	-	60,296	3.3	258,522	4.7
Broadcasting	-	-	-	-	-	-	6,509	7.3	10,180	6.3	9,995	2.6	134,904	7.4	128,326	2.3
Recording	-	-	-	-	-	-	-	-	-	-	3,100	0.8	41,467	2.3	187,776	3.4
Programme sales	426	5.9	171	1.9	187	1.3	191	0.2	2,078	1.3	5,406	1.4	11,700	0.6	47,677	0.9
Donations/Sponsorship	798	11.0	108	1.2	1,113	6.9	221	0.3	-	-	10,388	2.6	106,623	5.8	373,961	6.8
Membership subscriptions	18	0.3	28	0.3	34	0.2	387	0.4	788	0.5	4,237	1.1	6,810	0.4	34,605	0.6
Interest receivable	-	-	55	0.6	58	0.3	-	-	-	-	-	-	-	-	38,289	0.7
Sundry receipts	-	-	-	-	40	0.2	70	0.1	833	0.5	1,769	0.4	2,638	0.2	62,108	1.1
Income from Society's activities	5,981	82.7	6,208	71.2	12,594	78.0	51,497	58.2	83,880	52.1	173,195	44.3	996,597	54.6	3,232,450	58.5
Grants																
Arts Council	-	-	-	-	-	-	12,000	13.6	42,000	26.1	135,000	34.6	457,594	25.1	1,164,646	21.1
Birmingham City Council	1,250	17.3	2,500	28.8	3,542	22.0	25,000	28.2	35,000	21.8	82,380	21.1	369,235	20.3	1,125,000	20.4
Total Grants	1,250	17.3	2,500	28.8	3,542	22.0	37,000	41.8	77,000	47.9	217,380	55.7	826,829	45.4	2,289,646	41.5
Total Income	7,231	100	8,708	100	16,136	100	88,497	100	160,880	100	390,575	100	1,823,426	100	5,522,096	100
Expenditure																
Maintenance of orchestra	2,751	44.1	5,884	64.1	8,527	60.9	56,891	66.1	113,768	74.4	271,578	69.5	1,106,156	61.3	2,862,567	51.5
Concert expenses	2,679	42.9	2,743	29.9	4,319	30.9	22,340	25.9	27,098	17.7	85,875	22.0	516,821	28.6	1,883,952	33.9
Administration	811	13.0	557	6.0	1,145	8.2	6,540	7.6	11,736	7.7	30,847	7.9	164,750	9.1	749,272	13.5
Depreciation/Asset funding	-	-	-	-	-	-	311	0.4	317	0.2	2,275	0.6	18,264	1.0	60,448	1.1
Total Expenditure	6,241	100	9,184	100	13,991	100	86,082	100	152,919	100	390,575	100	1,805,991	100	5,556,239	100
Surplus/(Deficit)	990		(476)		2,145		2,415		7,961		-		17,435		(34,143)	
Accumulated Surplus/(Deficit)	(3,164)		943		4,150		(24,998)		16,733		-		-		(106,088)	

Notes

1. Programme income for the years 1934, 1944, 1954 is a net figure after deducting costs – no way of separating these.
2. The amount of £10,388 shown as Sponsorship in 1974 was a transfer from Capital Reserve.
3. Grant from Birmingham City Council in 1984 includes a grant from West Midlands County Council.

Notes

Preface and Acknowledgements

1. Alderman Byng Kenrick, Chairman of the City of Birmingham Orchestra (later the CBSO), 1931–50, writing to his successor in office, Councillor Stephen Lloyd, 8 May 1953.
2. Between 1945 and 1970, however, some forty days of 'School Visits' were undertaken each year for Birmingham Education Committee, in the course of which four or five different groups of players would visit four schools each; if all *those* concerts were to be taken into consideration, the total would be nearer 30,000 – a staggering record of musical endeavour.
3. Bona fide researchers may write to: The Archivist, CBSO, Paradise Place, Birmingham B3 3RP.

Chapter 1 Elgar's button-up boots

1. Beatrice Harrison soon became Elgar's favourite interpreter of the Cello Concerto; she had, indeed, made her first (acoustic) recording of the work with him, a few months before, but Salmond seems to have made a good impression at the première, despite very limited rehearsal time (Albert Coates having used most of the available time for the items he was to conduct in the same programme).
2. Letter to the author, September 1994.
3. Review by C. F. M., 11 November 1920.
4. Quoted in Michael Kennedy: *Portrait of Elgar* (Oxford University Press, 1968).
5. William C. Stockley: *Fifty Years of Music in Birmingham* (Hudson & Son, Birmingham, 1913), p. 41.
6. On 1 March 1915, at a Harrison Concert with the London Symphony Orchestra.
7. Malcolm MacDonald: *Havergal Brian on Music, Vol. 1* (Toccata Press).
8. CBSO house-magazine *Music Stand*, November 1980.

Chapter 2 William Stockley – George Halford

1. Sir Thomas Beecham: *A Mingled Chime – An Autobiography* (Hutchinson, 1944) ch. 6.

2. *The New Grove* (ed. Stanley Sadie) Vol. 2, p. 123.
3. David Brock: *The Birmingham School of Music – Its First Century* (Birmingham School of Music, 1986) p. 25.
4. Malcolm MacDonald: *op. cit.*, pp. 36–7.
5. *Birmingham Faces and Places, Vol. IV* (J. G. Hammond & Co, Scotland Passage, Birmingham, 1891) p. 69.
6. W. H. Priestley & Sons, Birmingham's principal music shop, at 71/3 Colmore Row. In her book *As I Remember*, the late Mildred Boulton wrote, 'In the late 1890s, and for a long time into this century, Priestley's was the hub of the City's musical life. In Mother's day, it was to Priestley's you went to get your concert tickets, buy your music, your piano and any other musical requirement you needed. The shop itself was, I remember, spacious, and there were music studios which could be hired by the hour, in rooms upstairs.'
7. William C. Stockley: *op cit.*, pp. 54–5.
8. Quoted in Christopher Fifield: *True Artist and True Friend* (Clarendon Press, 1993), p. 301.
9. *The Grimshaw Letters* (Archives Department, Birmingham Central Library), p. 139. They cover a period from 1829 to 1839 and include, *inter alia*, letters to Sam Grimshaw concerning musical festivals all over the country.
10. Quoted in Margaret Handford: *Sounds Unlikely – Six Hundred Years of Music in Birmingham* (Birmingham & Midland Institute, 1992), p. 102.
11. G. Bernard Shaw [*Corno di Bassetto*]: review dated 15 June 1892, quoted in *G.B.S. on Music* (Penguin Books, 1962) p. 102.
12. Sir Thomas Beecham: *op cit.* p. 67.
13. Richter's diary, 13 February 1900. Quoted in Christopher Fifield: *op cit.*, p. 301.
14. *Birmingham Daily Post*, 1 October 1897.
15. From 1901 onwards it was known as the Halford Concerts Society.
16. Henry J. Wood: *My Life of Music* (Victor Gollancz, 1938) p. 203.
17. 14 February 1933.
18. Malcolm MacDonald: *op. cit.* pp. 360–4.
19. *Midland Musician*, September 1926, pp. 22–3.
20. *Birmingham Daily Post*, 22 January 1902.
21. Robert J. Buckley, *Birmingham Gazette & Express*, 2 October 1907, p. 4. The mention of Siloti refers to the first British performance outside London of Rachmaninov's Piano Concerto No. 2 – see Margaret Handford: *op. cit.*, p. 184.
22. Max Mossel (1871–1929) also ran a series of Drawing-Room Concerts which became 'the most fashionable institution in the town's musical life' [*British Musician*, August 1929, p. 232]. He was a close friend of Elgar, and is one of the four musicians in the well-known photo, taken at the Three Choirs Festival, showing Elgar, Percy Hull and Sinclair (see note 27) with his bulldog Dan.
23. Archie Camden: *Blow by Blow* (Thames Publishing, 1982) pp. 41–4, 56–60. Camden earned £4.10.0 [£4.50] a week (inclusive of travel and subsistence) and felt 'immensely rich and independent'.
24. Bridget Duckenfield: *O Lovely Knight – A Biography of Sir Landon Ronald* (Thames Publishing, London, 1991), ch. 5.
25. Malcolm MacDonald: *op. cit.* p. 367.

26. 9 April 1907 – details on a silver tray, 'Presented . . . by the Members of his Orchestra as a token of esteem on the occasion of the 100th Concert, April 9th 1907', given to the CBSO by the Halford family, 1993, together with a salver, presented to Halford in 1889 to mark his retirement from Birmingham Choral and Orchestral Association.
27. Dr G. R. Sinclair of Hereford Cathedral – the 'G. R. S.' of the *Enigma Variations.*
28. In an interview with John Warrack in the *Observer Magazine*, 7 April 1974, Boult described Safonoff as 'the very greatest Tchaikovsky conductor of my experience'.

Chapter 3 *Granville Bantock – Thomas Beecham*

1. During the 1906–7 season, Wood conducted three City Choral concerts (*Messiah*, a Wagner programme and *The Kingdom*) and Beard conducted a Saturday 'Pop'. A letter from H. J. Lewis, Orchestral Steward, sets out the rehearsal schedule (two each for Wagner and Elgar) and the basic rates: 18/- [90p] per concert, 3/- [15p] for an extra rehearsal.
2. 30 October 1907 – unsigned but presumably written by Newman.
3. Malcolm MacDonald: *op. cit.*, pp. 36–7.
4. Margaret Handford: *op. cit.*, p. 236.
5. Sir Thomas Beecham: *op. cit.*, p. 154.
6. David Dilks: *Neville Chamberlain* (Cambridge University Press, 1984) Vol. 1, pp. 164, 389.
7. Letter (addressee unknown) dated 25 March 1916; a copy survives in the handwriting of Neville Chamberlain's son-in-law Stephen Lloyd, who seems to have used it when setting up the City of Birmingham Orchestral Endowment Fund, in the 1950s. A further series of six Hallé concerts was announced for the 1916–17 season, but only four seem to have taken place – two conducted by Beecham, one each by Ronald and Wood.
8. J. Sutcliffe Smith: *The Story of Music in Birmingham* (Cornish Brothers Ltd, Birmingham, 1945), p.70.
9. The title is inconsistent: the original advertisement for the principal Wednesday series of Nine Symphony Concerts describes it thus, as do some of the programmes, but a leaflet advertising another series of Ten Popular Sunday Concerts, and some later programmes, prefer 'The Birmingham Orchestra'.
10. David Dilks: *op cit.*, p. 185.
11. Sir Thomas Beecham, *op. cit.*, ch. 33.

Chapter 4 *Genesis*

1. Joseph McKenna: *Birmingham between the Wars* (Birmingham Library Services, 1991).
2. Bantock's dentist, *inter alia*, but according to John Crowder, 'Not much of a musician!'
3. Presumably the orchestra of the Beecham Opera Company.
4. 'A meeting of the Sub-Committee was held at the Council House on Tuesday July 3rd. Mr Bantock explained the difficulty of forming an orchestra this

season, & giving the proposed series of concerts. The Town Hall had been largely booked by the other societies, & most of the orchestral players being under contracts would be unable to accept our engagements. He further pointed out that at the moment we had no written constitution, & the legal point as to the liability of the guarantors had not been defined. It was proposed by him & seconded by Dr Russell – that the concerts be postponed until the season 1920–21.

Messrs Beale, Huxley & Warden were asked to draw up the form of constitution, & report to the Committee at a meeting to be held next October. Messrs Max Mossel & Gerald Forty were asked to prepare a revised estimate of the cost of the Concert scheme, & to report to the meeting to be held in October.

It was pointed out the great importance of having a competent Manager, & it was felt that the success or failure of the scheme would be largely determined by our choice in this matter. Members were therefore requested to consider carefully this question, & if possible be prepared to make nominations at our next meeting.'

5. In *The Times, Telegraph, Observer* and *Birmingham Post.*
6. Harrison had various irons in the fire, including the Beecham Opera Company; Bainton was Principal of the Newcastle-upon-Tyne Conservatoire. Both were composers of some note.
7. The Sub-Committee was evidently still aiming at a possible full-time contract orchestra, although this would have exceeded their remit from the Council.
8. Interview by Peter Spaull for BBC Radio Birmingham.
9. Letter in the *Birmingham Post*, 18 November 1982. The Ulsterman Charles Rafter became Birmingham's Chief Constable in 1899 and had taken command of crowd-control at the time of the notorious 'Lloyd George Riot' in Victoria Square, on 18 December 1901, when the great Liberal orator (considered pro-Boer and anti-Joseph Chamberlain, and therefore certain of an unfriendly reception in Birmingham) addressed a public meeting. Police over-reaction led to a baton-charge which resulted in the death of one youth (an innocent onlooker) and many injuries. Most of the windows in the Town Hall (where a Halford concert had taken place on the previous evening) were smashed by stone-throwing. The indestructible Rafter (later Sir Charles) remained in post for no less than 36 years.
10. In March 1920 Matthews also succeeded in 'upping' his annual salary from St Agnes's Church, Moseley, to £100.

Chapter 5 *Appleby Matthews – Innovator*

1. A letter to Matthews dated 20 March 1920, from the secretary of a local choral society, observes that it might prove hard to fix a choral/orchestral rehearsal, 'as so many play at the picture houses nowadays'.
2. Bands in those days normally played at the old sharp pitch, but in a radio interview with Peter Spaull for BBC Radio Birmingham, Sir Adrian Boult recalled that Rafter, the Chief Constable, had seen to it that his police bandsmen were equipped with low-pitch instruments, so that 'we could bring them

into the orchestra at any time. I think the third and fourth horns were always policemen'.

3. £160 of orchestra fees were budgeted per Symphony Concert, £80 per Popular Concert and £20 per Chamber Concert.
4. Stephen J. Pettitt: *Dennis Brain – A biography* (Robert Hale, 1989), p. 32.
5. Frank Forty recalls that the Yorkes 'were so short that when they stood up to play the National Anthem, they all disappeared behind their stands!'
6. Mr Arthur Rankin remembers that 'At the rehearsal a surprising thing occurred near the end of *En Saga*, after the cymbal clash. Matthews rushed up to Sibelius and apparently remonstrated with him; I can only think that it was for not slowing down for the remainder of the piece, as some conductors do.' (Letter to the author, dated January 1993.)
7. 5 September 1921, quoted in the CBO's Sunday programme, 11 September.
8. Approximately 6p in decimal currency. Twelve pennies made up one shilling, and twenty shillings made up one pound. A ticket costing one shilling and threepence could be expressed either as 1s. 3d. or as 1/3d.
9. Interview with the author, 1969. In a letter to the CBSO Office dated May 1982, Mrs Isabella Young recalled Beard's somewhat imperious manner, and his characteristic sitting posture, right leg straight out in front of him (as confirmed by extant photographs). 'On one occasion he kept the whole hall, including the conductor, waiting while he wiped his nose and slowly replaced his handkerchief in his trouser pocket – leg still out!'
10. In September 1922 Matthews listed 14 venues for the Committee: Burton-on-Trent, Cheltenham, Derby, Hanley, Kidderminster, Leamington, Malvern, Nottingham, Redditch, Stoke-on-Trent, Tamworth, Walsall, West Bromwich and Wolverhampton. These were to remain the core of the CBO's out-of-town concert promotions until the 1950s.
11. Michael Kennedy: *Adrian Boult* (Hamish Hamilton, 1987). Boult's appointment as conductor of the Festival Choral Society was announced in the *Birmingham Post* on 15 September 1923.
12. Carole Rosen: *The Goossens* (André Deutsch, 1993), p. 97.
13. Tax and costs were in addition to this sum, and Birkett's fee will have been substantial, too. In his book *Lord Justice Birkett* (Robert Hale, 1962) Dennis Bardens notes that shortly after this, in what *Punch* described as 'The Dustbin Case', his fee was £3000. It does not figure in the CBO's Accounts and one wonders who paid it? A possible clue is that Birkett's first job had been as private secretary to George Cadbury at Bournville. He later practised on the Midland Circuit, based at chambers in Temple Row, Birmingham.
14. Marion Appleby-Matthews: letter to the author, July 1994.

Chapter 6 *Adrian Boult – Orchestra builder*

1. Both references: 30 September 1924.
2. Throughout this and the following chapter I freely acknowledge my indebtedness to Michael Kennedy's excellent biography *Adrian Boult* (Hamish Hamilton Ltd, 1987). He in turn was able to draw upon documents in the CBSO's archives, including Sir Adrian's own Birmingham press-cuttings scrapbook, presented to the CBSO in the 1970s.

3. These included Lady Mills; Professor Ernest de Selincourt; C. H. Rafter (the Chief Constable); Barry Jackson (of Birmingham Repertory Theatre); Madame Zara Minadieu and George Halford. Lady Brooks was awarded a CBE for her efforts.
4. The orchestral breakdown was: 2/2/2/3 woodwind; 4/3/3/1 brass; timpani, percussion, harp + strings 11/9/6/6/5. For *The Planets* (25 November) the orchestra was enlarged to 75.
5. Another Boult conducting pupil at the Royal College of Music.
6. *BBC Yearbook, 1930*, p. 193. CBO Broadcasts gradually became more regular; in the following season the BBC took three concerts, at a guaranteed minimum fee of £40.
7. I am indebted to Brian Dixon and Robin Miller for copies of programmes of the CBO's annual concerts at Oundle School, 1925–30. Initially, Boult shared the conducting with the school's Director of Music, Clement Spurling, but after a while common sense prevailed and Boult would conduct the whole concert.
8. Harold Gray: Interview with the author, May 1973.
9. Myrrha Bantock: *Granville Bantock – A Personal Portrait* (J. M. Dent and Sons Ltd, 1972), p. 125.
10. *Midland Musician*, September 1926, p. 19.
11. Brian Wright: 'The civil servant', Classic CD, May 1991, p. 61.
12. Stephen J. Pettitt: *op. cit.*, p. 46.
13. I am indebted to Laura Gray for a transcript of Sibelius's draft letter, from Helsinki City Library.
14. Review in the *Midland Musician*, February 1926.
15. *Midland Musician*, September 1926, p. 19.
16. Both conditional, to some extent, on other sponsors coming forward.
17. In 1925–6 the CBO played for five Festival Choral Society concerts; Boult reported that Vaughan Williams's *Sea Symphony* on 11 February had been 'the greatest achievement of the season'.
18. A feature on the CBO in the *London Musical Courier* for January 1926 mentions a seating capacity of four or five thousand.

Chapter 7 Consolidation

1. His invitation to the (now much improved) Festival Choral Society to participate in No. 9 gave rise to some understandable resentment from the City Choir, which had been founded specifically to perform with the CBO.
2. Quoted by Lyndon Jenkins in *Sir Adrian Boult, Companion of Honour, A Tribute* edited by Nigel Simeone and Simon Mundy (Midas Books, 1980) p. 34.
3. *Birmingham Post*, 7 February 1927.
4. Boult had sensibly prepared the ground by including the work in one of his Sunday programmes, earlier in the season.
5. Hock's excellent little Birmingham String Orchestra, which gave many concerts and broadcasts from Queen's College Chambers, opposite the Town Hall, drew extensively on CBO players.

6. Composer of several operas, many songs and orchestral works (including a Symphony).
7. *Bristol Times & Mirror*, 21 October 1926.
8. The Annual Report explained that 'As we cannot yet engage musicians on a whole time basis', some of the musicians were freelance players.
9. The players' contracts stipulated 'Hotel expenses not exceeding ten shillings'.
10. Those who know the Town Hall well can empathise with this description; everyone I ever spoke to who remembered the hall prior to the alterations agreed that the resulting sound was greatly inferior to the original, especially at the back of the Ground Floor and Lower Gallery. It is good to hear that there are now plans to reverse the 1927 alterations by removing the upper gallery and reshaping the lower gallery 'similar to the original design' (*Birmingham Voice*, 1 March 1995).
11. On Boult's own admission, he had been working '7 days in the week', and in his autobiography [*op. cit.*, p. 58] he mentions that for his first three years in Birmingham he had also 'made a point of attending every concert given by local artists'.
12. Shephard's long-serving typist and assistant Miss Lycett received a rise, too – to 5/- per week!
13. Gerald Forty was asked to chair a sub-committee to look into this serious problem.
14. Sir Adrian Boult: *op. cit.*, p. 58.
15. Letter from A. H. Shephard to CBO violinist Victor Fleming.
16. Substantial cuts were made (one critic observed that to have Dorothy Silk present and not hear her sing '*Aus Liebe will mein Heiland sterben*' was a sad loss) but it was a splendid effort. Boult had engaged Wanda Landowska to play harpischord *continuo* (and a Bach Concerto on the previous Sunday) but she was ill and sent her distinguished pupil, Ruggiero Gerlin, in her place.
17. Pitt had worked closely with Richter on the first *Ring* cycle to be given in English (at Covent Garden, in January 1908) and with the Beecham Opera Co.
18. *Daily Express*, 21 May 1929.
19. The three not selected were Aylmer Buesst, Julian Clifford and Thomas McGuire.
20. Sargent liked to be 'Dr' as much as Boult preferred to be 'Mr'.
21. 13 February 1930.
22. Conductor of the Amsterdam Concertgebouw Orchestra and champion of Mahler's music.
23. *Birmingham Post*, 18 February 1930. Astra Desmond, who had come in for some stick in the same review, wrote to CBO committee member Mrs Coats, 'I'm glad my singing pleased you more than it did Mr Sheldon! I personally have enjoyed those two concerts, Bach [Boult's *St Matthew Passion*] and Mahler, as much as any I've sung this season, and more than most.'
24. The Royal Borough of Sutton Coldfield (as it then was) lies at Birmingham's north-eastern boundary. Promotion of the new series was soon taken over by the Borough and, later still, by the autonomous Philharmonic Society, which still exists.
25. *Birmingham Post*, 31 January 1930.

26. Alderman Berry.
27. CBSO principal cello Harry Stanier, whom Gwen was to marry, 34 years later.
28. 13 October 1930 – but how he will have squirmed a few moments later to hear his forthcoming rôle at the BBC described as 'the musical Mussolini of the British people'! The phrase (ill-chosen even then) was to take on an even hollower ring a decade later.

Chapter **8** *Leslie Heward – 'A very gifted musician'*

1. Published by the author, 1993, p. 147.
2. Eric Blom (ed.): *Leslie Heward 1897–1943* (J. M. Dent & Sons Ltd, 1944), p. 21.
3. Although Malcolm Sargent's reputation has suffered some decline since his death in 1967, as a young man he was regarded as probably the most gifted of all – an ARCO at the age of 16 and a Mus. D. at 24.
4. Details from a letter from Frank Young to Lyndon Jenkins, dated 12 January 1984. Mr Young visited the church, saw a printed programme of a later similar performance (1908) and spoke to a 92-year-old member of the congregation who clearly remembered the boy's prowess.
5. Eric Blom [*op. cit.*] includes reviews of a school concert at this time, contributed by Adrian Boult, Sydney Nicholson and Arthur Bliss.
6. Howells told Gordon Heard (at one time principal flute of the CBSO) that Heward was the most talented pupil he ever taught.
7. Heward's BNOC début took place in Birmingham's Prince of Wales Theatre, conducting Saint-Saëns's *Samson et Delilah*.
8. 'One of the most brilliant young conductors in the country is playing the piano in a West End theatre band – for a bad play, too!' Gordon Beckles, *Daily Express*, 21 May 1929.
9. Other local professionals regularly gave their services to augment the CBO for this event.
10. Mrs Florence Taylor (*née* Lycett), who worked in the CBO Office 1924–39 – interview with the author, October 1993.
11. Letter written from London, June 1930, to Mrs Coats, tireless CBO supporter and committee member.
12. Warlock [Philip Heseltine] wrote CBO notes for the last three months of 1930; in January 1931, following his tragic suicide, he was replaced by his friend Philip Page, music critic of the *Evening Standard*.
13. In a *Corno di Bassetto* review dated 13 December 1893, Bernard Shaw described this as 'the only real symphony that has been composed since Beethoven died'.
14. Harold Gray greatly appreciated Leslie introducing him to such artistic haunts as the Savage Club, Pagani's Restaurant, the Café Royal in Regent Street and the George (known to one and all as 'the Gluepot'), where he met many of the leading figures of London's musical world of the Thirties.
15. The job also involved writing programme notes, visiting schools and talking to head teachers. £1 per concert was deducted from Heward's salary, since these were really part of his responsibilities.

16. Interview with the author, 1979.
17. Garry O'Connor: *The Pursuit of Perfection – A Life of Maggie Teyte* (Victor Gollancz, 1979), p. 218. Cave was 'tall, dark-haired, big boned' and the passage which contains Teyte's remark also includes a description of his playing: 'he was lugubrious and hardly ever spoke a word. A musician, true, a violinist; a wonderful player, but it was not, as someone snidely said, the kind of playing anyone much liked to hear. After all, there is, in musical execution as in morals, a kind of perfection which is unutterably tedious.'
18. A printed table-card in the CBSO's archives lists the items to be played, with catalogue numbers of gramophone records of each number, 'obtainable in our Gramophone Department'. The fact that all the discs were either on the HMV or Columbia label suggests some early form of sponsorship.
19. Article quoted in Malcolm MacDonald: *op. cit.*, p. 209. 'LSD' was a shorthand for money (£.s.d. = pounds, shillings and pence).
20. Ignoring the ingenious suggestion of a CBO Committee member, Professor O. J. Kauffmann, who suggested placing a mirror inside each window to reflect light downwards. How that would have helped the situation on a dark winter's evening is not easy to understand. Kauffmann died only a few months later.

Chapter 9 *The BBC link*

1. According to Professor Ernest de Selincourt [Blom, *op. cit.*, p. 70], 'he was always helpful and conciliatory – adamant only on such points of principle as seemed to involve the integrity of the City Orchestra and his control over its policy and personnel.'
2. Havergal Brian 'Provincial Choral Societies (1937)' – article quoted in Malcolm MacDonald: *op. cit.*, pp. 381–2.
3. 7 March 1935 – a member of the audience recalls the occasion not only for a memorable reading of Beethoven's C minor Piano Concerto but because she happened to see Lamond leaving the Town Hall after the concert, with Heward, and thought 'how shabby and poor he looked. I wonder how much he was paid for his stupendous performance?' He was, in fact, paid 40 guineas.
4. A late replacement for Lisa Minghetti; Heward said that he gave 'a magnificent performance' of the Brahms Violin Concerto.
5. Despite some 'pulling in of horns': the previous season's 'Orchestra of 75 players' (80 for the *Planets* concert) had now shrunk to 70.
6. Following recent CBO performances of the Fourth Symphony and *Tapiola*, Heward wrote to the composer to ask whether Glockenspiel or tubular bells should be used in these two works. He replied, 'I thank you cordially for your interest in my music. Concerning your two technical questions I would suggest to you the using of Glockenspiel in the 4th Symphony and Stahlstäbe in *Oceanides.* With kind regards.' Since 'Stahlstäbe' is generally regarded as a synonym for 'Glockenspiel', Sibelius's reply was only partly informative, but at least it appeared clear enough that he did not want tubular bells in the Fourth Symphony.
7. 'Hay' was Sir Hamilton Harty's nickname.
8. Michael Kennedy: *Portrait of Walton* (Oxford University Press, 1989) p. 85.

9. Blom: *op. cit.*, p. 65.
10. Blom, *op. cit.*, p. 75.
11. Letter to the author, May 1994.
12. Malcolm Arnold played under Heward many times, as principal trumpet in the London Philharmonic: 'he was not only a reliable conductor, he even used to make you realise that *1812* was a piece of music and not just a damned noise!' (Interview with Lyndon Jenkins, *Classical Music*, 11 February 1984.)
13. *Birmingham Post*, 12 February 1937.
14. Oddly, this was billed both in the press and the printed programmes as 'First Public Performance'.
15. When David Willcocks finally persuaded the Three Choirs' Festival Committee that Walton's supposedly 'pagan' work could be performed (at Worcester, in the 1950s) it was again coupled with the Bloch.
16. Photos in Joseph McKenna: *Birmingham between the Wars* (Birmingham Library Services, 1991).
17. Eric Blom: *op. cit.*, p. 64ff.
18. Philip R. Henderson: letter to the author, July 1993. Extraneous noise has always been a problem in Birmingham Town Hall; as early as 1909, the music critic of the *Yorkshire Post* complained, 'At the Birmingham Festival last week a series of performances which I have never known surpassed for all-round excellence were frequently marred by the growing nuisance of the motor horn.' (Quoted in Christopher Fifield: *op. cit.*, p. 422.)
19. Harold Gray: article marking the CBSO's Jubilee in the *Birmingham Post*, 20 September 1969. This was one of Harold's favourite stories; he would always exaggerate Weingartner's thick accent: 'Ziss zenn voss holy groundt!'
20. Interview with the author, May 1994. Denison remembers the CBO's woodwind principals at this time: flautist George Barrett, oboist Lucy Vincent (who had a tendency to play sharp), clarinettist Richard Walthew and bassoonist Bill Foote ('A big man, brought up in Canada; he was a First World War veteran, and a real character').
21. 'I always found [Heward] a most inspiring collaborator.' Blom: *op. cit.*, p. 76.
22. Eric Blom: *op. cit.*, p. 48.
23. Letter to the author, May 1993.

Chapter **10** *The wartime years*

1. The last invoice from the BBC for the services of its 35 players was for a Cheltenham concert on 26 May.
2. All the local artists accepted 'expenses fees' only, to get things going.
3. Heward, who had taken a short holiday in Poole on leaving the sanatorium, actually returned to his Birmingham home on the 25th, but it seems very unlikely that he would yet have felt strong enough to attend this concert.
4. W. K. Stanton of the BBC also helped considerably with planning the 1939–40 series.
5. In an appreciation of Victor Hely-Hutchinson, written after his death in 1947, Sir Wilfrid Martineau described the Beethoven cycle as 'a godsend to lift us out of the awful present and to hope for better times to come'. Gerald Forty recalled that the Sonatas were 'memorised from week to week and performed

with impeccable artistry and without a single lapse of memory'. Interestingly, Hely-Hutchinson was not the only locally based pianist to perform the cycle at this time; Appleby Matthews did so in Birmingham Cathedral, and Tom Bromley broadcast all the sonatas for the BBC.

6. Here they were by no means immune from air raids, however. Sidonie Goossens recalled that Paul Beard (now Leader of the BBC Symphony Orchestra) 'was blown off his bicycle by a bomb blast, but was not seriously hurt'. Albert Cockerill, a founder member of the CBO and later its principal double bass, before joining the BBC Symphony at the outset of the war, was killed, along with his wife, when their Bristol flat suffered a direct hit. (See Carole Rosen: *op. cit.*, p. 193.)
7. Mrs Beryl Lawrence: letter to author, 17 August 1993.
8. Enough to wipe out the previous season's deficit of over £1000.
9. Concerts in Leamington, Bristol, Birmingham, Glasgow and Edinburgh.
10. All the CBO's wartime recordings, issued and unissued, are listed and described in *The Birmingham 78s, 1925–1947*, by the present author and Lyndon Jenkins (CBSO, 1983).
11. Apart from one of the regular 'Family Party' concerts, at which he shared the baton and two pianos, turn-and-turn-about, with Stanton, Hely-Hutchinson and Cunningham. This drew the best house of the season – over 1400.
12. Telephone conversation with the author, April 1994. The stories on p. 16 of Frank Downes's book *Around the Horn* (Birmingham City Council, 1994) refer to the New Midland Symphony Orchestra, not to the CBO.
13. Alton Douglas: *Birmingham at War* (Birmingham Post & Mail, 1982) p. 65.
14. These lived up to their name, with hundreds having to be turned away. By the following season, an additional 330 seats had been provided on the Ground Floor, and 30 in the Lower Gallery.
15. Heward noted in his diary that this 'went wrong' and had to be repeated a few days later.
16. On Sunday, 4 January 1942, a deleted diary entry reads, 'Cameron? if I'm not fit'.
17. Frank Young recalls that Heward had to interrupt the *Enigma Variations* during *Nimrod*, while a brass band marched very audibly through Victoria Square.
18. Alton Douglas, *op. cit.*, p. 12.
19. *British Musician*, October 1928, p. 216.
20. From the 'Musical Education' section of a CBO promotional brochure, 1947.
21. Heward had known Unger since 1938, but when he had conducted his Leningrad orchestra, two years earlier, Unger had been away on holiday. Heward was supposed to bring the score and parts of the orchestral extracts from Smetana's *Bartered Bride* with him, but Unger records that 'A week before he was due, a man came up to me during a break in rehearsal and said breathlessly: "Heward's not coming – his wife's dangerously ill. We've just received a telegram." "Have you got the telegram there?" In a a few minutes he brought it to me. It read: "Bartered Bride unobtainable Heward." ' The word 'bartered' was doubtless unfamiliar to the interpreter; the word 'battered' will have been more familiar.
22. Eric Blom: *op. cit.*, p. 80f.

23. Gordon Heard, in a letter to the author, May 1994, quoting his father, Syd Heard. Eli Fletcher's pub was a real old Brummie hostelry (sawdust on the floor, and a 'Gentlemen Only' bar) frequented by orchestral players since time immemorial, since it lay so close to the Town Hall.
24. The arithmetic looks wrong, but Heward had missed a whole season (1939–40) through illness.
25. Schumann's *Manfred* Overture, Saint-Saëns's Second Piano Concerto (Irene Kohler) and Tchaikovsky's Fourth Symphony. Heinz Unger had originally been announced as the conductor on this date.
26. The photographer Geoffrey G. Hoare remembers, 'I drove him to his last visit to the Clef Club in Birmingham, just before his death.'
27. Interview with the author, 1979.

Chapter 11 *George Weldon – Going for broke*

1. The address at his funeral was given by a younger colleague, John F. Waterhouse, whom we shall meet again as Eric Blom's successor at the *Birmingham Post*.
2. *Birmingham Mail*, 5 May 1943.
3. In 1927 Brunner had founded the Non-Competitive Schools Musical Festival movement in Shrewsbury; he was elected Chairman of the national body, when it was formed in 1938.
4. Son of the Julian Clifford who conducted the Birmingham Symphony Orchestra, *c.* 1909 (see end of Chapter 2).
5. He later revised his opinion and became a staunch friend and supporter of Weldon.
6. Dr Ruth Gipps: interview with the author, May 1994.
7. At its meeting on 10 August 1943, the Management Committee accepted the Executive Committee's recommendation to offer the series to Weldon. The Executive Meeting was started on 4 August and then adjourned to 6 August. The surviving correspondence, however, seems to imply that Mathieson (who had been asked, like Weldon, for a note of his availability during the ensuing season) was the second choice, rather than Neel.
8. The woefully inadequate entry on Weldon in *The New Grove* is at fault in giving his year of birth as 1906.
9. Weldon was in School House, 1922–6.
10. Extract from 'Conductor: George Weldon', a two-part article in *The Shirburnian* (Michaelmas 1951 issue, p. 212ff; Lent 1952 issue, p. 18ff).
11. Donald Brook: *Conductor's Gallery* (Rockliff, 1947), p. 143.
12. According to Ruth Gipps, he was paid £4.10.0 a week – less than a 'rank-and-file' violinist.
13. 9 October 1943.
14. That was, at any rate, the intention, but in the upshot both Stanton and Hely-Hutchinson were ill and had to be replaced.
15. Interview with the author, May 1993.
16. W. G. A. Russell: *The City of Birmingham Choir, 1921–1946* (The Bulletin Press, Hereford, 1946), p. 16.
17. On another occasion, a year later (1 April 1945), CBSO cellist Gwen Berry

noted in her diary that Matthews played 'very beautifully' and 'looked extremely young in his Air Force uniform'. James Langley, a regular member of the audience at this time, remembered many Mozart concertos played by Matthews 'with forage cap tucked into shoulder epaulettes'.

18. Alton Douglas: *op. cit.*, p. 88.
19. In January, Bill Taylor, in the course of a rave review of a Schubert *Great C major* performance in the *News*, wrote, 'we must have George Weldon as permanent conductor; we can't afford to let him go, on any consideration.'
20. Dated 22 September 1943. Forty wrote at the end, 'So far, so good – but what of the future?' The Liverpool Philharmonic also supplied much helpful information at this stage.
21. Letter to Brunner from the Midland Hotel, Manchester, probably written on 10 January 1944.
22. Kentner played Frank's *Symphonic Variations* and Liszt's *Hungarian Fantasia*; the Elgar was the First Symphony.
23. Leslie Heward's old friend Joseph Riley (a good friend of the CBO, also), who had recently died.
24. This is marked up on a different night each week. If (as appears to be the case) it took place on the Town Hall roof, the climb must have been extremely trying for Weldon. It is faithfully marked in the desk diary right through to the end of 1944, but in practice Birmingham's 50,000 volunteer Fire Guards were stood down in September, so hopefully his services will not have been called upon thereafter.
25. Entertainments National Service Association.
26. Interview with the author, May 1994.
27. A Minute of 6 July 1945 mentions 19 ENSA dates.
28. Including one familiar, if somewhat unexpected, name: the CBO's first conductor, Appleby Matthews, who engaged the orchestra for several of his Choral Union concerts. Evidently time had sufficiently healed the breach between him and the CBO Committee to enable this to take place.
29. The CBSO's archives contain a programme autographed by both Walton and Weldon.
30. George Weldon told a *Sunday Mercury* reporter that it was chosen because 'it was the quietest in the Midlands. No buses, trams, trains, birds or clock-strikings, and these are some of the disadvantages to be found in Birmingham Town Hall.'
31. Top price 3/6d, but a Lower Gallery Serial Ticket was available at 15/- for the six concerts.

Chapter **12** *Peace and productivity*

1. According to Kenneth Statham (letter of February 1993), the CBO 'regulars' called him 'Whacker Weldon'.
2. George Wheatley, Tribute to George Weldon in the *Music Teacher*, November 1963; also Ingvar Fredricksson (Rimbo, Sweden): letter to the author, October 1985.
3. *Op. cit.*, p. 145.
4. John Clayton: letter to the author, August 1994. Horn player Farquharson

Cousins recalled that principal bassoonist Vaughan Allin was also something of 'a speed merchant'. On out-of-town dates, the players would watch from the comparative safety of the orchestra coach, while 'two red sports cars would tear after one another in alarming fashion: George and Ronnie Allin, both excellent racing drivers, wagering who could get there first!' (Letter to the author, February 1984.)

5. Gerald Moore: *Furthermoore, Interludes in an Accompanist's Life* (Hamish Hamilton, 1983), p. 24.
6. Interview with Peter Wadland, quoted in Garry O'Connor: *op. cit.*
7. 3 January 1946, Brahms's Third Symphony the main work, with Irene Scharrer the soloist in Beethoven's Fourth Piano Concerto.
8. *Birmingham Post*, 25 July 1946.
9. *Penguin Music Magazine*, 1946, pp. 125–6.
10. 6 November 1945, Smethwick schools.
11. Not heard in Birmingham since Goossens had last conducted it with the CBO, in 1925. A few months later, the CBO's versatile principal oboist Mary Chandler played the concerto which Goossens had composed for his brother Leon.
12. Council for Education, Music and the Arts (later to become the Arts Council).
13. Interview with the author, 1979.
14. *Penguin Music Magazine*, 1947 (1st issue), p. 96.
15. *Penguin Music Magazine*, 1947 (2nd issue), p. 91.
16. *Birmingham Post*, 22 April 1947.
17. Hugo Rignold recorded works by Bliss, for Lyrita, in Kingsway Hall, January 1966.
18. John Farrington joined BBC Birmingham as Studio Manager in 1946: 'I remember we had a terrible listening-room at the back of the Town Hall, under the stage somewhere – it was awful! We made a fuss and eventually got a little studio built at the side of the platform for the Announcer – it's still there, in fact.' (Interview with the author in May 1994.)
19. As was often the case, the orchestra's busy schedule did not allow for a pre-rehearsal day, but an hour was found in Bristol for the Walton to be run through in preparation for the concert next day.
20. A small supply of these neat little stamps survives in the CBSO Archives.
21. *Penguin Music Magazine*, 1949 (1st issue), p. 119.
22. Ruth Gipps recalls that 'Eileen Joyce's fee was £150, but in Birmingham she would come for £100 provided that nobody else was paid more, so Dame Myra had to be beaten down to £90!'
23. 24 February 1948.
24. Elisabeth Schumann had, in fact, sung with Weldon and the City Orchestra before, at a concert in Wolverhampton on 13 September 1946.
25. Margaret Dennes, *Birmingham Gazette*, 2 August 1948.

Chapter **13** *Unlucky for some*

1. Ruth Gipps remembers visiting Weldon, with her husband Robert Baker, and finding him sitting on the doorstep in the sunshine, studying the score of this

work, which had just arrived in the post; he was very enthusiastic about it, and programmed it straight away.

2. Frank Downes: *op. cit.*, p. 78ff.
3. In a letter to John Waterhouse, dated 29 July 1948, John Perry (a regular CBSO concert-goer) remarked, 'The dismal progression of First Horns is an ideal example. One change can be expected in these days of housing shortage. Two changes may be a coincidence, but three in two years is just too many.'
4. The *Glasgow Herald* was enthusiastic; the *Scotsman* less so.
5. This still survives in one of his scrapbooks.
6. Letter, dated 12 July 1949, from CBSO secretary Betty Booth to a friend who sold programmes at the Proms. A newspaper review confirms that the egg was presented to Norris Stanley 'in token of his success in producing "a double-yolker" in the *Cocks and Hens* episode.' Weldon also presented buttonholes to the two pianists, Harold Gray and Barrs Partridge.
7. Later shortened to the more workable *Music You Love.*
8. Gerald Forty was too unwell to accept in person a silver salver, presented by the players, who held him in great affection, but in his letter of thanks to Norris Stanley he wrote, 'My long association with the orchestra . . . which has lasted over thirty years, has afforded me much happiness and has been one of the principal interests of my life, and I am very grieved that my ill-health should have brought it to a close.'
9. Joint General Manager of the Heath Street factory of the well-known Birmingham engineering firm Guest, Keen & Nettlefolds Ltd, and subsequently a GKN Director, Lloyd was, incidentally, Byng Kenrick's cousin.
10. A pillar of the City Choir (author of Volume I of its History), Senior Partner in the well-known Birmingham firm of accountants Russell, Durie Kerr, Watson & Co, and later Chairman of Glynwed Engineering.
11. Recently arrived from London to take over the Birmingham office of the accountants Cooper Brothers & Co.
12. John Waterhouse, *Birmingham Post*, 25 September 1950.
13. Letter from Russell to Lloyd, 11 November 1950.
14. David C. F. Wright, *Journal of the British Music Society, Vol. 13* (1991), pp. 3–13.
15. Denzil Walker reported to the Committee that during the 1949–50 season Weldon 'gave his services free for six Industrial Concerts and one Popular Concert. He also waived his fee for a concert in Dudley where the house was very poor', and agreed in February 1950, somewhat reluctantly, to accept a slightly reduced salary in view of the orchestra's financial difficulties. Walker wrote at that time to John Denison, Music Director of the Arts Council, to warn him, 'It is just possible that the present Musical Director will not accept the revised terms, and then, in any case, we are faced with a replacement.' Weldon had private means; according to Barrie Hall, CBSO Concert Manager in the 1950s, 'there was a tale told by the accounts office that in Weldon's day the books never balanced, and they traced the problem to the fact that he never cashed his salary cheques, leaving them in the tail pocket of his evening dress.' (Letter to the author, January 1995.) Gray, who had less bargaining power than Weldon, had seen his already derisory salary drastically reduced from £600 to £450 for the 1949–50 season.

16. Attendances over the period January-June 1950, not helped by a serious 'flu epidemic, fluctuated alarmingly between 685 (Weldon with Borodin, Delius, Holst, Grieg and Brahms); 1796 for Boult (a classical programme with Smith and Sellick) and a totally full house for a Weldon Viennese Night.
17. Ruth Gipps: interview with the author, May 1994.
18. Interview with the author, June 1994.
19. Letter to the author, 13 June 1994.
20. Every symphony orchestra in the country was invited to present two concerts, each of which was to include some British music. John Denison, Music Director of the Arts Council, masterminded this enterprising series.
21. A freelance body, formerly known as the 'City Orchestra Club'. It would eventually succumb to the orchestra's parent body – the CBSO Society – whose modest membership of 57 in October 1951 grew rapidly as its activities increased.
22. In Algeria, Belgium, Germany, Norway, Turkey and Yugoslavia.
23. Frank Downes: *op. cit.*, p. 84.

Chapter 14 *Rudolf Schwarz – Creativity and crisis*

1. Schwarz became a British citizen in 1952.
2. Interview with the author, October 1989. The November concert was actually Schwarz's second CBSO engagement within the space of a few months, but it is interesting that Stephen Lloyd had no recollection of either, and made it clear to the author that he would have seen no need for the players to work with their new conductor in advance of his appointment. This was normal practice in orchestra management at that time.
3. It speaks volumes for Schwarz's character and determination that he should have maintained vigorous health and a zest for life to the ripe old age of 89, dying quietly in his sleep on 30 January 1994.
4. John Boyden: *Stick to the Music* (Hutchinson, 1984), p. 114.
5. Interview with Lyndon Jenkins, 1980.
6. Conversation with the author, December 1993.
7. Schwarz's first concert as CBSO conductor included Schumann's Fourth Symphony.
8. Interview with Lyndon Jenkins, 1980.
9. 3 September 1951.
10. On 12 October 1951, John Waterhouse closed his enthusiastic *Post* review of Schwarz's first concert as Principal Conductor, 'Mr Schwarz's right hand clearly knows what his left hand does; and so does the orchestra, which is all that matters. To an observer in the background his methods are sometimes a little puzzling at first.' John Farrington worked with him many times as a BBC Studio Manager: 'Dear old Rudi – he had an extraordinary style of conducting. I never knew how the orchestra managed to keep with him; he always seemed to be half a bar ahead of them!' (Interview with the author, May 1994.)
11. £17,173, as at 31 March 1952. The Endowment Fund offered a £5000 guarantee and the BBC weighed in with 12 studio engagements, as against five in 1950–1, but the deficit on the 1951–2 season was still £8276.
12. Interview with the author, October 1989.

13. 'Statement by Councillor Lloyd, Chairman of the Management Committee', 1 April 1952. Neither the public nor the members of either orchestra were allowed to hear a whisper of the scheme until this day. Letters to Schwarz and Gray were sent out, on the same day, apprising them of the gravity of the situation, and later that week Lloyd and Walker met the Players' Committee; one thing that emerged was a plan for the CBSO to undertake a three-month summer residency in Eastbourne, but this too did not materialise.
14. Interview with the author, June 1994.
15. Little things often go wrong at concerts. Oboist Tony Miller remembers a concert in the Brangwyn Hall, Swansea, at which half the orchestra played 'Land of my Fathers', as intended, whilst the remainder forgot and played 'God save the Queen'. 'Rudi was furious! He *growled* at us and stamped his foot on the rostrum!'
16. Dudley, for example, offered £450, but Tamworth could only run to 10 guineas – indeed, its cheque was accidentally construed as an offering towards the Lord Mayor of Birmingham's 'Lynton & Lynmouth Flood Disaster Fund'. It had to be rescued and sent to the CBSO.
17. This rather unwieldy body now consisted of 15 elected CBSO Society members, six City Council and six Education Committee representatives, plus two player representatives, with power to co-opt two additional members if required.
18. Brain also played at a BBC studio concert at Queensbridge Road School, Moseley. Schwarz recalled that 'Very unusually, for him, Dennis arrived late at rehearsal. He always drove very fast, and on this occasion the radiator in his sports car started to boil. In taking the radiator cap off, he managed to scald his face quite badly, but his lips seemed to be OK, so he played – quite beautifully, as usual.' Barrie Hall, CBSO Concert Manager at that time, remembers the occasion well: 'I was there when Dennis arrived, his lips covered in some salve – the incident happened outside a doctor's house, and he had been instantly treated when calling to use the phone!' (Letter to the author, January 1995.)
19. *Birmingham Post*, 7 January 1952.
20. It was a condition of the gift that it should be used within the ensuing three years. It was made anonymously, but Payne's son Jack (for many years President of the City Choir) has now given permission for the donor to be named.
21. Morley Pooley of the *Bath Chronicle & Herald*, who had often heard the CBSO under Boult and Weldon, was full of praise for Schwarz, writing in July that 'this orchestra can rank with the best in the world'.
22. Matchett feels that at this time the Committee really wanted a glorified office-boy; a schedule of the 'Principal duties of the General Manager', given to him on his appointment, lists 16 major areas of responsibility, with a footnote: 'The above do not make any material demands on the time of the General Manager and Secretary.'
23. James Lloyd: letter to the author, December 1994.

Chapter 15 *'Ideas and ideals'*

1. *Music & Musicians*, September 1957. Barrie Hall was a well-liked CBSO Concert Manager in the 1950s, though oboist Tony Miller remembers him, too, as 'the man who on two separate occasions forgot to book the orchestra coaches; he had to book a fleet of taxis to get us to our school visits on time!' Barrie's comment: 'How wonderful to go down to posterity as the man who forgot to order the orchestra coaches!' (Letter to the author, January 1995.)
2. Top price 10/6, as against 7/6 on Thursdays. Denis Martineau remembers that the gentlemen of the orchestra were each given £10 to go out and buy themselves some evening dress.
3. *Birmingham Post*, 29 May 1954.
4. Interview with the author, October 1989.
5. Like Boult, Schwarz could be short-tempered on occasion; a few weeks later, Gwen noted, 'Rudi back, but in pleasant mood.'
6. Letter to the author, November 1990.
7. *Birmingham Evening Mail*, 30 August 1955.
8. 19–30 May 1955.
9. Letter to the author, November 1990.
10. Boult, Sargent, Bliss, Britten, Vaughan Williams, Rubbra and Maurice Johnstone (for the BBC) wrote appeals for the well-produced brochure. The response fell far short of the rather optimistic estimate, but it brought the Fund up to £36,000, and ongoing appeals increased the capital still further.
11. (1839–1905) Son of the founder of the *Birmingham Post* and for many years its proprietor.
12. *Birmingham Post*, 24 October 1955 (Navarra); 28 March 1956 (Monteux). The two most exciting weeks that Tony Miller remembers in the CBSO were those with Van Beinum and with Monteux.
13. Anyone who ever played for Rudolf Schwarz remembers his love of a lyrical *legato* line, as he crooned his favourite expression to the strings, 'Soostyne, my friends; Soos*tyne*!' He had a number of pet expressions, some of which were based on an incomplete English vocabulary; Stan Smith remembers that when the music was not going quite as he wanted it, he would say, 'No – it does not fire!'
14. Letter to Blyth Major dated 27 June 1955.
15. Peter Heyworth of the *Observer* called it 'a wretchedly slack and inadequate affair'.
16. *Forfar Dispatch*, 26 November 1992.
17. Interview with the author, 1979.
18. Interview with the author, August 1993.

Chapter 16 *Andrzej Panufnik – New thinking*

1. CBSO Players' Committee Newsletter No. 2, February 1977.
2. Methuen, (1987), p. 263.
3. Gwen's cello teacher, Johan Hock.
4. John Waterhouse's hilarious 'World of Music' article of 5 May 1958, entitled 'CBSO Calypso' is, alas, too long to reproduce here.

5. Andrzej Panufnik: interview with Lyndon Jenkins, 1980. In an interview with the author (November 1994), oboist Tony Miller recalled that Panufnik got Lewis to provide two versions of the Anthem, 'one for strings only and one for wind only, and we never knew until just before the concert which one it was going to be!'
6. Interview with the author, 1979.
7. 20 April 1958. This concert was in fact the subject of Waterhouse's article referred to above (Note 4).
8. Andrzej Panufnik: *op. cit.*, p. 266.
9. *Birmingham Evening Despatch*, 24 February 1958.
10. Andrzej Panufnik: *op. cit.*, p. 271. There can be little doubt that the 'business-man' was Harry Payne.
11. 21 April 1959.
12. Interview with the author, November 1994.
13. Telephone conversation with the author, September 1994. On 2 September 1959, Gwen Barry recorded that the CBSO's Concert Manager Colin Ratcliffe introduced Edwards to the players at rehearsal: 'He looks younger than I thought he would be, but sounds a good sincere sort of man.'
14. Andrzej Panufnik: *op. cit.*, p. 273.
15. Element was a friend and colleague from Sir Adrian's years with the CBO in the 1920s, and a distinguished Deputy Leader of the CBO during the late 1940s, eventually leaving to give himself more time for teaching, solo playing and chamber music.
16. *Musical Opinion*, March 1991.
17. *Birmingham Post*, 23 May 1960.
18. 'Too many cooks for Birmingham broth' was the headline in *The Times* on 6 October 1959.
19. It is natural that the players' subjective memories of that evening are terrible, but Alan Ward, one of the few who braved the fog to listen to the concert (and unaware of the drama backstage) remembers Vaughan Williams's *Job* as 'a wonderful performance – the thick haze in the hall only served to heighten the atmosphere'. (Recorded reminiscences, May 1994.)
20. 'I daren't tell you how quickly I generally do the run,' he told the *Evening Mail*.
21. Gray had been asked to do this so often, and at such short notice, that Gwen Berry noted in her diary, 'Once more into the breach'.
22. *Birmingham Post*, 25 April 1960.
23. Former CBSO violist Geoffrey Duggan recalls the occasion when Lehmann accepted with alacrity Sir Adrian's invitation to lunch with him, anticipating a sumptuous meal. 'Imagine his surprise when Boult approached him after rehearsal and beckoned him into the conductor's room. Here he was introduced to Lady Boult, who produced half a pork pie and a penknife. The pie was then cut into three!' (*Music Stand*, May 1985.)

Chapter 17 *Hugo Rignold – Complete professional*

1. Rignold's initial two-year contract was for sixty concerts a year at £50 per concert, £60 if he conducted more than that number.

2. *Birmingham Post*, 11 March 1957.
3. Rignold studied timpani, too, and, according to his daughter Jennifer, 'Henry Wood complimented him on his playing at Royal Academy orchestra rehearsals.'
4. Jennifer Rignold: letter to the author, November 1994.
5. Founded by Bronislaw Huberman, its initial concerts were conducted by Toscanini; after 1948 it became the Israel Philharmonic.
6. The first urban fox I remember seeing trotted nonchalantly across Hugo's back garden, while we were having morning coffee.
7. 17 December 1960.
8. The LPO performed the work in the Royal Festival Hall on the same evening, but Richard Butt remembers that the BBC (who were relaying the Birmingham concert) persuaded them to delay their performance so that the CBSO could rightly claim a 'British première' – by about 15 minutes.
9. In February 1995, Heather Harper stood in at the last moment to sing the *War Requiem* yet again, in St Paul's Cathedral – 33 years on.
10. 'It might be fair to them to point out that they were also learning Bliss's *Beatitudes*, in many ways more difficult than *War Requiem* . . . at rehearsals it was noticed that some of the old biddies were singing from the wrong work!' (Meredith Davies: letter to the author, November 1994.)
11. From the programme for a St Michael's Singers performance, Coventry Cathedral, 1987.
12. As Barry Lankester recalls, Richard Butt 'discovered that the vast audience was being admitted into the Cathedral through one single doorway. The queue stretched into the distance and it was quite obvious that many of them would not be in their places by the time we were due to start at 8 o'clock. It took a great deal of persuasion before more doors were eventually opened.' Butt's own description is 'a nightmare. Ben said, "We can't go on yet – it's like a marketplace out there!" And even when Ben and Meredith got to the podium, they found that the floodlights hadn't been switched on, so there was even more delay. In those days, if there was a gap of more than about 30 seconds with no signal, the transmitters were liable to cut out, so it was distinctly worrying.' (Interview with the author, January 1995.)
13. *Radio Times*, 14 August 1976.
14. 31 May 1962.
15. 1 June 1962.
16. 'I can recall his comment quite clearly: forthright, direct and unhesitating.' (Letter to the author, November 1994.)
17. One was the principal percussionist, Don Thomas, with whom Rignold had had a blazing and very public row at rehearsal; a knock-on effect of this was that Maggie Cotton found herself acting as principal for a performance of Nielsen's Fifth Symphony with Gray, in October 1962. 'I was struggling with that desperate *ad lib* snare drum part and at the rehearsal I remember Harold smiling up at me encouragingly and calling out, in broad Brummie, "*Gow* ber-serk, Margaret! *Gow* ber-serk!" '
18. A compromise was eventually reached in October 1962, resulting in a very substantial rise of £5 – virtually a one-third increase.
19. After acknowledging the applause at the end of her concerto at the first

concert, Miss Tsuji launched into the mighty Bach *Chaconne*, which lasts some twenty minutes, while Rignold fumed in the wings, 'Get her off! Get her off!' She was discouraged from a repeat performance.

20. Not all the notices were so good. Arthur Baker used to like to quote a Stuttgart headline: '*Beethoven kam nicht bis nach Birmingham.*'
21. Stan Smith remembers that 'the audience, who had just decided that we weren't coming, made a corridor for us and clapped us all the way from the coaches into the hall. We just played for them in our travelling clothes.'
22. The Chairman of the Cape Town Orchestra, C. O. Booth, remarked, 'I was very worried about him on Thursday in case his leg was troubling him, and nearly suggested that he should conduct sitting down in the second half.' (*Cape Argus*, 19 August 1963.) Weldon's suicide was confirmed in a letter to the author (February 1984) by ex-CBO horn player Farquharson Cousins, whose wife was a member of the Cape Town Orchestra at the time; Cousins described Weldon as 'never a Bruno Walter, but he was a fine working professional who had a grand rapport with his players'.
23. Sir Wilfrid, President of the City Choir (in which he sang) had been Lord Mayor of Birmingham, like his father, grandfather and great-grandfather before him; in due course Denis Martineau was himself elected to that high office.
24. Though Lyndon Jenkins, who was sitting at the side of the Lower Gallery behind the first violins, remembers that 'certain players were quite unable to cope with the battle scene!'
25. Letter to the author, November 1994.
26. Harry Van der Lyn volunteered to play the small but exacting mandolin part and the result was none too musical, giving rise to ribald comments from his colleagues about 'Van der Lyn handlin' the mandolin'.
27. Waterhouse's notice was mangled by a sub-editor; his description of Gerhard's music as 'eclectic' was printed as 'electric' and his subsequent use of 'eclectician' naturally emerged as 'What an opulent electrician Gerhard is'.
28. At the rehearsal in Cheltenham Town Hall, Horenstein got upset with the CBSO's double-bass section (which included at that time a number of delightful old gentlemen who had played in the CBSO since 1945 or before) over a passage in the Schoenberg which called for them to play *sul ponticello*. 'On ze bridge! Not *near* ze bridge – *on* ze bridge!', he said, pointing at Jeremiah Farmer, who was very short and stout, until Ken Burston, the section principal, explained to Horenstein that Jerry's arms were too short to reach the bridge at all!
29. *Evening Mail* notices dated 28 February and 1 December 1964. T. E. Bean, first General Manager of the Royal Festival Hall, ran for several years a column in his monthly lists of RFH concerts called 'Point – Counterpoint' in which diametrically opposing reviews of the same event were printed side by side, but so many critics complained that eventually he had to drop it.

Chapter 18 *Discord and Harmony*

1. It had become the custom at the 'Last Night of the Proms' for some of the audience to fold their programmes into paper darts, which whizzed around

the hall during the final celebrations; as soon as the Henry Wood *Sea Songs* had ended and Gray had started his speech, Parsons could be seen resolutely putting the wooden covers on to his beloved instruments; he would then stand glumly, with folded arms, throughout the concluding National Anthem.

2. Interview with the author, November 1994.
3. *Birmingham Post*, 13 December 1965.
4. Violinist Stan Smith remembers that 'Wilfrid Pook was rather a pedantic player; he rather fancied himself as an "early music" expert and he used to put in ornaments when they weren't in the music – that sort of thing. Some of the others got really fed up with him.'
5. The Arbitration took place in Martineau's Birmingham office on the following Saturday morning.
6. The competition brochure was multilingual.
7. There was a strict ban on taking sterling out of the country in 1965, but, with foresight, Martineau had pulled strings at the Bank of England to permit foreign artists to take their prize money abroad.
8. One reason was that the CBSO did not really have sufficient office staff to cope with the added administrative burden of organising an event of this kind, which kept Concert Assistant Betty Minors fully occupied for some three months.
9. *Music & Musicians*, December 1965.
10. *Guardian*, 29 March 1966.
11. *Birmingham Post*, 22 April 1967.
12. Interview with the author, May 1993.
13. Felix Kok recalls that 'He used to say, "Now look, I'm not going to fool you. Here's your beat – all you have to do is follow it", and if we *didn't* succeed in following him precisely, he would be very unhappy' and, according to Stan Smith, 'one of Hugo's favourite phrases was "You're all Leaders" – he wanted us all on the point of his stick.'
14. Interview with the author, November 1994.
15. Kenneth Dommett, *Birmingham Post*.
16. *Birmingham Post*, 24 February 1967.
17. 29 July 1967.
18. *Birmingham Post*, 30 December 1967.
19. *Music & Musicians*, April 1968.
20. Delivered in January 1968. Although for many years the orchestra had employed its own 'roadie', it had up to now engaged a local removal firm to move its instruments between Birmingham and out-of-town venues.
21. This involved dealing with the Cultural Agencies in each country, which had cumbersome titles such as 'Künstler-Agentur der Deutschen Demokratischen Republik'.
22. Our interpreter explained this as 'simply routine manœuvres'.
23. *Western Press*, 20 May 1968.
24. Interview with the author, 1979.
25. Percussionist Maggie Cotton, who played the bells, recalls that, very uncharacteristically, Rignold made a mistake and cued her a bar early. 'I ignored him and came in at the right place, but of course for the rest of the night I kept worrying and thinking, "Was I right?" About 11 o'clock that night, when

we'd just gone to bed, the phone rang and it was Hugo. "Maggie," he said, "you saved my bacon. Thank you very much indeed – I don't know what I was thinking about!" '

26. Interview with the author, November 1994.
27. Subtitled *Contra torrentum* ('Against the stream'). However, neither Wellesz's Sixth nor Seventh Symphonies made an immediate impression on the public comparable to that of the Fifth.
28. Peter Stadlen, *Daily Telegraph*, 22 March 1969.
29. Leitner was Wilhelm Kempff's preferred concerto accompanist; he created a considerable impression in London when Stuttgart Opera brought its celebrated Wieland Wagner productions of *Fidelio* and *Die Zauberflöte* to the Royal Festival Hall.
30. The Second Piano Concerto (Peter Frankl) and the Seventh and Eighth Symphonies.
31. For those of us in the hall there was a heart-stopping moment in the Bennett Concerto when the Steinway, which had not been properly secured, started to roll across the platform; somehow, without interrupting the broadcast performance, Bishop succeeded in stopping its progress, moving his stool to a new position and with one hand screwing up the foot-brake – a *tour de force* of cool thinking.

Chapter **19** *Louis Frémaux – 'A wrist second to none'*

1. At one time Frémaux's family hid an RAF pilot, Squadron-Leader James Frayne, whose aircraft had been shot down, and young Louis (working with the Maquis in Cugard) lent him his bicycle to escape. Many years later, at a CBSO concert in Cheltenham, he happened to mention this to the Mayor, an ex-RAF man, who succeeded in tracing Mr Frayne; after an abortive attempt to meet in Cheltenham the two were eventually reunited at a CBSO concert in London, where Louis was presented with a little silver bicycle as a memento.
2. Of Frémaux's first six recordings (1956–7), four were awarded a Grand Prix, which must surely be some sort of record. A Frémaux Discography, complete up to the end of 1974, appeared in the CBSO's house-magazine *Music Stand*, January 1975.
3. Interview with the author, 1979.
4. Interview with the author, November 1994.
5. *Cinq Métaboles* had been commissioned in 1964 for George Szell and the Cleveland Orchestra. Predictably, the work was rapidly christened 'Five Meat Balls' by the CBSO players. Dutilleux later dropped the prefix 'Cinq' from the title.
6. *Sunday Times*, 28 September 1969.
7. Bearing in mind that the first CBSO concert had taken place in September 1920, it would have been more correct to have waited until the 1970–1 season, but Frémaux's arrival was deemed to justify the celebration, and 1969–70 was, of course, technically the orchestra's 'fiftieth season'.
8. Two death scenes: Desdemona's from *Otello* and Mimi's from *La Bohème*.
9. The Education Committee grant had peaked at £16,000 in the early 1960s, falling to £11,000 in 1966–7, then to £5500 in the following season.

10. *Nuneaton Evening Tribune*, 3 December 1969.
11. 18 April 1970. It would be another twenty years before Dommett's wishful thinking would find fulfilment, in a hall even finer than De Doelen.
12. In an interview with the author (August 1993), Phyllis Sellick recalled that Arnold had some difficulty in getting the orchestra to play the tricky 'dotted' opening of the work together. After several wasted takes and amid mounting tension, 'finally Malcolm said, "We'll try it once more, and either we'll get it together or we bloody well won't!" Everyone laughed, the tension was broken, and a perfect take resulted!' Sadly, Cyril Smith died in August 1974.
13. *A Report on Orchestral Resources in Great Britain* (Arts Council of Great Britain, 1970).
14. Beresford King-Smith: *The First Fifty Years* (CBSO, 1970), p. 34.
15. Barbirolli died in July 1970 – the month of Handford's appointment to the CBSO.
16. First to come in were the County Boroughs of Walsall and Warley and the Boroughs of Halesowen and Sutton Coldfield.
17. *Midland Magazine*, 14 September 1968.
18. *A Concert Hall for Birmingham* – A Report commissioned from the John Madin Design Group for the Management Committee of the CBSO by the Trustees of the City of Birmingham Orchestral Endowment Fund, 1970.
19. Interview with the author, November 1994.
20. Felix Kok: interview with Lyndon Jenkins, 1989.
21. 7 October 1970.
22. Kenneth Dommett, *Birmingham Post*, 27 November 1971.
23. *Birmingham Post*, 25 June 1971.
24. Christopher Robinson, who played the *concertante* organ part, could be forgiven for feeling that the inclusive fee of £50 which he received for the two days of recording sessions was modest recompense, even then.
25. *Birmingham Post*, 29 April 1972.
26. An exhibition of Constantine's photos of the tour was shown during the 1972–3 season at several venues in Birmingham and around the Midlands; in the foyer of the Royal Festival Hall; at the Kodak Gallery in High Holborn; at the House of Photography in Chalon-sur-Sâone, France; and in Denver, Colorado.
27. The double-basses could at last be sited behind the cellos, not spread out behind the trombones.
28. In the CBSO's house-magazine *Music Stand*, March 1973.
29. 'Frémaux and the orchestra played it wonderfully well.' Lyndon Jenkins *Birmingham Post*, 19 January 1973.
30. Added spice was lent to Huddersfield concerts by the unscripted arrival of an elderly vagrant lady who would regularly come dancing down the aisle in the middle of the concert, until forcibly escorted out.
31. F.S., *Huddersfield Daily Examiner*, 21 December 1972.
32. Mrs Laverack's Arts Appreciation Agency also ran the successful H. Samuel International series of chamber concerts, rivalled only by the long-running series of Vincent's Celebrity Concerts; between the two, many top-flight international artists gave recitals in Birmingham Town Hall.
33. Interview with the author, November 1994. An editorial in the March 1973

issue of *Music Stand* noted that 'we are having a good season. In fact, we are pushing 90% average attendance.'

Chapter **20** *'The best French orchestra in the world'*

1. *Classical Music*, May 1978.
2. *Guardian*, 25 February 1972.
3. Edward Greenfield, *Guardian*, 17 May 1974.
4. A light-hearted piece in *Music Stand* (January 1974) explained that she 'showed an aptitude for the instrument from a very early age and later trained with the CBSO in Newhall Street, where she had been playing regularly for the past ten years'. The CBSO percussion player who fired the pistol-shots in *Parade* was the aptly named Annie Oakley.
5. *Birmingham Post*, 14 July 1973.
6. Gordon Clinton, *Music Stand*, November 1973.
7. Editorial in *Music Stand*, March 1973.
8. 17 February 1973.
9. There were generally a few vacancies amongst the strings; the normal playing strength was 80–85 at this time.
10. *Music Stand*, November 1974.
11. At its end, 'she put her bouquet on the stage, where it remained for the rest of the concert. I found this quite moving.' (Richard Ryland: letter to the author, November 1990.)
12. It was entirely characteristic of Richter-Haaser, a man of great integrity and humanity, that, on his one supposedly 'free' evening of the Festival, he should have insisted on coming to enjoy Frémaux's exciting reading of the *Missa Solemnis*.
13. *Financial Times*, 15 April 1975.
14. Both quotes: 18 April 1975.
15. Interview with the author, January 1995.
16. Peter Cox Associates, Leamington, July 1974.
17. Nicholas Kenyon: *Simon Rattle – The Making of a Conductor* (Faber and Faber, 1987), p. 110.
18. Richard Lawrence, *Early Music News*, November 1994.
19. Quoted in *Music Stand*, November 1976. Alison had attended the CBSO Young People's Concert called *The Art of Orchestration*, on Saturday, 9 October.
20. CBSO clarinettist Frank Allen must have taken part in most of the orchestra's regular Mahler performances, with Dorati, Frémaux, Handford, Uri Segal and other conductors, which had included in recent seasons practically all the symphonies and song cycles, and many of the big Strauss tone poems, so it is extraordinary to find him quoted as saying, in a 1993 interview, 'Before Simon Rattle came, the CBSO's repertoire was very limited and involved composers I was not greatly interested in playing: Saint-Saëns, Bizet, the French repertoire. Then Rattle came, of course, and brought in Mahler, Wagner and Richard Strauss, and if I'd still been with the CBSO when he arrived, I'd probably have stuck.' (*Classical Music*, 19 June 1993.)

Chapter **21** *All change*

1. Samuel French Ltd, 1950.
2. Interview with the author, November 1994.
3. A week or two before this concert, my office telephone rang and Sir Adrian's devoted secretary Gwen Beckett put him on the line. He wanted to do 'the version of the Prelude which Elgar recorded'. Apparently a folder of printed slips existed – one for each orchestral part – which had been prepared at Elgar's behest so that, in concert performances of the work, it would end in the correct key. We duly contacted Novello's, the publishers, who denied all knowledge of folder or slips. I rang Sir Adrian. 'Fiddlesticks! Saw it there myself.' 'When do you think you saw it there, Sir Adrian?' 'In 1934.' Sir Adrian rang the publishers himself, the folder *was* eventually found and the slips used – presumably for the first time since 1934.
4. Interviews with the author, November 1994 and February 1995. It is hard not to sympathise with Frémaux, but, in this instance, 'custom and practice' were on the players' side; sadly, politics sometimes overrule musical considerations.
5. 30 September and 18 November 1977; 26 January 1978.
6. Telephone conversation with the author, January 1995. Frémaux insists that the extent of Baker's work on his behalf has been greatly exaggerated ('He was never my agent in any real sense; in 1976 I undertook only three overseas concerts, and ten in 1977, and they were all arranged by my French agent'). Nevertheless, the fact remains that the link was *seen* as being too close, and that was unwise.
7. 25 February 1973.
8. Interview with the author, November 1994. Louis Frémaux's last concert with the CBSO took place in Birmingham Town Hall on Thursday, 8 March 1978. It ended with Tchaikovsky's Fourth Symphony ('Fate knocking at the door') and was broadcast live by the BBC.
9. The players' resolution had been aimed entirely at Baker. Paul Smith, Chairman of the Players' Committee, told the *Birmingham Post* (22 March 1978) that Frèmaux's resignation came as 'a complete bombshell'.
10. Interview with the author, February 1995.
11. Julianna Szekely, the CBSO's first full-time Marketing Manager, arrived to take up her position on the day when the news of the two resignations had been announced. I broke the news to her when she arrived in our third-floor offices in Newhall Street. 'My first instinct,' she says, 'was to go straight downstairs again and return to London. With hindsight, though, I'm glad that I stayed. I spent my first few days fending off reporters.'
12. CBSO Players' Committee Newsletter No. 2 (February 1977).
13. Baker had an extremely low level of musical tolerance – to sit next to him at countless CBSO concerts was an uncomfortable experience. If he was not enjoying the performance, he would pass the time by proofreading the programme, using a bold red marker to highlight any mistakes. As the person responsible for the programmes, which were supposed to be error-free, I did not greatly appreciate this.

14. Eventually a compromise was reached which left Kok leading the majority of CBSO concerts, with his Deputy Barrie Moore leading some others.
15. 12 May 1978.
16. CBSO programme, 8 March 1995.
17. At this time, Simon Clugston and Kenneth Cordingley.
18. New entrances, opened up on either side of the platform, cut disastrously into the performing space (already very limited); in consequence, a removable double stairway had to be provided in front of the rostrum.
19. In the October issue of the journal *Municipal Entertainment*, Cliff Bevan came up with the headline 'Change Makes Smith King – King-Smith Makes Change'.
20. Handley also conducted the CBSO's Christmas concerts, which coincided with the first snowfall of what *Music Stand* called 'a singularly wretched winter'. Marooned at his rural home near the Severn Bridge, and unable to negotiate the snowbound lanes by car, he trudged with his suitcase across several fields to the nearest main road, where the author picked him up at an agreed rendezvous and drove him up the M5 to Birmingham. A few weeks later a CBSO concert in Sheffield had to be cancelled as the result of blizzards.
21. Interview with the author, January 1995.
22. Somehow, news of the impending announcement reached the *Birmingham Post* in advance. On 22 June they headlined it: 'New Conductor Heralds CBSO Harmony'.
23. Harold Gray did, in fact, continue to conduct the CBSO at Sutton Coldfield Philharmonic Society concerts, up until March 1982, when the author had the privilege of playing a small part in his final concert. Gray told Barrie Grayson of the *Birmingham Post* that he was looking forward to having more time to himself: 'I shall still do some examining, and I have begun to practise the piano again.'
24. In 1979–80 the Council consisted of 15 elected members; six representatives of West Midlands County Council and five of Birmingham City Council; two players representatives (Simon Clugston and Paul Smith) and two co-opted members, plus Edward Smith *ex officio* and Eric Thompson, the Arts Council's Assessor. Senior members of the management team (the author as Smith's Deputy, Financial Controller Graham Escott and Marketing Manager Julianna Szekely) were now listed in the annual prospectus.
25. The Hotel Slavija, where the orchestra stayed overnight, kindly provided an English translation of its menu, which included 'Breaded Catfish', 'Sausages in Hogs' Grease' and 'Calves' Brains in Paper Sack'.
26. *Warwickshire and Worcestershire Life*, May 1980.
27. Appleby Matthews and the CBO had given the provincial première, in 1921, with baritone Herbert Simmonds.
28. Cleobury had at one time been Christopher Robinson's head chorister at Worcester Cathedral.
29. A new appointment; Richard Hartshorn was now promoted to the position of Treasurer.

Chapter **22** *Simon Rattle – Making music an adventure*

1. Conversation with the author, 1980.
2. Denis Rattle, quoted in Nicholas Kenyon: *op. cit.*, p. 28.
3. Faber and Faber, 1987. Currently out of print.
4. Compiled by the author (CBSO, 1980).
5. Beecham and Wood both featured (along with Sargent and Barbirolli) on a set of 'British Conductors' stamps issued by the Post Office in September 1980, which appeared on a commemorative CBSO Diamond Jubilee first-day cover. Sadly, Boult's longevity excluded him from this set, since living persons (HM the Queen excepted) may not be depicted on British stamps.
6. The idea was not entirely new; a Tuesday Celebrity Series had made an appearance for a few seasons, twenty years before.
7. The American company Chalfont, for which these Vaughan Williams items were made, subsequently ceased trading; the rights were bought by EMI, who eventually issued the disc.
8. Albrecht Jost, *Orpheus*, 11 December 1980.
9. Interview with the author, February 1995.
10. The van was replaced at a cost of £35,000. It was much in demand, for during the season only 55 out of 149 concerts took place in Birmingham.
11. Tenor soloist John Mitchinson, in fine voice at the concert, arrived at the sessions virtually voiceless, and there was nothing for it at that late stage but to record the work without him and to dub his crucially important contribution in later on.
12. *Classical Music*, 27 June 1981.
13. *Birmingham Post*, 6 May 1981.
14. 17 September 1981.
15. Reviewing Fauré's suite *Pelléas et Mélisande*, the reporter from the *Kidderminster Shuttle* doubtless intended to indicate that 'the story is one of a hapless maid'. Unfortunately, however, the word appeared as 'topless'.
16. Interview with the author, 1979.
17. The Arts Council now chipped in £360,000, with an additional guarantee of £50,000; West Midlands County Council gave £230,000 and Birmingham £38,250.
18. Thalben-Ball was by then 86, but his age was never mentioned; strictly speaking, he should have retired as City Organist at the age of 65!
19. *Guardian*, 7 December 1982.
20. 5 December 1982.
21. For technical reasons this was re-recorded in May 1984.
22. The programmes consisted of Nos. 1 and 4; 3 and 2; 6, 7, and 5. Subsequently, Rattle did this last programme on a number of occasions, but in the order 5, 6, 7.
23. At Rattle's request, the composer took some pre-rehearsals, both sectional and *tutti*.
24. Three of the most significant former conductors of the Birmingham orchestra died at 20-year intervals; Leslie Heward in 1943, George Weldon in 1963, and Adrian Boult (senior of the three) in 1983.
25. 30 August 1983.

26. 31 August 1983.
27. These were the work's first performances in Düsseldorf since Julius Buths of the Lower Rhine Music Festival had rescued it from possible oblivion in 1901.
28. Interview with the author, February 1995. Järvi has consistently championed the music of his compatriot Eduard Tubin (1905–82), and has now recorded all his symphonies.
29. 3 January 1984.
30. The CBSO appeared for the first time in St David's Hall in November 1983.
31. Interview with the author, January 1995.

Chapter **23** *The Development Plan*

1. Sir George died in 1987, at the age of 91.
2. The Trust celebrated thirty years of commissions for the CBSO with an exhibition of autograph scores of all 35 works to date, a symposium and a leaflet: *Creativity.*
3. 3 January 1985.
4. Interview with the author, January 1995. Tour repertoire included the Walton Viola Concerto and the Dvořák Cello Concerto, with Nobuko Imai and Yo Yo Ma respectively, the two combining in Strauss's *Don Quixote*, while the main orchestral works were the Tippett *Double String Concerto* and Debussy's *Ibéria*.
5. The Sutton connection went back as far as 1930. Concert-goers from the two towns were offered a coach service to attend the CBSO's Birmingham concerts.
6. January 1985.
7. Roger Cunningham: *Concert Conversations* (BHBN Press, 1986).
8. It was at this time, too, that the Endowment Fund began to build up a 'bank' of fine violins which could be made available to selected players, on a long-loan basis.
9. Iona Brown was awarded the OBE in the 1986 New Year's Honours.
10. Sadly, for financial reasons, BBC Radio's involvement with the orchestra was largely confined by this time to relays of the CBSO's own promotions.
11. Bartók's orchestral version of his Sonata for Two Pianos and Percussion, now recorded for the first time.
12. A *Bristol Evening Post* reporter was sufficiently confused to write about 'the huge Turangalîla Symphony Orchestra, under its personable principal conductor Simon Rattle'.
13. Interview with the author, February 1995.
14. Nicholas Kenyon: *op. cit.*, p. 136.
15. Roger Cunningham: *op. cit.*
16. Prize for the Most Tasteless Performance, however, undoubtedly went to Yuri Temirkanov; presumably he found Tchaikovsky's own ending to his *Manfred* Symphony too low-key for his taste, so he simply excised it and substituted a repeat of the energetic *coda* of the first movement.
17. Hutchinson (1986), p. 139.
18. In the TV documentary *Porgy, Bess and Simon Rattle.*
19. Quoted in Nicholas Kenyon: *op. cit.*, p. 131.
20. Simon Rattle says, 'Probably the main reason why the hall was built at all was Tom Caulcott's sheer native cunning in pretending that a hall was *not* going

to be built. It was to be a Convention Centre, and for a long time what we now call Symphony Hall was just known as "Hall 2".'

21. 70 strings (18/16/14/12/10); 12 woodwind (3/3/3/3); 13 brass (5/4/3/1); 2 timpanists, 3 percussion and 1 harp. The 'working' string-strength is generally 16/16/12/10/8.
22. The text is reproduced as Appendix I to Nicholas Kenyon's book, which also includes a detailed account of its impact on the musical scene.
23. Rattle also received the Distinguished Musician Award from the Incorporated Society of Musicians and an Honorary Fellowship from Birmingham Polytechnic.
24. 2 January 1987.
25. The average age of CBSO players at the beginning of 1987 was 38, but dropped still further during the next year or so.
26. Interview with the author, January 1995.
27. BBC Radio 4: *Desert Islands Discs*, November 1994.
28. 28 November 1987.

Chapter **24** *Symphony Hall*

1. *Independent*, 24 March 1989.
2. Review by P. S. of Mahler's Seventh Symphony, 1 May 1989.
3. Terry Grimley, *Classical Music*, 6 August 1988.
4. *Penguin Guide to Compact Discs*, Autumn 1989.
5. Also 'Best Orchestral' and 'Best Engineering' – a remarkable treble.
6. Iona Brown was, however, still Guest Director.
7. 20 September 1988, Cheltenham Town Hall, under David Atherton.
8. The day before this concert, Felix was installed as a Master of Music by the University of Birmingham. In June 1989, Chief Executive Edward Smith also received an honorary degree, when he was made a Fellow of Birmingham Conservatoire (formerly the School of Music).
9. *Birmingham Post*, 15 December 1988.
10. *Financial Times*, 20 January 1989.
11. Rattle brought back a Xerox copy of what Donald Mitchell called 'this legendary manuscript' and deposited it at the Aldeburgh Foundation, who gave permission for this solitary performance to take place.
12. Interview with the author, February 1995.
13. *Daily Telegraph*, 20 April 1989.
14. He also officially opened Birmingham Conservatoire, the former School of Music, whose building the CBSO administration shares.
15. The 'Friends of the CBSO' (formerly the CBSO Concert goers) provided librettos for every member of the audience in advance.
16. The BBC made three TV programmes about Berlioz at this time.
17. Christopher Morley, *Birmingham Post*, 10 July 1989. The performance was televised live by the BBC.
18. Interview with the author, February 1995.
19. Interview with the author, February 1995.
20. One wag in the CBSO Office (having in mind a favourite Rattle encore piece, by Sibelius) described it as 'just a *Scene with Cranes*'.

21. Later recorded for EMI.
22. The CBSO had played overseas at least once in every season since 1982–3 – a total of 66 concerts. No other regional orchestra approached this record, but it still fell far short of what the London orchestras were able to achieve. See *Cultural Trends 1990*, No. 7, p. 28.
23. George Jonas reported in *Music Stand* that after the performance in Zurich, the CBSO's former guest conductor Erich Schmid 'turned to me and said, "Such Mahler I have never heard!" '
24. Paul Griffiths, *The Times*, 23 December 1989.
25. Andrew Clements, *Sunday Correspondent*, 31 December 1989.
26. Marketvision Ltd, Coventry, January 1990.
27. With responsibilities which included the administration of the CBSO Chorus, printed programmes, *Music Stand*, archives and merchandising.
28. 26 September 1990.
29. *Sunday Correspondent*, 5 August 1990.
30. *Financial Times*, 1 August 1990.
31. Two gentlemen in their late eighties, who were guests of the Society, had attended CBO concerts in its first season. Mr Gilbert Woodhall's diary confirmed that he had taken his 'young lady' (whom he subsequently married) to the Theatre Royal on 31 October 1920, for an Appleby Matthews concert.
32. *Guardian*, 18 September 1990.
33. EMI's first use of the latest 20-bit digital technology.
34. Claire Briggs, on trial as principal horn, was appointed on the strength of her superb performance in *Odyssey.*
35. George Jonas's Foreword to the Report and Accounts, 1991.
36. The title was Smith's suggestion, but he had to fight long and hard to win acceptance for it.
37. Symphony Hall's capacity is approximately 2200, including the choir seats.
38. Interview with Robert Matthews, 21 April 1991.
39. Since the hall is built on top of one of the busiest railway tunnels in the UK, this was a bold claim, but its solid construction, and the massive rubber bearings on which it floats, effectively isolate all extraneous sound.
40. Interview with the author, February 1995.
41. *The Times*, 19 January 1991.
42. *Music Stand*, March 1991.
43. Michael Vyner, creator of the London Sinfonietta, who died in 1989.
44. Hugh Canning, *Sunday Times*, 30 December 1990.
45. £984,000, as against £1m for the Hallé, £1.2m for Liverpool, £1.3m for Bournemouth and £1.6m for the Royal Scottish. See *Cultural Trends 1991*, No. 12, p. 6.
46. CBSO Report and Accounts, 1991.

Chapter **25** *Towards the Millennium*

1. Foreword to the souvenir programme for the Symphony Hall opening concerts, 15 April 1991.
2. Interview with the author, February 1995.
3. *Leaving* demonstrated the enormous benefits of having a composer 'in associ-

ation'; Turnage worked closely with Simon Halsey, the Chorus and the instrumentalists, producing and rehearsing no fewer than four interim versions of this deeply satisfying work, before the final one was arrived at.

4. As an experiment, supertitles were back-projected on to a screen to help the audience follow the story-line.
5. *Financial Times*, 3 April 1995.
6. The planned West Coast element of the tour was scrapped.
7. Deputy Chairman Arthur Maddison and Treasurer Richard Hartshorn had both worked with Jonas throughout his term of office.
8. A Board member since 1980, whose musical interests outside the CBSO included close connections with the Midland Youth Orchestra and active membership of a local amateur band (the Birmingham Concert Orchestra). He presented George Jonas with a handsome silver salver, on behalf of the CBSO Society.
9. Proving that, if specially requested to do so beforehand, the audience is perfectly capable of maintaining an admirable degree of silence in this most acoustically sensitive of halls.
10. The list of charitable and voluntary organisations with which he had been associated filled one whole page in the service-sheet.
11. Polio from an early age, compounded by a succession of later fractures.
12. Interview with the author, February 1995.
13. Conducting a British chorus for the first time.
14. Rattle had prepared the orchestra himself, programming the work earlier in the season.
15. Ken Maslen: letter to the author, March 1995.
16. *Birmingham Post*, 12 July 1993.
17. *Daily Telegraph*, 1 April 1993.
18. In February 1991, Kate Walker had taken over from Julianna Szekely as Marketing Manager, leaving her free to concentrate on seeking sponsorship.
19. *Music Stand*, December 1993.
20. 'I learned so much from that; I shall never forget one little deaf boy. I'd been talking to them about Messiaen and bird-song – someone was "signing" for them, of course. Nobody had ever explained to them that birds actually sang – they'd seen them opening their mouths but they thought they were just breathing. This kid thought about it for a bit; then he said to me, "Simon, what's the song of a butterfly like?" '
21. Interview with the author, February 1995.
22. *Music Stand*, March 1994.
23. Interview with the author, April 1995.
24. Interview with the author, February 1995.
25. The première took place in Nottingham, 20 October 1993.
26. The first professional performances in Birmingham.
27. BBC Radio 3: *Choir Works*, 4 December 1994, in conversation with Brian Wright.
28. *Birmingham Post*, 11 June 1994.
29. *Music Stand*, December 1994.
30. Interview with the author, February 1995.
31. Sponsored by the Esmée Fairbairn Charitable Trust.

32. Interview with John Russell, *New York Times Magazine*, 12 April 1992.
33. Interview with the author, February 1995.
34. 20 January 1995.

Index

This is primarily an index of people, though composers have been included only selectively. A few organisations have been indexed, but the City of Birmingham [Symphony] Orchestra and CBSO Chorus have been omitted.

Abbado, Claudio 158
Abrahams, Pat 225
Adams, John 215, 223, 234, 237
Allen, Sir Hugh 36, 39, 41
Allen, Thomas 199, 233
Allin, 'Ronnie' Vaughan 87, 89, 91, 126
Allom, Sir Charles 43, 45
Amalgamated Musicians' Union 27
Ambrosian Singers 135
Ančerl, Karel 147
Anda, Géza 114, 119, 124
Ansermet, Ernest 40, 62
Aprahamian, Felix 155, 201
Argerich, Martha 173, 235
Arnold, Sir Malcolm 104, 124, 145, 162, 197
  conducting 158, 162
Arrau, Claudio 118, 124, 126, 133
Artec (company) 210, 224
Arts Council 211, 222, 233
  grants 106, 109, 139, 146, 157, 171, 203, 208, 209, 225
Ashkenazy, Vladimir 119, 195
Atherton, David 184, 199
Atkins, Sir Ivor 45
ATV 159
Atzmon, Moshe 184
Augér, Arleen 207, 215, 219
Austin, Richard 78
Avison, Charles 121

Bach, J.S. 47
Bachauer, Gina 156
Backhaus, Wilhelm 14
Baillie, Dame Isobel 72, 92
Bainton, Edgar 24
Baker, Arthur 136, 138, 139, 143, 144, 148, 149, 150, 152, 156, 158, 163, 168, 182
  disagreement with players, and resignation 178, 179–80
  view of 181
  death 218–19
Baker, Dame Janet 162, 177, 188, 201, 207, 209, 211, 215
Balakirev, Mily A. 118
Balfour, Margaret 47
Balkwill, Bryan 141, 164
Ballard, Jeremy 232
Bamber, Peter 149
Bantock, Sir Granville 5, 10, 28, 36, 39, 59, 89
  sponsor 13, 14–15
  and precursors of CBSO 16, 17–18, 19, 20
  and CBSO 21–2, 23, 24
Bantock, Myrrha 39
Barber, Samuel 89
Barbirolli, Sir John 100
Barenboim, Daniel 119
Barnell, Andrew 212
Barshai, Rudolf 195, 199
Bartók, Béla 42, 64, 104, 167
Bashmet, Yuri 235

Bauer, Harold 41
Bax, Sir Arnold 107
Baynes, Tom Hamilton 99
BBC 32, 38, 40, 45–6, 54–5, 60, 67
  Birmingham station 46, 54
BBC Midland Light Orchestra 82, 142
BBC Midland Orchestra 60, 64, 67
BBC Symphony Orchestra 47–8, 118
Beard, Albert 29
Beard, Fred 13
Beard, Paul 28–9, 31, 39, 41, 42, 46, 61, 92, 111
  joins LPO 57
  death 212
Beckles, Gordon 47
Beecham, Sir Thomas 5, 9, 13, 14, 15, 16, 52, 57, 61, 114, 118
  and origins of CBSO 16, 17, 18, 19–20
  death 133
Beek, Johanna 137
Beeson, William 29
Beethoven, Ludwig van 32, 43, 45
Beethoven Festivals 170, 182–3, 216
Ben-Tovim, Atarah 178, 183
Bennett, Richard Rodney 148, 152, 153, 156, 172
Berg, Alban 148, 201, 216, 228
Berglund, Paavo 199, 218
Berio, Luciano 211
Berkeley, Sir Lennox 116, 120, 126, 141
Berkeley, Michael 212
Berlin, Irving 200
Berlioz, Hector 29, 219–20
Bernstein, Leonard 173
Berrow, Jim 201
Berry, Gwen (Mrs Harry Stanier) 48–9, 50, 53, 71, 92, 93, 114–15, 119, 123, 124, 126, 129, 138
  on Panufnik 127
  on Rignold 131, 132–3
  retirement 133–4
Binns, Malcolm 174
Birmingham:
  cultural centre 5–6
  orchestras 9–10
  civic plans after World War I 21
  city centre changes 140, 186
Birmingham Arts Shop (Basil) 172
Birmingham Choral Union 141
'Birmingham Citizens' Orchestra' 57
Birmingham City Council, and orchestras 20, 22, 40, 65, 81, 136
  grants to CBSO 106, 109, 146, 157, 171, 203, 208, 233, 239–40
Birmingham Concerts Society 14
Birmingham Contemporary Music Group (BCMG) 212, 227, 232
Birmingham Ensemble 227–8
Birmingham (Evening) Mail 1, 36, 198
Birmingham Festival Choral Society (BFCS) 33, 61, 65
Birmingham International Convention Centre (ICC) 210, 220
Birmingham International Wind Competition 144–5
Birmingham Marketing Project 171
Birmingham National Exhibition Centre 199, 222
Birmingham Orchestral Concerts 13
Birmingham Philharmonic Society 14–15, 17
Birmingham Post 21, 23, 36, 43, 49, 65, 97, 158, 223
  see also Blom; Dommett; Falding; Newman; Sheldon; Waterhouse
Birmingham Symphony Orchestra (not CBSP) 12
Birmingham Town Hall 5, 42, 43, 45, 70
  Hill organ 4, 205
Birmingham Triennial Festival 152
Birmingham Workers' Music Club 87
Birtwistle, Harrison 205
Bishop (-Kovacevich), Stephen 152, 153, 184
Bizet, Georges 171
Black, Jack 101
Blech, Harry 188
Blenkinsop, David 152
Bliss, Sir Arthur 30, 116, 117, 145, 188
  conducting 62, 95, 138–9
Bloch, Ernest 63–4, 123
Blom, Dr Eric 51, 63, 76, 81, 87, 93, 96
  leaves Birmingham 88
  death 128
Blyth, May 58
Boothroyd, Philip 144
Borge, Victor 174
Borsdorf, Adolf 150
Boskovsky, Willi 157
Boughton, Rutland 30
Boulanger, Lili 147
Boulanger, Nadia 144, 147
Boulez, Pierre 190, 194, 231, 238
Boult, Sir Adrian 5, 12, 25–6, 37, 111, 191

conducting 29, 33, 58, 68, 69, 72, 76, 92, 93, 107, 118, 140, 144
Director and Conductor 36, 37–51
leaves CBO for BBC 47–8
farewell concert 50–1
honorary doctorate 51, 237
classes 53
Conductor again 128–30
further concerts 152, 156, 163, 169, 177
President, CBSO 159, 160
death 200
Hall named after 208
Boulton, Mildred 52
Bourgue, Maurice 145
Bournemouth Municipal Orchestra 106, 111
Bowen, Kenneth 174, 188
Bowen, Meirion 223
Bradbeer, Alderman 106, 113
Bradbury, Ernest 136, 193
Bradbury, John 158, 181
Brahms, Johannes 33, 38
Brailowsky, Alexander 66
Brain, Alfred 28, 30
Brain, Dennis 40, 110
Braithwaite, Warwick 73, 78
Brearley, John 174
Brendel, Alfred 164, 197, 209, 228
Brian, Havergal 2, 10, 11, 12, 14, 57–8
British Musician 48
Britten, Benjamin (Lord Britten) 107, 110, 113, 114, 115, 116, 129, 155, 201, 205
War Requiem 135, 137, 179, 186, 199
death 175
BRMB radio station 172, 174, 202
Brodsky, Adolf 11
Brook, Donald 86
Brooks, Sir David 22, 23, 32, 42
Brooks, Lady 26, 31
Brown, Christopher 184
Brown, Iona 200, 207, 212, 220
Browne, Sandra 174
Bruckner, Anton 44
Brüggen, Frans 220
Brunner, Ulric C. 78, 80, 81, 82, 83
Brymer, Jack 209
Bryn-Julson, Phyllis 234
Buckley, Michael 214, 222, 224–5, 230, 235
Buckley, Robert 11, 24, 29, 38, 40
Buckman, Rosina 25, 49
Buesst, Aylmer 79
Burley, Tony 174
Burnett, Harold 26, 197
Busch, Adolph 62
Bush, Geoffrey 114
business sponsorship 172, 209
Busoni, Ferrucio 11, 63
Butt, Dame Clara 6
Butt, Richard 144, 171
Butterworth, George 30

Cadbury, Mrs George 58
Camden, Archie 11, 145
Cameron, Basil 48, 53, 68, 70, 72, 73, 78
Campbell-White, Martin 185
Campoli, Alfredo 101, 102, 110, 133, 134, 141
Cannan, Phyllis 215
Canning, Hugh 225
Cantelli, Guido 142
Cantelo, April 129
Capetown Orchestra 52, 53, 138, 265
Capell, Richard 132
Cardus, Neville 145
Carewe, John 201
Casadeus, Robert 114, 126
Castelnuovo-Tedesco, Mario 155
Catley, Gwen 71
Catterall, Arthur 41, 55, 61, 68
Caulcott, Tom 210
Cave, Alfred 57, 58, 74
Central Independent Television 198, 212
Chaillez, Jacques 154
Chamberlain, Neville 15, 16, 17, 19, 20, 23, 36, 64, 66
death 69
Chandler, Mary 89, 115–16, 126
Chapple, Stanley 48
Checkland, Sir Michael 237
Cherkassky, Shura 107, 110, 152, 156, 160, 200
Chilcot, Susan 234
Chung Kyung-Wha 169, 188
Chung Myung-Wha 188
Chung Myung-Whun 188
Ciccolini, Aldo 156, 164
City of Birmingham Choir 30, 58, 61, 65, 95
City of Birmingham Police Band 26, 29, 30, 45, 47, 62
CBSO Concertgoers' Association 192
CBSO Listeners' Club 101–2
CBSO Society 117

City of Birmingham Symphony Youth Chorus 236
City Orchestra Club 63, 88
Clark, Douglas 138
Clements, Andrew 200, 206, 213, 219
Cleobury, Nicholas 188
Clifford, Julian (Jnr) 78, 256
Clifford, Julian (Snr) 12
Clinton, Gordon 167–8, 186, 188, 212
Clugston, Simon 212
Coates, Albert 30, 55
Coates, Edith 146
Cockerill family 29
Coghlan, Professor Brian 104
Cohen, Alex 28, 29, 113
Collett, Councillor Charles 165
Collins, Arthur 21
Conlon, James 195, 232
Constantine, Dennis 163
Cooke, Deryck 187
Cooper, Clayton 21–2, 30
Cooper, Imogen 197
Copland, Aaron 236
Corigliano, John 234
Cotton, Maggie 140, 177, 225, 232–3
Couzens, Brian and Ralph 217
Coward, Henry 12
Cox, Mike 170, 212
Cox, Peter 171
Crabbe, John 169
Craig, Charles 149
Cranmer, Arthur 47
Crowder, John 26, 32, 33
Crowther, Leslie 220
Cruft, John 144–5, 159
Cunard, Lady 19
Cunningham, Dr G.D. 58, 64, 80, 92, 95
Curzon, Clifford 102, 117, 133, 149, 156
Cziffra, Gyorgy 139

Davies, Fanny 39
Davies, Meredith 16, 24, 126, 128, 129, 130, 134, 135, 137, 141, 174, 186
  resignation 130
Davis, Andrew 166
Davis, Carl 197
Davis, Sir Colin 118–19, 124, 145
Dawson, Peter, 50
De Greef, Arthur 10, 14, 18, 55
De Vito, Gioconda 113, 118, 129
Debussy, Claude 15, 32, 37, 134
Del Mar, Norman 152, 188, 193
Delius, Frederic 11, 15, 18, 61
Deller, Alfred 167
Delogu, Gaetano 184
Delvaincourt, Claude 154
Denison, John 1, 66, 87
Desmond, Astra 49, 80
Dods, Marcus 186, 188
Dohnányi, Ernö 11, 48, 55
Dolmetsch, Arnold 4
Dommett, Kenneth W. 142, 147, 149, 151, 154, 157, 161, 162
  retires 163
Donohoe, Peter 195, 196, 197, 200, 213, 223
Dorati, Antal 139, 149, 153
D'Orsay, Dorothy 45
Dowd, Ronald 161, 162
Downes, Edward 184
Downes, Frank 71
Doyle, Pat 219
Draper, Haydn 28
Du Pré, Jacqueline 157
Duckenfield, Bridget 11
Duckworth, Leslie 161
Dudding, Paul 229
Dumling, Albrecht 204–5
Dutilleux, Henri 155, 166, 177, 215
Dvořák, Anton 8, 42

Eastern Authorities' Orchestral Association 157, 174
Easton, Robert 58
Eddison, Robert 163
Edgar, Percy 54, 55, 56
Edmunds, Dr Christopher 32, 143
Edward, Prince, patron 226
Edwards, Ernest E. 127–8, 130, 134, 135–6, 136
Edwards, Nick 224
Edwards, Sian 212
Elder, Mark 212, 228, 230, 234, 235, 238
Element, Ernest 81, 82–3, 129
Elgar, Sir Edward 4–5, 11, 13, 25, 80, 99, 188, 201
  conducting 1–2, 10, 12, 191
Elman, Mischa 14
EMI 199
ENSA concerts 83, 87
Ericsson, Eric 220
Escott, Graham 231
Evans, Tony 178
Ewing, Maria 209, 215, 222

Fachiri, Adila 68
Fagan, Gideon 78
Falding, John 163, 168–9, 170–1
Falla, Manuel de 46
Farkas, Ferenc 123
Fearon, Alan 197
Feeney, John 21, 116
Feeney Trust 29, 116, 117, 126, 134, 136, 137, 139, 141, 152, 156, 162, 174, 184, 194, 205, 221, 235
Ferras, Christian 164
Ferrier, Kathleen 92
Ffrancon-Davies, David 7
Ffrancon-Davies, Gwen 30
Fiedler, Max 13
Field, Helen 219
Field-Hyde, Margaret 167
Fielding, Fenella 163
Financial Times 200–1, 202–3, 206, 213
Fischer, Edwin 65
Fischer-Dieskau, Dietrich 135
Fisher, Sylvia 149
Fitton, Alan 84, 89, 96, 100, 114, 117, 123
Fitton, John 87
Flanders, Michael 163
Fleming, Robert 119
Fletcher, Lyn 223
Fogg, Nick 220
Forty, Gerald C. 17, 18, 20, 21, 22, 24, 31–2, 36, 38, 48, 50, 54, 55, 70, 76, 92, 97
  death 99
Foss, Hubert 62
Foster, Lawrence 184, 228, 236
Fourestier, Louis 154
Fournet, Jean 164
Fournier, Pierre 119
Fowke, Philip 196
Franck, César 164
Frémaux, Louis 152–3, 154
  Principal Conductor 153, 154–80
  view of 176
  and orchestral problems 178–80
  resignation 180
Frühbeck de Burgos, Rafael 220
Fuller-Maitland, J.A. 4
Furtwängler, Wilhelm 125, 142

Gál, Hans 117
Galway, James 145, 174
Gardiner, John Eliot 220
Gardner, John 134
Gavin, Barrie 200
Gay, Bram 127, 133
Geffen, Ivan 161, 164
Gelling, Councillor R.R. 30
Georgiadis, John 137, 139, 142
Gerhard, Robert 140
German, Edward 91
Gershwin, George 196, 198
Gibbs, Armstrong 38
Gibson, Sir Alexander 124, 192
Gielen, Michael 230
Gieseking, Walter 113
Gilels, Emil 156, 194
van Giltay, Lidus 41
Gipps, Dr Ruth 82–3, 89, 95, 97, 101
Giulini, Carlo-Maria 196
GKN 174
Glazunov, Alexander 30
Glock, William 144
Godowski, Leopold 11, 14
Goehr, Walter 98
Goetz, Hermann 55
Goldschmidt, Berthold 215, 237
Gomez, Jill 162, 197
Goodchild, Mark 216
Goodman, Arnold, (Lord Goodman) 109, 144
Goodwin, H.S. 31, 32
Goodwin, Noël 145
Goossens, Sir Eugene 19, 30, 33, 38, 39, 89, 113, 116, 145
Goossens, Leon 25, 28, 30, 66, 68, 113, 131
Goossens, Sidonie 113
Gounod, Charles 8
Grady, Keith 193
Graham, Desmond 222, 229
Grainger, Percy 11, 197, 201, 205–6
Gramophone 199, 217
Grant, Dr Willis 100
Gray, Cecil 76–7
Gray, Harold 37, 49–50, 55, 79, 91, 128, 139, 141
  Deputy Conductor 56, 58, 61, 64, 65, 66, 68, 78
  parting with CBO 71–2
  return to CBO 89, 92, 94, 95–6, 105, 107, 113, 118, 124, 126, 129, 130, 133, 134, 136, 143, 145, 146, 147–8, 149, 156, 158, 167, 169–70, 183
  retirement 186–7
  death 225–6

on Boult 200
on Frémaux 155
on Heward 57, 76, 77
on Panufnik 123
on Rignold 151
on Schwarz 119–20
on Schmid 196
Grayson, Barrie 38, 141
Greenfield, Edward 166, 198, 217
Greening, Dr Richard 188
Greensmith, Harold 90
Gregory, David 235
Grew, Sydney 10, 11, 48
Grieg, Edvard 6, 8, 91
Griffiths, Paul 212, 215, 225
Grimley, Terry 213
Grimshaw, Sam 7–8
Groves, Sir Charles 106, 129, 194, 201, 209
Gruber, H.K. 200
Guardian 160
Guabaidulina, Sofia 221, 235
Gulf Oil 229

Haas, Pavel 236
Haebler, Ingrid 124
Haefliger, Ernst 175
Haendel, Ida 92, 147, 149, 160, 187, 197, 200
Halford, George 7, 10–11, 13, 14
Hall, Barrie 112
Hallé, Charles 52
Hallé Orchestra 18, 109
Halsey, Louis 199
Halsey, Simon 199, 206, 211, 212, 218, 219, 220, 223, 236
Hambourg, Mark 80, 102
Hamer, Cathy 216
Hammond, Joan 71, 134
Handford, Margaret 15
Handford, Maurice 158, 160, 162, 163, 164, 165, 173, 192, 200, 205
death 212
Handley, Vernon 184, 188
Hann, Lewis 44–5
Harby, Rosemary 229
Harding, Daniel 235
Harper, Heather 135, 149, 150, 174
Harrell, Lynn 195, 228
Harris, Roy 234
Harrison, Beatrice and May 41
Harrison, Julius 24, 48, 68, 78, 79
Harrison, Percy and Thomas 5–6
Harry Payne Trust 174
Hart, Perry 127
Hartog, Howard 182
Hartshorn, Richard 183, 233
Harty, Sir Hamilton 'Hay' 11, 29, 30, 62
Haskil, Clara 110
Hatton, Ethel 102
Hayes, Alfred 21
Haywood, Lorna 175
Head, Philip 229
Heap, Dr Charles Swinnerton 607
Heard family 29
Heard, Gordon 62
Heinen, Ulrich 212
Hely-Hutchinson, Victor 53, 60, 63, 64, 66, 68, 69, 80, 81
leaves Birmingham 82
death 90
Hemming, Dorothy 83, 116
Hemsley, Thomas 115
Henderson, Philip 64
Henderson, Roy 58, 64, 80
Henninger, Richard 156
Herman, Peter 169
Hess, Dame Myra 69, 72, 74, 76, 80, 107, 114, 133
Heward, Herbert 52
Heward, Lenore 53, 55, 73, 76
Heward, Leslie 5, 37, 48, 50, 52–4, 67
Conductor 52–76
composer 56
illness 58, 61, 65, 67, 68, 69, 70, 72, 73
conductor, BBC Midland Orchestra 60
notice given to 68
back in operation 69–70
recording with CBO 70–1
and Hallé Orchestra 73, 75
last CBO concert 76
death 76
Hill-Smith, Marilyn 183
Hilton, Janet 196
Hindemith, Paul 107, 205
Hochhauser, Victor 157, 162
Hock, Johan C. 11, 19, 44, 48
Hodgson, Alfreda 197
Holliger, Heinz 1997, 220, 221
Holloway, Robin 211, 228
Holmes, Ralph 148
Holst, Gustav 36, 44, 58, 92
conducting 28, 41
Holst, Henry 61

Honegger, Arthur 122
Hopkins, Antony 161
Horder, Lord 73
Horenstein, Jascha 133, 140–1, 149, 153, 160
  death 164
Hough, Stephen 236
Howell, Gwynne 175
Howells, Anne 167
Howells, Herbert 53
Hubbard, G.W. 21
Hughes, David 158, 164
Hughes, Owain Arwel 184
Hunt, Donald 195
Hunter, Rita 235
Hurst, George 121, 124, 190

Iles, Edna 25
Imperial Metal Industries (IMI) 172, 174
d'Indy, Vincent 164
Inoue, Michi 182, 184
Ireland, John 104
Ives, Charles 225, 228, 234

Jackson, Judith 180
Jacob, Gordon 117
Jaguar Cars 212, 225
James, Wilfred 28
Janáček, Leoš 193, 194, 198
Janowski, Marek 238
Jansons, Mariss 199
Järvi, Neeme 160, 196, 199, 201–2, 207
Jenkins, Lyndon 42, 74, 123, 166, 175, 187, 195
Jennings, Paul 135
Joachim, Joseph 11
John Madin Design Group 159
Johnson, Councillor George 24
Johnson, John 164
Johnson, Russell 224
Johnston, David 174
Johnston, Robert 177
Johnstone, George Hope 13
Johnstone, Maurice 75
Jonas, George 152, 161, 168, 172, 178, 179, 180, 183, 185, 186, 197, 198, 206, 218
  retirement 229
Jones, Gwyneth 141
Jones, Trefor 58
Joubert, John 162, 184
Jowett, Andrew 224
Joyce, Eileen 68, 80, 93, 102

Kabos, Ilona 130
Kahn, Charles 74
Kamu, Okko 186, 195, 207, 211, 212, 218
Karajan, Herbert von 125, 142
Katchen, Julius 116, 117, 133
Katsaris, Cyprien 173
Keep, Harry 45
Kempe, Rudolf 133
Kempff, Wilhelm 115, 149, 160
Kennedy, Michael 33, 129, 215, 219
Kennedy, Nigel 211
Kenrick, Alderman W. Byng 56, 58, 61, 81, 88, 98, 99
Kenrick, Sir George 18, 23, 41, 45
Kentner, Louis 68, 82, 119
Kenyon, Nicholas, on Simon Rattle 173, 191, 213
Kernis, Aaron Jay 237
Ketèlbey, Albert 207
Keys, Professor Ivor 148
King, Peter 212
King-Smith, Beresford 139, 158, 184, 222–3
  retirement 231–2
Kirby, James 113
Klemperer, Otto 125, 142
Kletzki, Paul 156
Knapp, Arthur 229, 233, 238
Knight, Arthur 83
Knussen, Oliver 199, 215, 237
Kodály, Zoltán 130, 134
Koechlin, Charles 207
Kogan, Leonid 156
Kohler, Irene 80
Kok, Felix 141, 144, 158, 181–2, 185, 188, 204, 208, 229
  on Frémaux 160
  retirement 218
Kraemer, Nicholas 220
Kraus, Lili 164
Kreisler, Fritz 11
Kremer, Gidon 221, 235
Krips, Henry 125, 152

Labèque, Katia and Marielle 207
Lackland, John 163
Lalandi, Lina 165
Lalo, Edouard 18, 74
Lambert, Constant 37, 59, 71, 73
Lamond, Frederic 11, 61

Lanchbery, John 130, 135
Langdon, Michael 149
Lankester, Barry 135
Larner, Gerald 160, 201
Laverack, Elizabeth 165, 172
Lebrecht, Norman 231, 236
Lee, Justin 236
Leeds Municipal Orchestra 57–8
LeFanu, Nicola 172
Legge, Walter 71, 84, 87, 91
Lehmann, Wilfred 127, 130
Leighton, Kenneth 156
Leitner, Ferdinand 153, 182
Leslie Heward Memorial Fund 81
Levi, Yoel 218
Lewin, Kurt 113
Lewis, Professor Anthony 90, 91, 100, 116, 133, 152
  music by 123, 126
  retirement from Birmingham 148
Lewis, Joseph 30, 31, 46, 55
Liwes, Richard 140, 175
Lewis's, sponsor 45
Liberman, Victor 214, 220
Lill, John 162, 164, 170, 184, 187, 223
Lindars, Herman 95
Liverpool Philharmonic Orchestra 109, 132
Listener 209
Liszt, Franz 118, 167
Llangollen, International Eisteddfod 118
Lloyd family 22
Lloyd, David 71
Lloyd, Dorothy (née Chamberlain) 72
Lloyd, Stephen 99, 100–1, 106, 108, 111, 115, 116, 128, 136, 138, 159, 181, 197, 229
  retirements 151, 206
  death 230
London Wind Quintet 28
Long, Kathleen 68, 80
Loppert, Max 170, 223, 228
Los Angeles, Victoria de 160
Los Angeles Philharmonic Orchestra 196
Lott, Felicity 236
Loveland, Kenneth 192
Lowe, John 100, 134–5
Lucas Industries 174, 188
Ludford, Ian 216
Lumby, Herbert 74
Luxon, Benjamin 187, 236
Lympany, Moura 80, 102
Lyon, Joseph 8

McBurney, Gerard 228
McCabe, John 162, 171
McCormack, John 14
Macdonald, Councillor G.F. 31, 38, 48, 50, 55
McGegan, Nicholas 220
Mackerras, Sir Charles 139
Macklin, Elsie 88, 101–2
MacMahon, Dr Desmond 88, 105
Maconchy, Elizabeth 139
Maddison, Arthur 99, 101, 106, 136, 179, 180, 183, 188
  retirement 235
Magaloff, Nikita 110
Mahler, Gustav 44, 49, 110, 173, 187, 193
Maitland, Robert 58
Major, Blyth 99, 112, 117–18, 119, 121–2, 126
  resignation 127–8
Major, Margaret 127
Malipiero, Gian Francesco 123
Malko, Nicolai 63, 116, 133
Manchester Guardian 30
Mandell, Robert 172–3, 174
Manduell, John 140, 144
Manns, August 52
Marsh, Roger 194
Martin, Frank 126
Martineau, A. Denis 139, 142, 144, 146, 150–1, 152, 153, 155, 159, 165, 177, 211
  retirement 168
Martineau, Sir Wilfrid 81, 138
Martins, João Carlos 139
Martinů, Bohuslav 170, 205
Mata, Eduardo 212
Maslen, Ken 205
Massenet, Jules 160
Massey, Roy 173–4
Masur, Kurt 227, 236
Matchett, Kenneth 108, 109, 110, 136, 155, 181
  resignation 111
Mathieson, Muir 79
Matthew-Walker, Robert 129
Matthews, Arthur 101
Matthews, (Thomas) Appleby 3, 5, 18, 20, 24–5, 38–9, 81
  Conductor, CBO 25–9
  recording and prize 30

Berlin Philharmonic 30–1
against the Committee 33
last concert 33–4
assessment 34–5
later, and death 57, 97
Matthews, Denis 68, 80, 86, 115
Maude, John 82, 83, 84
Maw, Nicholas 224
Maycock, Robert 217
Mayer, John 174
Measham, David 137, 142
Mehta, Zubin 157
Melba, Dame Nellie 5, 6, 14
Melos Ensemble 135
Mendelssohn, Felix 8
Elijah 8, 65, 161–2
Menges, Isolde 63
Menuhin, Sir Yehudi 126, 137, 140, 157, 174, 186, 191
Merrill Lynch & Co Inc 216, 221
Messiaen, Olivier 177, 195
Turangalîla Symphony 197, 207–8
Midland Authorities' Orchestral Association 158
Midland Bank 174
Midland Youth Orchestra 117–18
Milanova, Stoika 170
Miles, Maurice 78
Miles, Philip Napier 44
Milhaud, Darius 126
Miller, Tony 108, 127
Milne, Betty 167, 226
Milstein, Nathan 152
Minton, Yvonne 175
Mitchell, Donald 135
Mitchells & Butlers 45
Mitchinson, John 177, 197, 211, 235
Moeran, E.J. 55, 66
Moiseiwitsch, Benno 18, 66, 69, 80, 81, 113, 147
Möller, Inge 113
Monteux, Pierre 40, 64, 116, 117
Monthly Musical Record 51
Moody, John 146
Moore, Dudley 156
Moore, Gerald 87
Moores, Michael 183
Morley, Christopher 218, 223, 231, 235
Moroney, Tony 164
Morris, Frederic C. 88
Morrison, Elsie 115
Morton, Albert 101
Mossel, Max 11, 13, 24
Mozart, W.A. 44, 56
Mukle, May 55, 66
Mullinar, Michael 39
Mullings, Frank 41, 49, 58
Murdoch, William 56
Murphy, Stan 80
Music Stand 183, 184, 192
Musicians' Union 27, 46, 47, 85, 96, 108, 109, 124, 143, 181–2, 213, 214
Mutter, Anne-Sophie 235

Nash, Heddle 80
Navarra, André 117
Neaman, Yfrah 140
Neel, Boyd 78–9
Neuhold, Gunther 219
New Philharmonic Society 15–18
Newbould, Brian 217
Newman, Ernest 13, 14, 15, 16, 17. 18, 21, 23, 25, 40
Ney, Elly 137
Nicholson, Sydney 52
Nielsen, Carl 113, 126, 133, 147, 156, 184, 228
Nikisch, Artur 37, 53
Nørby, Erik 205
Norman, Jessye 170, 200, 207
Norrington, Roger 221
Norris, Geoffrey 231

Oakes, Meredith 209
Observer 213
O'Farrell, Sean 193
Ogdon, John 148, 174, 200
Oistrakh, David 164, 170
Oistrakh, Igor 156, 164, 170
Ord, Bernhard 44
Orloff, Nikolai 55
Osborn, Franz 107
Ousset, Cécile 196, 198, 199, 222

de Pachmann, Vladimir 7
Paderewski, Ignacy 6
Palmer, Felicity 186
Panufnik, Sir Andrzej 122, 123
new Conductor 121–2
quarrel with Norris Stanley 125–6
own music 126, 205
resignation 127, 128
conducting later 195, 205
death 229–30
Parikian, Manoug 139

Parry, Sir Hubert 50, 53
Parsons, Albert 142
Parsons, Ernest 119, 142
Parsons, William 101
Partridge, Ian 149
Patrick, John 161
patronage, private and public 22–3
Pattison's patisserie 47
Pauk, Gyorgy 175, 195, 216
Pavarotti, Luciano 222
Payne, Harry 110, 113, 117
Peacock report, on regional orchestras 158
Pears, Sir Peter 110, 113, 114, 115, 129, 135, 186
Penguin Music Magazine 88
Pennario, Leonard 133
Pernel, Orrea 66
Petherbridge, Edward 163
Petri, Egon 11, 61, 63
Pettitt, Stephen 40
Peyton, Richard 13
Philharmonia Orchestra 196
Pickett, Philip 218
Pini, Anthony 61
Pitt, Percy 47, 53
Pizarro, Artur 223
Play On 97
Players' Committee 47, 178, 179–80
Police Band *see* City of Birmingham Police Band
Pollini, Maurizio 223, 234
Pook, Wilfrid 143–4
Pougnet, Jean 63
Pouishnoff, Leff 41, 102
Poulter, Eileen 149
Pratt, Peter 183
Preston, Simon 205
Prideaux-Lightfoot, Gerard 138
Priestley (W.H.) music shop 18
Primrose, William 63
Pritchard, John 202
Prokofiev, Sergei 146, 170
Puccini, Giacomo 146

Rachmaninov, Sergei 11
Radcliffe Trust 228
Rafter, Sir Charles 26, 45, 55
Rankl, Karl 132
Ratcliffe, Colin 116
Rattle, Eliot 221
Rattle, Elise *see* Ross, Elise
Rattle, Sacha 201
Rattle, Sir Simon 185, 190–1, 198–9, 240
  on CBSO 166, 207
  conducting 173, 184–5
  appointment to CBSO 185
  Conductor, CBSO 190–241
  honours 206, 213, 229, 232, 234, 241
Rattle, Susan 190
Ravel, Maurice 134, 228
Rawnsley, John 174
Rawsthorne, Alan 116, 126
Raybould, Clarence 68, 70, 72
Read, Cyril 186
Reiss, Thelma 68
Reith, John (Lord Reith) 48, 54
Richter, Hans 6, 7, 9, 12, 13, 52
Richter-Haaser, Hans 147, 149, 153, 156, 164, 170
  death 195
Rigg, Diana 146
Rignold, Hugo 118, 121, 129, 131
  Conductor 131–51
  recording 145
  resignation 150–1
  death 173
Rignold, Jennifer (Jennifer Gay) 132, 150
Riley, Joseph 22
Rimsky-Korsakov, Nikolai 18, 93
Rippon, Michael 188
Robinson, Christopher 141, 146, 152, 166–7, 195, 219, 235
Rodway, Philip 27
Rodzinski, Arthur 201
Rogers, Paul 161
Roll, Michael 124
Ronald, Sir Landon 5, 11, 12, 13, 18, 27, 29, 38, 41, 52
Ross, Elise 190, 195, 197, 205, 219, 228, 240
Rossini, Gioacchino 146
Rostal, Max 99, 125
Rostropovich, Mstislav 152
Rotterdam Philharmonic Orchestra 157
Roussel, Albert 104, 167
Royal College of Music 39
Rozhdestvensky, Gennadi 119, 138
Rubbra, Edmund 104, 114, 116
Russell, Albert 'Rus' 97, 115, 117, 129
Russell, W.G.A. 'Bill' 99, 100, 101, 102, 103, 108, 128, 136, 138
  death 197

Safonoff, Vassily Ilyich 12, 15
St John-Stevas, Norman 191–2
Saint-Saëns, Camille 8, 162, 171, 177
Salmond, Felix 1
Salonen, Esa Pekka 211
Sammons, Albert 18, 62, 66, 73
Samuel (H) Ltd 172, 174
Sanderling, Kurt 164, 195
Santley, Charles 14
Sargent, Sir Malcolm 49, 50, 70, 73, 79, 93, 118, 132
Satie, Erik 167
Sauer, Emil 236
Sawallisch, Wolfgang 212
Scharrer, Irene 14, 68–9, 102
Scharwenka, Xaver 236
Schmid, Erich 182–3, 187, 194–5, 196, 205
Schnabel, Artur 58–9
Schnittke, Alfred 235
Schoenberg, Arnold 134, 219, 228
Schønwandt, Michael 205
Schubert, Franz 43
Schumann, Elisabeth 94
Schwarz, Greta 103
Schwarz, Rudolf 98, 99, 103–4
  Conductor 99–100, 102, 104–18
  character 112, 119–20
  resignation 118
  later 149, 195
  death 235
Schwarzkopf, Elisabeth 156
Scott, Cyril 41
Seaman, Christopher 187–8, 192, 200
Searle, Humphrey 136–7
Seckerson, Edward 223
Seefried, Irmgard 145
Segal, Uri 164
de Selincourt, Ernest 78
Sellick, Phyllis 80, 107, 120, 158
Serocki, Kazimierz 167
Shafir, Shulamith 80
Shaw, Bernard 8
Shaw, Robert 220, 230, 238
Sheldon, A.J. 23, 24, 28, 29, 33, 38, 40, 43, 44, 45, 49, 50, 51
Shephard, Albert H. 19, 20, 37–8, 46, 60, 68, 78
Shirley-Quirk, John 186, 211
Shostakovich, Dmitry 63, 147, 174
Shostakovich, Maxim 212
Shufflebotham, Gilbert 92
Sibelius, Jean 8, 29, 41, 55, 61, 62, 63, 117, 134, 145, 199, 200, 214
Silk, Dorothy 44, 47
Siloti, Alexander 7, 11, 14
Silvestri, Constantin 142, 147, 155
Simpson, Robert 129, 137, 148
Sinclair, Dr G.R. 12
Sinigaglia, Leone 55
Sippings, Andrew 178–9
Sitkovetsky, Dmitri 201
Skalkottas, Nikos 124
Smart, Clive 128
Smith, Cyril 72, 80, 102, 120, 158
Smith, Edward 184, 185, 194, 202, 203, 206, 211, 214, 218, 222, 224, 230, 233, 235, 238, 241
Smith, Paul 178, 179–80
Smith, Stan 134, 147, 181
  on Schwarz 120, 121
Smith, T.H. 19
Smyth, Dame Ethel 36, 44, 55
Söderström, Elisabeth 199, 214
Solomon 63
Solomon, John 131
Soltesz, Stefan 232
Spiegl, Fritz 155
Stanford, Sir Charles Villiers 14, 44, 53
Stanier, Harry 58, 148
Stanley, Norris 74, 82–3, 96, 99, 110, 115
  retired 125–6
  death 173
Stanton, Walter 65, 68, 70, 72, 76, 80
Steele, Arthur 127, 171, 183
Steinbach, Heribert 175
Stern, Isaac 152, 215
Stevenson, Evelyn 58
Stevenson, Mathew, jr 16, 19
Stockhausen, Karlheinz 231
Stockley, William 1–2, 6
Stolow, Meyer 130, 134, 137
Stolzman, Richard 234
Stratton, Wymark 12
Strauss, Richard 11, 15, 31, 139
Stravinsky, Igor 18, 199, 228
Strebing, James 162
Suggia, Guilhermina 66
Suk, Josef 170, 225
Sullivan, Sir Arthur 4
Sumitomo Corporation 225
Susskind, Walter 147, 152, 153
Sutherland, Joan 128
Sydney Symphony Orchestra 176

Symphony Hall, Birmingham 224, 226, 227
Szekely, Julianna 188, 193, 231
Szering, Henryk 133, 164, 216
Szigeti, Joseph 14, 126
Szymanowski, Karol 170, 193, 228, 237

Takemitsu, Toru 205, 221
Talich, Vačlav 41
Tavener, John 184
Tawaststjerna, Professor Erik 214
Taylor, Kendall 68, 80, 147
Taylor, W.S.A. 80
Tchaikovsky, Pyotr Ilyich 12, 28, 143
Te Kanawa, Dame Kiri 164
Tear, Robert 188, 199
Temirkanov, Yuri 164, 184
Tennant, Ann 229
Tertis, Lionel 131
Teyte, Maggie 57, 87
Thalben-Ball, Sir George 95, 114, 198, 205
Thau, Pierre 167
Theatre Royal, New Street, Birmingham 27, 118
Thomas, Bryden 205
Thomas, Marjorie 140
Thomas, Peter 218, 220, 227
Thonnes, Mathilde 122
Thorpe, Jeremy 174
Three Choirs Festivals:
  Gloucester 143, 177
  Hereford 159, 166, 173
  Worcester 130, 146, 147, 163
TI (Tube Investments Ltd) 186, 188
The Times 47, 201
Tinsley, Pauline 141, 146
Tippett, Sir Michael 116, 117, 199, 166, 178, 193, 219, 228
Tookey, Muriel 62, 64
Tortelier, Paul 149, 164, 177
Tourel, Jennie 113
Tovey, Bramwell 229
Trotter, Thomas 205
Tsuji, Hisako 137
Tučapsky, Antonin 194
Tureck, Rosalyn 116, 124
Turnage, Mark Anthony 221, 226, 228, 234, 237
Turnovsky, Martin 205

Uchida, Mitsuko 168
Unger, Heinz 75, 78

Vale, E.F. 66
Van Beinum, Eduard 114
Van der Lyn, Harry 115
Varèse, Edgard 231, 234
Vaughan Williams, Ralph 29, 49, 59, 92, 107, 115, 116, 163, 199
  Conductor 115
  spoof on *Fantasia on Greensleeves* 87
  death 126
Veale, John 95
Verbrugghen, Henri 14
Vickers, John 207
Vyner, Michael 225
Vyvyan, Jennifer 113, 116

Wagner, Richard 28, 33–4, 49
Walden, Peter 205
Waldhans, Jiři 150, 160
Walker, Major Denzil 83, 85, 90, 91, 92, 94
  on Weldon 138
  resignation 107–8
Walker, Kate 222
Wall, Charles 183
Wallace, William 55
Wallenstein, Alfred 147
Walls, Tom 183
Walter, Bruno 38, 40, 43
Walton, Sir William 58, 59, 62, 64, 83–4, 93, 133, 164, 175
  death 199
Wangenheim, Volker 184
Ward, John 190
Warden, W.Ellary 17, 20, 21, 22, 24
Wardle, Dr A.D. 187
Warlock, Peter (Philip Heseltine) 54, 75
Wassell, Richard 20, 24–8, 45
  death 97
Waterhouse, John F. 88, 90, 91, 92, 93, 96, 97, 100, 105, 110, 113, 116, 117, 118, 121, 126, 129, 130, 131, 133
  retirement 141
Weber, Carl Maria von 123
Webern, Anton 58, 200
Weigall, Richard 162, 232
Weill, Kurt 195, 199, 228
Weingartner, Felix 65, 122
Weir, Judith 237
Weldon, George 79
  Conductor 79–80
  Music Director and Conductor 82–102

recordings 84, 91
character 86, 138
Conductor, City of Birmingham Choir 95
resigns from choir 99–102
guest conductor 130
death 138
Weller, Walter 216, 217, 223, 226, 238, 239
Wellesz, Egon 145, 147, 153
Welsh National Opera 141,143, 146
Wendt, Theo 53
Wessely, Hans 131
West Midlands Arts 212
West Midlands County Council 171, 203
Westrup, Professor Jack 82,90
White, Willard 196, 201, 209, 215, 233
Whitehead, Alan 133
Whittaker, Bill 101
Wick, Denis 117
Willcocks, Sir David 113, 124
Williams, Grace 146
Williams, John 155, 205
Williams, Laverne 196
Wilson, Sir Steuart 47, 49
Winn, Dr Rowland M. 7
Wishart, Peter 116, 126
Wolf, Hugo 117
Wolff, Ernst 61
Wolff, Hugh 237
Wolverhampton Contemporary Music Festival 97
Wood, Anne 113
Wood, Sir Henry 5, 12, 13, 15, 18, 33, 52, 56
on Halford 10
and CBSO 22
Wood, R.W. 130
World of Music 40
Wright, Brian 184
Xenakis, Iannis 204
York, Richard 229
Yorke family 29
Yorke, W.S. 66
Yorkshire Post 217
Young, Alexander 118, 134
Ysaÿe, Eugene, 11, 14
Zehetmair, Thomas 237
Zimbalist, Efrem 14
Zissman, Councillor 198